Student Manual

WinSuperSite.com - ck out windows Vista

Scintilla Text Editor (Free)
Windows Defender (Free) Spyware (Part of Vista)

A+™ Certification

Operating Systems Third Edition – A CompTIA Certification

Rozanne Murphy Whalen

A+™ Certification: Operating Systems Third Edition – A CompTIA Certification

Part Number: 085812
Course Edition: 2.0

ACKNOWLEDGMENTS

Project Team

Content Developer: Rozanne Murphy Whalen • **Development Assistance:** Nancy Curtis, Judith A Kling, Andrew LaPage, Taryn Manuele and Sue San Filippo • **Content Manager:** Clare Dygert • **Copy Editors:** Angie French and Laura Thomas • **Material Editor:** Lance Anderson • **Graphic/Print Designer:** Isolina Salgado Toner • **Project Technical Support:** Mike Toscano

NOTICES

The logo of the CompTIA Authorized Curriculum Program and the status of this or other training material as "Authorized" under the CompTIA Authorized Curriculum Program signifies that, in CompTIA's opinion, such training material covers the content of the CompTIA's related certification exam. CompTIA has not reviewed or approved the accuracy of the contents of this training material and specifically disclaims any warranties of merchantability or fitness for a particular purpose. CompTIA makes no guarantee concerning the success of persons using any such "Authorized" or other training material in order to prepare for any CompTIA certification exam. The contents of this training material were created for the CompTIA A+ exam covering CompTIA certification exam objectives that were current as of April, 2003.

How to Become CompTIA Certified: This training material can help you prepare for and pass a related CompTIA certification exam or exams. In order to achieve CompTIA certification, you must register for and pass a CompTIA certification exam or exams. In order to become CompTIA certified, you must:

1. Select a certification exam provider. For more information please visit http://www.comptia.org/certification/genral_information/test_locations.asp.

2. Register for and schedule a time to take the CompTIA certification exam(s) at a convenient location.

3. Read and sign the Candidate Agreement, which will be presented at the time of the exam(s). The text of the Candidate Agreement can be found at http://www.comptia.org/certification/general_information/candidate_agreement.asp.

4. Take and pass the CompTIA certification exam(s).

For more information about CompTIA's certifications, such as their industry acceptance, benefits, or program news, please visit http://www.comptia.org/certification/default.asp. CompTIA is a non-profit information technology (IT) trade association. CompTIA's certifications are designed by subject matter experts from across the IT industry. Each CompTIA certification is vendor-neutral, covers multiple technologies, and requires demonstration of skills and knowledge widely sought after by the IT industry. To contact CompTIA with any questions or comments: Please call + 1 630 268 1818 questions@comptia.org

HELP US IMPROVE OUR COURSEWARE

Your comments are important to us. Please contact us at Element K Press LLC, 1-800-478-7788, 500 Canal View Boulevard, Rochester, NY 14623, Attention: Product Planning, or through our Web site at **http://support.elementkcourseware.com.**

KNOWLEDGE²

by Element K Courseware

Knowledge², available exclusively from Element K Courseware, gives you two great ways to learn using our best-in-class content.

This courseware includes a companion online ID. Use your online ID to reinforce what you've learned in the classroom, prepare for certification tests, or as a reference guide. It's easy, and available to you anytime, 24x7, at www.elementk.com.

To use your Knowledge² online ID, follow these five easy steps:

1. Log on to www.elementk.com

2. Click on Student Enrollment

3. Enter the following Enrollment Key

    1523-APLUSOSH-1255

4. Choose a user name and password, complete personal information, and then click Submit.

5. Your profile has been set up successfully. You may now proceed to Login to Element K.

Your Knowledge² online ID is valid for 90-days from initial logon.

A+™ CERTIFICATION: OPERATING SYSTEMS THIRD EDITION - A COMPTIA CERTIFICATION

LESSON 1: WINDOWS TOOLS

Contents

CONTENTS

A+™ Certification: Operating Systems Third Edition – A CompTIA Certification

LESSON 6: MANAGING FILE AND PRINT RESOURCES IN WINDOWS 9X

LESSON 7: MANAGING DISK RESOURCES IN WINDOWS 2000/NT/XP

LESSON 8: MANAGING DISK RESOURCES IN WINDOWS 9X

CONTENTS

LESSON 11: PREPARING FOR DISASTER RECOVERY

LESSON 12: RECOVERING FROM DISASTER

CONTENTS

APPENDIX A: UPGRADE FROM WINDOWS 95 TO WINDOWS 98

APPENDIX B: UPGRADE FROM WINDOWS NT TO WINDOWS 2000 OR WINDOWS XP

APPENDIX C: DYNAMIC DISKS

APPENDIX D: A+ OS TECHNOLOGIES EXAM OBJECTIVES

ABOUT THIS COURSE

A+ Certification: Operating Systems is the course you should take if your job responsibilities include the support of computers running the Windows 9x, Windows 2000, and Windows XP operating systems. This course, along with the *A+ Certification: Hardware* course, prepares you for the CompTIA A+ Operating Systems certification exam. In this course, you'll build on your skills with using a Windows-based operating system to learn the specific skills you need to install, maintain, and troubleshoot the Windows 9x, Windows 2000, and Windows XP operating systems.

You'll find that this course benefits you in two ways. First, if you want to pass the A+: Operating Systems exam (CompTIA exam number 220-302), this course will help you significantly in preparing for this exam. Second, and even more important, this course will provide you with the skills you need to be successful as an A+ technician. Certification alone doesn't ensure your professional success. You also need to be able to perform the skills on which the certification is based.

Course Description

Target Student

This course is targeted to an individual with basic end-user skills using Windows-based personal computers, who wishes to begin a career in information technology by becoming a personal computer service technician, or who wants to prepare to take the CompTIA A+ Operating Systems examination.

Course Prerequisites

To ensure your success in this course, we recommend that you know how to complete the following tasks:

- Start up and shut down the computer.
- Log on to a computer or computer network.
- Run applications.
- Move, copy, delete, and rename files in Windows Explorer.
- Browse and search for information on the Internet.
- Send and receive email.

- Basic knowledge of computing concepts, including:
  — The difference between hardware and software.
  — The functions of software components such as the operating system, applications, and file system.
  — The function of a computer network.

You can obtain this level of skills and knowledge by taking any of the following Element K courses:

- *Introduction to Personal Computers Using Windows 98*
- *Introduction to Personal Computers Using Windows 2000*
- *Introduction to Personal Computers Using Windows XP*
- In addition, *Hard Disk Management for DOS 6.22* is a required prerequisite for this course.

Although it is not a requirement, it is strongly recommended that you take *A+ Certification: Core Hardware* prior to taking this course.

It is also strongly recommended that you have a minimum of six months experience working with computers.

How to Use This Book

As a Learning Guide

Each lesson covers one broad topic or set of related topics. Lessons are arranged in order of increasing proficiency with *A+ Operating Systems*; skills you acquire in one lesson are used and developed in subsequent lessons. For this reason, you should work through the lessons in sequence.

We organized each lesson into results-oriented topics. Topics include all the relevant and supporting information you need to master *A+ Operating Systems*, and activities allow you to apply this information to practical hands-on examples.

You get to try out each new skill on a specially prepared sample file. This saves you typing time and allows you to concentrate on the skill at hand. Through the use of sample files, hands-on activities, illustrations that give you feedback at crucial steps, and supporting background information, this book provides you with the foundation and structure to learn *A+ Operating Systems* quickly and easily.

As a Review Tool

Any method of instruction is only as effective as the time and effort you are willing to invest in it. In addition, some of the information that you learn in class may not be important to you immediately, but it may become important later on. For this reason, we encourage you to spend some time reviewing the topics and activities after the course. For additional challenge when reviewing activities, try the "What You Do" column before looking at the "How You Do It" column.

As a Reference

The organization and layout of the book make it easy to use as a learning tool and as an after-class reference. You can use this book as a first source for definitions of terms, background information on given topics, and summaries of procedures.

Course Objectives

In this course, you will support Windows 9x, Windows NT 4.0, Windows 2000, and Windows XP computers.

You will:

- list Windows and command-line tools.
- manage applications.
- install network components.
- implement local security in Windows 2000/NT/XP.
- manage file and print resources in Windows 2000/NT/XP.
- manage file and print resources in Windows 9x.
- manage disk resources in Windows 2000/NT/XP.
- manage disk resources in Windows 9x.
- connect to Internet and intranet resources.
- implement virus protection.
- prepare for disaster recovery.
- recover from disaster.
- install client operating systems.
- automate client operating system installations.

Course Requirements

Hardware

Except where noted, the requirements listed are for the student and instructor computers.

- 300 Mhz Pentium processor or higher.
- 10 GB hard disk or larger for the student and instructor computers.
- 12 GB hard disk or larger for the classroom domain controller. (You will need an even larger hard disk if you want each student to use Ghost to create an image of his computer in Lesson 14. You will need approximately 2 GB of disk space per computer image stored on the server.)
- 128 MB of RAM or more. For the classroom domain controller, 256 MB of RAM or more.
- 800 x 600-capable display adapter and monitor.
- Floppy disk drive and bootable CD-ROM drive.

- One computer installed as a Windows 2000-based classroom domain controller. This computer's hardware must be on the Windows 2000 Hardware Compatibility List (HCL).
- Network adapter and cabling connecting each classroom computer.
- A projector system to display the instructor's screen output.
- 17 3.5" floppy disks for each student and the instructor.
- Bootable Windows XP Professional CD-ROMs for the ASR recovery topic.
- Internet access.

Software

- For the classroom domain controller, you can use either Windows 2000 Server or Windows 2000 Advanced Server. Make sure you have enough per-server licenses for the classroom.
- Windows XP Professional for each student and instructor computer. Be sure you have met the licensing or activation requirements for your situation.
- Windows 2000 Professional for each student and instructor computer. Be sure you have met the licensing or activation requirements for your situation.
- Service Pack 2 or later for Windows 2000.
- Bootable Windows 98 Second Edition CD-ROM for each student and instructor computer. Be sure you have met the licensing or activation requirements for your situation.
- Norton AntiVirus 2002 Professional Edition or McAfee VirusScan Professional Edition. If you choose to use McAfee VirusScan, students will not be able to manually update their virus definitions unless they register their software.
- Norton Ghost.
- PowerQuest Partition Magic or Norton Disk Commander.
- If you want to teach students how to install and configure Netscape Navigator instead of Internet Explorer, you will need Netscape Navigator 7.01 or later. You can download Netscape Navigator at **http://channels.netscape.com/ns/borwsers/download.asp**.
- There are additional requirements for some of the lesson-level lab activities. Please see the setup procedures for each lab activity for these requirements.
- You will need an email account for each student. Obtain these accounts either by installing Microsoft Exchange Server on the classroom domain controller and creating the necessary accounts or by creating the accounts with one of the free email services such as Hotmail. You can create one account for each student or create a single account and have students share this account.

Class Setup

For the Classroom Domain Controller:

1. Perform a clean installation of Windows 2000 Server or Advanced Server on the C drive in the default installation location. To start the Windows 2000 Server Setup program, you can either boot the computer from the Windows 2000 Server installation CD-ROM, create Setup boot disks by using the appropriate command (Makeboot.exe or Makebt32.exe) and then boot from the Setup boot disks, or create a network boot disk and install from a network share. Use the following installation parameters:

   - Create a single C partition using the entire disk.
   - Format the C partition to use NTFS.
   - Set the appropriate regional settings for your country.
   - Enter the appropriate user name and organization for your environment.
   - Enter the product key.
   - Configure enough per-server licenses so that all classroom computers can connect.
   - Use a computer name of 2000SRV.
   - Set the administrator's password to password.
   - Install the Domain Name System (DNS), Dynamic Host Configuration Protocol (DHCP), and Windows Internet Name Service (WINS) networking services.
   - Configure the date and time settings that are appropriate for your locale.
   - Select Custom networking settings. Assign a static IP address of 192.168.200.200 and a subnet mask of 255.255.255.0. Enter this IP address as the Preferred DNS Server address and also the WINS server address.
   - Accept the default workgroup membership.
   - When installation is complete, log on as Administrator.
   - Uncheck Show This Screen At Startup and close the Windows 2000 Configure Your Server window.

2. Configure the DNS domain name properties for this computer to be class.com.

   - Open the Properties for My Computer.
   - Select the Network Identification tab.
   - Click Properties, and then click More.
   - In the Primary DNS Suffix Of This Computer text box, type class.com and click OK.
   - Click OK to close all open windows.
   - Restart the computer when prompted and log on as Administrator.

3. Using the DNS console, create a standard primary forward lookup zone and a reverse lookup zone for the class.com domain.

   - From the Start menu, choose Programs→Administrative Tools→DNS.
   - In the console tree, expand and select your 2000SRV computer.
   - Choose Action→Configure the Server.
   - Click Next.
   - Make sure that Yes, Create A Forward Lookup Zone is selected and click Next.

- In the Zone Type portion of the wizard, verify that Standard Primary is selected and click Next.
- In the Zone Name portion of the wizard, in the Name text box, type class.com and click Next.
- In the Zone File portion of the wizard, verify that Create A New File With This File Name is selected along with a file name of class.com.dns, and then click Next.
- Verify that Yes, Create A Reverse Lookup Zone is selected and click Next.
- In the Zone Type portion of the wizard, verify that Standard Primary is selected and click Next.
- In the Network ID text box, type 192.168.200 and click Next.
- On the Zone File Page, click Next to accept the default file name of 200.168.192.in-addr.arpa.dns.
- Click Finish.

4. Configure the class.com forward lookup zone and the 200.168.192 reverse lookup zone to accept dynamic updates.
   - Select and right-click each zone and choose Properties.
   - On the General page, from the Allow Dynamic Updates drop-down list, choose Yes.
   - Click OK to configure the zone to accept dynamic updates.
   - Close the DNS console.

5. Promote this computer to Active Directory domain controller status for the class.com domain.
   - From the Start menu, choose Run. Enter dcpromo and click OK.
   - Click Next to advance through the Welcome To The Active Directory Installation Wizard page.
   - Create a domain controller for a new domain.
   - Create a new domain tree.
   - Create a new forest of domain trees.
   - In the Full DNS Name For New Domain text box, type class.com.
   - Accept the default NetBIOS name, database, and log locations.
   - Accept the default location for the Shared System Volume.
   - Set the permissions to be compatible with only Windows 2000 servers.
   - Enter password for the Directory Services Restore Mode password.
   - When prompted, restart the computer and log on as Administrator.
   - If necessary, close the Windows 2000 Configure Your Server window.
   - If desired, configure the W32Time Service.

6. Configure DHCP so that this server can assign IP addresses to the instructor and student computers.
   - From the Start menu, choose Programs→Administrative Tools→DHCP.
   - Select and right-click 2000srv.class.com and choose New Scope.
   - On the Welcome page, click Next.
   - In the Name text box, type Class Scope and click Next.
   - In the Start IP Address text box, type 192.168.200.1.

- In the End IP Address text box, type 192.168.200.199.
- Verify that the Length is 24 and the Subnet Mask is 255.255.255.0, and then click Next.
- Do not create any exclusions (unless required by your network).
- Accept the default lease duration of eight days.
- When prompted as to whether you want to define options, verify that Yes, I Want To Configure These Options Now is selected, and then click Next.
- If you're using a router to access the Internet from the classroom, on the Router page, enter the IP address of the router and click Add. Click Next to continue.
- On the Domain Name And DNS Servers page, in the Parent Domain text box, type class.com. In the IP Address text box, type 192.168.200.200 and click Add. Click Next.
- On the WINS Servers page, in the IP Address text box, type 192.168.200.200 and click Add. Click Next to continue.
- Verify that Yes, I Want To Activate This Scope Now is selected and click Next.
- Click Finish.
- Right-click 2000srv.class.com and choose Authorize to authorize the DHCP server in the Active Directory.
- Close DHCP.

7. In Active Directory Users And Computers, create two users for each student. Name the first user Admin#, where # is a unique number for each student. Assign each user the password of password. Add these users to the Domain Admins group. Grant the Dial-In Permission to each of these users. Name the second user User#, where # is a unique number for each student. Assign each user the password of password.

8. Install an HP Laser Jet 5si MX printer on this server. Share the printer as NetPrint.

9. Install the server as a VPN server.
   - Configuring the server as a VPN server requires the server to have two network cards. You can install the Microsoft Loopback Adapter to simulate a second network card if your server doesn't have two network cards. (You're going to use this network card to simulate a connection to the Internet.)
     - In Control Panel, double-click Add/Remove Hardware.
     - Click Next.
     - Verify that Add/Troubleshoot A Device is selected and click Next.
     - Select Add A New Device and click Next.
     - Select No, I Want To Select The Hardware From A List and click Next.
     - Select Network Adapters and click Next.
     - Below Manufacturers, select Microsoft.
     - Below Network Adapter, verify that Microsoft Loopback Adapter is selected and click Next.
     - Click Next.
     - Click Finish.
     - On the desktop, right-click My Network Places and choose Properties.
     - Right-click Local Area Connection 2 and choose Properties.
     - Select Internet Protocol (TCP/IP) and click Properties.

- - Choose Use The Following IP Address. In the IP Address text box, type 10.0.0.1. Verify that the Subnet Mask is 255.0.0.0. Click OK.
  - Click OK to close the Local Area Connection 2 Properties dialog box.
  - Close Network And Dial-Up Connections and Control Panel.
- From the Start menu, choose Programs→Administrative Tools→Routing And Remote Access.
- In the console tree, right-click 2000SRV and choose Configure And Enable Routing And Remote Access.
- Click Next.
- On the Common Configurations page, select Virtual Private Network (VPN) Server and click Next.
- On the Remote Client Protocols page, verify that TCP/IP is selected and click Next.
- Below Internet Connections, select Local Area Connection 2 (the one with Microsoft Loopback Adapter in the Description column) and click Next.
- On the IP Address Assignment page, verify that Automatically is selected and click Next.
- Do not specify that you have a RADIUS server. Click Next.
- Click Finish.
- Click OK to close the message box about the DHCP Relay Agent.
- In Routing And Remote Access, configure the DHCP Relay Agent.
  - In the console tree, expand the 2000SRV (local) object
  - Right-click DHCP Relay Agent and choose Properties.
  - In the Server Address text box, type 192.168.200.200.
  - Click Add.
  - Click OK.
- Close Routing And Remote Access.

10. Install the latest Service Pack for Windows 2000.

11. Create a directory named C:\Support and share it as Support. Copy the contents of the \Support\Tools folder from the Windows 2000 Professional CD-ROM to the C:\Support folder.

12. Create a directory named C:\AntiVirus and share it as AntiVirus. Copy the installation files for Norton AntiVirus to this share.

13. Create a directory named C:\VirusScan and share it as VirusScan. Copy the installation files for Norton AntiVirus to this share.

14. Create a directory named C:\Ghost and share it as Ghost. Copy the installation files for Norton Ghost to this share.

15. Create a directory named C:\Images and share it as Images. Copy C:\Ghost\Ghost.exe and C:\Ghost\Ghost.env to C:\Images.

16. Create at least one email account for students to use in Activity 8-4. Create these accounts on your own mail server (such as Microsoft Exchange Server) or by using a free email service such as Hotmail.

17. Create a directory named C:\Win2000 and share it as Win2000. Copy the contents of the \i386 folder from the Windows 2000 installation CD-ROM to this folder.

18. Create a directory named C:\WinXP and share it as WinXP. Copy the contents of the \i386 folder from the Windows XP installation CD-ROM to this folder.

For the Student and Instructor Computers:

1. Delete all partitions on the computers' hard disks.

    ⚠ Do not use all of the available disk space when you install Windows 98.

2. Perform a clean installation of Windows 98 using the following parameters:
    - Create a C partition of 2 GB in size. Do not enable large disk support on this partition or Setup will use all available disk space.
    - Install Windows 98 Second Edition to the default C:\Windows folder.
    - Perform a Typical installation.
    - Select the Install The Most Common Components (Recommended) option.
    - Name the computer WIN98-#, where # is a unique number for each student (such as 1, 2, 3, and so on). Install the computer into the default workgroup (named Workgroup).
    - Select the appropriate country or region for your location.
    - When prompted, restart the computer.
    - On the User Information page, enter the appropriate Name and Company information.
    - Accept the Windows 98 license agreement.
    - If necessary, type your Windows 98 product key. After copying some additional files, Setup will restart your computer again.
    - Select your time zone.
    - After configuring the startup environment, Setup will restart your computer again.
    - Log on to the computer as Admin# (where # is the same number you assigned to the computer) with a password of password. When prompted, re-enter the password.
    - In the Welcome To Windows 98 dialog box, uncheck Show This Screen Each Time Windows 98 Starts. Close the dialog box.
    - Close the Channels bar. Click No to configure Windows 98 to no longer display the Channels bar when Windows 98 starts.
    - Rename the My Computer icon to WIN98-#, where # is the number you assigned to the computer.
    - In the Network dialog box, enable File and Printer Sharing for Microsoft Networks.

3. In Windows 98, create a folder named C:\WIN98. Copy the contents of the \WIN98 folder from the Windows 98 CD-ROM to the C:\WIN98 folder.

4. Configure Windows 98 so that the computer can connect to the Internet. Open Internet Explorer and configure it to use this connection.

    ⚠ You must use Partition Magic or Norton Disk Commander to create these partitions. If you create the partitions during the installation of Windows 2000 and Windows XP, setup will create a single extended partition using all of the remaining free space on the disk. A single extended partition will prevent students from creating partitions later on in the course.

5. Use Partition Magic or Norton Disk Commander to create two additional 2 GB primary partitions on the hard disk.

   ⚠️ Do not upgrade Windows 98 to Windows 2000 Professional. Perform a clean install instead.

6. After you've successfully installed Windows 98 and created the two additional primary partitions, insert the Windows 2000 Professional CD-ROM. When you're prompted to upgrade to Windows 2000, click No. Click Install Windows 2000 to install Windows 2000 Professional with the following parameters:

   - Choose Install A New Copy Of Windows 2000 (Clean Install).

   - Enter the appropriate product key.

   - If you need to install additional languages for your location, click Language Options and make the appropriate selections.

   - On the Windows Setup page, click Advanced Options. Check I Want To Choose The Installation Partition During Setup so that you can create a new partition on which you can install Windows 2000.

   - If you need to install Accessibility Options, click Accessibility Options and make the appropriate selections.

   - Install Windows 2000 into the D primary partition. Format this partition to use the NTFS file system.

   - Configure the regional settings that are appropriate for your country.

   - Enter the appropriate user name and organization for your environment.

   - Name the computer WIN2000-#, where # is the same number you chose for this computer when installing Windows 98.

   - Set the Administrator's password to password.

   - If the computer on which you're installing Windows 2000 has a modem, you'll be prompted to configure the modem dialing options. Enter the appropriate area code and number for accessing an outside line for your environment.

   - Configure the date and time settings that are appropriate for your locale.

   - Select Typical Settings for the network configuration.

   - Install the computer into the default workgroup.

   - When the installation is complete, restart the computer. In the Network Identification Wizard, on the Users Of This Computer page, select Users Must Enter A User Name And Password To Use This Computer.

   - Rename the My Computer icon to WIN2000-#, where # is the number you assigned to this computer.

   - In Computer Management, create a user account named Admin#, where # is the computer's assigned number. Assign a password of password to this user. Configure the password so that it never expires. Add the Admin# account to the Administrators group.

    If you find that you need to load hardware drivers from the manufacturers' disks instead of the Windows 2000 Professional installation CD-ROM, students will need these drivers during Lessons 13 and 14.

7. Configure Windows 2000 so that the computer can connect to the Internet. Open Internet Explorer and configure it to use this connection.

8. After you've completed the installation of Windows 2000, install Windows XP Professional with the following parameters:

    - Select New Installation (Advanced) as the installation type.

    - Enter the appropriate product key.

    - On the Setup Options page, click Advanced Options. Check I Want To Choose The Install Drive Letter And Partition During Setup so that you can create a new partition on which you can install Windows XP.

    - Configure the Accessibility Options and Language as appropriate for your environment.

    - Do not upgrade the Windows 98 FAT partition to NTFS.

    - Do not download updated Setup files.

    - Install Windows XP into the E primary partition. Format this partition to use the NTFS file system.

    - Configure the regional and language options that are appropriate for your locale.

    - Enter the appropriate user and organization names.

    - Name the computer WINXP-#, where # is the same number you assigned to this computer for the other operating system installations.

    - Set the Administrator's password to password.

    - If necessary, enter the appropriate area code and number for accessing an outside line for your environment.

    - Configure the date and time settings that are appropriate for your locale.

    - Select Typical Settings for the network configuration.

    - Install the computer into the default workgroup.

    - After the computer restarts, use the Setup program to create a user account named Admin#, where # matches the computer number. Set the password to password. (This account should become a member of the local Administrators group by default.) Use the following steps to set the password:

        - Open Control Panel.

        - Click User Accounts.

        - Click the Admin# user account.

        - Click Create A Password.

         If you find that you need to load hardware drivers from the manufacturers' disks instead of the Windows XP Professional installation CD-ROM, students will need these drivers during Lessons 13 and 14.

9. Configure Windows 2000 Professional as the default operating system.

    - In Windows XP, from the Start menu, choose Control Panel.

    - Click Performance And Maintenance.

    - Below Or Pick A Control Panel Icon, click System.

    - In the System Properties dialog box, select the Advanced tab.

    - Below Startup And Recovery, click Settings.

    - From the Default Operating System drop-down list, select Windows 2000 Professional.

10. Configure the C, D, and E drives with the following drive labels:

- In Windows 2000, open Computer Management. In the console tree, select the Disk Management tool.

- In the right pane, right-click C: and choose Properties. In the Label text box, type Win98. Click OK to save your changes.

- In the right pane, right-click D: and choose Properties. In the Label text box, type Win2000. Click OK to save your changes.

- In the right pane, right-click E: and choose Properties. In the Label text box, type WinXP. Click OK to save your changes.

11. Configure Windows XP so that the computer can connect to the Internet. Open Internet Explorer and configure it to use this connection.

12. Extract the data files to both the C and D drives on each student and instructor computer prior to class. Remove the Read-only attribute from the data files after extracting them.

For the Instructor's Computer Only:

1. If you've chosen to use McAfee VirusScan and you want to be able to demonstrate manually updating virus definitions during the class, install McAfee VirusScan on the instructor's computer.

2. Register the McAfee VirusScan software.

To Provide Data File and Overhead Access:

1. Keep the courseware CD-ROM available at the instructor computer to display PowerPoint slides. The CD-ROM includes the PowerPoint viewer.

   IMPORTANT: The following instructions are for the optional Lesson Labs at the end of this book. Lesson Labs are meant to be self-guided practice activities for students to reinforce what they learned in class and are completely separate from the activities you'll present in the classroom. You do not need to set up the Lesson Labs in order to successfully teach this course.

For Lesson 2, Lab 1:

If students will be keying this lab immediately following Lesson 2, you will need to provide them with access to the Windows 98 Resource Kit installation files. Complete the following tasks:

1. Copy the \Tools\Reskit folder and its contents from the Windows 98 installation CD-ROM to C:\Tools\Reskit on the classroom domain controller.

2. Share the C:\Tools\Reskit folder as Reskit.

3. Have students restart their computers to Windows 98 and log on.

If students will be keying this lab outside of the pre-established classroom environment, you will need to provide the following:

- A computer with the default installation of Windows 98.

- Access to the student data files.

- Access to the \Tools\Reskit folder and its contents from the Windows 98 installation CD-ROM. You can provide this access by sharing the files on another computer, copying them to the local hard disk on the Windows 98 computer, or by giving the students the Windows 98 installation CD-ROM.

For Lesson 3, Lab 1:

If students will be keying this lab immediately following Lesson 3, there is no additional setup that is required. Students should boot into Windows XP and begin the lab. If students will be keying this lab outside of the pre-established classroom environment, you will need to provide the following:

- A networked computer with the default installation of Windows XP.
- A second networked computer so that students can test the network configuration of the computers.
- A DHCP server.
- Access to the Internet.

For Lesson 4, Lab 1:

If students will be keying this lab immediately following Lesson 4, there is no additional setup that is required. Students should boot into Windows XP and begin the lab. If students will be keying this lab outside of the pre-established classroom environment, you will need to provide a computer with the default installation of Windows XP.

For Lesson 5, Lab 1:

If students will be keying this lab immediately following Lesson 5, there is no additional setup that is required. Students should boot into Windows XP and begin the lab. If students will be keying this lab outside of the pre-established classroom environment, you will need to provide the following:

- A networked computer with the default installation of Windows XP.
- A domain controller. Follow the steps outlined in the "For the Classroom Domain Controller" setup procedure.

For Lesson 6, Lab 1:

If students will be keying this lab immediately following Lesson 6, there is no additional setup that is required. Students should boot into Windows 98 and begin the lab.

If students will be keying this lab outside of the pre-established classroom environment, you will need to provide the following:

- A networked computer with a default installation of Windows 98.
- A second computer with a network connection so that students can test the share permissions they have set up on the Windows 98 computer's resources.

For Lesson 7, Lab 1:

If students will be keying this lab immediately following Lesson 7, you will need to have them delete the Z drive created during the lesson. Students should then boot into Windows XP and begin the lab.

If students will be keying this lab outside of the pre-established classroom environment, you will need to provide the following:

- A computer with a 4 GB or larger hard disk that contains one 3 GB partition with a default installation of Windows XP and the rest of the disk left as free space.

For Lesson 8, Lab 1:

Students will not be able to key this lab immediately following Lesson 8 because they will have already completed the tasks that make up this lab in the activities within the lesson. In addition, students cannot complete this lab on the classroom computers because the tasks in the lab will prevent them from running Windows 2000 and Windows XP. To provide additional practice for this lesson outside of the pre-established classroom environment, you will need to provide the following:

1. A computer with a 3 GB or larger hard disk that contains one 2 GB partition with a default installation of Windows 98 and the rest left as free space.

For Lesson 9, Lab 1:

If students will be keying this lab immediately following Lesson 9, there is no additional setup that is required. Students should boot into Windows 98 and begin the lab. If students will be keying this lab outside of the pre-established classroom environment, you will need to provide the following:

1. A networked computer with a default installation of Windows 98.

2. An email account for each student completing the lab. You can obtain these accounts either by installing Microsoft Exchange Server on an accessible domain controller and creating the necessary accounts, or by creating the accounts with one of the free email services such as Hotmail.

For Lesson 10, Lab 1:

If students will be keying this lab immediately following the Implementing Virus Protection lesson, there is no additional setup that is required. Students should boot into Windows 98 and begin the lab. If students will be keying this lab outside of the pre-established classroom environment, you will need to provide the following:

1. A computer with a default installation of Windows 98.

2. A copy of Norton AntiVirus 2003.

3. An Internet connection so that students can obtain the latest virus definition files from the Symantec security Web site.

For Lesson 11, Lab 1:

Students cannot complete this activity using the computers configured for the classroom. This activity requires a client computer configured to dual-boot between Windows 2000 and Windows XP. This computer should have a 6 GB or larger hard disk. Prepare the client computer as follows:

1. Perform a default installation of Windows 2000 Professional.

    *   During the installation, create a C partition that is 2 GB in size and uses the NTFS file system.

    *   Install Windows 2000 Professional into the C partition.

    *   Install the course data files into the C partition.

2. After you have completed this installation, in Windows 2000 Professional, create two additional primary partitions that are each 2 GB in size. Format these partitions to use the NTFS file system.

3. Install Windows XP Professional into the second primary partition on the computer.

4. Provide the students with three blank floppy disks for use in the lab.

For Lesson 12, Lab 1:

Students cannot complete this activity using the computers configured for the classroom. You will need to provide the following:

1. A networked computer with a default installation of Windows 2000.

2. A bootable Windows 2000 Professional installation CD-ROM.

3. An Internet connection so that students can research error messages.

4. Access to the Lab student data files.

For Lesson 13, Lab 1:

Students cannot complete this activity using the computers configured for the classroom. You will need to provide the following:

1. A computer that meets the minimum hardware requirements for both Windows 2000 and Windows XP. This computer should have a hard disk that is 4 GB or larger.

2. Access to the Windows 2000 Professional and Windows XP Professional installation CD-ROMs. If the drivers for your computers' hardware are not included on the installation CD-ROMs, you will also need to provide students with access to the hardware drivers.

3. Access to the Internet so that students can update their computers after completing the installations.

4. A domain controller. Use the "For the Classroom Domain Controller" setup procedure to set up the domain controller.

For Lesson 14, Lab 1:

Students cannot complete this activity using the computers configured for the classroom. You will need to provide the following:

1. A computer that meets the minimum hardware requirements for Windows XP.

2. A computer on which to create the unattended answer file. This can be the same computer on which they're going to install Windows XP as long as the computer has an operating system.

3. Access to the Windows XP Professional installation CD-ROM.

4. If the drivers for your computers' hardware are not included on the installation CD-ROMs, you will also need to provide students with access to the hardware drivers.

5. Access to the Internet so that students can update their computers after completing the installation.

List of Additional Files

Printed with each activity is a list of files students open to complete that activity. Many activities also require additional files that students do not open, but are needed to support the file(s) students are working with. These supporting files are included with the student data files on the course CD-ROM or data disk. Do not delete these files.

LESSON 1
Windows Tools

Lesson Objectives:

In this lesson, you will list Windows and command-line tools.

You will:

- Describe Windows graphical tools.
- Describe command-line tools.

Introduction

As an A+ technician supporting Windows computers, when you sit down at a computer the first thing you need to know is which tools you need to use to accomplish a particular task. So before you begin to learn how to administer and support a Windows computer, you need to learn which tools you have at your disposal and when to use them.

Imagine having to troubleshoot a user's network connection, or having to copy a file from a floppy disk to a hard drive. And picture the situation where you need to install a new network card or a new application. Which tools do you use? Where do you find them? Are they the same tools in Windows NT Workstation 4.0 as they are in Windows XP? You can't do your job, or even learn to do your job, without knowing which tools to use and how to find them. So in this lesson, you'll learn about two sets of tools: graphical tools and command-line tools. Once you know the basics, you can sit down at any Windows computer and instantly find the tools you need.

The following CompTIA A+ Operating System Technologies (2003) Examination objectives are covered in this lesson:

- Topic A:
    - 1.1 Contrasts between Windows 9x/ME, Windows NT 4.0 Workstation, Windows 2000 Professional, and Windows XP.
    - 1.1 Major Operating System Interfaces: Windows Explorer, My Computer, Control Panel, Computer Management Console, Accessories/System Tools, Network Neighborhood/My Network Places, Task Bar/Systray, Start Menu, Device Manager.
    - 1.4 Directory Structure (root directory, subdirectories, etc): Maximum Depth.
    - 1.4 Files: File naming conventions, File types (text vs binary file).
    - 1.5 Disk Management Tools: Disk Cleanup.
    - 1.5 System Management Tools: Device Manager, Event Viewer.
    - 1.5 File Management Tools: Windows Explorer.
    - 2.5 Caches.
- Topic B:
    - 1.1 Major Operating System Interfaces: Command line.
    - 1.3 Command line functions and utilities include: Command/CMD, DIR, ATTRIB, VER, MEM, SCANDISK, DEFRAG, EDIT, XCOPY, COPY, FORMAT, FDISK, SETVER, MD/CD/RD, Delete/Rename, DELTREE, TYPE, ECHO, SET.
    - 1.5 Disk Management Tools: ScanDisk, CHKDSK, Format.
    - 1.5 System Management Tools: COMMAND/CMD.
    - 3.2 Diagnostic tools, utilities and resources: MSD.

Topic A

Windows Graphical Tools

When you sit down in front of a Windows computer to perform routing maintenance, because Windows has a graphical interface, most times you're going to open a graphical tool. Because the most common Windows tools are graphical, we're going to cover them first in this lesson.

There are a wide variety of graphical tools available in the Windows operating systems, so knowing which one to use and when to use it is important for any Windows support personnel. If you don't know which tools are available, and which tools perform which functions, you'll find you won't get very far as an A+ technician.

Graphical Tools

Definition:

A graphical tool is a program that is opened within a Windows operating system and is displayed in a colorful window with a mixture of text and icons to represent files and programs on the computer. Graphical tools enable users to manage operating systems using a combination of input from mouse clicks and a keyboard. Output from the computer is displayed in the same window or new windows, which represent the results of the user's input.

Example: My Computer

As you can see in Figure 1-1, My Computer is an example of a graphical utility. The tool is opened from within the operating system by double-clicking the My Computer icon on the desktop. The tool combines text and icons to represent files and programs on the computer. Users can use a mouse to click the files and programs to open them, or they can use the keyboard to open files and programs by pressing Enter. Results are displayed right in the My Computer window or in new windows that open when a user launches a program.

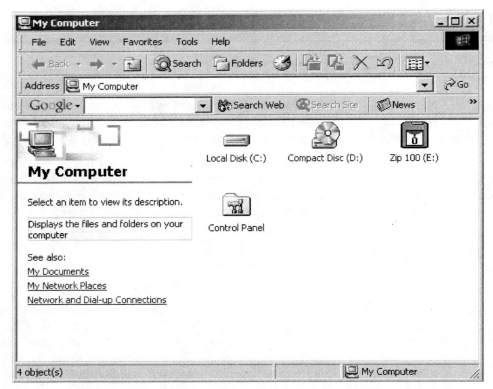

Figure 1-1: *My Computer graphical tool in Windows 2000.*

Taskbar

The taskbar is located at the bottom of a Windows screen, as shown in Figure 1-2. It contains the following items:

- The Start button.

- The Quick Launch toolbar (Windows 98 and Windows 2000), which has icons that let you quickly launch the most often used programs, including Internet Explorer and Outlook Express. You can add other programs to this toolbar by dragging shortcuts onto it.

- Buttons for any open programs.

- The system tray, which includes the clock, and icons for any programs that have been configured to add an icon to the system tray. You can often access the properties of these programs by clicking or right-clicking the icons in the system tray.

taskbar

Figure 1-2: *The taskbar in Windows XP Professional.*

While the taskbar might appear slightly different in the various versions of the Windows operating systems, it's default location and function is the same.

Start Menu

The Start menu, shown in Figure 1-3, is the main starting point in the Windows operating system. You can access almost any graphical tool you need on the Start menu, including Windows Explorer and Control Panel, by choosing it directly from the Start menu or from one of the sub-menus that open off of it. You can open the Start menu by clicking the Start button on the taskbar, in the lower-left corner of the Windows screen. While the Start menu might have a slightly different appearance from one version of Windows to the next, it still provides a central location for all the important system tools you'll need to manage the operating system.

Figure 1-3: *The Windows Start menu in Windows 98.*

The default installations of the different Windows operating systems will arrange the Start menu in slightly different ways. Table 1-1 shows which menus and items you'll see when you open the Start menu in fresh installations of Windows 98, Windows NT 4.0, Windows 2000, and Windows XP. In addition to these items, the Start menu might also contain programs that have been configured to add menu items to it.

Table 1-1: *Start Menu Contents*

Operating System	What's on the Start Menu When You Open It
Windows 98	Windows Update, Programs menu, Favorites menu, Documents menu, Settings menu, Find menu, Help, Run, Log Off *username*, and Shut Down.
Windows NT Workstation 4.0	Programs menu, Documents menu, Settings menu, Find menu, Help, Run, and Shut Down.
Windows 2000 Professional	Windows Update, Programs menu, Documents menu, Settings menu, Search menu, Help, Run, and Shut Down.
Windows XP Professional	Internet Explorer, Outlook Express, MSN Explorer, Windows Media Player, Windows Movie Maker, Tour Windows XP, Files And Settings Transfer Wizard, All Programs menu, My Documents, My Recent Documents menu, My Pictures, My Music, My Computer, My Network Places (if networking properties have been configured), Control Panel, Printers And Faxes, Help And Support, Search, Run, Log Off, and Turn Off Computer. The Start menu might also contain any commonly used programs (added automatically).

In Windows 98, Windows 2000, and Windows XP, the Programs menu has an Accessories submenu, which itself contains a System Tools submenu. You can use the System Tools menu to open a variety of tools, which are listed in Table 1-2. System Tools, such as Disk Cleanup, which is used to find and delete unnecessary temporary files or Internet cache files to help recover disk space, are important management tools that you can use to optimize a computer's performance.

Table 1-2: *System Tools on Windows Operating Systems*

Operating System	System Tools Menu Contents
Windows 98	Backup, Disk Cleanup, Disk Defragmenter, Drive Converter, Maintenance Wizard, ScanDisk, Scheduled Tasks, System Information, and Welcome To Windows.
Windows 2000	Backup, Character Map, Disk Cleanup, Disk Defragmenter, Getting Started, Scheduled Tasks, and System Information.
Windows XP	Activate Windows, Backup, Character Map, Disk Cleanup, Disk Defragmenter, Files And Settings Transfer Wizard, Scheduled Tasks, System Information, and System Restore.

Windows Explorer

You use Windows Explorer, shown in Figure 1-4, to manage files and folders on your computer, including the contents of your hard disk, floppy drives, CD-ROM/CD-R/CD-RW drives, DVD/DVD-R drives, and any other storage device attached to your computer. Windows Explorer might look slightly different on the different versions of Windows, but you still use it for the same purpose. You can find Windows Explorer on the Programs menu in Windows 98 and Windows NT 4.0, and you can find it on the Accessories menu off the Start menu in Windows 2000 and Windows XP.

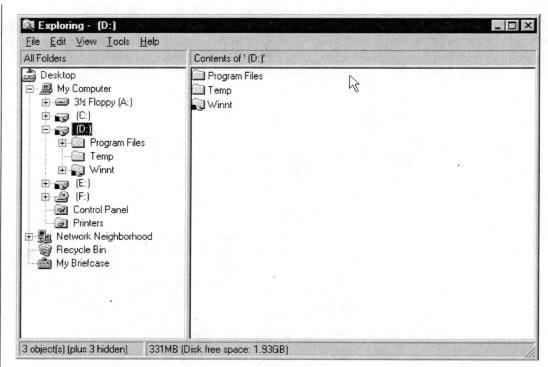

Figure 1-4: *Windows Explorer in Windows NT Workstation 4.0.*

When naming files and folders in Windows Explorer, keep in mind that the maximum depth of a folder structure is dictated by the maximum number of characters in a file path, which is 255. Included in this total is the character representing the C drive and any file extension. The three-letter file extension is used to represent the contents of the file. Some of the more common file name extensions are listed in Table 1-3. In Windows, file extensions are used to associate files with applications, such as text documents with Word or spreadsheets with Excel. If you alter a file name extension, you might find that the file won't run properly or that you can't open it with its associated application, so take care when modifying file names to preserve their extensions.

 Text files can be read using a common text editor, such as Notepad, while binary files (executable programs) can be read only by the computer.

Table 1-3: *Common File Extensions*

File Extension	File Type
bat	Batch file
bin	Binary file
com	Command file
exe	Programs/applications
hlp, chm	Help files
htm, html	HyperText Markup Language (HTML) files
inf	Setup configuration settings
ini	Configuration settings
msi	Windows Installer package
sys	System files

File Extension	File Type
tif, jpg, jpeg, gif, bmp	Image files
txt, rtf	Text files
vbs	VBScript file

My Computer

Like Windows Explorer, My Computer is used to manage files and folders on your computer and on any storage devices attached to your computer. You can also access other Windows tools, such as Control Panel, using My Computer, which you can open by double-clicking the My Computer icon on the desktop in Windows 98, Windows NT 4.0, and Windows 2000. You can open My Computer from the Start menu in Windows XP.

Control Panel

Control Panel contains programs that you use to configure the Windows operating system or the computer's hardware. In Table 1-4, we list the most commonly used Control Panel programs.

 You'll sometimes hear the Control Panel programs referred to as applets.

Table 1-4: *Control Panel Programs*

Applet	Use To
Add New Hardware (Windows 9x); Add/Remove Hardware (Windows 2000); Add Hardware (Windows XP)	Install or remove hardware devices from the computer.
Add/Remove Programs (Windows 9x, Windows NT/2000); Add or Remove Programs (Windows XP)	Install or remove application software from the computer.
Display	Configure the wallpaper, screen saver, color scheme, and screen resolution for the computer's monitor.
Mouse	Configure mouse properties such as whether you're using the mouse left-handed or right-handed, the double-click speed, pointer style, and acceleration.
Passwords (only in Windows 9x)	Change the current user's password and to implement user profiles in Windows 9x.
System	Configure hardware profiles, devices (Windows 9x/2000/XP), and performance settings such as virtual memory.

Figure 1-5: *Control Panel in Windows 2000.*

Like other graphical tools, Control Panel may look slightly different from one Windows version to the next, but essentially its function is the same. Control Panel in Windows 2000, shown in Figure 1-5, looks much the same as it does in Windows 98 and Windows NT 4.0. However, Control Panel in Windows XP, shown in Figure 1-6, looks different because similar tools are grouped together in categories, and it is the categories and not the programs that you see when you first open Control Panel in Windows XP.

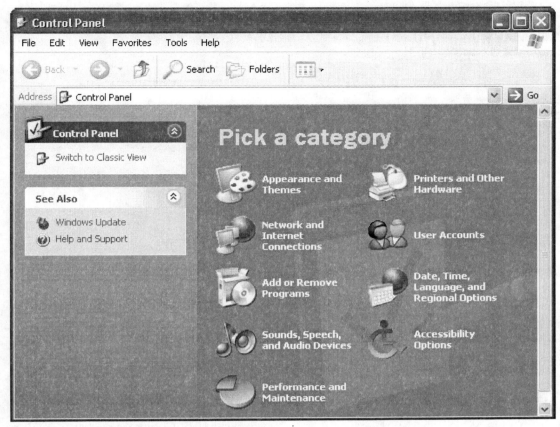

Figure 1-6: *Control Panel in Windows XP.*

You can find Control Panel off the Settings submenu on the Start menu in Windows 98, Windows NT 4.0, and Windows 2000. In Windows XP, Control Panel can be opened directly from the Start menu.

Computer Management in Windows 2000/XP

One central place to find just about every system administration or information tool in Windows 2000 and Windows XP is Computer Management, shown in Figure 1-7. You can open Computer Management by right-clicking My Computer and choosing Manage. You can use Computer Management to perform a wide variety of administrative tasks, including:

- View and manage logs in Event Viewer.
- View system information, such as processor speed and RAM configuration.
- View and configure performance monitors.
- Manage shared folders.
- Manage and configure devices.
- Manage local user and group accounts.
- Configure hard disks and partitions.
- Defragment the hard disk.
- Manage logical drives.
- Configure removable storage devices.

- Configure system services.

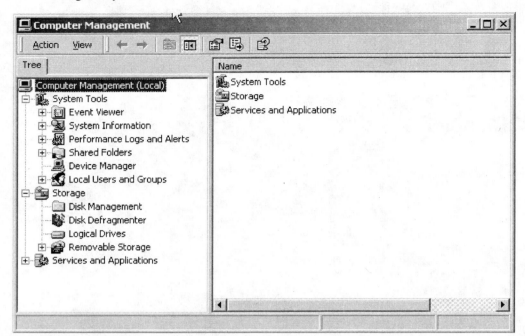

Figure 1-7: *The Computer Management screen.*

Network Neighborhood and My Network Places

Network Neighborhood and My Network Places are similar to My Computer in that they allow you to manage files and folders. The difference is you use Network Neighborhood and My Network Places to manage files and folders on other computers in the network. Of course, you must have the necessary permissions to connect to another computer and manage files and folders on that computer.

You can use Network Neighborhood and My Network Places to perform the following tasks:

- Connect to another computer on the network.
- Transfer files and folders from another computer to your computer.
- Transfer files and folders from your computer to another computer.
- Manage files and folders on another computer in the network.

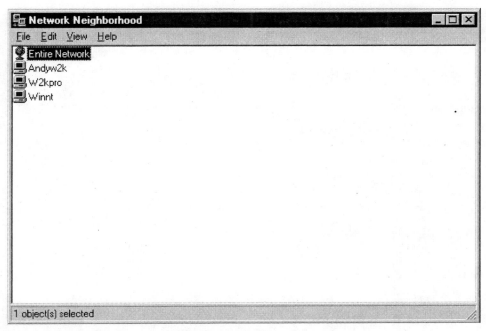

Figure 1-8: *Network Neighborhood in Windows NT 4.0.*

Network Neighborhood, shown in Figure 1-8, is the tool you use in Windows 98 and Windows NT 4.0. My Network Places, shown in Figure 1-9, is the tool you use in Windows 2000 and Windows XP. You can find the tool in the desktop in Windows 98, Windows NT 4.0, and Windows 2000. You can find the tool in Windows XP in the Network And Internet Connections category in Control Panel. To access any of the computers or shared folders you see in Network Neighborhood and My Network Places, just double-click them. (You might be prompted to enter another user name and password to access the resources in Windows NT 4.0, Windows 2000, or Windows XP.)

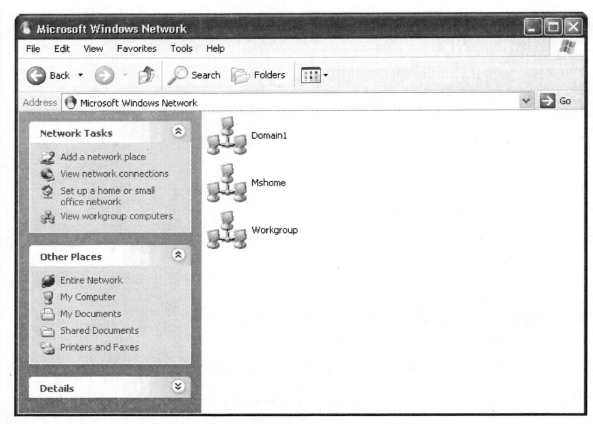

Figure 1-9: *My Network Places in Windows XP.*

Device Manager

In Windows 9x, Windows 2000, and Windows XP, you can determine the hardware devices currently installed in a computer by using the Device Manager. Device Manager is not available in Windows NT. You can use Device Manager to determine the following information:

- The name of a particular hardware component installed in a computer.
- The status of each hardware device.
- The hardware driver installed for each component.
- The hardware resources in use by each component.

You can also use Device Manager to determine the status of your hardware devices. If Device Manager detects a problem, it displays one of the following icons next to the device:

- A red X over a device if it's disabled, as shown in Figure 1-10.
- A yellow circle with an exclamation point if a device's driver is not installed.
- A question mark if a device's configuration conflicts with another device in the computer.

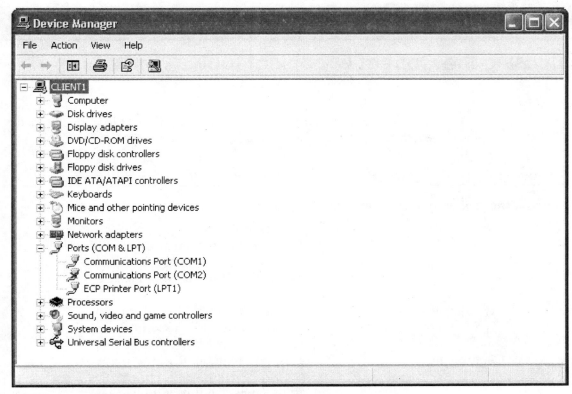

Figure 1-10: *Device Manager in Windows XP.*

Disk Management Tools

In Windows 2000 and Windows XP, you manage hard disks by using the Disk Management utility within the Computer Management console. In Windows NT, you manage hard disks by using the Disk Manager administrative tool. Regardless of which operating system you're using, you access the disk management tool from Administrative Tools.

Account Management Tools

Windows 2000, Windows XP, and Windows NT each include a utility for creating, managing, and deleting user and group accounts. In Windows 2000 and Windows XP, you use Computer Management. In Windows NT, you use User Manager.

ACTIVITY 1-1

Choosing the Correct Graphical Tool

Scenario:

As part of a job interview for an A+ technician position, you've been asked to correctly identify a list of graphical tools that you'd use to manage a Windows computer.

What You Do	**How You Do It**

1. **Match the tool with its description.**

___ Windows Explorer

a. Found in Windows 2000 and Windows XP, this tool contains just about every system administration or information tool you'd need to manage both operating systems.

___ My Computer

b. Found in Windows 98 and Windows NT 4.0, this tools is used to connect to other computers on the network.

___ Control Panel

c. This tool, found in the lower-left corner of a Windows desktop, contains all the tools you'd need to manage the computer.

___ Computer Management

d. Found in Windows 98, Windows 2000, and Windows XP, this tool is used to gather information about the hardware attached to a computer.

___ My Network Places

e. Opened directly from the Start menu in Windows XP, this tool contains programs used to configure the Windows operating system or the computer's hardware.

___ Network Neighborhood

f. Opened from the desktop in Windows 98, Windows NT 4.0, and Windows 2000, this tool is used to manage files and folders on your computer.

___ Device Manager

g. Found in Windows 2000 and Windows XP, this tool is used to connect to other computers on the network.

___ Start menu

h. Opened from the Programs menu in Windows 98 and Windows NT 4.0, this tool is used to manage files and folders on your computer.

TOPIC B

Windows Command-line Tools

Command-line tools are an additional set of tools that you can use to manage Windows computers. You won't use them as often as graphical tools, but they can be just as important in successfully managing the Windows environment.

What happens when your computer won't boot to Windows? Or what do you do when you find a graphical tool too clumsy to use? Fortunately, the command-line tools are available for use within a Windows operating system and outside the operating system in a DOS environment if you can't boot to Windows or if a graphical tool doesn't provide the functionality you need to perform a simple task. In this lesson, you'll learn which command-line tools are available to help you manage your Windows computers.

Command-line Tool

Definition:

A command-line tool is a program that is run by entering appropriate command syntax at a command prompt. The command prompt can be either a command prompt in a DOS environment or in a Command Prompt window in a Windows environment. Command-line tools accept only text input, and they output information in text format or sometimes by opening a window to display information in graphical form. Some command-line tools can only be run in a DOS environment and some can be run in both a DOS and Windows environment. You can also use command-line tools to automate certain administrative functions, such as defragmenting a hard drive, with custom made scripts, such as a batch file or a Visual Basic script.

Example: Format

Format is a program that you run by entering the correct command syntax at a command prompt. You can use Format in a DOS environment or in a Command Prompt window in a Windows environment, which you can see in Figure 1-11. Format accepts text input, and it outputs information in text format.

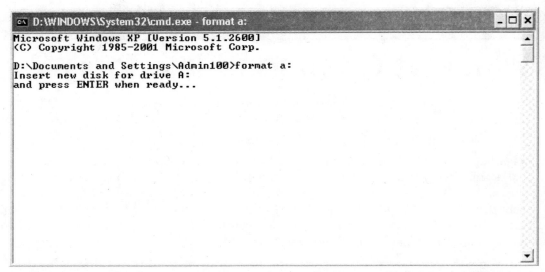

Figure 1-11: *The Format command-line tool in a Windows XP Command Prompt window.*

Popular Command-line Tools

There are a variety of command-line tools you can use to manage your Windows computers. Some popular command-line tools are listed in Table 1-5. Because the syntax may vary slightly in the different operating systems, you should check online help for the exact syntax. To view online help, enter the command followed by a forward slash and a question mark (/?). For a list of all the available commands, type `help` at the command prompt in Windows NT 4.0, Windows 2000, and Windows XP.

 Not all tools are available in all operating systems.

Table 1-5: *Popular Command-line Tools*

Tool	Used to	Sample Syntax	Supported Operating Systems
Cd	Change to another folder (directory).	cd *drive:path*	Windows 98, Windows NT, Windows 2000, and Windows XP
Cmd	Open the command interpreter.	cmd	Windows NT, Windows 2000, and Windows XP
Command	Open the command interpreter.	command *drive:path*	Windows 98
Copy	Copy files.	copy *source_files destination*	Windows 98, Windows NT, Windows 2000, and Windows XP
Defrag	Defragment hard drives.	defrag *volume*	Windows 98 and Windows XP
Del	Delete files.	del *filename*	Windows 98, Windows NT, Windows 2000, and Windows XP

Tool	Used to	Sample Syntax	Supported Operating Systems
Deltree	Delete a directory structure (a directory and all its subdirectories).	`deltree filepath`	DOS and Windows 98
Echo	Display a message or enable/disable echoing.	`echo on	off` or `echo message`	Windows 98, Windows NT, Windows 2000, and Windows XP
Extract	Extract cabinet (.cab) files	`extract cabinet filename`	Windows 98, and Windows 2000 (with download)
Md	Create a folder (directory).	`md foldername`	Windows 98, Windows NT, Windows 2000, and Windows XP
Rd	Delete a folder (directory).	`rd foldername`	Windows 98, Windows NT, Windows 2000, and Windows XP
Rename	Rename a file.	`rename drive:path oldfilename newfilename`	Windows 98, Windows NT, Windows 2000, and Windows XP
Set	Configure environment variables.	`set variable=string`	Windows 98, Windows NT, Windows 2000, and Windows XP
Setver	Configure the version of DOS Windows reports to a program. Used to simulate an older version of DOS if an application won't run in Windows 2000/ XP/NT.)	`setver drive:path filename DOSversion`	Windows 98, Windows NT, Windows 2000, and Windows XP
Type	Display a text file.	`type drive:path filename`	Windows 98, Windows NT, Windows 2000, and Windows XP
Ver	Display operating system version.	`ver`	Windows 98, Windows NT, Windows 2000, and Windows XP
Xcopy	Copy files, folders, and directory trees.	`xcopy source destination`	Windows 98, Windows NT, Windows 2000, and Windows XP

Command-line Troubleshooting Tools

One of the common problems you can encounter is a hard disk that won't boot to Windows or won't boot at all. There are several tools that you can use to troubleshoot problems that are preventing a computer from booting. In Table 1-6, you'll find a list of these tools, a description that includes an explanation of when you might use the tool, and the command's syntax if applicable. You can also use many of these tools within a Command Prompt window; check the operating system Help files for more information.

 Use a DOS boot disk to boot a computer that otherwise won't boot from the hard disk.

Table 1-6: *DOS Boot Troubleshooting Tools*

Tool	Purpose	Syntax
Attrib	Enables you to change the attributes of files. You might use this command if you need to edit a file that has the read-only attribute.	Enter attrib *filename + or - attribute*. For example, to remove the read-only attribute from the boot.ini file, you would enter attrib boot.ini -r.
chkdsk	Enables you to check the hard disk for errors. If any errors are reported, you can then use other tools such as ScanDisk to repair those errors.	Enter chkdsk *drive letter*. For example, to check the C drive, enter chkdsk C:.
Dir	Use to view the contents of a directory. For example, you might use the dir command to verify that a file exists in a directory.	Enter dir *path options*. For example, to view a list of the files in the C:\ directory, you would enter dir C:\. If you want to display the list of files in alphabetical order, enter dir C:\ /on. (/on in this syntax stands for "order by name.")
Edit	Use to edit a file. For example, you might use edit to correct problems with the Autoexec.bat or Config.sys files.	Enter edit *filename*. For example, if you need to edit the boot.ini file, enter edit boot.ini.
Fdisk	Use to view, create, or delete partitions, and to mark a primary partition as active.	
Format	Use to format a disk. You can also use it to format a disk and make it bootable.	Enter format A: /s to format a floppy disk and make it bootable.
Mem	View the memory usage on a computer including the conventional, upper memory, and high memory area segments.	Enter mem.
Msd	View system information.	Enter msd to start the Msd utility.
Scandisk	Performs a thorough check of a hard disk and repairs any errors it encounters.	Enter scandisk *drive letter*.
Sys.com	Transfer the Io.sys and Msdos.sys files from a bootable floppy disk to a hard disk so that the computer can boot from the hard disk.	Enter sys C:.

ACTIVITY 1-2

Scenario:

As the second part of a job interview for an A+ technician position, you've been asked to correctly identify a list of command-line tools that you'd use to manage a Windows computer.

What You Do	How You Do It

1. **Match the command-line tool with its description.**

___	Md	a.	Copies files, folders, and directory trees.
___	Deltree	b.	Displays the operating system version.
___	Ver	c.	Creates a new directory.
___	Xcopy	d.	Displays the memory usage on a computer.
___	Dir	e.	Configures environment variables.
___	Mem	f.	Changes file attributes.
___	Attrib	g.	Deletes a specified directory structure (a directory and all its subdirectories).
___	Set	h.	Displays the contents of a directory.

Lesson 1 Follow-up

In this lesson, you learned about Windows graphical and command-line tools that an A+ technician needs to perform his or her job. Knowing which tools to use is a given situation and how to find them is an important skill that every technician who supports Windows computers needs to have in order to perform such basic functions as installing applications and troubleshooting network connections. And now that you know which tools you have at your disposal, you're ready to begin managing and supporting Windows computers.

1. **Which Windows tools do you think you'll be using most often?**

2. **Which command-line tools do you think you'll use most often?**

LESSON 2
Managing Applications

Lesson Time
1 hour(s), 30 minutes

Lesson Objectives:

In this lesson, you will manage applications.

You will:

- Install a Windows application.
- Configure virtual memory.
- Install a non-Windows application.
- Configure a non-Windows application.
- Remove an application.

Introduction

Because they're some of the tasks you'll perform most often as an A+ technician, you're going to begin learning how to be an A+ technician by learning how to install, configure, and remove applications on users' computers. Applications such as Microsoft Office or Lotus Notes enable your users to use their computers to perform the tasks required by their jobs. In this lesson, you'll learn how to install, configure, and remove applications.

Without properly installed applications, your users won't be able to get any work done on their computers. If your users can't get any work done, your company won't be productive—which means your company might lose money until the users can access the applications they need to perform their jobs. For these reasons, it's important that you know how to install, configure, and remove applications so that your users can be productive.

The following CompTIA A+ Operating System Technologies (2003) Examination objectives are covered in this lesson:

- Topic A:
  — 1.1 Major Operating System components: Registry
  — 1.2 Windows 9x-specific files: Registry data files: SYSTEM.DAT, USER.DAT.
  — 1.2 Windows NT-based specific files: NTUSER.DAT, Registry data files.
  — 1.5 System Management Tools: REGEDIT.EXE (View information/Backup registry), REGEDT32.EXE
  — 2.5 Virtual Memory Management.
  — 2.2 Verify application compatibility.
- Topic B:
  — 1.1 Major Operating System components: Virtual Memory.
  — 2.5 Files and Buffers.
- Topic D:
  — 1.2 Windows 9x-specific files: HIMEM.SYS, EMM386.exe,
  — 2.5 Temporary file management.

TOPIC A

Install a Windows Application

This lesson focuses on managing applications. The first step in managing applications is to install them on computers. Windows applications are the most common type of application you'll encounter in the workplace. So, in this topic, you'll learn how to install a Windows application on your users' computers.

Before your users can work with an application, you must install it so that it's available for the user on the Start menu. Not only must you install the application, but you must also make sure that you install it correctly. Installing the application correctly the first time around will prevent you from having to spend time later troubleshooting or even re-installing the application.

Installation Types

You have three choices for installing an application: Autorun, Executable File (Local), and Executable File (Network). In Table 2-1, we describe the different installation types from which you can choose.

Table 2-1: *Installation Types*

Installation Source	Installation Type	Enables You to Perform an Installation Using
Local	Autorun	The application's installation CD-ROM. If a CD-ROM contains an Autorun file, the Windows computer automatically runs this file whenever you insert the CD-ROM. The Autorun file typically launches a wizard that guides you through installing that application.
Local	Executable file	An executable file such as Setup.exe or Install.exe or an installation package (.msi) file; this file can be stored on local media such as the computer's local hard disk, the application's installation CD-ROM, or a floppy disk. When you double-click the executable file for installing an application, it typically launches a wizard that guides you through installing that application.
Network	Shared folder or CD-ROM	An executable file such as Setup.exe or Install.exe or an installation package (.msi) file stored on a shared network folder or CD-ROM. When you connect to the shared folder and double-click the application's installation executable file, it typically launches a wizard that guides you through installing that application.

 Many companies share their application's installation files on a server so that those applications can be easily installed on computers throughout the network. Installing an application from a shared folder makes the installation easier because you won't have to insert the installation CD-ROM in each computer.

The Background Logon Authentication Process

When you connect to a shared resource, such as a shared folder or printer on a network, Windows verifies that you're authorized to access that share.

1. Your computer provides the user name and password you used to log on to the local computer to the computer containing the shared resource to which you're attempting to connect. (This authentication process takes place in the background. You are prompted to interact with the authentication process only when the credentials you provided on your computer are not valid on the computer to which you're attempting to connect.)

2. The computer with the shared resource checks either its user account database or the domain's account database to verify that your user name and password are valid.

3. If your user name and password are valid, the computer with the shared resource checks the resource's access permissions list to verify that you have sufficient permissions to connect to the shared resource.

    If your user name and password are not valid, you receive an unknown user name or password error message and must enter valid credentials.

4. If you have sufficient permissions, you're permitted to access the shared resource.

    If you do not have sufficient permissions to access the resource, you receive an Access Denied error message.

Registry

Definition:

The *Registry* is a configuration database in the Windows 9x, Windows NT, Windows 2000, and Windows XP operating systems that specifies how the computer is configured. This database contains configuration information for:

*   Applications that are installed on the computer.

*   The computer's hardware.

*   Security settings.

In Windows 9x, the Registry consists of two files: system.dat and user.dat; these files are stored in the \Windows folder. In Windows NT, Windows 2000, and Windows XP, the Registry consists of five files stored in the \Winnt\System32\Config folder: Default, SAM, Security, Software, and System, plus a file named Ntuser.dat that's unique for each user who logs on to the computer. This file is stored in the user's profile folder.

If you're using Windows 9x, Windows NT, Windows 2000, or Windows XP, the Registry consists of the HKEY_CLASSES_ROOT, HKEY_CURRENT_USER, HKEY_LOCAL_MACHINE, HKEY_USERS, and HKEY_CURRENT_CONFIG subtrees. Windows 9x contains an additional subtree, HKEY_DYN_DATA. Table 2-2 describes the purpose of each of these subtrees.

Table 2-2: *The Registry Subtrees*

Subtree	Contains
HKEY_CLASSES_ROOT	All the file association information. Windows 9x uses this information to determine which application it should open whenever you double-click a file with a specific extension. For example, Windows 9x automatically opens Notepad whenever you double-click a file with the extension .txt.

Subtree	Contains
HKEY_CURRENT_USER	The user-specific configuration information for the user currently logged on to the computer. For example, information about the user's selected color scheme and wallpaper is stored in this subtree.
HKEY_LOCAL_MACHINE	All the configuration information for the computer's hardware. For example, this subtree contains information about any modems installed in the computer, any defined hardware profiles, and the networking configuration.
HKEY_USERS	User-specific configuration information for all users who have ever logged on at the computer.
HKEY_CURRENT_CONFIG	Information about the current configuration of the computer's hardware. Because Windows 9x supports Plug and Play, the configuration of the hardware can vary even while the computer is running.
HKEY_DYN_DATA	Information that's stored in RAM on the computer for fast retrieval. For example, Windows 98 stores performance statistics in this subtree. Please note that this subtree is present only in the Windows 9x Registry.

Example:

In Figure 2-1, you find an example of application configuration information in the Windows 2000 Registry.

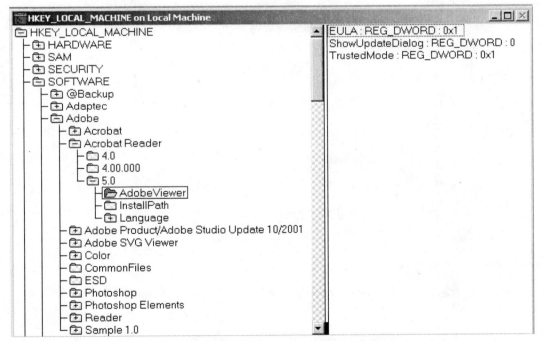

Figure 2-1: *The Registry with application configuration information.*

In Figure 2-2, you see the hardware configuration information as it's stored in the Registry.

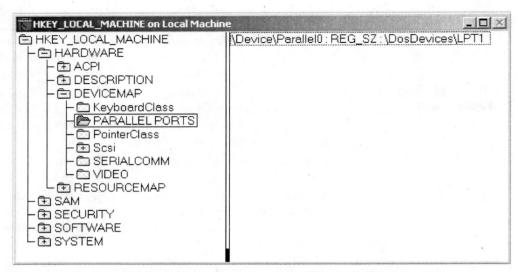

Figure 2-2: *The Registry with hardware configuration information.*

In Figure 2-3, you see the security information stored in the Registry.

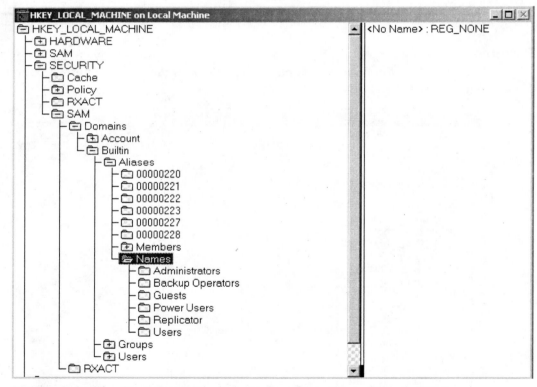

Figure 2-3: *The Registry with security configuration information.*

Registry Entries

Definition:

A Registry entry is a configuration specification that defines how the computer's hardware, software, or security settings are configured. A Registry entry must have a *key* and a value. You can optionally create a key to contain other keys and values. A key consists of only a name. A *value* consists of a name, a data type, and the *data* stored in the value. The data types you can assign to values include string, multiple strings, binary, and hexadecimal.

Data Types

In Windows 9x, you can assign the String, Binary, or Dword data types to a value. In Windows NT, Windows 2000, and Windows XP, you can assign the REG_BINARY, REG_SZ, REG_DWORD, REG_MULTI_SZ, or REG_EXPAND_SZ data types to a value. We describe each of these data types in Table 2-3.

Table 2-3: *Registry Value Data Types*

Supported Types of Data	Value Data Type
An alphanumeric string	String (Windows 9x); REG_SZ (Windows NT/2000/XP)
Multiple alphanumeric strings	REG_MULTI_SZ (Windows NT/2000/XP)
An expandable alphanumeric string	REG_EXPAND_SZ (Windows NT/2000/XP)
A binary value	Binary (Windows 9x); REG_BINARY (Windows NT/2000/XP)
A hexadecimal value	Dword (Windows 9x); REG_DWORD (Windows NT/2000/XP)

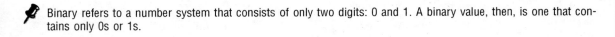

Binary refers to a number system that consists of only two digits: 0 and 1. A binary value, then, is one that contains only 0s or 1s.

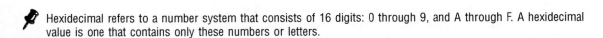

Hexidecimal refers to a number system that consists of 16 digits: 0 through 9, and A through F. A hexidecimal value is one that contains only these numbers or letters.

Example:

Figure 2-4 shows an example of a Registry key that contains several values.

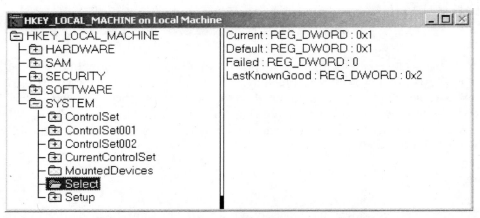

Figure 2-4: *A Registry key containing four values, each with a data type of REG_DWORD.*

Editing the Registry

Procedure Reference: Edit the Registry in Windows 9x

To edit the Registry in Windows 9x:

You should back up the Registry before making any changes to it.

1. From the Start menu, choose Run.
2. In the Open text box, type `regedit` and click OK.
3. Navigate to the location where you want to make a change to the Registry.
4. If you want to change the data for a Registry value:
   a. Double-click the value.
   b. In the Value Data text box, type the data for this value.
   c. Click OK.

   If you want to rename a key or value:
   a. Right-click the key or value and choose Rename.
   b. Enter a new name.

   If you want to add a new value to the Registry:
   a. Choose Edit→New, and then select the appropriate value type (String, Binary, or DWORD).
   b. Enter the name for the value.
   c. Double-click the new value.
   d. In the Value Data text box, type the data for this value and click OK.

   If you want to add a new key to the Registry:
   a. Choose Edit→New→Key.
   b. Enter a name for the new key.

   If you want to remove a key or value from the Registry:

    a.   Right-click the key or value you want to remove.

    b.   From the shortcut menu, choose Delete.

    c.   Click Yes to confirm the deletion.

5.   Close Registry Editor.

Procedure Reference: Edit the Registry in Windows NT, Windows 2000, and Windows XP

To edit the Registry in Windows NT, Windows 2000, and Windows XP:

You should back up the Registry before making any changes to it.

1.   Log on as a user with administrator privileges.

2.   From the Start menu, choose Run.

3.   In the Open text box, type `regedt32` and click OK.

4.   Navigate to the location where you want to make a change to the Registry.

5.   If you want to change the data for a Registry value:

    a.   Double-click the value.

    b.   In the text box, type the data for this value.

    c.   Click OK.

If you want to add a new value to the Registry:

    a.   Choose Edit→Add Value.

    b.   In the Value Name text box, type a name for the value.

    c.   From the Data Type drop-down list, select the data type for the value.

    d.   Click OK.

    e.   Enter the data for the new value and click OK.

If you want to add a new key to the Registry:

    a.   Choose Edit→Add Key.

    b.   Enter a name for the new key and click OK.

If you want to remove a key or value from the Registry:

    a.   Select the key or value you want to remove.

    b.   Choose Edit→Delete.

    c.   Click Yes to confirm the deletion.

6.   Close Registry Editor.

ACTIVITY 2-1

Examining the Registry

Setup:

Your user name is Admin#, where # is the number assigned to your computer. The password for this account is password.

Scenario:

You manage several Windows 2000 computers. You're planning to install new applications on those computers. You have just read an article that stated that when you install an application, that application's setup program updates the HKEY_LOCAL_MACHINE\Software key with information about that application. Before you install the new applications, you want to review the Windows 2000 Registry so that you can identify the changes installing the applications makes to the Registry.

What You Do	How You Do It
1. As a local administrator, **review the contents of the HKEY_LOCAL_MACHINE\Software key.**	a. **Turn on the power to the computer.** The computer boots into Windows 2000 Professional by default.
	b. If necessary, in the User Name text box, **type *Admin#*** where # is your assigned student number.
	c. In the Password text box, **type *password* and click OK** to log on to Windows 2000.
	d. From the Start menu, **choose Run.**
	e. In the Open text box, **type regedt32 and click OK** to open Registry Editor.
	f. If necessary, **choose Windows→HKEY_LOCAL_MACHINE** to make the HKEY_LOCAL_MACHINE subtree window the current window.

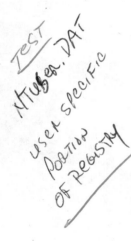

Test
NTuser.DAT
user specific
portion
of registry

g. In the left pane, **double-click the Software key** to expand the folder. You see a list of the keys within the Software key.

h. **Close Registry Editor.**

Installation Changes

When you install a new application, you'll find several changes to your computer. These changes include:

- A new menu on the Programs menu with one or more shortcuts for launching the application.
- Optionally, a shortcut on the computer's desktop that you can use to launch the application.
- One or more folders within the \Program Files folder for storing the application's files.
- Modifications to the computer's Registry. These changes include any new file associations for the application (for example, if you install Microsoft Excel, you'll find an association linking .xls files to Excel in HKEY_CLASSES_ROOT).

User Profiles

Definition:

A user profile is a specific grouping of folders, files, and configuration settings created by the operating system to store the user interface configuration for each user who logs on to the computer. In Windows NT, Windows 2000, and Windows XP, the operating system automatically creates a profile for each user who logs on to the computer. In Windows 9x, each user shares the same user profile unless you explicitly set up Windows 9x to maintain separate profiles for each user. A user profile contains:

- All desktop appearance settings such as color scheme, wallpaper, and screen saver.
- The Start menu and taskbar settings.
- The contents of several folders.

A user profile might also contain:

- Shortcuts on the desktop.
- User-specific application configuration settings.
- Any Web sites added to the Favorites menu in Internet Explorer.
- Connections to network printers.
- Connections to shared network folders.

- Internet Explorer configuration settings.

A user profile stores configuration information such as the selected color scheme or the Start menu configuration settings. In Windows 9x, these settings are stored in a file named user.dat. In Windows NT, Windows 2000, and Windows XP, these same settings are stored in a file named ntuser.dat.

Example:

In Figure 2-5, you see the Display Properties that are stored in a user profile.

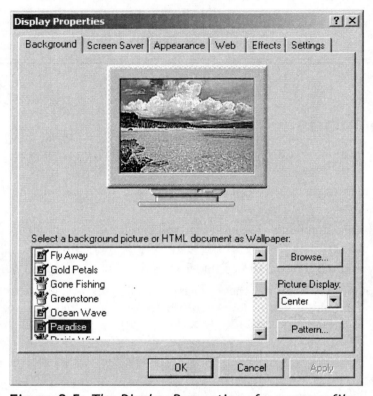

Figure 2-5: *The Display Properties of a user profile.*

In Figure 2-6, you see the Start menu and Taskbar properties that are stored in a user profile.

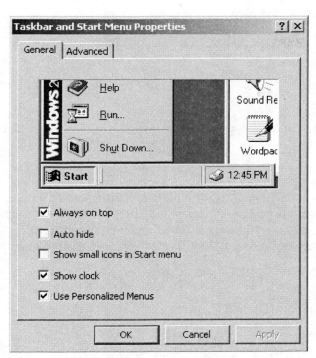

Figure 2-6: *The Start menu and Taskbar properties of a user profile.*

In Figure 2-7, you see the My Documents folder that is part of a user profile.

Figure 2-7: *The My Documents folder in a user profile.*

ACTIVITY 2-2

Examining User Profiles

Setup:

In addition to your Admin# user, you can also log in as Administrator with a password of password.

Scenario:

You have just been hired to work as a member of the Help Desk department at a company that only has Windows 2000 computers. In the past, you've supported only Windows 9x computers. One of your duties will be to respond to questions users have about configuring their desktops. You want to familiarize yourself with the Windows 2000 user profiles so that you can be prepared for users' questions.

What You Do	How You Do It

1. **Verify that Windows 2000 automatically retains each user's wallpaper settings.**

   a. On the desktop, **right-click and choose Properties** to open the Display Properties dialog box.

   b. Below Select A Background Picture Or HTML Document As Wallpaper, **select a wallpaper.**

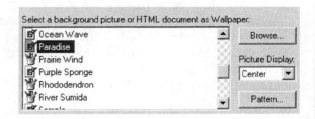

   c. **Click OK** to save your changes.

   d. If necessary, **click Yes** to enable Active Desktop.

    Depending on the wallpaper you select, Windows 2000 might require you to enable Active Desktop.

   e. From the Start menu, **choose Shut Down.**

   f. From the What Do You Want Your Computer To Do drop-down list, **select Log Off Admin# and click OK.**

   g. **Log on as Administrator with a password of password.** Notice that you don't see the wallpaper you selected for the other user. Windows 2000 stores the wallpaper selection as part of the user's profile.

   h. **Log off and log back on as Admin#.**

User Profile Folder Locations

A user profile consists of the following folders:

- \My Documents
- \Application Data
- \Cookies

- \Desktop
- \Favorites
- \NetHood
- \Recent
- \SendTo
- \Start Menu

In Windows 9x, all of these folders are stored within the \Windows folder with the exception of the \My Documents folder—it's stored in the root directory of the hard disk. In Windows NT, the user profile folders are stored within the \Winnt\Profiles folder. In Windows 2000 and Windows XP, the user profile folders are stored within the \Documents and Settings folder. In Windows 9x, the user.dat file is stored in the \Windows folder. In Windows NT, the ntuser.dat file is stored in the \Winnt\Profiles*username* folder. In Windows 2000 and Windows XP, the ntuser.dat file is stored in the \Documents and Settings*username* folder.

In Windows 2000 and Windows XP, you'll find two special user profiles within the \Documents and Settings folder: Default User and All Users. Windows 2000 and Windows XP use the Default User profile as a template for creating new users' profiles. So, whatever folders, files, and configuration settings are contained within this profile are automatically copied to a new user's profile whenever that user first logs on to the computer. By default, Windows 2000 and Windows XP automatically hide the Default User profile. You can use the All Users profile in Windows 2000 and Windows XP to store folders, files, and configuration settings you want to be accessible to all users who log on to the computer.

ACTIVITY 2-3

Examining User Profile Folders

Scenario:

As a new technician for your company, you are responsible for managing user profiles. You think user profiles have been created on your company's Windows 2000 computers. You want to examine the folder structure so that you know where to look for profile components in case you run into any problems.

What You Do	How You Do It
1. Review the contents of the user profiles folders, including the Default User profile.	a. From the Start menu, **choose Programs→ Accessories→Windows Explorer.**

b. **Open the D:\Documents and Settings folder** to display the profiles on the computer. You see a folder for Admin#, Administrator, and All Users.

c. **Choose Tools→Folder Options.** You must configure Windows Explorer to display hidden files in order to see the Default User profile.

d. In the Folder Options dialog box, **select the View tab.**

e. Below Hidden Files And Folders, **select Show Hidden Files And Folders.**

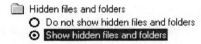

f. **Click OK** to save your changes.

g. **Review the contents of the D:\Documents and Settings folder.** You now see the Default User profile.

h. **Select your Admin#'s profile folder.** It contains various subfolders that define the contents of the profile.

i. **Select the Start Menu\Programs subfolder for your profile.** This enables you to identify the Start menu items that are specific to your user account.

j. **Select your user's Desktop folder.** This

folder will contain the user-specific shortcuts on your desktop.

k. **Close Windows Explorer.**

How to Install a Windows Application

Procedure Reference: Install a Windows Application on Windows 2000

To install a Windows application on Windows 2000:

1. Log on as a user with sufficient permissions to install an application.

2. If the application has an installation CD-ROM with an Autorun file:

    a. Insert the CD-ROM.

    b. The Autorun file automatically starts the installation wizard. Follow the
        prompts in the installation wizard to install the application.

3. If the application does not have an Autorun file on its installation CD-ROM or
    you're installing the application from floppy disk, you can use either of the fol-
    lowing methods to install it:

    *   Install the application using Control Panel, as follows:

        a. In Control Panel, double-click Add/Remove Programs.

        b. Click Add New Programs.

        c. Perform one of the following tasks, depending on your installation
            source:

            To install a program from an installation file, click CD Or Floppy (even
            if the file is on your hard disk or on a shared network folder).

            To download programs from Microsoft's Web site, click Windows
            Update and follow the instructions on the Web site.

            🖈 We're going to cover Windows Update in more detail in Lesson 13.

        d. If you clicked CD Or Floppy, a wizard will run. Click Next.

        e. If the wizard doesn't find an installation file on a CD or floppy disk,
            enter or browse for the path to the installation file and click Finish.

        f. If you choose to install an application from a network share, you might
            see a Connect As dialog box prompting you for a valid user name and
            password for the computer on which the share resides. Enter a valid
            user name and password and click OK.

        g. An installation wizard might run, depending on the application you're
            installing. If so, follow the prompts in the software program's installa-
            tion wizard to install the software.

        h. Close Control Panel.

    *   Install the application by accessing its installation files directly:

        a. Double-click the installation file. (This file typically ends in .exe or
            .msi.)

b.   Follow the prompts in the installation wizard to install the application.

4.   Test the application to verify that it works properly.

Procedure Reference: Install a Windows Application on Windows XP

To install a Windows application on Windows XP:

1.   Log on as a user with sufficient permissions to install an application.

2.   If the application has an installation CD-ROM with an Autorun file:

a.   Insert the CD-ROM.

b.   The Autorun file automatically starts the installation wizard. Follow the prompts in the installation wizard to install the application.

3.   If the application does not have an Autorun file on its installation CD-ROM or you're installing the application from floppy disk, you can use either of the following methods to install it:

- Install the application using Control Panel, as follows:

a.   In Control Panel, click Add Or Remove Programs.

b.   Click Add New Programs.

c.   Perform one of the following tasks, depending on your installation source:

To install a program from an installation file, click CD Or Floppy (even if the file is on your hard disk or on a shared network folder).

To download programs from Microsoft's Web site, click Windows Update and follow the instructions on the Web site.

> We're going to cover Windows Update in more detail in Lesson 13.

d.   If you clicked CD Or Floppy, a wizard will run. Click Next.

e.   If the wizard doesn't find an installation file on a CD or floppy disk, enter or browse for the path to the installation file and click Finish.

f.   If you choose to install an application from a network share, you might see a Connect As dialog box prompting you for a valid user name and password for the computer on which the share resides. Enter a valid user name and password and click OK.

g.   An installation wizard might run, depending on the application you're installing. If so, follow the prompts in the software program's installation wizard to install the software.

h.   Close Control Panel.

- Install the application by accessing its installation files directly:

a.   Double-click the installation file. (This file typically ends in .exe or .msi.)

b.   Follow the prompts in the installation wizard to install the application.

4.   Test the application to verify that it works properly.

Procedure Reference: Install a Windows Application on Windows NT

To install a Windows application on Windows NT:

1. Log on as a user with sufficient permissions to install an application.

2. If the application has an installation CD-ROM with an Autorun file:

   a. Insert the CD-ROM.

   b. The Autorun file automatically starts the installation wizard. Follow the prompts in the installation wizard to install the application.

3. If the application does not have an Autorun file on its installation CD-ROM or you're installing the application from floppy disk, you can use either of the following methods to install it:

   - Install the application using Control Panel, as follows:

     a. In Control Panel, double-click Add/Remove Programs.

     b. Click Install.

     c. Click Next to install a program from either a CD or a floppy disk (even if the file is on your hard disk or on a shared network folder).

     d. If the wizard doesn't find an installation file on a CD or floppy disk, enter or browse for the path to the installation file and click Finish.

     e. If you choose to install an application from a network share, you might see a Connect As dialog box prompting you for a valid user name and password for the computer on which the share resides. Enter a valid user name and password and click OK.

     f. An installation wizard might run, depending on the application you're installing. If so, follow the prompts in the software program's installation wizard to install the software.

     g. Close Control Panel.

   - Install the application by accessing its installation files directly:

     a. Double-click the installation file. (This file typically ends in .exe or .msi.)

     b. Follow the prompts in the installation wizard to install the application.

4. Test the application to verify that it works properly.

Procedure Reference: Install a Windows Application on Windows 98

To install a Windows application on Windows 98:

1. If the application has an installation CD-ROM with an Autorun file:

   a. Insert the CD-ROM.

   b. The Autorun file automatically starts the installation wizard. Follow the prompts in the installation wizard to install the application.

2. If the application does not have an Autorun file on its installation CD-ROM or you're installing the application from floppy disk, you can use either of the following methods to install it:

   - Install the application using Control Panel, as follows:

     a. In Control Panel, double-click Add/Remove Programs.

     b. Click Install.

c. Click Next to install a program from either a CD or a floppy disk (even if the file is on your hard disk or on a shared network folder).

d. If the wizard doesn't find an installation file on a CD or floppy disk, enter or browse for the path to the installation file and click Finish.

e. If you choose to install an application from a network share, your Windows 98 user account must be defined on the computer on which the share resides (if that computer is running the Windows 2000, Windows XP, or Windows NT operating systems). If the password for this account is different on Windows 98 from the password on the computer with the shared folder, enter the password and click OK.

f. An installation wizard might run, depending on the application you're installing. If so, follow the prompts in the software program's installation wizard to install the software.

g. Close Control Panel.

- Install the application by accessing its installation files directly:

a. Double-click the installation file. (This file typically ends in .exe or .msi.)

b. Follow the prompts in the installation wizard to install the application.

3. Test the application to verify that it works properly.

ACTIVITY 2-4

Installing the Windows 2000 Professional Support Tools

Setup:

The installation file for the Windows 2000 Professional Support Tools is in the \\2000srv\ Support folder. Your user account is defined on 2000srv and has the necessary permissions to access the Support share.

Scenario:

You would like to have a tool available to you on your Windows 2000 computer that you can use to determine if an application is compatible with the Windows operating systems. You know that the Application Compatibility Program (Apcompat.exe), which is included in a typical installation of the Windows 2000 Support Tools, can provide this information for you.

What You Do	How You Do It
1. Install the Windows 2000 Professional Support Tools.	a. From the Start menu, choose Settings→ Control Panel.
	b. Double-click Add/Remove Programs.

c. **Click Add New Programs.**

d. Even though you will be installing your program from a network share, **click CD Or Floppy.**

e. **Click Next.** The wizard will now search your local drives for an installation program. When it doesn't find such a program, it will prompt you to locate the installation program manually.

f. In the Open text box, **enter the path \\2000srv\support\setup.exe** or browse to locate this program.

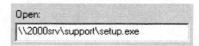

g. **Click Finish.**

h. In the Windows 2000 Support Tools Wizard, **click Next.**

i. On the User Information page, **click Next** to accept the Name and Organization defined when Windows 2000 was installed on your computer.

j. **Verify that the Typical installation type is selected and click Next.**

k. **Click Next** to install the tools onto your computer.

l. When the installation is complete, **click Finish.**

m. **Close Add/Remove Programs and Control**

Panel.

2. **Verify that the tools were installed and that you can run the Application Compatibility Tool.**

a. From the Start menu, **choose Programs→ Windows 2000 Support Tools→Tools Help.** The Windows 2000 Support Tools Help window opens with an alphabetical list of all the support tools.

A

Acldiag.exe

Adsiedit.msc

Apcompat.exe

Apmstat.exe

b. In the right pane, **click the Apcompat.exe link** to display the help information about the Application Compatibility program.

c. **Click the Run Application Compatibility Tool Now link** to verify that you can run the Application Compatibility program.

Run Application Compatibility tool now.

Open command prompt now.

d. **Click Cancel** to close the Application Compatibility program.

e. **Close the Windows 2000 Support Tools Help window.**

TOPIC B

Configure Virtual Memory

In the previous topic, you learned how to install a Windows application. But, to make many Windows applications run the way they're intended, you'll need to configure virtual memory to meet the requirements of each application. In this topic, you'll learn how to configure a Windows-based computer's virtual memory.

Configuring virtual memory properly enables you to optimize the performance of your users' computers for running applications. You can also configure virtual memory to optimize the performance of the Windows operating system itself. For example, before you optimize a computer's virtual memory, a user who is a data entry clerk would see very slow performance in the company's point-of-sale system and would have to spend her day apologizing to customers. By optimizing this computer's virtual memory, you can make the data entry clerk's application run much faster. Optimizing the performance of your users' applications as well as their operating systems enables your users to be more productive with their computers.

Virtual Memory

Virtual memory enables the computer to use hard disk space as if it is Random Access Memory (RAM). Virtual memory must be assigned to at least one drive and have a minimum size. In Windows 9x, Microsoft recommends that you let the operating system configure the virtual memory settings. In Windows NT, Windows 2000, and Windows XP, you can configure the drive, minimum, and maximum size of virtual memory. You can also configure virtual memory to use multiple hard disks. Virtual memory accesses the hard disk space through a file called the *paging file*; this file is named *pagefile.sys*. The paging file is created by default in the root of the drive on which Windows is installed. You can optionally move the virtual memory file to a different hard drive.

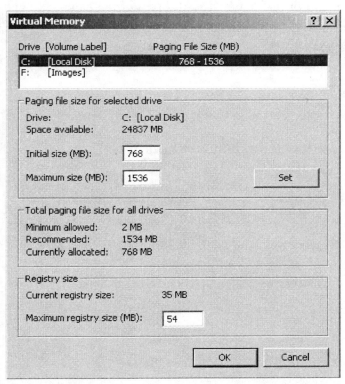

Figure 2-8: *Windows 2000 Virtual Memory settings.*

How to Configure Virtual Memory

Procedure Reference: Configure Virtual Memory in Windows 2000

To configure virtual memory in Windows 2000:

1. Log on as a user with sufficient permissions to configure the computer.

2. Open the System Properties dialog box:
   - In Control Panel, double-click System.
   - On the desktop, right-click the My Computer icon and choose Properties.

3. Select the Advanced tab.

4. Click Performance Options.

5. In the Virtual Memory portion of the Performance Options dialog box, click Change.

6. Modify the Virtual Memory settings:
   - To add a page file, begin by selecting the drive on which you want to place the new page file. Enter both an initial size and a maximum size for the page file and then click Set.
   - To move the page file to a different hard drive, begin by selecting the drive on which you want to place the page file. Enter both an initial size and a maximum size for the page file and then click Set. Next, select the drive from which you want to remove the page file. Set its initial and maximum sizes to 0 and click Set.

- To change either the initial or maximum size (or both) of the page file, begin by selecting the drive on which they are stored. Enter the value for the Initial Size or Maximum Size and then click Set.

7. Click OK to close all open dialog boxes.

8. If necessary, close Control Panel.

9. Test your change by restarting the computer and verifying that it works.

Procedure Reference: Configure Virtual Memory in Windows XP

To configure virtual memory in Windows XP:

1. Log on as a user with sufficient permissions to configure the computer.

2. Open the System Properties dialog box by using either of the following methods:
   - In the Category view of Control Panel, click the Performance and Maintenance link. In Performance and Maintenance, click the System link.
   - In the Classic view of Control Panel, double-click System.

3. In the System Properties dialog box, select the Advanced tab.

4. Below Performance, click Settings.

5. In the Performance Options dialog box, select the Advanced tab.

6. Below Virtual Memory, click Change.

7. Modify the Virtual Memory settings:
   - To add a page file, begin by selecting the drive on which you want to place the new page file. Enter both an initial size and a maximum size for the page file and then click Set.
   - To move the page file to a different hard drive, begin by selecting the drive on which you want to place the page file. Enter both an initial size and a maximum size for the page file and then click Set. Next, select the drive from which you want to remove the page file. Set its initial and maximum sizes to 0 and click Set.
   - To change either the initial or maximum size (or both) of the page file, begin by selecting the drive on which they are stored. Enter the value for the Initial Size or Maximum Size and then click Set.

8. Click OK to save your changes.

9. Click OK to close all open dialog boxes.

10. If necessary, close Control Panel.

11. Test your change by restarting the computer and verifying that it works.

Procedure Reference: Configure Virtual Memory in Windows NT

To configure virtual memory in Windows NT:

1. Log on as a user with sufficient permissions to configure the computer.

2. Open the System Properties dialog box by using either of the following methods:
   - In Control Panel, double-click System.
   - On the desktop, right-click the My Computer icon and choose Properties.

3. Select the Performance tab.

4. Below Virtual Memory, click Change.

5. Modify the Virtual Memory settings:

   - To add a page file, begin by selecting the drive on which you want to place the new page file. Enter both an initial size and a maximum size for the page file and then click Set.

   - To move the page file to a different hard drive, begin by selecting the drive on which you want to place the page file. Enter both an initial size and a maximum size for the page file and then click Set. Next, select the drive from which you want to remove the page file. Set its initial and maximum sizes to 0 and click Set.

   - To change either the initial or maximum size (or both) of the page file, begin by selecting the drive on which they are stored. Enter the value for the Initial Size or Maximum Size and then click Set.

6. Click OK twice.

7. If necessary, close Control Panel.

8. Test your change by restarting the computer and verifying that it works.

Procedure Reference: Configure Virtual Memory in Windows 98

To configure virtual memory in Windows 98:

1. Open the System Properties dialog box by using either of the following methods:
   - In Control Panel, double-click System.
   - On the desktop, right-click the My Computer icon and choose Properties.

2. Select the Performance tab.

3. Click Virtual Memory.

4. In the Virtual Memory portion of the Performance Options dialog box, click Change.

5. Choose Let Me Specify My Own Virtual Memory Settings.

6. Modify the Virtual Memory settings:

   - To move the page file to a different hard drive, from the Hard Disk drop-down list, select the disk on which you want Windows 98 to place the page file.

   - To limit the size of the page file, specify a maximum size. By default, Windows 98 sets the maximum page file size equal to the amount of free space on the hard drive.

   - To change the initial size of the page file, specify a minimum size.

7. Click OK to save your changes.

8. Click OK to close the System Properties dialog box.

9. If necessary, close Control Panel.

10. Test your change by restarting the computer and verifying that it works.

If a computer is running low on RAM and you want to increase the available memory by using virtual memory, use trial and error to determine the appropriate value. For example, you might try increasing virtual memory by 128 MB if you have enough available disk space on the computer.

ACTIVITY 2-5

Configuring Virtual Memory in Windows 2000

Scenario:

You're responsible for managing the Windows 2000-based computers for users who run AutoCAD. The current project your users are working on is quite large, and the users are receiving out-of-memory errors when they work on this project. You have an additional 128 MB of RAM on order for each computer, but you would like the users to be able to continue working on the project until you're able to upgrade their computers' RAM.

What You Do	How You Do It
1. **Increase the page file size.**	a. If necessary, **log on as Admin#.**
	b. In Control Panel, **open the System Properties dialog box.**
	c. **Select the Advanced tab.**
	d. **Click Performance Options.**
	e. In the Performance Options dialog box, **click Change.**
	f. In the Drive list, **select the drive on which the page file is stored.**

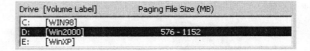

	g. In the Initial Size text box, **type a value that is 128 MB greater than the current initial size.**
	h. **Increase the maximum size of the page file by 128 MB.**
	i. **Click Set.**
	j. **Click OK three times.**
	k. **Close Control Panel.**

2. Test your changes to the virtual memory configuration.

   a. Restart the computer.

   b. When prompted, **log on as Admin#.**

   c. In Control Panel, **double-click System.**

   d. Select the Advanced tab and click Performance Options.

   e. Verify that the settings are correct for virtual memory.

   f. Close all open windows.

TOPIC C

Install a Non-Windows Application

In Topic 2A, you learned how to install a Windows application. A second type of application you might be expected to install is an application that wasn't written for the Windows operating system. In many cases, the non-Windows applications are custom applications developed for a company by either an in-house programmer or a consultant. These applications were typically designed to run on older computers. In fact, computers have changed faster than companies can update these custom applications. Because such applications are so common, in this topic, you'll learn the steps you should use to install a non-Windows application.

If a company has invested a lot of money in a custom application, they will want to continue using that application even though it wasn't designed to run on a Windows-based operating system. Custom applications typically do just the tasks users need to perform their jobs. In fact, companies typically invest in custom applications when there aren't any available applications to perform these tasks. Having the skills to install a non-Windows application will enable you to install such custom applications properly. By installing the application properly, the company's users will be able to work productively in the non-Windows application.

Non-Windows Applications

Definition:

A non-Windows application is a software program that was written to run in the MS-DOS environment. Non-Windows applications do not have a graphical interface; you navigate the application by using the arrow keys or letters on the computer's keyboard. When you run a non-Windows application on a Windows-based computer, Windows simulates the MS-DOS environment for that application.

Example:

Figure 2-9 shows you an example of a non-Windows application.

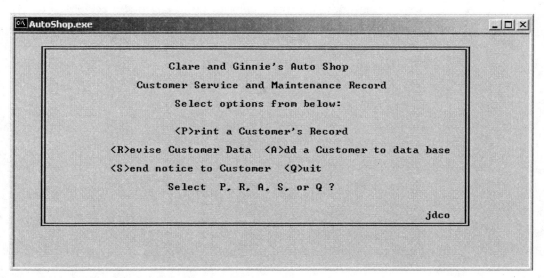

Figure 2-9: *A non-Windows application.*

How to Install a Non-Windows Application

Procedure Reference: Install a Non-Windows Application Without a Setup Program

To install a non-Windows application without a setup program:

1. Create a folder on the computer's hard disk in which to store the non-Windows application.

2. Copy the non-Windows application's files to this folder.

3. Choose where you want to create a shortcut to run the non-Windows application.

    *   In Windows 2000 or Windows XP, if you want the shortcut to be available only to a specific user, create the shortcut in either the \Documents And Settings*username*\Start Menu\Programs folder or the \Documents And Settings*username*\Desktop folder. If you want the shortcut to be available to all users, create the shortcut in either the \Documents And Settings\All Users\ Start Menu\Programs folder or the \Documents And Settings\All Users\ Desktop folder.

    *   In Windows NT, if you want the shortcut to be available only to a specific user, create the shortcut in either the \Winnt\Profiles*username*\Start Menu\ Programs folder or the \Winnt\Profiles*username*\Desktop folder. If you want the shortcut to be available to all users, create the shortcut in either the \Winnt\Profiles\All Users\Start Menu\Programs folder or the \Winnt\ Profiles\All Users\Desktop folder.

    *   In Windows 98, if you want the shortcut to be available on the Start menu, create the shortcut in the \Windows\Start Menu folder. If you want the shortcut to be available on the desktop, create it in the \Windows\Desktop folder.

4. To create a shortcut, complete the following steps:

    a. In the appropriate folder or on the desktop, right-click and choose New→ Shortcut.

    b. Specify the location of the program's executable file:

- If you know the exact path to the program's executable file, type it in the Type The Location Of The Item text box.

- If you do not know the exact path to the program's executable file, click Browse and browse the hard disk until you find the executable file. Double-click this file to select it.

c. Click Next.

d. In the Type A Name For This Shortcut text box, type the name you want to appear under the shortcut (on the desktop or Start menu).

e. Click Next.

f. Below Select An Icon For The Shortcut, select the icon you want to use for the shortcut.

g. Click Finish.

5. Test the application to verify that it works properly. If you're installing the application for use by multiple users, test it by logging on as each user.

Procedure Reference: Install a Non-Windows Application With a Setup Program

To install a non-Windows application with a setup program:

1. In Control Panel, use the appropriate utility for installing an application on the computer's operating system.

   - If you're using Windows 2000, double-click Add/Remove Programs and then click Add New Programs. Click CD Or Floppy.

   - If you're using Windows XP, click the Add Or Remove Programs link and then click Add New Programs. Click CD Or Floppy.

   - If you're using Windows NT, double-click Add/Remove Programs and then click Install. Click Next to install from either a CD or a floppy disk.

   - If you're using Windows 98, double-click Add/Remove Programs and then click Install. Click Next to install from either a CD or a floppy disk.

2. If the wizard doesn't find a setup program on a CD or floppy disk, a wizard will run. Enter or browse for the path to the setup program and click Finish.

3. An installation wizard might run, depending on the non-Windows application you're installing. If so, follow the prompts in the software program's installation wizard to install the software.

4. Close Control Panel.

5. If necessary, create a shortcut on the Start menu or the user's desktop to run the non-Windows application.

6. Test the application to verify that it works properly. If you're installing the application for use by multiple users, test it by logging on as each user.

ACTIVITY 2-6

Installing a Non-Windows Application Without a Setup Program

Data Files:

- AutoShop.exe

Setup:

You'll find the AutoShop folder and the program within it in the C:\Data folder. You have a user named User# on your computer.

Scenario:

All users at one of the Windows 2000 computers in your company need access to a small command-line utility, AutoShop, that has no setup program.

What You Do	How You Do It
1. Install AutoShop.	a. **Open Windows Explorer.**
	b. **Copy the D:\Data\AutoShop folder and its contents to D:\.**
	c. In the left pane, **select the D:\Documents And Settings\All Users\Desktop folder.**

d. In the right pane, **right-click and choose New→Shortcut.**

e. In the Type The Location Of The Item text
box, **type** *D:\AutoShop\Autoshop.exe* or
browse to locate this file.

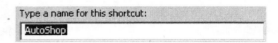

Type the location of the item:

d:\AutoShop\AutoShop.exe

f. **Click Next.**

g. **Click Next** to accept the default name of
AutoShop for this shortcut.

Type a name for this shortcut:

AutoShop

h. **Select an icon for the shortcut.**

i. **Click Finish** to create the shortcut to the
AutoShop program.

j. **Close Windows Explorer.**

2. **Verify that the installation of AutoShop was successful.**

a. While logged on as Admin#, **verify that you see the AutoShop shortcut on your desktop.**

b. **Double-click AutoShop** to verify that you can run the non-Windows application.

c. **Press Q** to quit AutoShop.

d. **Log off as Admin#.**

e. **Log on as User# with a password of password** (replace # with your assigned student number).

f. **Verify that you see the AutoShop shortcut on your desktop.**

g. **Double-click AutoShop** to verify that you can run the non-Windows application.

h. **Press Q** to quit AutoShop.

TOPIC D

Configure a Non-Windows Application

In Topic 2C, you learned how to install a non-Windows application. But, you'll often find that such applications require additional configuration before they will run properly on your users' computers. In this topic, you'll learn the skills you need to configure non-Windows applications.

Non-Windows applications, along with their installation programs, typically aren't very user-friendly. This means that you'll frequently find that you'll have to perform additional configuration tasks in order for the application to meet your users' needs. Knowing the techniques for configuring non-Windows applications will help you get your users working in their non-Windows applications faster. In addition, configuring the non-Windows applications properly the first time will help you avoid having to make repeated visits to your users' computers to change the configuration of the applications.

Operating System Startup Files

DOS and Windows 9x use two startup files: C:\autoexec.bat and C:\config.sys. In DOS, you use these files to configure the operating system, load drivers such as the CD-ROM driver, and configure memory. In Windows 9x, you use these files primarily to configure settings required by non-Windows applications. Both DOS and Windows 9x execute the startup files each time you boot the computer.

Windows NT, Windows 2000, and Windows XP support two startup files: autoexec.nt and config.nt. These files are stored in the \Winnt\System32 folder on the drive on which Windows is installed. These startup files are executed only when you run a non-Windows application within Windows NT, Windows 2000, or Windows XP.

DOS Memory Segments

There are five memory segments in MS-DOS: conventional memory, upper memory, high memory, extended memory, and expanded memory. When you run a non-Windows application in Windows, you might find that you will need to configure some of these five memory segments in order for the application to run. We describe the DOS memory segments in Table 2-4. You configure the DOS memory segments for a non-Windows application by modifying the properties of the shortcut you use to run the application.

Table 2-4: *DOS Memory Segments*

Memory Segment	Size	Description
Conventional Memory	640 KB	Because of the limitations of MS-DOS and the processors for which it was originally designed, DOS could address only the first 640 KB of RAM. For each non-Windows application you run on a computer, Windows must allocate a certain portion of the computer's RAM to simulate conventional memory.
Upper Memory Area	384 KB	This segment of RAM, the memory between 640 KB and 1 MB, was designed for use by hardware devices. In DOS, you could use memory management techniques to force DOS to use the available memory (called *upper memory blocks* or UMB) within the upper memory area. When you run a non-Windows application on a Windows-based computer, Windows also simulates the upper memory area for that application.
High Memory Area	64 KB	This segment of RAM represents the memory between 1,024 KB and 1,088 KB. In DOS, you could use this memory segment to store a single *terminate-and-stay-resident (TSR)* program, a device driver, or DOS itself. Windows does not simulate this segment of memory when you run a non-Windows application.

Memory Segment	Size	Description
Extended Memory (XMS)	All memory above 1,088 KB in the computer	This segment of RAM corresponds to all memory in the computer above 1,088 KB. When you run a non-Windows application, Windows can provide extended memory for the application on an as-needed basis. In Windows, extended memory is automatically available. In DOS, you must load the *himem.sys* driver in the config.sys file to make the extended memory accessible. Himem.sys is a driver that enables DOS to access extended memory.
Expanded Memory (EMS)	Limited to the size of the expanded memory card	Unlike the other DOS memory segments, expanded memory refers to an older specification that enabled you to install an expansion card containing memory in the computer. DOS accessed the memory on this card by using a 64 KB upper memory block. Although you won't encounter computers with expanded memory anymore, you might encounter applications that were written to use it. If so, you can configure Windows to provide the non-Windows application with expanded memory. In DOS, if you want to make expanded memory accessible, you must load the *emm386.exe* driver in the config.sys file. Emm386.exe is a driver that must be loaded before DOS can access expanded memory. You can also use the emm386.exe driver to make the upper memory area accessible for storing TSRs by modifying Config.sys.

Environment Variables

Both MS-DOS and the Windows operating systems support a variety of environment variables that control the behavior of the operating system or an application (or both). Table 2-5 lists some of the common environment variables and how they are used. In Windows 9x, you configure these environment variables by modifying the Windows startup files. In Windows NT, Windows 2000, and Windows XP, you configure environment variables using the System applet within Control Panel.

Table 2-5: *Common Environment Variables*

Environment Variable	Use To
Path	Identify the folders in which you want the operating system to search for executable files.
Temp	Specify the folder in which you want the operating system or application to store temporary files.
Tmp	Define the folder in which you want an application to store temporary files.

 Some applications use the Temp environment variable to identify the folder in which they should store temporary files. Alternatively, other applications use the Tmp environment variable instead.

Files and Buffers

The *files* configuration setting controls how much memory is reserved for the number of files opened by a DOS application. The *buffers* configuration setting specifies how much memory is reserved for transferring temporary information between a non-Windows application's data in RAM and an I/O device such as the monitor. In Windows, you configure the files and buffers configuration settings by modifying the appropriate Windows startup files.

How to Configure a Non-Windows Application

Procedure Reference: Configure DOS Memory Segments in Any Windows Operating System

To configure DOS memory segments in any Windows operating system:

1. Right-click the shortcut for starting the non-Windows application and choose Properties.

2. Select the Memory tab.

3. Use the Conventional Memory, Expanded (EMS) Memory, Extended (XMS) Memory, and MS-DOS Protected Mode (DPMI) Memory text boxes to configure memory to meet the requirements of the non-Windows application. Notice that you can use either a drop-down list to select pre-defined memory settings or type in a specific value in MB in each of the text boxes.

4. Click OK to save your changes.

5. Test the application to verify that it works properly.

Procedure Reference: Configure Environment Variables in Windows 2000

To configure environment variables in Windows 2000:

1. Open the System Properties dialog box by using either of the following methods:
   - In Control Panel, double-click System.
   - On the desktop, right-click the My Computer icon and choose Properties.

2. Select the Advanced tab.

3. Click Environment Variables. You can modify the variables as follows:
   - To edit an existing variable, select the variable and click Edit. Enter the changes and click OK.
   - To delete a variable, select the variable and click Delete.
   - To add a new user variable, click New in the User Variables section. Enter the variable name and value and click OK.
   - To add a new system variable, click New in the System Variables section. Enter the variable name and value and click OK.

4. Click OK twice.

5. If necessary, close Control Panel.

6. Test any non-Windows applications to verify that they work properly.

Procedure Reference: Configure Environment Variables in Windows XP

To configure environment variables in Windows XP:

1. Open the System Properties dialog box by using either of the following methods:
   - In the Category view of Control Panel, click the Performance and Maintenance link. In Performance and Maintenance, click the System link.
   - In the Classic view of Control Panel, double-click System.

2. Select the Advanced tab.

3. Click Environment Variables. You can modify the variables as follows:
   - To edit an existing variable, select the variable and click Edit. Enter the changes and click OK.
   - To delete a variable, select the variable and click Delete.
   - To add a new user variable, click New in the User Variables section. Enter the variable name and value and click OK.
   - To add a new system variable, click New in the System Variables section. Enter the variable name and value and click OK.

4. Click OK twice.

5. If necessary, close Control Panel.

6. Test any non-Windows applications to verify that they work properly.

Procedure Reference: Configure Environment Variables in Windows NT

To configure environment variables in Windows NT:

1. Open the System Properties dialog box by using either of the following methods:
   - In Control Panel, double-click System.
   - On the desktop, right-click the My Computer icon and choose Properties.

2. Select the Environment tab. You can modify the variables as follows:
   - To edit an existing variable, select the variable and click Edit. Enter the changes and click OK.
   - To delete a variable, select the variable and click Delete.
   - To add a new user variable, click New in the User Variables section. Enter the variable name and value and click OK.
   - To add a new system variable, click New in the System Variables section. Enter the variable name and value and click OK.

3. Click OK to save your changes.

4. If necessary, close Control Panel.

5. Test any non-Windows applications to verify that they work properly.

Procedure Reference: Configure Environment Variables in Windows 98

To configure environment variables in Windows 98:

1. From the Start menu, choose Run.

2. In the Open text box, type sysedit and click OK to run the System Configuration Editor.

3. Select the C:\AUTOEXEC.BAT window.

4. Add or edit the statements for configuring the PATH and TEMP variables.

   - To add a PATH variable, type PATH= followed by the folder for which you want Windows 98 to search for executable files.

   - To add a new folder to an existing path statement, type a semi-colon (;) after the current path and then the path to the folder for which you want Windows 98 to search for executable files.

   - To add a TEMP variable, type TEMP= followed by the path to the folder in which you want Windows 98 to store temporary files.

   - To change the folder in which you want Windows 98 to store temporary files, edit the line containing the TEMP= statement in the AUTOEXEC.BAT file.

5. Choose File→Save to save your changes to the AUTOEXEC.BAT file.

6. Close System Configuration Editor.

7. Restart the computer so that Windows 98 will execute the changes you made in the AUTOEXEC.BAT file.

8. Test any non-Windows applications to verify that they work properly.

Procedure Reference: Configure Files and Buffers in Windows 2000, Windows XP, and Windows NT

To configure files and buffers in Windows 2000, Windows XP, and Windows NT:

1. In Notepad, open *X*:*%SystemRoot%*\System32\Config.NT. (Replace *X* with the drive letter on which the operating system is installed; replace *%SystemRoot%* with the folder in which the operating system is installed—typically Winnt.)

2. Scroll to the end of the file.

3. If necessary, add the line files= followed by the number of files the non-Windows application needs. If the line files= already exists, edit the value as needed.

4. Add the line buffers= followed by the number of buffers required by the non-Windows application.

5. Save the file.

6. Test any non-Windows applications to verify that they work properly.

Procedure Reference: Configure Files and Buffers in Windows 98

To configure files and buffers in Windows 98:

1. In Notepad, open C:\CONFIG.SYS.

2. Scroll to the end of the file.

3. If necessary, add the line files= followed by the number of files the non-Windows application needs. If the line files= already exists, edit the value as needed.

4. Add the line buffers= followed by the number of buffers required by the non-Windows application.

5. Save the file.

6. Restart the computer so that Windows 98 will execute the changes you made in the CONFIG.SYS file.

7. Test any non-Windows applications to verify that they work properly.

ACTIVITY 2-7

Configuring a Non-Windows Application's Memory Usage

Scenario:

Users of the AutoShop MS-DOS application are reporting that they're getting out-of-memory errors when they try to run the application. After researching the problem, you've determined that you need to reserve 480 KB of conventional memory and 2048 KB of extended memory for the program to run properly.

LESSON 2

What You Do	How You Do It
1. **Configure the non-Windows application.**	a. **Log on as your Admin# account.**
	b. On the desktop, **right-click the AutoShop shortcut and choose Properties.**
	c. **Select the Memory tab.**
	d. From the Conventional Memory drop-down list, **select 480.**
	e. From the Extended (XMS) Memory drop-down list, **select 2048.**

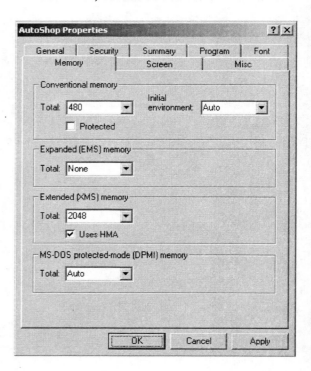

	f. **Click OK** to save your changes.
2. **Test AutoShop.**	a. On the desktop, **double-click AutoShop** to run the application.
	b. **Press Q** to close the AutoShop application.

TOPIC E

Remove an Application

Up to this point in the lesson, we've focused on what you need to do to install, configure, and troubleshoot applications. But what happens if you need to remove an application from a computer? You might run into this problem if you're upgrading users' computers to a new application or if your users no longer need an application on their computers. In this topic, you'll learn how to remove both Windows and non-Windows applications.

It's important that you know how to remove both Windows and non-Windows applications so that you can avoid problems such as unused program files using up the computer's disk space. Removing an application properly enables you to make sure that you've reclaimed the space used by that application on a user's computer. Another situation that might require you to remove an application is during an upgrade of that application. In some cases, you might need to remove the old version of the application before you'll be able to install the new version of that application.

How to Remove an Application

Procedure Reference: Remove an Application in Windows 2000

To remove an application in Windows 2000:

1. In Control Panel, double-click Add/Remove Programs.

2. Select the installed program and click Remove.

3. Follow the prompts to remove the application.

4. Close Add/Remove Programs and Control Panel.

5. Verify that the application was removed successfully.

Procedure Reference: Remove an Application in Windows XP

To remove an application in Windows XP:

1. In Control Panel, click Add Or Remove Programs.

2. Select the installed program and click Change/Remove.

3. Follow the prompts to remove the application.

4. Close Add Or Remove Programs and Control Panel.

5. Verify that the application was removed successfully.

Procedure Reference: Remove an Application in Windows NT

To remove an application in Windows NT:

1. In Control Panel, double-click Add/Remove Programs.

2. Select the installed program and click Add/Remove.

3. Follow the prompts to remove the application.

4. Close Add/Remove Programs and Control Panel.

5. Verify that the application was removed successfully.

Procedure Reference: Remove an Application in Windows 98

To remove an application in Windows 98:

1. In Control Panel, double-click Add/Remove Programs.

2. Select the installed program and click Add/Remove.

3. Follow the prompts to remove the application.

4. Close Add/Remove Programs and Control Panel.

5. Verify that the application was removed successfully.

ACTIVITY 2-8

Removing the Windows 2000 Support Tools

Scenario:

A user is running out of disk space on her computer. You have a new hard disk on order but it won't be in until next week. The user is unable to run a critical application on her computer because it has so little free space. After examining the applications installed on her computer, you've determined that she no longer needs to run the Windows 2000 Support Tools.

What You Do	How You Do It
1. **Remove the Windows 2000 Support Tools.**	a. **Verify that you're logged on as Admin#.**
	b. In Control Panel, **double-click Add/ Remove Programs.**
	c. **Select the Windows 2000 Support Tools and click Remove.**

	d. **Click Yes** to confirm that you want to remove the tools from your computer.
	e. **Close Add/Remove Programs and Control Panel.**

2. **Verify that the application was removed.**

    a. From the Start menu, **choose Programs.**

    b. **Review the list of programs** to verify that the Windows 2000 Support Tools are no longer installed.

Lesson 2 Follow-up

In this lesson, you learned how to install and remove both Windows and non-Windows applications. In addition, you also learned how to configure the properties of non-Windows applications and virtual memory to optimize application performance. With these skills, you can install any application in the Windows 2000, Windows XP, Windows NT, and Windows 9x environments.

1. **In your work environment, what types of applications will you be expected to install?**

2. **If you have any non-Windows applications, have you been required to customize their properties in order for the applications to run successfully? If so, what properties have you had to customize?**

LESSON 3

Installing Network Components

Lesson Time
3 hour(s)

Lesson Objectives:

In this lesson, you will install network components.

You will:

*   Update a network card driver.
*   Install TCP/IP.
*   Troubleshoot IP connectivity.
*   Install NetBEUI.
*   Install IPX/SPX.
*   Install a NetWare client.
*   Configure a network connection in Windows 9x.

Introduction

Most companies don't use stand-alone computers. Instead, they network computers together so that users can share resources such as programs, data, and printers. Because the majority of companies have networks, as an A+ technician, you'll be expected to configure networked computers. In this lesson, you'll learn how to configure the network software components that provide basic connectivity from each PC to the network. In addition, you'll learn how to troubleshoot problems with network connectivity.

Without network connectivity, users can't access the shared resources they need to perform their jobs. Installing and configuring network components correctly will ensure that your users will have the access they need.

The following CompTIA A+ Operating System Technologies (2003) Examination objectives are covered in this lesson:

- Topic A:
  - 2.1 Device Driver Configuration: Load default drivers, Find updated drivers.
  - 2.4 Device Driver Installation: Plug and Play (PNP) and non-PNP devices, Install and configure device drivers, Install different device drivers, Manually install a device driver, Search the Internet for updated device drivers, Using unsigned drivers (driver signing).

- Topic B:
  - 1.3 Command line functions and utilities include: PING.
  - 4.1 Configure Protocols: TCP/IP: Gateway, Subnet mask, DNS (and domain suffix), WINS, Static address assignment, Automatic address assignment (APIPA, DHCP), Appletalk.
  - 4.1 Understand the use of the following tools: IPCONFIG.EXE, PING.
  - 4.2 Protocols and terminologies: ISP, TCP/IP, DNS.

- Topic C:
  - 3.2 Eliciting problem symptoms from customers, Having customer reproduce error as part of the diagnostic process, Identifying recent changes to the computer environment from the user.
  - 3.3 Other Common problems: Option (Sound card, modem, input device) or will not function.
  - 4.1 Understand the use of the following tools: IPCONFIG.EXE, PING, TRACERT. EXE, NSLOOKUP.EXE.

- Topic D:
  - 4.1 Configure protocols: NetBEUI / NetBIOS.

- Topic E:
  - 4.1 Configure protocols: IPX/SPX (NWLink).

- Topic F:
  - 4.1 Configure client options: Novell. Verify the configuration.

- Topic G:
  - 4.1 Configure client options: Microsoft. Verify the configuration.
  - 4.1 Understand the use of the foolwing tools: WINIPCFG.EXE.

TOPIC A

Update a Network Card Driver

There are several network components that must be working properly before you can connect a computer to the network. Before you can configure a network connection, the network card driver must be installed and functioning correctly. In this topic, you'll learn how to update a network card driver in the Windows NT, Windows 2000, and Windows XP operating systems.

Until the network card driver is functioning properly, you can't install or configure any of the other network software components. And until you can configure the necessary network software components, you won't be able to connect the computer to a network—which means that the computer's user won't be able to access the network's resources. Installing the network card driver properly enables you to get that much closer to connecting a computer to the network so that the computer's user can access the network resources he needs to be productive.

Hardware Driver

The Windows operating systems use hardware *drivers* to communicate with the specific hardware in your computer. Depending on the manufacturer of a particular hardware component, the methods by which Windows must communicate with that component can vary. For example, you can install an Ethernet network card made by manufacturers such as 3Com or Intel. Even though both are Ethernet network cards, the methods by which your computer communicates with each network card varies. For this reason, you must install the appropriate hardware driver for the particular network card you're using.

Some hardware drivers are digitally signed to indicate that the drivers have been tested and are of a certain level of quality. With the release of Windows 98, Microsoft began signing drivers that passed Windows Hardware Quality Labs (WHQL) testing. You can use unsigned drivers, but be aware that unsigned drivers have not been tested and certified as compatible with the Windows 98, Windows Me, Windows 2000, or Windows XP operating systems. If a driver hasn't been signed, you will be prompted whether to continue installation when you try to install it on one of your Windows operating systems. While many unsigned drivers are safe and compatible with Windows, you must decide whether you need to use them or whether you can find another driver that has been tested and signed.

Plug and Play

Beginning with Windows 95, and with the exception of Windows NT, Microsoft implemented support for *Plug and Play*. Plug and Play enables the computer's BIOS and the Windows operating system to work together to identify any new hardware you install or attach to a computer. For example, many printers now support Plug and Play. This means that when you attach such a printer to a Windows-based computer, the operating system will automatically detect the new printer and attempt to install the correct printer hardware driver.

How to Use Device Manager

Procedure Reference: Use Device Manager to Identify Hardware Devices

To use Device Manager to identify the hardware devices in a computer:

1. If you're using Windows 2000 or Windows XP, log on as a local administrator.

2. Open Device Manager.

- In Windows 2000:

    a. Open Control Panel.

    b. Double-click System.

    c. Select the Hardware tab.

    d. Click Device Manager.

    You can also open the System dialog box by right-clicking the My Computer icon on the desktop and choosing Properties.

- In Windows 9x:

    a. Open Control Panel.

    b. Double-click System.

    c. Select the Device Manager tab.

- In Windows XP:

    a. On the Start menu, right-click My Computer.

    b. Choose Properties.

    c. Select the Hardware tab.

    d. Click Device Manager.

3. Expand the category of a hardware device (for example, Network Adapters). The name of the hardware device is listed below its category.

Procedure Reference: Use Device Manager to Verify Hardware Device Status

To use Device Manager to verify that a hardware device is working properly:

1. If you're using Windows 2000 or Windows XP, log on as a local administrator.

2. Open Device Manager.

- In Windows 2000:

    a. Open Control Panel.

    b. Double-click System.

    c. Select the Hardware tab.

    d. Click Device Manager.

- In Windows 9x:

    a. Open Control Panel.

    b. Double-click System.

    c. Select the Device Manager tab.

    You can also open the System dialog box by right-clicking the My Computer icon on the desktop and choosing Properties.

- In Windows XP:

    a. On the Start menu, right-click My Computer.

    b. Choose Properties.

    c. Select the Hardware tab.

    d.   Click Device Manager.

3.   Expand the category of a hardware device (for example, Network Adapters).

4.   Right-click the hardware device and choose Properties.

5.   Review the Device Status portion of the Properties dialog box. You use this information to determine if the device is working properly.

Procedure Reference: Use Device Manager to Install a Different Device Driver

1.   To install a different device driver in Windows 98:

    a.   Open Device Manager.

    b.   Right-click a device and choose Properties.

    c.   In the device's Properties dialog box, select the Driver tab.

    d.   Click Update Driver to start the Update Device Driver Wizard. Click Next.

    e.   Select Search For A Better Driver Than The One Your Device Is Now Using. Click Next.

    f.   Select the locations where you want the wizard to search. You can choose to search the floppy disk drive, the CD-ROM drive, the Microsoft Windows Update site on the Internet, or you can specify a location on the local computer or the network. Click Next.

    g.   If the wizard finds another driver, you'll be prompted to use that driver or keep the current driver. Make your selection and click Next.

    h.   Complete the wizard to install the selected driver.

2.   To install a different device driver in Windows 2000:

    1.   Log on as a local administrator.

    2.   Open Device Manager.

    3.   Right-click a device and choose Properties.

    4.   In the device's Properties dialog box, select the Driver tab.

    5.   Click Update Driver to start the Update Device Driver Wizard. Click Next.

    6.   Select Search For A Suitable Driver For My Device. Click Next.

    7.   Select the locations where you want the wizard to search. You can choose to search floppy disk drives, CD-ROM drives, a specific location on the local computer or network, or the Microsoft Windows Update site on the Internet. Click Next.

    8.   If the wizard finds another driver, you'll be prompted to use that driver or keep the current driver. Make your selection and click Next.

    9.   Complete the wizard to install the selected driver.

3.   To install a different device driver in Windows XP:

    1.   Log on as a local administrator.

    2.   Open Device Manager.

    3.   Right-click on a device and choose Update Driver.

    4.   Choose Install From A List Or Specific Location. Click Next.

    5.   Select Search Removable Media or specify a location to search, or both. Click Next.

6. If the wizard finds another driver, you'll be prompted to use that driver or keep the current driver. Make your selection and click Next and complete the wizard to install the driver.

7. If the wizard can't find a driver, the wizard will end. Click Finish.

Procedure Reference: Use Device Manager to Configure Driver Signing Options

1. To configure driver signing options in Windows 2000 and Windows XP:

    a. Right-click My Computer and choose Properties.

    b. Select the Hardware tab.

    c. In the Device Manager section, click Driver Signing.

    d. Configure Windows 2000 to ignore file signatures, prompt you before installing unsigned drivers, or block the installation of unsigned drivers.

ACTIVITY 3-1

Examining Device Manager

Scenario:

You've just been hired to work as a member of the Help Desk department at a company that has Windows 2000 computers. Your boss has told you that you will be primarily fielding network support calls. Because you're new to these computers, you want to familiarize yourself with their hardware so that you can be prepared for any support calls that might come your way.

What You Do	How You Do It
1. Determine the type of network card installed in the computer and that it is working properly.	a. If necessary, **log on as Admin#.**
	b. In Control Panel, **double-click System.**
	c. **Select the Hardware tab.**
	d. **Click Device Manager.**
	e. In the list of devices, **expand Network Adapters.**
	⊟ ▦ Network adapters ▦ Realtek RTL8139(A/B/C/8130) PCI Fast Ethernet NIC
	f. **Right-click the network adapter driver and choose Properties.**

g. **Review the Device Status portion of the dialog box** to determine if the device is working properly.

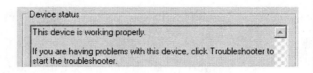

h. **Click Cancel** to close the network driver's Properties dialog box.

i. **Close Device Manager, System Properties, and Control Panel.**

How to Update a Network Card Driver

Procedure Reference: Update a Network Card Driver in Windows 2000

To update a network card driver in Windows 2000:

1. Log on as a user with administrative permissions.

2. From the Start menu, choose Settings→Network And Dial-up Connections.

3. Right-click Local Area Connection and choose Properties.

4. In the Local Area Connection Properties dialog box, click Configure.

5. Select the Driver tab.

6. Click Update Driver.

7. On the Welcome To The Upgrade Device Driver Wizard page, click Next.

8. In the Upgrade Device Driver Wizard, verify that Search For A Suitable Driver For My Device is selected and click Next.

9. On the Locate Driver Files page, select the locations you want the Wizard to search for a new driver. You can install the updated driver from any of the following locations:

   - Floppy Disk
   - CD-ROM
   - Local or shared network folder
   - The Microsoft Windows Update Web site

   🖈 You might find it necessary to obtain an updated driver for the computer's network card by going directly to the manufacturer's Web site.

10. Click Next to begin the search.

11. If necessary, insert the appropriate disk in either the computer's floppy disk drive or the CD-ROM drive.

12. Click Next to install the updated driver (or to continue with the Wizard if no new driver was found).

13. Click Finish to close the Wizard.

14. Click Close to close the Properties dialog box for your network card.

15. Click OK to close the Local Area Connection Properties dialog box.

16. Verify that the network card and its driver are working properly by right-clicking Local Area Connection and choosing Status. You should see a status of Connected. Click Close to close the Local Area Connection Status dialog box.

17. Close Network And Dial-Up Connections.

Procedure Reference: Update a Network Card Driver in Windows XP

To update a network card driver in Windows XP:

1. Log on as a user with administrative permissions.

2. From the Start menu, choose My Network Places→View Network Connections.

3. Right-click Local Area Connection and choose Properties.

4. In the Local Area Connection Properties dialog box, click Configure.

5. Select the Driver tab.

6. Click Update Driver to start the Hardware Update Wizard.

7. If you want to load the new driver from CD-ROM or floppy disk, complete the following steps:
   a. Choose Install The Software Automatically.
   b. Click Next.
   c. If the Hardware Update Wizard finds an updated driver, click Next to install it.
   d. Click Finish to close the Hardware Update Wizard.

   The Hardware Update Wizard doesn't include an option to search for a new driver on the Microsoft Windows Update Web site. We cover how you can access the Windows Update Web site to search for not only updated network card drivers but also other Windows updates in Lesson 13.

8. If you want to load the new driver from a local or shared network folder, complete the following steps:
   a. Choose Install From A List Or Specific Location.
   b. Click Next.
   c. Uncheck Search Removable Media.
   d. Check Include This Location In The Search.
   e. Click Browse to select the local or shared network folder from which you want to update the driver.
   f. Select the folder that contains the driver.
   g. Click OK to close the Browse For Folder dialog box.
   h. Click Next to begin searching for a new driver.

     i.   If the Hardware Update Wizard finds an updated driver, click Next to install it.

     j.   Click Finish to close the Hardware Update Wizard.

9.   Click Close to close the Properties dialog box for your network card.

10.   Verify that network card and its driver are working properly by right-clicking Local Area Connection and choosing Status. You should see a status of Connected. Click Close to close the Local Area Connection Status dialog box.

11.   Close Network Connections.

Procedure Reference: Update a Network Card Driver in Windows NT

To update a network card driver in Windows NT:

1.   Log on as a user with administrative permissions.

2.   From the Start menu, choose Settings→Control Panel.

3.   Double-click Network.

4.   Select the Adapters tab.

5.   In the list of Network Adapters, select the driver you want to update.

6.   Click Update.

7.   In the Windows NT Setup dialog box, enter the path to the updated driver files. (You can load the updated driver from floppy disk, CD-ROM, local folder, or shared network folder.)

 You can't update the network card driver from the Microsoft Windows Update Web site using this procedure. You'll learn how to update Windows NT including its network card driver in Lesson 13.

8.   Click Continue.

9.   Click Close to close the Network dialog box.

10.   When prompted, click Yes to restart the computer.

11.   Log back on to the computer.

12.   Close Control Panel.

13.   Verify that network card and its driver are working properly by using Network Neighborhood to browse the network.

     a.   On the desktop, double-click Network Neighborhood.

     b.   Verify that you see other computers listed in the Network Neighborhood.

     c.   Close the window.

ACTIVITY 3-2

Updating a Network Card Driver

Scenario:

You're the on-site A+ technician for a company with a large network. After researching on Microsoft's Web site, you've determined that Microsoft has posted an updated driver on their Web site for the network card in one of the Windows 2000-based computers you're responsible for supporting.

What You Do	How You Do It
1. Update the network card driver.	a. From the Start menu, **choose Settings→ Network And Dial-up Connections.**
	b. **Right-click Local Area Connection and choose Properties.**
	c. In the Local Area Connection Properties dialog box, **click Configure.**

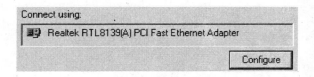

	d. **Select the Driver tab.**
	e. **Click Update Driver.**
	f. In the Upgrade Device Driver Wizard, **click Next.**
	g. **Verify that Search For A Suitable Driver For My Device is selected and click Next.**

h. On the Locate Driver Files page, **check Microsoft Windows Update and uncheck all other search locations.**

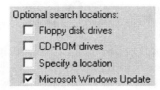

i. **Click Next.**

j. On the Driver Files Search Results page, **click Next** to install the new device driver or to continue with the wizard.

k. **Click Finish.**

l. **Click Close** to close the Properties dialog box for your network card.

m. **Click OK** to close the Local Area Connection Properties dialog box.

---

2. **Verify that the network card and driver are working properly.**

a. In Network And Dial-up Connections, **right-click Local Area Connection and choose Status.**

b. **Verify that the connection's status states Connected.**

c. **Click Close** to close the Local Area Connection Status dialog box.

d. **Close Network And Dial-Up Connections.**

TOPIC B

Configure TCP/IP

Now that you've seen how to verify that you have a working network card driver, the next step in configuring network connectivity is to install and configure a network protocol. The primary protocol for both Windows-based networks and the Internet is TCP/IP. In this lesson, you'll learn how to configure TCP/IP in the Windows NT, Windows 2000, and Windows XP operating systems.

Without TCP/IP properly configured on their computers, your users won't be able to communicate with other TCP/IP-based computers on their local network. They also won't be able to access resources on the Internet. Because TCP/IP is so critical, both for connecting to local network resources and the Internet, you can expect frequent requests from your users to install TCP/IP. Knowing how to install TCP/IP properly will help you to get your users up and running quickly, and avoid spending time correcting mistakes.

Network Protocols

A network protocol is responsible for formatting the data packets that are sent between computers on a network. In order for two computers to communicate over a network, they must have a network protocol in common. Windows 9x, Windows NT, and Windows 2000 support the TCP/IP, NWLink IPX/SPX, and NetBEUI network protocols. Windows XP supports the TCP/IP and NWLink IPX/SPX network protocols.

IP Address

Definition:

An IP address is a series of four numbers that you assign to a computer on a TCP/IP network. These four numbers will look something like this: 192.168.200.200. The IP address must consist of four numbers, separated by periods. Each number can be from 0 to 255, with the exception that the first number in the series cannot be 0. In addition, all four numbers cannot be 0 (0.0.0.0) or 255 (255.255.255.255).

Analogy:

An IP address is like a mailing address. A portion of the numbers in the IP address identify the network on which a computer resides, just as a person's mailing address uses a street name to identify the street on which they live. The other portion of the numbers in the IP address uniquely identify the computer on the network, just as the house number uniquely identifies a specific house on a street. So, just as your mailing address consists of both a street name and a house number, so does an IP address consist of numbers to identify the network and numbers to identify the computer on the network.

Example:

In Figure 3-1, you see an example of an IP address with the network and computer portions of the address labeled.

192.168.200.200

| Network address | Computer address |

Figure 3-1: *An IP address.*

Subnet Mask

Definition:

A subnet mask is a series of four numbers that the computer uses to determine how many of the four numbers in the IP address are being used to specify the computer's network address. A subnet mask typically looks like this: 255.255.0.0. The first number of the subnet mask must be 255; the remaining three numbers can be any of the following numbers:

- 255
- 254
- 252
- 248
- 240
- 224
- 192
- 0

The four numbers in the subnet mask cannot consist of all 255s (255.255.255.255).

Where you see a number other than zero in the subnet mask, you can determine that the number in the same position in the IP address is part of the computer's network address. For example, if the computer's IP address is 192.168.200.200 and the subnet mask is 255.255.255.0, the numbers in the subnet mask tell you that the first three numbers in the IP address are being used to identify the network on which the computer resides. Likewise, where you see a zero in the subnet mask, this tells you that the number in the same position in the IP address is being used to identify the computer itself.

Example:

In Figure 3-2, you see an example of a subnet mask. The subnet mask is 255.255.255.0, which means that the first three numbers in the computer's IP address are being used to identify the network on which the computer resides.

IP Address = 192.168.200.200
SubnetMask = 255.255.255.0

The network address is 192.168.200.

Figure 3-2: *A subnet mask.*

TCP/IP

Definition:

TCP/IP is a non-proprietary, routable network protocol that enables computers to communicate over a network. (A protocol is called routable if it is able to communicate across routers.) The TCP/IP protocol is the foundation for the Internet. In order to communicate on the Internet, a computer must be using the TCP/IP protocol. When you install TCP/IP, you must configure the following properties:

- *IP address*—Four numbers that uniquely identifies the network on which the computer is installed and the computer itself.

- *Subnet mask*—Four numbers used to identify how much of the IP address is being used to identify the network on which the computer is installed.

You might optionally be called upon to configure the following properties for TCP/IP:

- *Default gateway* address. This is the IP address of a router on the network. The computer uses this address to access computers on the other side of the router.

- Preferred and alternate DNS server addresses. Computers use the DNS server address(es) to enable users to access network or Internet resources by name (such as **www.elementk.com**) instead of IP address.

- One or more WINS server addresses. Computers use the WINS server address to access Microsoft Windows network resources by name.

Example:

In Figure 3-3, you find an example of the required and some of the optional TCP/IP configuration properties.

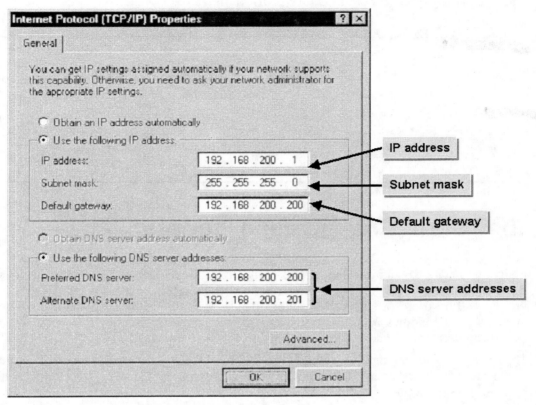

Figure 3-3: *TCP/IP configuration properties.*

Name Servers

On a TCP/IP-based network and even the Internet, you connect to computers by using their names, not their IP addresses. For example, you connect to a computer on your network by using a name such as 2000srv; on the Internet, you connect to computers by using names such as **www.cnn.com**. In order for you to communicate with another computer, however, your computer must know that computer's IP address. There are two ways computers find the IP addresses for specific computer names: *Domain Name System (DNS)* and *Windows Internet Naming System (WINS)* servers. These servers contain databases that consist of computer names and their associated IP addresses.

 You'll sometimes hear computer names referred to as host names.

Automatic TCP/IP Configuration Methods

Windows 98, Windows 2000, and Windows XP support two methods for automatically assigning IP addresses to computers: by using a *Dynamic Host Configuration Protocol (DHCP)* server or by using *Automatic Private IP Addressing*. Windows NT supports automatic IP address assignment only through a DHCP server. Table 3-1 describes each of these configuration methods. Using an automatic TCP/IP configuration method reduces your workload because you won't have to manually assign an IP address and subnet mask to each computer you configure with TCP/IP.

Table 3-1: *Automatic TCP/IP Configuration Methods*

Method	Description
DHCP Server	A server that a network administrator configures with a pool of IP addresses (along with other IP addressing information such as the subnet mask, default gateway, and so on) to assign to clients.
APIPA	A service that automatically configures a computer with an IP address on the 169.254.0.0 network. For example, this service might configure a computer with the IP address of 169.254.217.5.

[handwritten: Small or local only]

The TCP/IP Configuration Process

When you configure TCP/IP on a computer, you can configure its properties manually, by assigning a static IP address, subnet mask, and any optional IP addressing parameters such as the default gateway, DNS server address(es), or WINS server address(es). You can also configure the TCP/IP protocol's properties automatically. When you select automatic configuration in Windows 98, Windows 2000, and Windows XP, the computer uses the following process to obtain the necessary IP addressing information for the computer:

1. The computer attempts to communicate with a DHCP server to obtain an IP address. If a DHCP server responds with an offer of IP addressing information, the computer uses the information to automatically configure its IP address, subnet mask, and any other optional properties assigned by the DHCP server.

2. If the computer does not receive a response from a DHCP server, it will use an IP address within the 169.254.0.1 to 169.254.255.254 address range. The computer will also automatically set its subnet mask to 255.255.0.0. The computer does not configure any optional IP addressing parameters such as the default gateway.

If you are configuring the TCP/IP protocol on a Windows NT computer, you can configure its properties manually or automatically. If the Windows NT computer does not find a DHCP server, the computer will not have an IP address and will be unable to communicate on the network. Windows NT does not support APIPA.

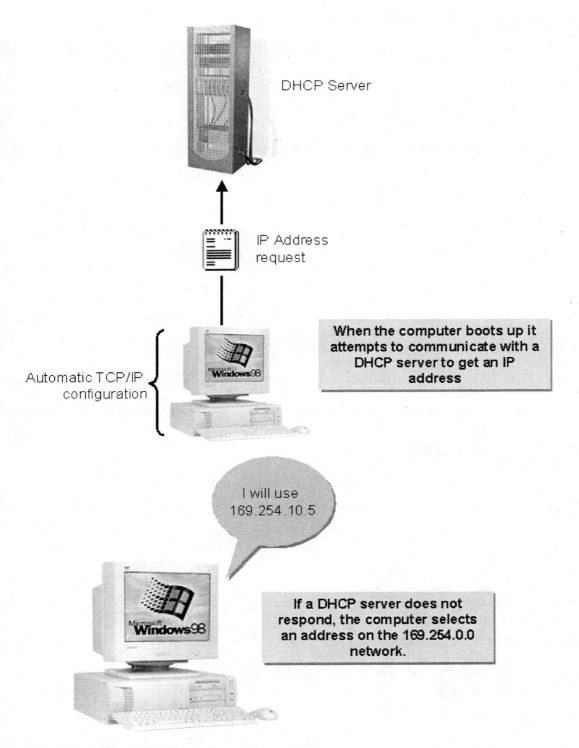

DHCP Server

IP Address request

Automatic TCP/IP configuration

When the computer boots up it attempts to communicate with a DHCP server to get an IP address

I will use 169.254.10.5

If a DHCP server does not respond, the computer selects an address on the 169.254.0.0 network.

Figure 3-4: *The TCP/IP configuration process.*

The IPConfig Command

You use the ipconfig command to verify the configuration of TCP/IP on a computer. In Table 3-2, we list the configuration parameters you can use with the ipconfig command along with a description of what each does.

Table 3-2: *IPConfig Command Parameters*

Parameter	Enables You To
ipconfig	View the computer's DNS domain name, IP address, subnet mask, and default gateway information.
ipconfig /all	View the computer's host name, DNS domain name, network card driver, IP address, subnet mask, default gateway, DNS server(s), and WINS server(s). In addition, you can use this display to determine whether the computer was configured through DHCP or APIPA. If the computer obtained its addressing through DHCP, you also see the IP address of the DHCP server.
ipconfig /release	Release the IP addressing information assigned to the computer by the DHCP server or APIPA.
ipconfig /renew	Obtain IP addressing information from a DHCP server or APIPA.

The Ping Command

The ping command enables you to verify that a computer can communicate across the network using the TCP/IP protocol. The syntax of ping is ping *IP address*, where *IP address* is the IP address of another computer on the network. When you use the ping command, your computer sends four queries out to the computer associated with the IP address you specified. If your computer can successfully communicate with that computer, you'll see four replies to the ping command, as shown in Figure 3-5.

```
C:\WINNT\System32\cmd.exe                              _ □ ×

C:\>ping 200.200.200.117

Pinging 200.200.200.117 with 32 bytes of data:

Reply from 200.200.200.117: bytes=32 time<10ms TTL=128
Reply from 200.200.200.117: bytes=32 time<10ms TTL=128
Reply from 200.200.200.117: bytes=32 time<10ms TTL=128
Reply from 200.200.200.117: bytes=32 time<10ms TTL=128

Ping statistics for 200.200.200.117:
    Packets: Sent = 4, Received = 4, Lost = 0 (0% loss),
Approximate round trip times in milli-seconds:
    Minimum = 0ms, Maximum =  0ms, Average =  0ms

C:\>
```

Figure 3-5: *A successful test of TCP/IP connectivity using the ping command.*

Internet Service Provider (ISP)

When you connect a computer or network to the Internet, you typically connect it via a modem to a company that provides Internet access; this company is called an Internet Service Provider (ISP). Most ISPs charge a fee for this connection and, in turn, provide you with a user name, password, email address, and a list of access phone numbers. You connect to the Internet by dialing one of these access phone numbers; the ISP then connects you to the Internet.

 The modem you use to connect to an ISP can be the typical dial-up modem, or it can be a DSL or cable modem for higher-speed connections.

How to Configure TCP/IP

Procedure Reference: Configure TCP/IP in Windows 2000

To configure TCP/IP in Windows 2000:

1. Consult the network administrator to determine if you should manually assign the IP addressing information to the computer or use either DHCP or APIPA. If you're going to manually assign the IP addressing information, obtain the following required information:

   - IP address
   - Subnet mask
   - Default gateway address (if applicable)
   - Preferred and alternate DNS server addresses (if applicable)

2. Log on as a user with administrative permissions.

3. Open Network And Dial-Up Connections. (From the Start menu, choose Settings→Network And Dial-up Connections.)

4. Right-click Local Area Connection and choose Properties.

5. Select the Internet Protocol (TCP/IP) and click Properties.

6. Configure the TCP/IP properties.

   - If you're configuring the IP address information for the computer manually, select Use The Following IP Address and type in the IP address and subnet mask at a minimum. Optionally, type in a default gateway address, preferred DNS server address, and an alternate DNS server address (if available).

   - If you're configuring the computer to use either DHCP or APIPA, select Obtain An IP Address Automatically and Obtain A DNS Server Address Automatically.

7. Click OK to save your configuration changes.

8. Click OK to close the Local Area Connection Properties dialog box.

9. Close Network And Dial-up Connections.

10. Verify the TCP/IP configuration.

    a. From the Start menu, choose Programs→Accessories→Command Prompt.

    b. Enter `ipconfig /all`.

    c. Verify that the TCP/IP addressing parameters are correct.

     d.   Close the Command Prompt window.

11. Use ping to verify the TCP/IP configuration. (See the following procedure for how to use ping.)

Procedure Reference: Configure TCP/IP in Windows XP

To configure TCP/IP in Windows XP:

1. Consult the network administrator to determine if you should manually assign the IP addressing information to the computer or use either DHCP or APIPA. If you're going to manually assign the IP addressing information, obtain the following required information:

- IP address
- Subnet mask
- Default gateway address (if necessary)
- Preferred and alternate DNS server addresses (if necessary)

2. Log on as a user with administrative permissions.

3. Open Network Connections. (From the Start menu, choose My Network Places→ View Network Connections.)

4. Right-click Local Area Connection and choose Properties.

5. Select the Internet Protocol (TCP/IP) and click Properties.

6. Configure the TCP/IP properties.

- If you're configuring the IP address information for the computer manually, select Use The Following IP Address and type in the IP address and subnet mask at a minimum. Optionally, type in a default gateway address, preferred DNS server address, and an alternate DNS server address (if available).
- If you're configuring the computer to use either DHCP or APIPA, select Obtain An IP Address Automatically and Obtain A DNS Server Address Automatically.

7. Click OK to save your configuration changes.

8. Click OK to close the Local Area Connection Properties dialog box.

9. Close Network Connections.

10. Verify the TCP/IP configuration.

     a.   From the Start menu, choose All Programs→Accessories→Command Prompt.

     b.   Enter ipconfig /all.

     c.   Verify that the TCP/IP addressing parameters are correct.

     d.   Close the Command Prompt window.

11. Use ping to test the TCP/IP configuration. (See the procedure below for how to use ping.)

Procedure Reference: Configure TCP/IP in Windows NT

To configure TCP/IP in Windows NT:

Windows NT does not support Automatic Private IP Addressing (APIPA).

1. Consult the network administrator to determine if you should manually assign the IP addressing information to the computer or use DHCP. If you're going to manually assign the IP addressing information, obtain the following required information.

   - IP address
   - Subnet mask
   - Default gateway address (if necessary)
   - Preferred and alternate DNS server addresses (if necessary)

2. Log on as a user with administrative permissions.

3. Open the Network dialog box. (From the Start menu, choose Settings→Control Panel. Double-click Network.)

4. Select the Protocols tab.

5. In the Network Protocols list, select TCP/IP Protocol.

6. Click Properties.

7. Configure the TCP/IP properties as follows:

   - If you're configuring the IP address information for the computer manually, complete the following steps:

     1. Select Specify An IP Address and type in the IP address, subnet mask, and, optionally, a default gateway address.
     2. If you have DNS server addresses to configure, select the DNS tab.
     3. In the DNS Service Search Order portion of the dialog box, click Add.
     4. In the DNS Server text box, type the IP address of the first DNS server.
     5. Click Add.
     6. Add any additional DNS server addresses.

   - If you're configuring the computer to use DHCP, select Obtain An IP Address From A DHCP Server. (This setting will also automatically configure the computer's DNS server addresses.)

8. Click OK to close the Microsoft TCP/IP Properties dialog box.

9. Click OK to close the Network dialog box.

10. Close Control Panel.

11. Click Yes to restart the computer.

12. When prompted, log back on to the computer.

13. Verify the TCP/IP configuration.

    a. From the Start menu, choose Programs→Accessories→Command Prompt.
    b. Enter `ipconfig /all`.
    c. Verify that the TCP/IP addressing parameters are correct.
    d. Close the Command Prompt window.

14. Use `ping` to test and verify the TCP/IP configuration. (See the procedure below for how to use `ping`.)

Procedure Reference: Test Connectivity Using Ping

To use ping to test and verify TCP/IP connectivity:

1. Obtain the IP address of another computer on the network.

2. From the Start menu, choose Programs→Accessories→Command Prompt to open a Command Prompt window.

3. Enter ping *another computer's IP address*. By pinging the IP address of another computer on the network, you verify that the network portion of the computer's IP address and its subnet mask are correct, and that it can communicate with other computers on its network segment.

4. Close the Command Prompt window.

AppleTalk Protocol

Windows NT and Windows 2000 computers natively support the AppleTalk protocol. AppleTalk is the routable network protocol for Macintosh networks. AppleTalk arranges network components into three main subsets:

*   Nodes, which are individual devices, such as computers or printers, that have network access. Nodes are addressed by a single 8-bit binary number, represented by the decimal numbers 1 to 254 (the number 255 is reserved for broadcasting). Each node generates its own node number when it comes online, but before using it, the node broadcasts a request to make sure there is no duplicate address.

*   Networks, which are the physical segments (network cables).

*   Zones, which are workgroups arranged by the administrator to aid in the sharing and access of resources. Members of a zone don't need to be on the same network (physical segment).

Newer Apple computers, including those with the Mac OS X (version 10.2 and higher) operating system, support TCP/IP connectivity, which makes it easier to share files and printers in a Windows network.

ACTIVITY 3-3

Configuring TCP/IP Manually

Setup:

Use an IP address of 192.168.200.#, where # is your computer number. The subnet mask is 255.255.255.0. The preferred DNS server's address is 192.168.200.200.

Scenario:

As an A+ technician, you receive a support call from a client stating that her new Windows 2000 Professional laptop can't connect to her office's small network. When you review the computer's configuration, you determine that it's attempting to obtain an IP address from a DHCP server. Your client's network doesn't have a DHCP server. Instead, all computers are configured manually with IP addresses.

What You Do	How You Do It
1. Configure the TCP/IP protocol.	a. **Open Network And Dial-up Connections.**
	b. **Right-click the Local Area Connection and choose Properties.**
	c. In the list of network components, **select Internet Protocol (TCP/IP).**
	☑ ᛏ Internet Protocol (TCP/IP)
	d. **Click Properties.**
	e. **Select Use The Following IP Address.**
	f. In the IP Address text box, **type *192.168.200.#,*** where # is your assigned computer number.
	g. In the Subnet Mask text box, **verify that the subnet mask is 255.255.255.0.**

h. In the Preferred DNS Server text box, **type** *192.168.200.200*

```
┌─ⓒ Use the following IP address: ─────────────────┐
│  IP address:                    192 . 168 . 200 .  1  │
│                                                        │
│  Subnet mask:                   255 . 255 . 255 .  0  │
│                                                        │
│  Default gateway:                 .     .     .        │
│                                                        │
│  ○ Obtain DNS server address automatically            │
│  ─ⓒ Use the following DNS server addresses: ─────     │
│  Preferred DNS server:          192 . 168 . 200 . 200 │
│                                                        │
│  Alternate DNS server:            .     .     .        │
└────────────────────────────────────────────────────┘
```

i. **Click OK twice.**

j. **Close Network And Dial-Up Connections.**

2. **Verify the IP addressing configuration.**

a. From the Start menu, **choose Programs→ Accessories→Command Prompt.**

b. **Enter** `ipconfig /all`

c. **Verify that the IP address, subnet mask, and DNS server address information are correct.**

```
IP Address. . . . . . . . . . . . : 192.168.200.1
Subnet Mask . . . . . . . . . . . : 255.255.255.0
Default Gateway . . . . . . . . . :
DNS Servers . . . . . . . . . . . : 192.168.200.200
```

3. **Test TCP/IP connectivity.**

a. In the Command Prompt window, **type** `ping 192.168.200.200` to verify that you can communicate on the network using the TCP/IP protocol.

b. **Close the Command Prompt window.**

DISCOVERY ACTIVITY 3-4

Configuring TCP/IP Automatically

Activity Time:

5 minutes

Scenario:

One of your clients, a growing company, has just implemented DHCP servers to reduce the administrative workload for assigning IP addresses. The network administrator has configured the DHCP server to provide computers with an appropriate IP address, subnet mask, and DNS server address. As an A+ technician, you've been called in to assist with configuring the client's Windows 2000 computers to use DHCP.

---

1. **Configure your computer to obtain its IP address and DNS server address information automatically.**

---

2. **Verify and test the IP addressing configuration.**

TOPIC C

Troubleshoot TCP/IP Connectivity

As an A+ technician, you'll find that many of the calls you receive for troubleshooting involve problems with network connectivity. The majority of these support calls are due to mistakes in configuring the network connectivity, not a failure in the network hardware itself. Now that you've seen how to install TCP/IP on client computers, you need to learn the steps you can take to troubleshoot problems with the TCP/IP configuration. In this topic, you'll learn how to troubleshoot the TCP/IP configuration on Windows NT-, Windows 2000-, and Windows XP-based computers.

The goal with network connectivity is for your users to be able to be productive by accessing network resources. When your users encounter network connectivity problems, it's important for you to be able to diagnose and resolve these problems as soon as possible. In many cases, you'll be able to resolve these problems by troubleshooting the TCP/IP configuration. Knowing the steps to troubleshooting TCP/IP, along with the tools you can use to help you identify problems, will help you resolve TCP/IP connectivity problems quickly so that your users can get back to work.

The Troubleshooting Process

The troubleshooting process consists of the following phases:

1. The Collect Phase: You should gather information about the computer you're troubleshooting. This information includes:

   - For each computer that is experiencing the problem, obtain detailed information about its hardware, including the manufacturer, processor type and speed, RAM, hard disks, and any peripheral devices such as tape and CD-ROM drives.

   - If all computers on a network are experiencing the problem, document the type of network hardware in use, such as the network cards and cabling. If possible, obtain a diagram with the layout of the network cabling.

   - Document the software in use on the computers affected by the problem. Make sure you record not only the version of Windows, but also any updates installed. If the problem occurs when you run a specific application, record the application's version also.

   - Wherever possible, record the exact steps that result in the problem. Also record any error messages displayed on the screen.

   - Check the System and Application Logs in Windows 2000, Windows NT, or Windows XP for any error messages.

   - Collect the necessary resources to troubleshoot the problem, such as boot disks and diagnostic utilities.

2. The Isolate Phase: Use a series of questions to isolate the potential causes of the problem. Questions to ask include:

   - Is the computer's hardware on the Windows Hardware Compatibility List?

   - Have you installed the latest updates for the version of Windows you're using?

   - Is the problem happening to all users or only one user? If the problem is with only a particular computer, you can focus your attention on that computer. In contrast, if the problem is occurring on all computers, focus on the network configuration.

   - Is the problem happening when you attempt to access shared resources on one computer or shared resources on multiple computers? If the problem is happening when you attempt to access shared resources on multiple computers, focus on the network configuration of your computer. If the problem is happening when you attempt to access shared resources on only one computer, focus on the computer to which you're trying to connect. Can other users access this computer? If so, it might be a permissions problem. If no other users can access this computer, then suspect a problem with the computer's network configuration.

   - Were you ever able to do the task you're attempting to do? If not, the problem is probably that the application or operating system isn't properly configured.

   - Have you changed anything or installed any new software or hardware? If so, the problem might be caused by a conflict between your computer and the new software or hardware.

3. The Correct Phase: When you have narrowed down the scope of the problem to a specific area, you can then develop a plan for resolving the problem. When correcting the problem, make sure that you attempt only one change at a time so that you can determine which solution worked.

The TCP/IP Connectivity Process

When you attempt to connect to a computer on a TCP/IP-based network, Windows completes the following steps:

1. Your computer first attempts to find the IP address associated with the name of the computer to which you're attempting to connect.

    - If you're connecting to a computer on the Internet, your computer queries a DNS server to find the computer's IP address.

    - If you're connecting to a computer on the local network and you're using Windows 9x or Windows NT, your computer queries a WINS server to find the computer's IP address.

    - If you're connecting to a computer on the local network and you're using Windows 2000 or Windows XP, your computer queries a DNS server to find the computer's IP address.

    - If you're connecting to a computer on the local network and neither a DNS server nor a WINS server is available (or installed), your computer will broadcast a request to find the computer's IP address. If the computer to which you're attempting to connect responds, your computer can communicate with that computer.

2. Next, your computer determines if you're attempting to connect to a computer on another network. If you are, your computer forwards your communication attempt to the IP address of its default gateway.

3. Your computer establishes a connection with the remote computer. Depending on the computer, your computer might be required to provide your user name and password before you're granted access.

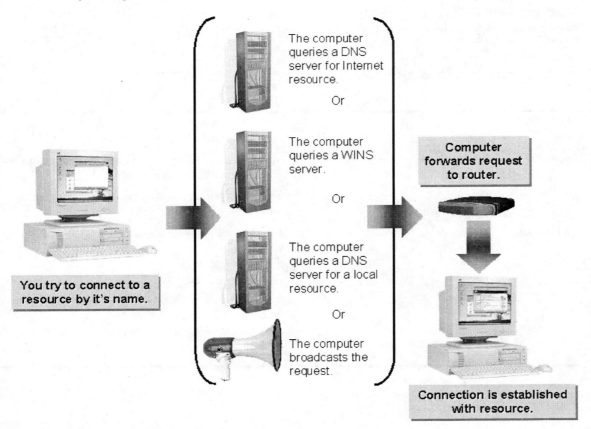

Figure 3-6: *The TCP/IP connectivity process.*

Common Connectivity Problems

There are several common problems you can encounter when troubleshooting TCP/IP. In Table 3-3, you find a list of the common problems and their symptoms.

Table 3-3: *Common TCP/IP Connectivity Problems*

Problem	Symptom
Incorrect subnet mask	Cannot communicate with other hosts. Usually can't communicate with other hosts on the same subnet at all.
Duplicate host address exists on network	Unable to initialize TCP/IP.
Incorrect default gateway address	Cannot communicate with remote networks.
DHCP server unavailable	Cannot obtain an IP address. In Windows 98, Windows 2000, and Windows XP, TCP/IP initializes with an IP address in the APIPA range (169.254.#.#).
Physical connectivity problems	Unable to communicate past the point of the connectivity break.
Incorrect DNS server address; DNS server unavailable	Cannot resolve host names or Internet URLs.
Incorrect WINS server address; WINS server unavailable	Cannot resolve NetBIOS names.

Troubleshooting Tools

Microsoft includes a variety of tools in its Windows operating systems that you can use to troubleshoot TCP/IP. In Table 3-4, you find a description of each of these tools and why you might use them.

Table 3-4: *Troubleshooting Tools*

Tool	Use To
`ipconfig`	Verify the configuration of TCP/IP and to release or renew DHCP IP address leases.
Local Area Connection Status	Verify that the Local Area Connection is connected to the network and able to send and receive data.
`ping`	Test communications between two TCP/IP-based hosts.
`nslookup`	Verify that the computer can connect to a DNS server and successfully find an IP address for a given computer name.
`tracert`	Determine the route the computer uses to send a packet to its destination. If `tracert` is unsuccessful, you can use the results generated to determine at what point communications are failing.

How to Troubleshoot TCP/IP Connectivity

Procedure Reference: Troubleshoot TCP/IP Connectivity Problems:

To troubleshoot TCP/IP connectivity problems:

1. Identify the scope of the problem. Is it happening to only one user? If so, you should troubleshoot only that user's computer. On the other hand, is the problem happening on multiple computers? If so, the problem might be the network hardware such as the cabling, hubs, or routers.

2. Ask the user questions and use troubleshooting tools (such as `ping` and `ipconfig`) to isolate the problem. You'll find that most of the TCP/IP connectivity problems fit into one of the following categories:

    *   IP addressing problems—Verify that the client has addressing information that matches your network's configuration.

    *   Physical network problems—Suspect this if the client's IP configuration otherwise appears correct. Make sure that the computer's network cable is plugged in and check its connection to the wall jack. Verify that the network card is functioning properly. Use `tracert` to verify that you can communicate with other computers across routers.

    *   Name resolution problems—See if your client can connect to a target computer by IP address instead of by name. Use `nslookup` to verify that the computer can communicate with the DNS server and obtain the target computer's IP address.

3. Correct the problem.

    *   For IP addressing problems, use `ipconfig /release` and `ipconfig /renew` to attempt to lease an IP address on dynamically configured clients. If the clients are manually configured, enter the correct addressing information.

    *   For physical network problems, replace or reconnect the network card, cable, jack, or hub.

    *   For name resolution problems, correct either the DNS and WINS server addresses in the TCP/IP configuration for manually configured clients. If the DNS or WINS server addresses are incorrect on dynamically configured clients, bring it to the network administrator's attention.

4. Use `ipconfig` and `ping` to verify that you can communicate with other hosts on the network.

5. Document your solution for future reference.

Procedure Reference: Troubleshoot Connectivity Using Ping

To use `ping` to troubleshoot TCP/IP connectivity:

1. Open a Command Prompt window.

2. Enter `ping 127.0.0.1`. Pinging the IP address of 127.0.0.1 (also called the loopback address) generates a response from the IP protocol on your own computer. This verifies that TCP/IP is installed and working, even if the computer doesn't yet have a valid IP address. The loopback address is a standard address that's reserved by the TCP/IP protocol for testing. An equivalent command is `ping localhost`.

3. Enter ping *your IP address*. (Replace "your IP address" with the IP address of the computer.) Pinging the computer's own IP address enables you to verify that the IP address is unique and valid.

4. Enter ping *default gateway address*. (Replace "default gateway address" with the IP address of the default gateway.) By pinging the IP address of the default gateway (or another computer on the computer's network segment if you don't have a default gateway), you verify that the network portion of the computer's IP address and its subnet mask are correct, and that it can communicate with other hosts on its network segment.

5. Enter ping *remote IP address*. (Replace "remote IP address" with the IP address of a host on a different network segment; in other words, a host with a different network address from the computer's own.) Pinging a remote IP address verifies that the computer can communicate across the router (default gateway).

6. Close the Command Prompt window.

Procedure Reference: Troubleshoot Name Resolution Problems Using Ping

To use ping to troubleshoot TCP/IP name resolution:

1. Open a Command Prompt window.

2. Enter ping *host name*. (Replace host name with the name of a computer on the network or an Internet URL such as **www.cnn.com**.) If the computer on which you're working attempts to ping a computer (even if that computer doesn't respond), the computer is successfully able to access either a DNS or WINS server to resolve the host name.

3. Close the Command Prompt window.

Procedure Reference: Troubleshoot Name Resolution Problems Using NSLookup

To use nslookup to troubleshoot TCP/IP name resolution:

1. Open a Command Prompt window.

2. Enter nslookup *computer name*. For example, if you're testing name resolution for a computer named server1 on your own network, enter nslookup *server1*. If you're testing name resolution for Internet addresses, enter nslookup *www.cnn.com*.

3. Close the Command Prompt window.

Procedure Reference: Troubleshoot Connectivity Using Tracert

To use tracert to troubleshoot TCP/IP connectivity:

1. Open a Command Prompt window.

2. Enter tracert *IP address or computer name*.

3. Close the Command Prompt window.

Procedure Reference: Troubleshoot Connectivity Using IPConfig

To use IPConfig to verify your IP addressing information:

1. Open a Command Prompt window.

2. Enter `ipconfig /all`. This command displays not only the computer's IP address, but also information about its DNS server addresses as well as the IP address of the DHCP server from which it leased an address (if applicable).

3. Close the Command Prompt Window.

Procedure Reference: Troubleshoot Automatic TCP/IP Configuration Using IPConfig

To use IPConfig to troubleshoot dynamic IP addressing:

1. Open a Command Prompt window.

2. Enter `ipconfig /release` to release the IP address you leased from the DHCP server.

3. Enter `ipconfig /renew` to attempt to lease a new IP address.

4. Close the Command Prompt window.

DISCOVERY ACTIVITY 3-5

Troubleshooting TCP/IP Problems

Scenario:

Your company provides technical support to a number of different clients. These clients have networks that range in size from only a few computers to as many as hundreds of computers. As an A+ technician, your job is to troubleshoot connectivity problems that your clients report.

1. One of your clients calls to report that he is unable to connect to any network resources or the Internet. After questioning him, you've determined that someone accidentally unplugged the DHCP server. The client reports that the DHCP server is up and running, but he's still unable to connect to any resources. You have the client type in `ipconfig /all`, and here's what he reports:

- IP address: 169.254.225.48
- Subnet mask: 255.255.0.0
- Default gateway: None
- DNS server: None

After reviewing your company's documentation for this client's network, you've determined that the client's IP address should be on the 192.168.200.# network with a subnet mask of 255.255.255.0. The default gateway address is 192.168.200.1.

What should you try next to attempt to solve the problem?

a) Have the client open a Command Prompt window and enter `ping 127.0.0.1`.

b) Have the client open a Command Prompt window and enter `ping 192.168.200.1`.

c) Have the client open a Command Prompt window and enter `ipconfig /release` and `ipconfig /renew`.

d) Have the client manually configure his IP address to one on the 192.168.200.# network, a subnet mask of 255.255.255.0, and a default gateway address of 192.168.200.1.

2. You receive a call from a client who reports that she's unable to access any Web sites in Internet Explorer. While talking with this user, you verify that she can ping the server's IP address on her network segment, the IP address of the default gateway, and the IP address of a computer on another network segment. You also determine that none of the other users on her network can connect to Web sites in Internet Explorer.

   What might be the problem?

   a) Her network's WINS server is down.

   b) Her network's DNS server is down.

   c) Her computer is configured with the wrong default gateway address.

   d) Her computer is configured with the wrong subnet mask.

3. One of your clients reports that he is unable to see computers when he double-clicks Computers Near Me in My Network Places.

   Which step should you take first?

   a) Ask the client to ping another computer on his network.

   b) Ask the client if any of the other users on the network are experiencing problems.

   c) Ask the client to verify that the DHCP server is running.

   d) Ask the client to run `ipconfig /release` and `ipconfig /renew`.

4. A client reports that he's unable to connect to any computers on the network or the Internet. You have him run the IPConfig command, and all his TCP/IP addressing parameters are correct. When you have him ping other computers on the network, his computer is unable to reach them. This computer is the only one that's experiencing a problem.

   What should you check next?

   a) That his computer's network cable is plugged in to both the network card and the wall jack.

   b) That the router is on and functioning properly.

   c) That the hub is on and functioning properly.

   d) That the DHCP server is on and functioning properly.

5. Your client tells you that she has just installed a new server on her network. This server has a CD-ROM tower in it that she wants to share with all users on the network. No users can connect to this computer. All of her users can connect to other resources on the network and the Internet.

   Which configuration parameter might be the cause of this problem?

   a) The server's IP address

   b) The users' IP addresses

   c) The users' subnet masks

   d) The server's default gateway address

TOPIC D

Install or Remove NetBEUI

As you've seen in this lesson, a network protocol is required for clients to be able to communicate on a network. Just as you might install TCP/IP as a client's network protocol, so might you install NetBEUI. On the other hand, you might encounter a computer on which unnecessary protocols for the user's network environment have been installed. So, in this topic, you'll learn how to install or remove NetBEUI as a network protocol on your users' Windows 2000- and Windows NT-based computers.

There are some situations in which using NetBEUI as the only network protocol might be the best choice for a network. For example, a network administrator might choose to use NetBEUI on a small network that doesn't connect to the Internet. Alternatively, you might encounter situations where you need to install NetBEUI as an additional network protocol in order for your clients to be able to access older, NetBEUI-based resources. Regardless of whether NetBEUI is the only network protocol or an additional protocol, it's important for you to know how to install it properly so that your users will be able to communicate with your network's resources. Conversely, network protocols do use additional resources such as RAM and network bandwidth on a computer. If the network environment doesn't require a particular protocol such as NetBEUI, you should be prepared to remove it from any clients to improve their performance.

The NetBEUI Protocol

The *NetBEUI* protocol is a small, *non-routable*, proprietary Microsoft network protocol. (A non-routable protocol cannot send data across routers.) It is supported by Windows 9x, Windows NT, and Windows 2000, but not Windows XP. When you install NetBEUI, it has no parameters to configure.

 By default, Windows XP does not include support for the NetBEUI protocol. If you're interested in configuring NetBEUI on Windows XP, refer to the Knowledge Base article # Q301041at **http://support.microsoft.com/ default.aspx?scid=kb;en-us;Q301041**.

How to Install or Remove NetBEUI

Procedure Reference: Install NetBEUI in Windows 2000

To install NetBEUI in Windows 2000:

1. Log on as a user with administrative permissions.

2. Open Network And Dial-Up Connections.

3. Right-click Local Area Connection and choose Properties.

4. Click Install to install a new network component.

5. In the Select Network Component Type dialog box, select Protocol.

6. Click Add.

7. In the Network Protocol list, select NetBEUI Protocol.

8. Click OK to install the NetBEUI protocol.

9. Click Close to close the Local Area Connection Properties dialog box.

10. Close Network And Dial-Up Connections.

11. Test the NetBEUI protocol by verifying that you can see other NetBEUI-based computers in My Network Places.

    a. On the desktop, double-click My Network Places.

    b. Double-click Computers Near Me.

    c. Verify that you see other computers listed in Computers Near Me.

    d. Close the window.

Procedure Reference: Remove NetBEUI from Windows 2000

To remove NetBEUI from Windows 2000:

1. Log on as a user with administrative permissions.

2. Open Network And Dial-Up Connections.

3. Right-click Local Area Connection and choose Properties.

4. In the list of network components, select NetBEUI Protocol.

5. Click Uninstall to remove the protocol.

6. Click Yes to confirm that you want to remove the protocol.

7. Click Yes to confirm that you want to restart the computer.

8. Log back on to the computer.

9. Verify that the protocol is removed.

    a. Display the properties of the Local Area Connection.

    b. Make sure that the NetBEUI protocol is no longer displayed in the list of installed network components.

    c. Close any open dialog boxes and windows.

Procedure Reference: Install NetBEUI in Windows NT

To install NetBEUI in Windows NT:

1. Log on as a user with administrative permissions.

2. Open the Network dialog box. (From the Start menu, choose Settings→Control Panel. Double-click Network.)

3. Select the Protocols tab.

4. Click Add so that you can install a new protocol.

5. In the Network Protocol list, select NetBEUI Protocol and click OK.

6. In the Windows NT Setup dialog box, enter the path to the Windows NT installation files. (If necessary, insert the Windows NT CD-ROM into the computer's CD-ROM drive.)

7. Click Continue.

8. Click Close to close the Network dialog box.

9. When prompted, click Yes to restart the computer.

10. Log back on to the computer.

11. Test the NetBEUI protocol by verifying that you can see other NetBEUI-based computers in the Network Neighborhood.

    a.   On the desktop, double-click Network Neighborhood.

    b.   Verify that you see other computers listed in the Network Neighborhood.

    c.   Close the window.

Procedure Reference: Remove NetBEUI from Windows NT

To remove NetBEUI from Windows NT:

1. Log on as a user with administrative permissions.

2. Open the Network dialog box.

3. Select the Protocols tab.

4. In the list of protocols, select NetBEUI Protocol.

5. Click Remove.

6. Click Yes to confirm that you want to remove the protocol.

7. Click Close to close the Network dialog box.

8. When prompted, click Yes to restart the computer.

9. Log back on to the computer.

10. Verify that the protocol is removed.

    a.   In the Network dialog box, select the Protocols tab.

    b.   Verify that you do not see the NetBEUI protocol listed.

    c.   Close all open dialog boxes.

ACTIVITY 3-6

Installing the NetBEUI Protocol

Scenario:

Your client, a non-profit agency, has just received a donation of a legacy CD-ROM tower that supports only the NetBEUI protocol. He would like you to configure his network's Windows 2000 computers so that they can access this CD-ROM tower. Currently, your client uses only the TCP/IP protocol on the network.

What You Do	How You Do It
1. Install NetBEUI.	a. **Display the Properties of the Local Area Connection.**
	b. **Click Install** to install a new network component.
	c. In the Select Network Component Type dialog box, **select Protocol.**
	d. **Click Add.**
	e. In the Network Protocol list, **select NetBEUI Protocol.**
	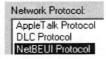
	f. **Click OK** to install the NetBEUI protocol.
	g. **Click Close** to close the Local Area Connection Properties dialog box.
	h. **Close Network And Dial-up Connections.**

2. How do you verify connectivity after installing the NetBEUI protocol?

DISCOVERY ACTIVITY 3-7

Removing the NetBEUI Protocol

Scenario:

Your client is an elementary school. The principal would like to make sure that the students cannot access the administrative computers. All of the computers are running Windows 2000 Professional. The students' computers are running the NetBEUI protocol. The administrative computers are running both the NetBEUI protocol and the TCP/IP protocol so that they can access the Internet.

1. **Remove the NetBEUI protocol.**

2. **Verify that the NetBEUI protocol is no longer installed.**

TOPIC E

Install or Remove NWLink IPX/SPX

So far in this lesson, you've learned how to install, configure, and troubleshoot the TCP/IP and NetBEUI protocols. But these aren't the only protocols you can use on a network. In this topic, you'll learn how to install the NWLink IPX/SPX protocol in Windows NT, Windows 2000, and Windows XP. And in case you encounter a computer on which the NWlink IPX/SPX protocol isn't needed, you'll also learn how to remove the protocol from these operating systems.

Although TCP/IP is the network protocol most commonly used on today's networks, it's possible that you'll encounter a situation where you'll need to install an alternative or additional protocol such as NWLink IPX/SPX. For example, you might be responsible for configuring clients to connect to older Novell NetWare servers that are running the IPX/SPX protocol. Knowing how to install NWLink IPX/SPX will enable you to configure computers to successfully communicate with IPX/SPX-based resources. You might also encounter computers on which the NWLink IPX/SPX protocol is no longer needed. Knowing how to remove the protocol will enable you to free up both memory and network bandwidth.

The NWLink IPX/SPX Protocol

The *NWLink IPX/SPX* network protocol is Microsoft's implementation of Novell's proprietary transport protocol, Internet Packet Exchange/Sequenced Packet Exchange (IPX/SPX). IPX/SPX was the default network protocol for older versions of Novell NetWare (all versions prior to NetWare 5). NetWare 5 and later versions use TCP/IP as their network protocol instead of IPX/SPX. You'll typically install NWLink IPX/SPX only if your Windows computers need access to an older NetWare server for file and print services or for accessing an application such as a database server.

NWLink IPX/SPX Configuration Settings

Table 3-5 provides you with a guide to the properties you might configure when you install the NWLink IPX/SPX protocol.

Table 3-5: *NWLink IPX/SPX Configuration Settings*

Setting	Description
Frame Type	Determines the format in which the computer sends data and expects to receive data. Computers running different frame types can't communicate. By default, Windows automatically attempts to find the frame type in use on the network and configures the computer to use this frame type. If Windows detects more than one frame type in use on the network, it configures the computer to use the default Ethernet frame type (called 802.2). If you have a mix of servers running different frame types, you might need to set the frame type manually.
External Network Number	Identifies the number assigned to the network. (This number is configured on the NetWare server.) By default, Windows automatically detects the External Network Number.
Internal Network Number	Uniquely identifies the computer; this number is also autodetected by Windows. You configure the Internal Network Number only if you are installing a computer with multiple network cards or running specialized network services on that computer.

How to Install or Remove NWLink IPX/SPX

Procedure Reference: Install NWLink IPX/SPX in Windows 2000

To install NWLink IPX/SPX in Windows 2000:

1. Log on as a user with administrative permissions.

2. Display the properties for the Local Area Connection. (In Network And Dial-up Connections, right-click Local Area Connection and choose Properties.)

3. Click Install to install a new network component.

4. In the Select Network Component Type dialog box, select Protocol.

5. Click Add.

6. In the Network Protocol list, select NWLink IPX/SPX/NetBIOS Compatible Transport Protocol.

7. Click OK to install the protocol.

8. If necessary, configure the frame type.

    a. In the list of network components, select the NWLink IPX/SPX/NetBIOS Compatible Transport Protocol.

    b. Click Properties.

    c. From the Frame Type drop-down list, select the appropriate frame type for the network.

    d. Click OK to save your changes.

9. Click Close to close the Local Area Connection Properties dialog box.

10. Close Network And Dial-Up Connections.

11. Test the NWLink IPX/SPX protocol by verifying that you can see other computers in My Network Places.

    a. On the desktop, double-click My Network Places.

    b. Double-click Computers Near Me.

    c. Verify that you see other NWLink IPX/SPX-based computers listed in Computers Near Me.

    d. Close the window.

Procedure Reference: Remove NWLink IPX/SPX from Windows 2000

To remove NWLink IPX/SPX from Windows 2000:

1. Log on as a user with administrative permissions.

2. Display the properties for the Local Area Connection. (In Network And Dial-up Connections, right-click Local Area Connection and choose Properties.)

3. In the list of network components, select NWLink IPX/SPX/NetBIOS Compatible Transport Protocol.

4. Click Uninstall.

5. Click Yes to confirm that you want to remove the protocol.

6. Click Yes to restart the computer.

7. Log back on to the computer.

8. Close Network And Dial-Up Connections.

9. Verify that the protocol is removed.

    a. Display the properties of the Local Area Connection.

    b. Make sure that the NWLink IPX/SPX/NetBIOS Compatible Transport Protocol is no longer displayed in the list of installed network components.

    c. Close any open dialog boxes and windows.

Procedure Reference: Install NWLink IPX/SPX in Windows XP

To install NWLink IPX/SPX in Windows XP:

1. Log on as a user with administrative permissions.

2. Display the properties for the Local Area Connection. (In Network Connections, right-click Local Area Connection and choose Properties.)

3. Click Install to install a new network component.

4. In the Select Network Component Type dialog box, select Protocol.

5. Click Add.

6. In the Network Protocol list, select NWLink IPX/SPX/NetBIOS Compatible Transport Protocol.

7. Click OK to install the protocol.

8. If necessary, configure the frame type.

   a. In the list of network components, select the NWLink IPX/SPX/NetBIOS Compatible Transport Protocol.

   b. Click Properties.

   c. From the Frame Type drop-down list, select the appropriate frame type for the network.

   d. Click OK to save your changes.

9. Click Close to close the Local Area Connection Properties dialog box.

10. Close Network Connections.

11. Test the NWLink IPX/SPX protocol by verifying that you can see other computers in My Network Places.

   a. On the Start menu, click My Network Places.

   b. Click View Workgroup Computers.

   c. Verify that you see other NWLink IPX/SPX-based computers listed.

   d. Close the window.

Procedure Reference: Remove NWLink IPX/SPX from Windows XP

To remove NWLink IPX/SPX from Windows XP:

1. Log on as a user with administrative permissions.

2. Display the properties for the Local Area Connection. (In Network Connections, right-click Local Area Connection and choose Properties.)

3. Select the NWLink IPX/SPX/NetBIOS Compatible Transport Protocol.

4. Click Uninstall to remove the protocol.

5. Click Yes to confirm that you want to remove the protocol.

6. Click Yes to restart the computer.

7. Log back on to the computer.

8. Verify that the protocol is removed.

   a. Display the properties of the Local Area Connection.

   b. Make sure that the NWLink IPX/SPX/NetBIOS Compatible Transport Protocol is no longer displayed in the list of installed network components.

   c. Close any open dialog boxes and windows.

Procedure Reference: Install NWLink IPX/SPX on Windows NT

To install NWLink IPX/SPX on Windows NT:

1. Log on as a user with administrative permissions.

2. Open the Network dialog box.

3. Select the Protocols tab.

4. Click Add so that you can install a new protocol.

5. In the Network Protocol list, select NWLink IPX/SPX Compatible Transport and click OK.

6. In the Windows NT Setup dialog box, enter the path to the Windows NT installation files. (If necessary, insert the Windows NT CD-ROM into the computer's CD-ROM drive.)

7. Click Continue.

8. If necessary, configure the frame type.

   a. In the list of network protocols, select the NWLink IPX/SPX Compatible Transport.

   b. Click Properties.

   c. From the Frame Type drop-down list, select the appropriate frame type for the network.

   d. Click OK to save your changes.

9. Click Close to close the Network dialog box.

10. When prompted, click Yes to restart the computer.

11. Log back on to the computer.

12. Test the NWLink IPX/SPX protocol by verifying that you can browse the Network Neighborhood.

    a. On the desktop, double-click Network Neighborhood.

    b. Verify that you see other NWLink IPX/SPX-based computers listed in the Network Neighborhood.

    c. Close the window.

Procedure Reference: Remove NWLink IPX/SPX from Windows NT

To remove NWLink IPX/SPX from Windows NT:

1. Log on as a user with administrative permissions.

2. Open the Network dialog box.

3. Select the Protocols tab.

4. In the list of protocols, select NWLink IPX/SPX Compatible Transport.

5. Click Remove.

6. Click Yes to confirm that you want to remove the protocol.

7. Click Close to close the Network dialog box.

8. When prompted, click Yes to restart the computer.

9. Log back on to the computer.

10. Verify that the protocol is removed.

    a. In the Network dialog box, select the Protocols tab.

    b. Verify that you do not see the NWLink IPX/SPX Compatible Transport protocol listed.

    c. Close all open dialog boxes.

ACTIVITY 3-8

Installing NWLink IPX/SPX

Scenario:

Your client has a custom database application that runs only on a Novell NetWare 3.12 server. You're in the process of configuring new Windows 2000-based computers for your client's network.

What You Do	How You Do It
1. Install the NWLink IPX/SPX protocol.	a. **Display the properties of the Local Area Connection.**
	b. **Click Install** to install a new network component.
	c. In the Select Network Component Type dialog box, **select Protocol.**
	d. **Click Add.**
	e. In the Network Protocol list, **select NWLink IPX/SPX/NetBIOS Compatible Transport Protocol.**
	NetBEUI Protocol Network Monitor Driver NWLink IPX/SPX/NetBIOS Compatible Transport Protocol
	f. **Click OK** to install the protocol.
	g. **Click Close** to close the Local Area Connection Properties dialog box.
	h. **Close Network And Dial-up Connections.**

2. How can you verify that the NWLink IPX/SPX protocol is installed successfully?

TOPIC F

Install a NetWare Client

As you saw in Topic 3E, installing the IPX/SPX protocol enables your clients to access applications on servers that are using the IPX/SPX protocol. But what if your clients also need to access shared file and print resources on these servers? If so, you'll need to install the NetWare client to enable your clients to access the servers' file and print resources. In this topic, you'll learn how to install the Windows NT, Windows 2000, and Windows XP clients for connecting to a NetWare server.

By default, all of the Windows operating systems automatically install a client for connecting to shared resources on Windows-based computers. But if you have NetWare servers on your network, without a NetWare client, your users won't be able to connect to the shared file and print resources on the NetWare servers. Installing the NetWare client on your users' computers will provide them with easy access to the resources on a NetWare server.

Network Client

Definition:

A *network client* is a software component that enables a computer to access a shared resource on another computer. The network client redirects requests for accessing shared resources to the appropriate computer on the network. By default, Windows 2000 and Windows XP automatically load Microsoft Client For Networks if Windows setup detects a network card in the computer during installation. This client enables you to connect to shared resources on other Windows-based computers. (In Windows NT, the equivalent of Microsoft Client For Networks is the Workstation service.) You can optionally install the Novell NetWare network client, the Client Service For NetWare, if you need to connect to shared resources on a NetWare server.

Example:

In Figure 3-7, you see an example of how a network client sends a user's request for accessing a shared folder to the appropriate server on the network.

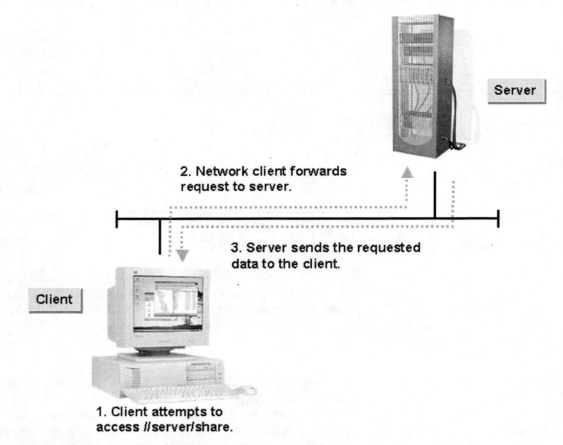

Figure 3-7: *A network client.*

NetWare Client Properties

When you install Client Service For NetWare, you can configure the properties listed in Table 3-6.

Table 3-6: *NetWare Client Properties*

Property	Description
Add Form Feed	This option configures Client Service For NetWare to add a form feed at the end of the user's print jobs to force the paper to feed out of the printer. With most application software, the applications send a form feed to force the paper out of the printer. So, if you enable this option, you'll typically see a blank sheet after each of the user's print jobs.
Default Tree And Context	If you're connecting the computer to NetWare 4.0 or a later version, use this property to specify the name of the NetWare server's directory tree and context.
Notify When Printed	By default, Client Service For NetWare configures the computer so that you're automatically notified when your print jobs are complete.

Property	Description
Preferred Server	If you're connecting the computer to a NetWare 3.12 server or earlier version, use the Preferred Server property to specify the name of the server to which you want to log on.
Print Banner	By default, Client Service For NetWare configures the computer to automatically print a banner page (a page that displays the user's login name for the NetWare server) whenever the user prints to a NetWare printer.
Run Login Script	This property enables you to choose whether you want the computer to run the NetWare server's login script whenever the user logs on to the computer.

How to Install a NetWare Client

Procedure Reference: Install NetWare Client in Windows 2000 and Windows XP

To install NetWare Client in Windows 2000 and Windows XP:

1. Log on as a user with administrative permissions.

2. Open the properties for the Local Area Connection.

3. If necessary, install the NWLink IPX/SPX/NetBIOS Compatible Transport Protocol.

4. Click Install.

5. Verify that Client is selected and click Add.

6. Select Client Service For NetWare and click OK.

7. If you're using Windows 2000, after a moment, in the Select NetWare Logon dialog box, configure the NetWare logon location information for the current user account.

   - If you're logging on to a NetWare 3.12 server or earlier version, verify that Preferred Server is selected. From the Preferred Server drop-down list, select the name of your NetWare server. Click OK.

   - If you're logging on to a NetWare 4.0 server or later version, select Default Tree And Context. In the Tree text box, type the name of the NDS tree. In the Context text box, type the context within that tree where the user account exists. Click OK.

   - If you don't currently have a NetWare server available to you, verify that <None> is selected in the Preferred Server drop-down list. Click OK.

8. Click Yes to restart the computer.

9. Log back on to the computer.

10. If you're using Windows XP, in the Select NetWare Logon dialog box, configure the NetWare logon location information for the current user account.

- If you're logging on to a NetWare 3.12 server or earlier version, verify that Preferred Server is selected. From the Preferred Server drop-down list, select the name of your NetWare server. Click OK.

- If you're logging on to a NetWare 4.0 server or later version, select Default Tree And Context. In the Tree text box, type the name of the NDS tree. In the Context text box, type the context within that tree where the user account exists. Click OK.

- If you don't currently have a NetWare server available to you, verify that <None> is selected in the Preferred Server drop-down list. Click OK.

11. Configure the Print Options as necessary.

    a.   Open Control Panel.

    b.   If you're using Windows 2000, double-click CSNW.

        If you're using Windows XP, click the Other Control Panel Options link and then click CSNW.

    c.   Below Print Options, uncheck Print Banner if you do not want to include a banner page in each print job.

    d.   Uncheck Notify When Printed to prevent Windows from sending notifications when the print jobs are complete.

    e.   Check Add Form Feed if you want the Client Service For NetWare to add a form feed at the end of the user's print jobs.

    f.   Click OK to save your changes.

12. Close all open windows.

Procedure Reference: Remove NetWare Client in Windows 2000 and Windows XP

To remove NetWare Client from Windows 2000 and Windows XP:

1. Log on as a user with administrative permissions.

2. Open the properties for the Local Area Connection.

3. Select Client Service For NetWare and click Uninstall.

4. Click Yes to confirm that you want to uninstall Client Service For NetWare.

5. Click Yes to restart the computer.

6. Log back on to the computer.

7. Remove the NWLink IPX/SPX protocol if you no longer need it.

Procedure Reference: Install NetWare Client in Windows NT

To install NetWare Client in Windows NT:

1. Log on as a user with administrative permissions.

2. Open the Network dialog box.

3. If necessary, install the NWLink IPX/SPX Compatible Transport protocol.

4. Select the Services tab.

5. Click Add so that you can install a new network service.

6. In the Network Service list, select Client Service For NetWare.

7. Click OK to install the client.

8. In the Windows NT Setup dialog box, enter the path to the Windows NT installation files. (If necessary, insert the Windows NT CD-ROM into the computer's CD-ROM drive.)

9. Click Continue.

10. Click Close to close the Network dialog box.

11. Click Yes to restart the computer.

12. Log back on to the computer.

13. In the Select NetWare Logon dialog box, configure the NetWare logon location information for the current user account as follows:

   • If you're logging on to a NetWare 3.12 server or earlier version, verify that Preferred Server is selected. From the Preferred Server drop-down list, select the name of your NetWare server. Click OK.

   • If you're logging on to a NetWare 4.0 server or later version, select Default Tree And Context. In the Tree text box, type the name of the NDS tree. In the Context text box, type the context within that tree where the user account exists. Click OK.

   • If you don't currently have a NetWare server available to you, verify that <None> is selected in the Preferred Server drop-down list. Click OK.

14. Configure the Print Options as necessary.

   a. Open Control Panel.

   b. Double-click CSNW.

   c. Below Print Options, uncheck Print Banner if you do not want to include a banner page in each print job.

   d. Uncheck Notify When Printed to prevent Windows from sending notifications when the print jobs are complete.

   e. Check Add Form Feed if you want the Client Service For NetWare to add a form feed at the end of the user's print jobs.

   f. Click OK to save your changes.

Procedure Reference: Remove NetWare Client from Windows NT

To remove NetWare Client from Windows NT:

1. Log on as a user with administrative permissions.

2. Open the Network dialog box.

3. Select the Services tab.

4. In the Network Service list, select Client Service For NetWare.

5. Click Remove.

6. Click Yes to confirm that you want to remove Client Service For NetWare.

7. Remove the NWLink IPX/SPX protocol if you no longer need it.

8. Click Close to close the Network dialog box.

9. Click Yes to restart the computer.

10. Log back on to the computer.

ACTIVITY 3-9

Installing NetWare Client

Scenario:

One of your clients has ordered a custom application from a software programming company. This application runs only on a Novell NetWare server. As part of their contract, the software programming company is going to install and configure a Novell NetWare server on which to run the custom application. Your client has asked you to prepare his users' Windows 2000 computers so that they can access the NetWare server when the software programming company delivers it. The NetWare server has not been delivered yet.

What You Do	How You Do It
1. Install Client Service For NetWare.	a. **Open the properties for the Local Area Connection.**
	b. **Click Install.**
	c. **Verify that Client is selected and click Add.**
	d. **Select Client Service For NetWare and click OK.**

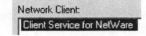

e.   Wait until you see the Select Netware Logon dialog box (the Shutdown dialog box may appear first). **Verify that <None> is selected in the Preferred Server drop-down list.**

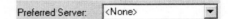

f.   **Click OK** to close the Select NetWare Logon dialog box.

g.   **Click Yes** to restart the computer.

h.   **Log back on to the computer as Admin#.**

i.   **Close all open windows.**

ACTIVITY 3-10

Removing NetWare Client

Scenario:

A client just called to say that she has migrated all of her users' data and applications from the NetWare server to the Windows 2000 server. She configured the Windows 2000 server to use only the TCP/IP protocol. She plans to remove the NetWare server from the network, and she would like you to make sure that the users' Windows 2000 computers have only the network components installed that are necessary for accessing the Windows 2000 server.

What You Do	How You Do It
1. **Remove NetWare Client and NWLink IPX/SPX protocol.**	a. **Display the properties for the Local Area Connection.**
	b. **Select Client Service For NetWare and click Uninstall.**
	c. **Click Yes** to confirm that you want to uninstall Client Service For NetWare.
	d. **Click Yes to restart the computer.**
	e. When prompted, **log on as Admin#.**
	f. **Remove the NWLink IPX/SPX protocol.**

TOPIC G

Configure a Network Connection in Windows 9x

Up to this point in the lesson, you've learned the steps for configuring the various network components for connecting Windows NT-, Windows 2000-, and Windows XP-based computers to a network. But what if you're called in to configure a network connection on a Windows 9x-based computer? To make sure you're prepared for such a call, in this topic, you'll learn the steps for configuring a network connection on a Windows 9x-based computer.

Not all companies have the latest and greatest computers for their users. In fact, it's quite common to encounter companies with older computers—and thus older operating systems such as Windows 98. As an A+ technician, you'll need to have the skills necessary for configuring network connections on such computers so that the computers' users can access the network resources they need to perform their jobs.

Primary Network Logon Types

Windows 98 supports four *primary network logon types*: Client For Microsoft Networks, Client For NetWare Networks, Microsoft Family Logon, and Windows Logon. These logon types are described in Table 3-7.

Table 3-7: *Windows 98 Network Logon Types*

Logon Type	Select as Primary Logon Type If You Want to Configure
Client For Microsoft Networks	The computer to log on to a Windows NT or Windows 2000 domain.
Client For NetWare Networks	The computer to log on to a NetWare server.
Microsoft Family Logon	The computer to list all user profiles on the computer. Use this option if you want users to be able to select their account names from a list and you have enabled user profiles.
Windows Logon	The computer to prompt for a user name and password, but not display a list of users on the computer.

 If you do not configure Client For Microsoft Networks with the name of a domain, there is no difference between using Client For Microsoft Networks and Windows Logon as the primary network logon type.

How to Configure a Network Connection in Windows 9x

Procedure Reference: Configure a Network Connection in Windows 9x

To configure a network connection in Windows 9x:

1. If necessary, update the network card driver.
   a. From the Start menu, choose Settings→Control Panel.
   b. Double-click System.

c.   Select the Device Manager tab.

d.   In the list of devices, expand Network Adapters.

e.   Select the network card driver and click Properties.

f.   Select the Driver tab.

g.   Click Update Driver.

h.   In the Update Device Driver Wizard, click Next.

i.   Verify that Search For A Better Driver Than The One Your Device Is Using Now is selected and click Next.

j.   Select the locations you want the wizard to search for a new driver. You can install the updated driver from any of the following locations:

   • Floppy disk

   • CD-ROM

   • The Microsoft Windows Update Web site

   • Local or shared network folder

k.   Click Next to search for an updated driver.

l.   If the wizard found an updated driver, click Next.

m.   Click Continue.

n.   Click Finish to close the Update Device Driver Wizard.

o.   Click Close to close the Properties dialog box for the network card.

p.   Click Close to close System Properties.

q.   Close Control Panel.

2.   Configure the TCP/IP protocol.

a.   From the Start menu, choose Settings→Control Panel.

b.   Double-click Network.

c.   In the list of network components, select the TCP/IP→*network card type* component, where "network card type" is the name of the computer's network card.

d.   Click Properties.

e.   On the IP Address tab, configure the IP addressing information.

   • If you're configuring TCP/IP manually, select Specify An IP Address. Type the computer's IP address in the IP Address text box and the subnet mask in the Subnet Mask text box.

   • If you're configuring TCP/IP dynamically, select Obtain An IP Address Automatically.

f.   If you're configuring TCP/IP manually and the computer is on a network with a default gateway, configure the default gateway.

   1.   Select the Gateway tab.

   2.   In the New Gateway text box, type the IP address of the default gateway.

   3.   Click Add.

g.   If you're configuring TCP/IP manually and the computer is on a network with DNS servers, enable and configure DNS.

   1.   Select Enable DNS.

2. In the Host text box, type the computer name.

3. In the DNS Server Search Order text box, type the DNS server address and click Add.

4. If another DNS server is available, type the IP address of the server in the DNS Server Search Order text box and click Add.

(If you're configuring TCP/IP dynamically, you don't have to change anything on the DNS Configuration page. The DHCP server will automatically assign the IP addresses of the DNS servers to the computer.)

h. If you're configuring TCP/IP manually and the computer is on a network with WINS servers, use the WINS Configuration tab to configure the WINS server information.

1. Select Enable WINS Resolution.

2. In the WINS Server Search Order text box, type the WINS server address and click Add.

3. If another WINS server is available, type the IP address of the server in the WINS Server Search Order text box and click Add.

(If you're configuring TCP/IP dynamically, you don't have to change anything on the WINS Configuration page. The DHCP server will automatically assign the IP addresses of the WINS servers to the computer.)

i. Click OK to save your TCP/IP configuration changes.

j. Click OK to close the Network dialog box.

k. When prompted, click Yes to restart the computer.

l. Log back on to the computer.

m. Close Control Panel.

3. If necessary, install the NetBEUI protocol.

a. Open the Network dialog box (from the Start menu, choose Settings→ Control Panel. Double-click Network).

b. Click Add.

c. In the Select Network Component Type dialog box, select Protocol and click Add.

d. In the Manufacturers list, select Microsoft.

e. In the Network Protocols list, select NetBEUI.

f. Click OK to install the protocol.

g. Click OK to close the Network dialog box.

h. In the Insert Disk message box, click OK.

i. In the Copying Files dialog box, enter the path to the Windows 98 installation files (if necessary, insert the Windows 98 CD-ROM into the computer's CD-ROM drive).

j. When prompted, click Yes to restart the computer.

k. Log back on to the computer.

l. Close Control Panel.

4. If necessary, install the IPX/SPX-compatible Protocol.

a. Open the Network dialog box (from the Start menu, choose Settings→ Control Panel. Double-click Network).

b. Click Add.

c. In the Select Network Component Type dialog box, select Protocol and click Add.

d. In the Manufacturers list, select Microsoft.

e. In the Network Protocols list, select IPX/SPX-compatible Protocol.

f. Click OK to install the protocol.

g. Click OK to close the Network dialog box.

h. On the Insert Disk message box, click OK.

i. In the Copying Files dialog box, enter the path to the Windows 98 installation files and click OK (if necessary, insert the Windows 98 CD-ROM into the computer's CD-ROM drive).

j. When prompted, click Yes to restart the computer.

k. Log back on to the computer.

l. Close Control Panel.

5. If necessary, install Client For NetWare Networks.

> If you install Client For NetWare Networks and you do not have the IPX/SPX-Compatible Protocol installed, Windows 9x automatically installs it for you.

a. Open the Network dialog box.

b. In the Manufacturers list, select Microsoft.

c. In the Network Clients list, select Client For NetWare Networks.

d. Click OK to install the client.

e. Click OK to close the Network dialog box.

f. On the Insert Disk message box, click OK.

g. In the Copying Files dialog box, enter the path to the Windows 98 installation files and click OK. (If necessary, insert the Windows 98 CD-ROM into the computer's CD-ROM drive.)

h. When prompted, click Yes to restart the computer.

i. Log back on to the computer.

6. If necessary, configure the Primary Network Logon.

a. Open the Network dialog box.

b. From the Primary Network Logon drop-down list, select the logon type appropriate for the computer.

- Use Client For Microsoft Networks if you want the computer to log on to a Windows NT or Windows 2000 domain.

- Use Client For NetWare Networks if you want the computer to log on to a NetWare server.

- Use Microsoft Family Logon if you want to provide users with a list of available user accounts from which to choose.

- Use Windows Logon if you want to have Windows 98 prompt the user for a user name and password.

     c.   Click OK to save your changes.

     d.   When prompted, click Yes to restart the computer.

     e.   Log back on to the computer.

7.   Test the network connection by using a utility such as the IP Configuration utility (Winipcfg) or browsing the Network Neighborhood.

Procedure Reference: Test TCP/IP Connectivity with the IP Configuration Utility (Winipcfg)

To test TCP/IP connectivity with the IP Configuration Utility:

1.   From the Start menu, choose Run.

2.   In the Open text box, type winipcfg.

3.   Click OK to run Winipcfg.

4.   Click More Info to display detailed IP addressing information.

5.   If necessary, from the drop-down list, select the computer's network card.

6.   Review the IP addressing information.

7.   If the computer's IP address is assigned dynamically and you're experiencing problems, you can click the Release and Renew buttons to force it to renew its IP address lease.

8.   Click OK to close the IP Configuration dialog box.

ACTIVITY 3-11

Configuring a Network Connection in Windows 9x

Setup:

The Windows 98 installation files are in C:\Win98.

Scenario:

Your client, a non-profit organization, has just received a donation of a Windows 98 computer. They have asked you to make sure that the computer works properly and to configure it to work on their network. The network consists of Windows 2000 and NetWare 3.12 servers. All users obtain their IP addresses from a DHCP server. In addition, the network has a shared CD-ROM tower that supports only the NetBEUI protocol. Although the client does not yet want the Windows 98 computer to log on to the Windows 2000 domain, they plan to later configure the computer to do so.

What You Do	How You Do It
1. **Update the network card driver.**	a. **Reboot the computer.** From the boot menu, **select Microsoft Windows** to load the Windows 98 operating system.
	b. **Log on as Admin#.**
	c. From the Start menu, **choose Settings→ Control Panel.**
	d. **Double-click System.**
	e. **Select the Device Manager tab.**
	f. In the list of devices, **expand Network Adapters.**

```
⊟ ▦ Network adapters
    ▦ Dial-Up Adapter
    ▦ Realtek RTL8139/810X Family PCI Fast Ethernet NIC
```

	g. **Select the network card driver and click Properties.**
	h. **Select the Driver tab.**
	i. **Click Update Driver.**

	j. In the Update Device Driver Wizard, **click Next.**
	k. **Verify that Search For A Better Driver Than The One Your Device Is Using Now is selected and click Next.**

l. **Check Microsoft Windows Update.**

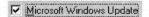

m. **Click Next.**

n. **If the Wizard found an updated driver, click Next and then click Continue, otherwise click Next.**

o. **Click Finish** to close the Update Device Driver Wizard.

p. **Click Close** to close the Properties dialog box for the network card.

q. **Click Close** to close System Properties.

r. **Close Control Panel.**

---

2. **Verify that TCP/IP is configured to obtain an IP address automatically.**

a. **Open Control Panel.**

b. **Double-click Network.**

c. In the network components list, **select TCP/IP→network card name.**

d. **Click Properties.**

e. **Verify that Obtain An IP Address Automatically is selected.**

f. **Select the Gateway tab.**

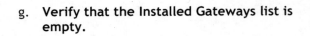
g. Verify that the Installed Gateways list is empty.

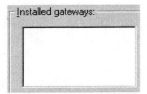

h. Select the DNS Configuration tab.

i. Verify that Disable DNS is selected.

j. Select the WINS Configuration tab.

k. Verify that neither Disable WINS Configuration nor Enable WINS Configuration is selected.

l. **Click OK** to save your changes.

---

3. **Install the NetBEUI protocol.**

a. In the Network dialog box, **click Add.**

b. **Select Protocol and click Add.**

c. In the Manufacturers list, **select Microsoft.**

d. In the Network Protocols list, **select NetBEUI.**

e. **Click OK** to install the protocol.

---

4. **Install the IPX/SPX-compatible Protocol.**

a. In the Network dialog box, **click Add.**

b. **Select Protocol and click Add.**

c. In the Manufacturers list, **select Microsoft.**

d. In the Network Protocols list, **select IPX/SPX-compatible Protocol.**

e. **Click OK** to install the protocol.

f. **Click OK** to close the Network dialog box.

g. When prompted, **click Yes** to restart the computer.

h. From the boot menu, **choose Microsoft Windows.**

i. **Log back on as Admin#.**

j. **Close Control Panel.**

---

5. **Set the primary network logon.**

a. In the Network dialog box, from the Primary Network Logon drop-down list, **select Client For Microsoft Networks.**

b. **Click OK** to save your changes.

c. In the Insert Disk message box, **click OK.**

d. In the Copying Files dialog box, **enter C:\Win98 and click OK.**

Copy files from:

C:\Win98

e. **Click Yes** to restart the computer.

f. From the boot menu, **choose Microsoft Windows.**

g. **Log back on as Admin#.**

---

6. **Test TCP/IP connectivity.**

a. From the Start menu, **choose Run.**

b. In the Open text box, **type winipcfg**

Open: winipcfg

c. **Click OK.**

d. In the IP Configuration dialog box, **click More Info** to display all the IP addressing information.

e. If necessary, from the drop-down list, **select the computer's network card.**

Ethernet Adapter Information

Realtek 8139-series PCI NIC

f. **Review the IP addressing information** to verify that the computer received the correct IP address, subnet mask, and, optionally, default gateway and WINS server addresses from the DHCP server.

g. **Click OK** to close the IP Configuration dialog box.

Lesson 3 Follow-up

In this lesson, you learned how to install the components necessary for connecting Windows 2000, Windows 9x, Windows NT, and Windows XP computers to a network. For example, you learned how to make sure a computer is using the latest driver for its network card and how to install any of the supported network protocols. In addition, you learned how to troubleshoot problems with TCP/IP. By mastering all of these skills, you'll be able to quickly and easily set up users' connections to the network.

1. **In your work environment, what network protocols will you be using?**

2. **If you have worked with TCP/IP in a network environment, what types of problems have you encountered? How did you troubleshoot these problems?**

NOTES

LESSON 4

Implementing Local Security in Windows 2000/NT/XP

Lesson Time
2 hour(s)

Lesson Objectives:

In this lesson, you will implement local security in Windows 2000/NT/XP.

You will:

- Create or delete local user accounts.
- Modify user account properties.
- Set the workgroup or domain membership.
- Configure file and folder security.
- Encrypt files and folders.

LESSON 4

Introduction

As an A+ technician, one of the big concerns you'll be expected to address for your users and clients is how to secure their computers. Security is important for both networked and stand-alone computers. In this lesson, you'll learn the techniques and strategies you can use to secure a Windows 2000-, Windows NT-, or Windows XP-based computer.

If you don't properly secure a computer and its data, you leave it vulnerable to accidental or intentional loss and misuse. It is essential, as an A+ technician, that you implement security to prevent these threats from resulting in costly intrusions, loss of critical data, and lost productivity.

The following CompTIA A+ Operating System Technologies (2003) Examination objectives are covered in this lesson:

- Topic A:
  - — 1.5 System Management Tools: Computer Manager.
- Topic D:
  - — 1.1 Major Operating System components: File System.
  - — 1.4 File Systems: FAT16, FAT32, NTFS4, NTFS5.x.
  - — 1.4 Files: File Permissions.
  - — 2.1 Determine OS installation options: File system type.
- Topic E:
  - — 1.4 Files: File Encryption.

TOPIC A

Create or Delete Local User Accounts

One of the first things a user must do when she sits down at a Windows 2000-, Windows XP-, or Windows NT-based computer is to log on. In these operating systems, any activity the user performs must be in the context of a logged-on user account. Before your users can log on, they must have user accounts. On the other hand, you also need to know how to delete a local user account so that you can protect the computer from unauthorized access. In this topic, you'll learn how to create and delete local user accounts.

Logging on to a computer is like giving a user a key to unlock your company's front door. Without the key, the user won't be able to get to her office to begin working. And without being able to log on to her computer, the user won't be able to do the tasks she needs to perform her job. As an A+ technician, setting up and configuring local user logon accounts will be one of the tasks you'll be expected to perform. Setting up these logon accounts properly for any situation will help your users gain access to their computers so that they can get their work done. Knowing how to delete user accounts enables you to protect the computer from situations such as preventing a user who leaves the company (especially if the user is fired) from logging on to a computer. Such disgruntled users may attempt to damage the computer's data—which can cost your company a lot of time and money due to the loss of productivity.

Local Security

Windows 2000, Windows XP, and Windows NT are secure operating systems, which means that you cannot access a computer running one of these operating systems without logging on as a valid user. A valid user is one that has an account in the Windows 2000, Windows XP, or Windows NT user database on the specific computer to which you're attempting to log on. Such a user account is called "local," because it must be created in the user database on the computer where you log on.

The Built-in User and Group Accounts

Windows 2000 Professional, Windows NT Workstation, and Windows XP Professional include two user and six group accounts that are created automatically when you install the operating system. The *built-in user accounts* are Administrator and Guest. These accounts are described in Table 4-1. Windows XP comes with two additional built-in user accounts; we describe them in Table 4-2. The group accounts are Administrators, Backup Operators, Guests, Power Users, Replicator, and Users. The *built-in groups*, along with their default members, are described in Table 4-3. As you saw with user accounts, Windows XP includes three additional built-in groups. We describe these groups in Table 4-4.

Table 4-1: *Built-in User Accounts*

User Account	Provides
Administrator	Complete administrative access to the computer.
Guest	Limited computer access to persons without a logon user account. By default, the Guest account is disabled when you install the operating system. You enable this account only if you want to permit users to log on as Guest.

Table 4-2: *Windows XP-only Built-in User Accounts*

User Account	Provides
HelpAssistant	Access to the computer during a Remote Assistance session.
Support	Access to Microsoft's Web-based Help and Support services.

Table 4-3: *Built-in Group Accounts*

Group Account	Enables Members To	Default Members
Administrators	Perform all administrative tasks on the computer.	Administrator. In Windows XP, this group also includes an account you create during installation.
Backup Operators	Back up and restore files to which the members do not otherwise have permissions.	None
Guests	Perform any tasks for which the group has permissions.	Guest

Group Account	Enables Members To	Default Members
Power Users	Run pre-Windows 2000 applications, modify some system-wide settings (such as the time), install some programs, and manage some local accounts.	None
Replicator	Participate in domain-based file replication.	None
Users	Run applications and perform other day-to-day computer tasks. Perform any task for which the group has been granted permissions.	All user accounts

Table 4-4: *Windows XP-only Built-in Group Accounts*

Group Account	Enables Members To	Default Members
Network Configuration Operators	Manage network configuration.	None
Remote Desktop Users	Log on to the computer remotely.	None
HelpServicesGroup	Connect to Microsoft's Web-based Help and Support service.	Support user account

How to Create or Delete Local User Accounts

Procedure Reference: Create a Local User Account in Windows 2000

To create a local user account in Windows 2000:

1. Log on as a local computer administrator.
2. From the Start menu, choose Settings→Control Panel.
3. Double-click Administrative Tools.
4. Double-click Computer Management.
5. Below System Tools, expand Local Users And Groups.
6. Select the Users folder.
7. Right-click Users and choose New User.
8. In the User Name text box, type the new user's account name.
9. In the Full Name text box, type the user's full name.
10. In the Password text box, type the user's password.
11. In the Confirm Password text box, re-type the user's password.
12. Select the desired account options. (See Table 4-5.)
13. Click Create to create the new user account.
14. Click Close to close the New User dialog box.

15. Close Computer Management.

16. Close Control Panel.

17. Test the account by logging on as the user.

Table 4-5: *Local Account Options*

Check This Box	Use To
User Must Change Password At Next Logon	Force the user to change the password you assign when you create the account.
User Cannot Change Password	Prevent the user from changing the password you assign to the account.
Password Never Expires	Prevent the user's password from expiring, regardless of any password-expiration policies you establish.
Account Is Disabled	Prevent someone from logging on as this user.

Procedure Reference: Delete a Local User Account in Windows 2000

To delete a local user account in Windows 2000:

1. Log on as a local computer administrator.

2. Open Computer Management. (In Control Panel, double-click Administrative Tools and then double-click Computer Management. Alternatively, you can right-click the My Computer icon and choose Manage.)

3. Below System Tools, expand Local Users And Groups.

4. In the console tree, select Users.

5. In the details pane, right-click the user you want to delete and choose Delete.

6. Click Yes to confirm that you want to delete this user account.

7. Close Computer Management (and Control Panel if necessary).

Procedure Reference: Create a Local User Account in Windows XP

To create a local user account in Windows XP:

1. Log on as a local computer administrator.

2. In Control Panel, select the Performance And Maintenance category.

3. Click Administrative Tools.

4. Double-click Computer Management.

5. Below System Tools, expand Local Users And Groups.

6. Select the Users folder.

7. Right-click the Users folder and choose New User.

8. In the User Name text box, type the new user's account name.

9. In the Full Name text box, type the user's full name.

10. In the Password text box, type the user's password.

11. In the Confirm Password text box, re-type the user's password.

12. Select the desired account options. (See Table Table 4-5.)

13. Click Create to create the new user account.

14. Click Close.

15. Close Computer Management and Control Panel.

16. Test the account by logging on as the user.

Procedure Reference: Delete a Local User Account in Windows XP

To delete a local user account in Windows XP:

1. Log on as a local computer administrator.

2. In Control Panel, select the Performance And Maintenance category.

3. Click Administrative Tools.

4. Double-click Computer Management.

5. Below System Tools, expand Local Users And Groups.

6. Select the Users folder.

7. In the details pane, right-click the user you want to delete and choose Delete.

8. Click Yes to confirm that you want to delete this user.

9. Close Computer Management and Control Panel.

Procedure Reference: Create a Local User Account in Windows NT

To create a local user account in Windows NT:

1. Log on as a local computer administrator.

2. From the Start menu, choose Programs→Administrative Tools→User Manager.

3. Choose User→New User.

4. In the Username text box, type the new user's account name.

5. In the Full Name text box, type the user's full name.

6. In the Password text box, type the user's password.

7. In the Confirm Password text box, re-type the user's password.

8. Select the desired account options. (See Table 4-5.)

9. Click OK to create the new user account.

10. Close User Manager.

11. Test the account by logging on as the user.

Procedure Reference: Delete a Local User Account in Windows NT

To delete a local user account in Windows NT:

1. Log on as a local computer administrator.

2. From the Start menu, choose Programs→Administrative Tools→User Manager.

3. Select the user you want to delete.

4. Choose User→Delete.

5. Click OK to acknowledge the warning message about deleting user accounts.

6. Click Yes to delete the account.

7. Close User Manager.

Procedure Reference: Delete a Local User Profile in Windows 2000

To delete a local user profile in Windows 2000:

1. Log on as a local computer administrator.

2. Open Control Panel and double-click System. (Alternatively, you can right-click the My Computer icon and choose Properties.)

3. Select the User Profiles tab.

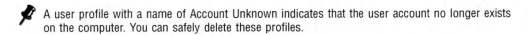 A user profile with a name of Account Unknown indicates that the user account no longer exists on the computer. You can safely delete these profiles.

4. Select a profile with the name of Account Unknown.

5. Click Delete.

6. Click Yes to confirm that you want to delete the profile.

7. Repeat these steps to delete any other profiles with the name of Account Unknown.

8. Click OK to close System Properties.

9. Close Control Panel.

10. In Windows Explorer, verify that you no longer see folders within \Documents and Settings for users whose accounts you have deleted.

Procedure Reference: Delete a Local User Profile in Windows XP

To delete a local user profile in Windows XP:

1. Log on as a local computer administrator.

2. On the Start menu, right-click My Computer and choose Properties.

3. Select the Advanced tab.

4. Below User Profiles, click Settings.

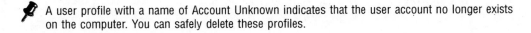 A user profile with a name of Account Unknown indicates that the user account no longer exists on the computer. You can safely delete these profiles.

5. Select a profile with the name of Account Unknown.

6. Click Delete.

7. Click Yes to confirm that you want to delete the profile.

8. Repeat these steps to delete any other profiles with the name of Account Unknown.

9. Click OK to close the User Profiles dialog box.

10. Click OK to close System Properties.

11. In Windows Explorer, verify that you no longer see folders within \Documents and Settings for users whose accounts you have deleted.

Procedure Reference: Delete a Local User Profile in Windows NT

To delete a local user profile in Windows NT:

1. Log on as a local computer administrator.

2. Open Control Panel and double-click System. (You can also right-click the My Computer icon and choose Properties.)

3. Select the User Profiles tab.

> A user profile with a name of Account Unknown indicates that the user account no longer exists on the computer. You can safely delete these profiles.

4. Select a profile with the name of Account Unknown.

5. Click Delete.

6. Click Yes to confirm that you want to delete the profile.

7. Repeat these steps to delete any other profiles with the name of Account Unknown.

8. Click OK to close System Properties.

9. In Windows Explorer, verify that you no longer see folders within the \Winnt\ Profiles folder for users whose accounts you have deleted.

ACTIVITY 4-1

Creating Local Accounts

Setup:

There are two administrative user accounts on the computer: the default Administrator account and an account named Admin# which was created when the computer was installed.

Scenario:

You have been called in to configure a client's new Windows 2000 computer. After interviewing the client, you've determined that she needs accounts on the computer for the following users:

*   Susan Williams (the client)
*   Jeff Bernard
*   Sally Thomas

After talking to the network administrator, you discover that he uses the following naming convention for naming all user accounts: the user's first name plus the first initial of their last names. In addition, the network administrator prefers that you assign each user a password of password, and that each user not be able to change his or her password.

What You Do	How You Do It
1. Create the local accounts.	a. **Restart Windows 2000 Professional.**
	b. **Log on as Admin#.**
	c. **Open Control Panel.**
	d. **Double-click Administrative Tools.**
	e. **Double-click Computer Management.**
	f. **Expand Local Users And Groups.**

g. **Select the Users folder.**

h. **Right-click Users and choose New User.**

i. In the User Name text box, **type** *SusanW*

j. In the Full Name text box, **type** *Susan Williams*

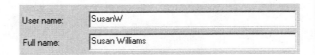

k. In the Password text box, **type** *password*

l. In the Confirm Password text box, **type** *password*

m. **Uncheck User Must Change Password At Next Logon.**

n. **Check User Cannot Change Password.**

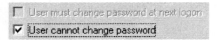

o. **Click Create** to create Susan Williams' account.

p. **Enter the account information for the user Jeff Bernard.**

User name:	JeffB
Full name:	Jeff Bernard
Description:	
Password:	********
Confirm password:	********

☐ User must change password at next logon
☑ User cannot change password

q. **Click Create.**

r. **Enter the account information for the user Sally Thomas.**

s. **Click Create.**

t. **Click Close** to close the New User dialog box.

u. In the details pane, **verify that you see the three new user accounts.**

JeffB	Jeff Bernard
SallyT	Sally Thomas
SusanW	Susan Williams

v. **Close Computer Management and Administrative Tools.**

2. Verify that you can log on with each new user account.

   a. **Press Ctrl+Alt+Delete.**

   b. **Click Log Off.**

   c. **Click Yes** to confirm that you want to log off.

   d. In the User Name text box, **type** *SusanW*

   e. In the Password text box, **type** *password*

   f. **Click OK** to log on as SusanW.

   g. **Repeat these steps to log off as each user and then log on as JeffB and SallyT.**

3. **What would happen if you attempted to log on as JeffB to the class.com domain?**

ACTIVITY 4-2

Deleting a Local Account

Scenario:

The user Sally Thomas no longer works for your client's company. Your client has asked you to make sure that Sally can no longer access her computer and to prevent her user profile from using up disk space.

What You Do	How You Do It
1. Delete the local user account.	a. **Log on as Admin#.**
	b. **Open Computer Management.** (On your desktop, right-click My Computer and choose Manage.)
	c. **Expand Local Users And Groups.**
	d. **Select the Users folder.**

e. **Right-click SallyT and choose Delete.**

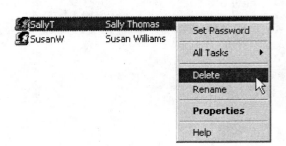

f. **Click Yes** to confirm that you want to delete the account.

g. **Close Computer Management.**

---

2. **Delete any unnecessary user profiles.**

a. If necessary, **log on as Admin#.**

b. **Open the System Properties dialog box.** (Right-click the My Computer icon and choose Properties.)

c. **Select the User Profiles tab.**

d. **Select a user profile with the name of Account Unknown.**

e. **Click Delete.**

f. **Click Yes** to confirm that you want to delete the profile.

g. **Click OK** to close the System Properties dialog box.

h. **Close the Control Panel.**

---

3. Verify that the profile was removed from the hard disk.

   a. Open Windows Explorer.

   b. Expand the drive on which Windows 2000 is installed.

   c. Expand Documents And Settings.

   d. Verify that you don't see any folders for users who no longer have accounts on the server.

   e. Close Windows Explorer.

TOPIC B

Modify User Account Properties

In Topic 4A, you learned how to both create and delete user accounts with the default set of properties. In many cases, these default properties won't fit the needs of your company. In this topic, you'll learn how to modify the properties of local user accounts.

You're bound to run into situations where a user doesn't like his logon name or another user forgets her password after her two-week vacation. You'll also encounter situations such as a user not having the privileges he needs. As an A+ technician, it will be your job to straighten out these problems. The good news is that you can solve these problems by modifying the user accounts.

User Account Properties

After you have created a user account, there are several properties for the user account you can change. Some of the properties you can change include:

* Renaming the account. You might do so if a user leaves your company and a new person takes the user's job. Instead of creating a new account for the new person, you can provide them with access to the computer by renaming the old user's account.

* Changing the user's password. You'll typically be asked to change a user's password when he forgets it.

* Adding the user as a member of a group or removing the user from a group.

How to Modify User Account Properties

Procedure Reference: Rename a User Account in Windows 2000/XP/NT

To rename a user account in Windows 2000, Windows XP, and Windows NT:

1. Log on as a local computer administrator.

2. Open the appropriate user account management tool for the computer's operating system:

   - If you're using Windows 2000 or Windows XP, open Computer Management.
   - If you're using Windows NT, open User Manager.

3. If you're using Windows 2000 or Windows XP, complete the following steps:

   a. Expand Local Users And Groups.

   b. Select the Users folder.

   c. Right-click the user you want to rename and choose Rename.

   d. Type the new name for the user and press Enter.

4. If you're using Windows NT, complete the following steps:

   a. In the list of users, select the user you want to rename.

   b. Choose User→Rename.

   c. In the Change To text box, type the new name for the user.

   d. Click OK.

5. Close the user account management tool.

Procedure Reference: Rename a User's Profile in Windows 2000 or Windows XP

To rename a user's profile in Windows 2000 or Windows XP:

1. Log on as a local computer administrator.

2. Open Windows Explorer.

3. Select the appropriate user profiles folder.

   - If you're using Windows 2000 or Windows XP, select \Documents And Settings.
   - If you're using Windows NT, select \Winnt\Profiles.

4. Right-click the folder you want to rename and choose Rename.

5. Enter a new name for the folder.

6. Close Windows Explorer.

Procedure Reference: Change a User's Password in Windows 2000/XP/NT

To change a user's password in Windows 2000, Windows XP, and Windows NT:

1. Log on as a local computer administrator.

2. Open the appropriate user account management tool for the computer's operating system:

   - If you're using Windows 2000 or Windows XP, open Computer Management.
   - If you're using Windows NT, open User Manager.

   ⚠ In Windows XP, resetting a user's password will prevent them from accessing any encrypted files. You should reset a user's password only as a last resort.

3. If you're using Windows 2000 or Windows XP, complete the following steps:

   a. Expand Local Users And Groups.

    b.   Select the Users folder.

    c.   Right-click the user for whom you want to change the password and choose Set Password.

    d.   If you're using Windows XP, click Proceed.

    e.   In the New Password text box, type the new password for the user.

    f.   In the Confirm Password text box, type the password again.

    g.   Click OK.

4.   If you're using Windows NT, complete the following steps:

    a.   In the list of users, double-click the user whose password you want to reset.

    b.   In the Password text box, type the new password for the user.

    c.   In the Confirm Password text box, type the password again.

    d.   Click OK.

5.   Close the user account management tool.

Procedure Reference: Modify a User's Group Memberships in Windows 2000/XP/NT

To modify a user's group memberships in Windows 2000, Windows XP, and Windows NT:

1.   Log on as a local computer administrator.

2.   Open the appropriate user account management tool for the computer's operating system:

- If you're using Windows 2000 or Windows XP, open Computer Management.
- If you're using Windows NT, open User Manager.

3.   If you're using Windows 2000 and you want to add the user as a member of a group, complete the following steps:

    a.   Expand Local Users And Groups.

    b.   Select the Users folder.

    c.   Double-click the user for whom you want to change group memberships.

    d.   Select the Member Of tab.

    e.   Click Add.

    f.   Select the group or groups to which you want to add the user and click Add.

    g.   Click OK to close the Select Groups dialog box.

    h.   Click OK to close the user's Properties dialog box.

4.   If you're using Windows XP and you want to add the user as a member of a group, complete the following steps:

    a.   Expand Local Users And Groups.

    b.   Select the Users folder.

    c.   Double-click the user for whom you want to change group memberships.

    d.   Select the Member Of tab.

    e.   Click Add.

    f.   If you know the name of the group to which you want to add the user, enter it under Enter The Object Names To Select and click OK.

g.   If you want to search for the group to which you want to add the user:

    1.   Click Advanced.

    2.   Click Find Now to display a list of groups.

    3.   Select the desired group or groups and click OK.

h.   Click OK to close the Select Groups dialog box.

i.   Click OK to close the user's Properties dialog box.

5.   If you're using Windows NT and you want to add the user as a member of a group, complete the following steps:

   a.   Double-click the user.

   b.   Click Groups.

   c.   From the Not Member Of list, select the group to which you want to add the user and click Add.

   d.   Click OK to close the Group Memberships dialog box.

   e.   Click OK to close the user's Properties dialog box.

6.   If you're using Windows 2000 or Windows XP and you want to remove the user from a group, complete the following steps:

   a.   Expand Local Users And Groups.

   b.   Select the Users folder.

   c.   Double-click the user for whom you want to change group memberships.

   d.   Select the Member Of tab.

   e.   Select the group from which you want to remove the user.

   f.   Click Remove.

   g.   Click OK to close the user's Properties dialog box.

7.   If you're using Windows NT and you want to remove the user from a group, complete the following steps:

   a.   Double-click the user.

   b.   Click Groups.

   c.   From the Member Of list, select the group from which you want to remove the user and click Remove.

   d.   Click OK to close the Group Memberships dialog box.

   e.   Click OK to close the user's Properties dialog box.

8.   Close the user account management tool.

Procedure Reference: Modify Other User Account Properties in Windows 2000/ XP/NT

To modify other user account properties in Windows 2000, Windows XP, and Windows NT:

1.   Log on as a local computer administrator.

2.   Open the appropriate user account management tool for the computer's operating system:

   •   If you're using Windows 2000 or Windows XP, open Computer Management.

   •   If you're using Windows NT, open User Manager.

3. If you're using Windows 2000 or Windows XP and you want to modify the user's full name, description, or password options, complete the following steps:

   a. Expand Local Users And Groups.

   b. Select the Users folder.

   c. Double-click the user for whom you want to change properties.

   d. On the General page, enter the new full name, description, or desired password options.

   e. Click OK to close the user's Properties dialog box.

4. If you're using Windows NT and you want to modify the user's full name, description, or password options, complete the following steps:

   a. Double-click the user.

   b. Enter the new full name, description, or desired password options.

   c. Click OK to close the user's Properties dialog box.

5. Close the user account management tool.

ACTIVITY 4-3

Modifying User Account Properties

Setup:

You have created a user named SusanW.

Scenario:

Your client, Susan Williams, calls to tell you that she just got married and would like her account name to reflect her new last name of Hill. In addition, she would like sufficient permissions so that she can perform all administrative tasks on her computer.

What You Do	How You Do It
1. **Change the account's user name and full name.**	a. **Open Computer Management** (on the desktop, right-click the My Computer icon and choose Manage).
	b. **Expand Local Users And Groups.**
	c. **Select the Users folder.**

d. Right-click SusanW and choose Rename.

e. Enter *SusanH* and press Enter.

f. Double-click SusanH to open the Properties dialog box.

g. In the Full Name text box, **change the user's name to Susan Hill.**

h. Click OK to save your changes.

2. Add the user to the Administrators group.

a. In the details pane, **double-click SusanH.**

b. In the SusanH Properties dialog box, **select the Member Of tab.**

c. Click Add.

d. Select the Administrators group and click Add.

e. Click OK to close the Select Groups dialog box.

f. Click OK.

g. Close Computer Management.

3.	Rename Susan Hill's profile folder to reflect her new user account name.	a.	Open Windows Explorer.
		b.	Select D:\Documents And Settings.
		c.	In the right pane, **right-click the SusanW folder and choose Rename.**
		d.	**Enter** *SusanH*
		e.	Close Windows Explorer.

4.	Test Susan Hill's administrative privileges.	a.	Log on as SusanH.
		b.	Open Computer Management.
		c.	Expand Local Users And Groups.
		d.	Right-click Users and choose New User.
		e.	**Create a new user named TestUser with a password of password.** By creating a new user, you verify that Susan Hill has administrative privileges on the computer.
		f.	Close the New User dialog box.
		g.	Close all open windows.

TOPIC C

Set Workgroup or Domain Membership

Another security task you might be called to do is to configure the local computer's workgroup or domain membership. As an A+ technician, you'll need the skills for setting and changing a computer's workgroup or domain membership. For example, you might be assigned the task of configuring the workstations on a network to join a new domain that the network administrator has just installed. In this topic, you'll identify the differences between a workgroup and a domain and learn how to configure a computer as a member of each.

Configuring a computer as a member of a domain or a workgroup enables you to make sure that the shared resources on the computer are available to the appropriate users. For example, by configuring the computer's domain or workgroup membership, you make it possible for users to connect to that computer by browsing the appropriate domain or workgroup in either My Network Places (in Windows 2000) or the Network Neighborhood (in Windows NT).

Workgroup

Definition:

A *workgroup* is a Microsoft network model that groups computers together for organizational purposes. The computers that make up a workgroup appear together when you browse the Network Neighborhood in Windows NT or My Network Places in Windows 2000 and Windows XP. In addition, each Windows 2000, Windows XP, and Windows NT computer in the workgroup maintains its own user account database. This means that if a user wants to log on at any computer within the workgroup, you must create the user's account on each computer in the workgroup.

Example:

In Figure 4-1, you see an example of a workgroup. Notice that each computer has its own user account database.

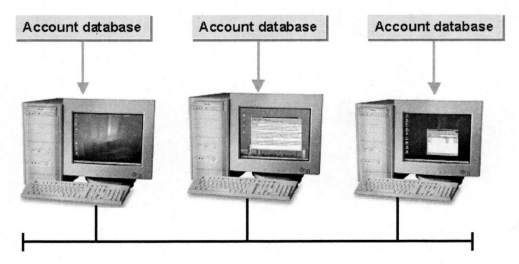

Figure 4-1: *Computers in a workgroup.*

Domain

Definition:

A *domain* is a Microsoft network model that groups computers together for security and to centralize administration. Computers that are members of a domain have access to a shared central user account database, which means that a user can use a single user account to log on at any computer within the domain. Administration is centralized because you need to create the user accounts only in the domain, not on each computer. The shared central user account database is stored on specialized servers called *domain controllers*. Like a workgroup, computers that are members of a domain appear together when you browse the Network Neighborhood in Windows NT or My Network Places in Windows 2000 and Windows XP.

Example:

In Figure 4-2, you see an example of a domain. Notice that each computer has access to the shared domain user account database.

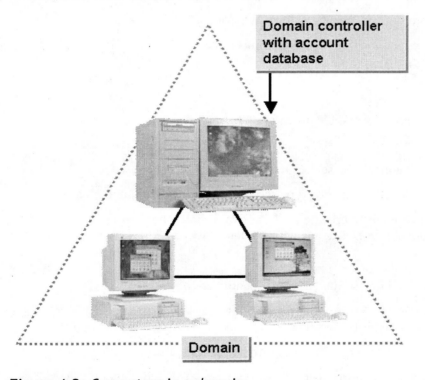

Figure 4-2: *Computers in a domain.*

How to Set the Workgroup or Domain Membership

Procedure Reference: Configure Workgroup Membership in Windows 2000

To configure workgroup membership in Windows 2000:

1. Log on as a local computer administrator.

2. Open Control Panel.

3. Double-click System.

4. Select the Network Identification tab.

5. Click Properties.

6. In the Workgroup Name text box, type the name of the workgroup and click OK. The default workgroup name is WORKGROUP.

7. Click OK to close the Network Identification message.

8. Click OK to close the message stating that you must reboot the computer before your change will take effect.

9. Click OK to close the System Properties dialog box.

10. Click Yes to confirm that you want to reboot the computer.

11. Log back on to the computer.

12. Close Control Panel.

Procedure Reference: Configure Domain Membership in Windows 2000

To configure domain membership in Windows 2000:

1. Log on as a local computer administrator.

2. Open Control Panel.

3. Double-click System.

4. Select the Network Identification tab.

5. Click Properties.

6. Below Member Of, select Domain.

7. In the Domain text box, type the name of the domain and click OK.

8. In the Domain Username And Password dialog box, enter the name and password of a domain user account with the authority to add a computer to the domain.

9. Click OK.

10. Click OK to close the Network Identification message.

11. Click OK to close the message stating that you must reboot the computer before your change will take effect.

12. Click OK to close the System Properties dialog box.

13. Click Yes to confirm that you want to reboot the computer.

14. Verify that you can log on to the domain.

    a. When the Welcome To Windows dialog box is displayed, press Ctrl+Alt+Delete.

    b. In the User Name text box, type the domain user account name.

    c. In the Password text box, type the domain user account's password.

    d. From the Log On To drop-down list, select the domain name.

    e. Click OK to log on to the domain.

Procedure Reference: Configure Workgroup Membership in Windows XP

To configure workgroup membership in Windows XP:

1. Log on as a local computer administrator.

2. From the Start menu, right-click My Computer and choose Properties.

3. Select the Computer Name tab.

4. Click Change.

5. In the Workgroup Name text box, type the name of the workgroup and click OK. The default workgroup name is WORKGROUP.

6. Click OK to close the Computer Name Changes message.

7. Click OK to close the message stating that you must reboot the computer before your change will take effect.

8. Click OK to close the System Properties dialog box.

9. Click Yes to confirm that you want to reboot the computer.

10. Log back on to the computer.

Procedure Reference: Configure Domain Membership in Windows XP

To configure domain membership in Windows XP:

1. Log on as a local computer administrator.

2. From the Start menu, right-click My Computer and choose Properties.

3. Select the Computer Name tab.

4. Click Change.

5. Below Member Of, select Domain.

6. In the Domain text box, type the name of the domain and click OK.

7. In the Domain Username And Password dialog box, enter the name and password of a domain user account with the authority to add a computer to the domain.

8. Click OK.

9. Click OK to close the Computer Name Changes message.

10. Click OK to close the message stating that you must reboot the computer before your change will take effect.

11. Click OK to close the System Properties dialog box.

12. Click Yes to confirm that you want to reboot the computer.

13. Verify that you can log on to the domain.

    a. When the Welcome To Windows dialog box is displayed, press Ctrl+Alt+Delete.

    b. In the User Name text box, type the domain user account name.

    c. In the Password text box, type the domain user account's password.

    d. Click Options.

    e. From the Log On To drop-down list, select the domain name.

    f. Click OK to log on to the domain.

Procedure Reference: Configure Workgroup Membership in Windows NT

To configure workgroup membership in Windows NT:

1.   Log on as a local computer administrator.

2.   Open Control Panel.

3.   Double-click Network.

4.   Click Change.

5.   In the Workgroup text box, type the name of the workgroup and click OK. The default workgroup name is WORKGROUP.

6.   Click OK to close the Network Configuration message box.

7.   Click Close to close the Network dialog box.

8.   Click Yes to confirm that you want to reboot the computer.

9.   Log back on to the computer.

10. Close Control Panel.

Procedure Reference: Configure Domain Membership in Windows NT

To configure domain membership in Windows NT:

1.   Log on as a local computer administrator.

2.   Open Control Panel.

3.   Double-click Network.

4.   Click Change.

5.   Below Member Of, select Domain.

6.   In the Domain text box, type the name of the domain. If you're joining a Windows NT computer to a Windows 2000 Active Directory domain, type the NetBIOS name for the domain, not the DNS name. For example, if the name of the Active Directory domain is "company.com," type "company" for the domain name.

7.   If a computer account hasn't already been created for this computer in the domain, check Create A Computer Account In The Domain. In the User Name and Password text boxes, enter the credentials of a user with the authority to create a computer account in the domain.

8.   Click OK.

9.   Click OK to close the Network Configuration message box.

10. Click Close to close the Network dialog box.

11. Click Yes to confirm that you want to reboot the computer.

12. Verify that you can log on to the domain as follows:

   a.   When the Welcome To Windows dialog box is displayed, press Ctrl+Alt+Delete.

   b.   In the User Name text box, type the domain user account name.

   c.   In the Password text box, type the domain user account's password.

   d.   From the Log On To drop-down list, select the domain name.

e.   Click OK to log on to the domain.

ACTIVITY 4-4

Setting Domain Membership

Setup:

You have an Active Directory domain on your network. The domain name is class.com. In the domain, you have a domain user account named Admin#. This account is a member of the Domain Admins group, which gives you the necessary authority to add computers to the domain. The password for the Admin# domain user account is also password.

Scenario:

You've been called in on a contract basis to assist a large company with configuring its Windows 2000 client computers to access a Windows 2000 Active Directory domain. (The company is in the midst of migrating its servers from Novell NetWare 4.12 to Windows 2000.) The Windows 2000 computers are all currently members of the default workgroup (WORKGROUP).

What You Do	How You Do It
1. Join the Class.com domain.	a. **Log on as Admin#.**
	b. **Open Control Panel.**
	c. **Double-click System.**
	d. **Select the Network Identification tab.**
	e. **Click Properties.**
	f. Below Member Of, **select Domain.**
	g. In the Domain text box, **type** *class.com* **and click OK.**

	h. In the Name text box, **type** *Admin#*
	i. In the Password text box, **type** *password*
	j. **Click OK** to log on to the class.com domain.
	k. **Click OK** to close the Network Identification message.

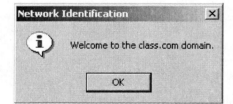

l. **Click OK** to close the second Network Identification message.

m. **Click OK** to close the System Properties dialog box.

n. **Close Control Panel.**

o. **Click Yes** to confirm that you want to reboot the computer.

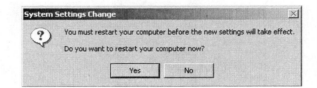

p. From the boot menu, **select Windows 2000 Professional.**

2. **Verify that you can log on to the domain.**

   a. When the Welcome To Windows dialog box is displayed, **press Ctrl+Alt+Delete.**

   b. In the User Name text box, **type** *Admin#*

   c. In the Password text box, **type** *password*

   d. **Click the Options >> button.**

   e. From the Log On To drop-down list, **select Class.**

   f. **Click OK** to log on to the domain.

   g. In the Getting Started With Windows 2000 wizard, **uncheck Show This Screen At Startup.**

   h. **Close the Getting Started With Windows 2000 wizard.**

 When you log on for the first time, Windows 2000 automatically displays a Click On The Start Button message bubble. You can close this message bubble by clicking anywhere in the bubble.

Policies

When a computer is a member of a domain, it's possible for the administrator of the domain to create policies to restrict the activities that a user can perform on the computer. For example, an administrator can establish a policy that prevents users from changing the color scheme or wallpaper on the computer. In a Windows 2000 or Windows Server 2003 Active Directory domain, this type of policy is called a *group policy object* and is administered as part of the Active Directory. In a Windows NT domain, the equivalent policy is called a *system policy*; the domain administrator implements this system policy by creating a file with the necessary restrictions. As an A+ technician, it's possible that you might encounter a scenario where you are restricted from performing a specific configuration task due to a policy assigned by the domain administrator.

TOPIC D

Configure File and Folder Security

Up to this point in the lesson, you've worked with how to secure a computer through logon accounts. But once the user logs on to the computer, you might not want the user to have access to all files and folders on the computer. In this topic, you'll learn how to secure files and folders.

On almost all of the computers you'll work with, you'll encounter multiple user accounts. You might just see the user's account plus the Administrator; on the other hand, you might encounter multiple users sharing the same computer. In any situation where you have multiple users of the same computers, you can encounter problems with users accessing and modifying each other's files. You need to be sure that each of the users of the computer can access only their own files. You might also need to configure a folder to which all the users of the computer have access so that they can share files with each other. By assigning the file and folder permissions properly, you make sure that the users of the computer can access the files and folders they need without accessing the files and folders they shouldn't.

File Systems

Operating systems use a file system to determine how to store files on a computer's hard disk. There are six different file systems: File Allocation Table (FAT), File Allocation Table 32 (FAT32), NT File System version 4 (NTFS4), NT File System version 5 (NTFS5), High Performance File System (HPFS), and CD File System (CDFS). Each Windows operating system supports some of the available file systems. In Table 4-6, you find a description of each file system along with the versions of Windows that support it.

 You'll sometimes hear the FAT file system referred to as FAT16.

Table 4-6: *File Systems*

File System	Description	Supported By
FAT	The FAT file system is an older file system that's best suited for use with drives that are less than 4 GB in size. Advantages to the FAT file system include: it uses very little overhead on a disk and it's compatible with many different operating systems. If you want to configure a dual-boot computer between Windows 9x and Windows 2000/NT/XP, you must configure the C drive to use the FAT file system.	Windows 9x, Windows NT, Windows 2000, Windows XP
FAT32	The FAT32 file system is an enhanced version of the FAT file system. It scales better to large hard disks (up to 2 TB in size), and uses a smaller cluster size than FAT for more efficient space usage.	Windows 98, Windows 2000, Windows XP

File System	Description	Supported By
NTFS4	NTFS4 is the native file system Microsoft introduced in the Windows NT operating system. It offers many advantages over the FAT-based file systems including support for very large hard disks, file- and folder-level security, and disk compression.	Windows NT, Windows 2000, Windows XP
NTFS5	NTFS5 is an enhanced version of NTFS that adds support for encryption and disk quotas (for limiting users' disk space).	Windows NT with Service Pack 6, Windows 2000, Windows XP
HPFS	HPFS is a file system created by IBM for the OS/2 operating system. This file system enhanced the FAT file system by adding support for larger hard disks and using a smaller cluster size. Microsoft added support for this file system to the Windows NT operating system.	Windows NT
CDFS	CDFS is a specialized 32-bit file system that enables the Windows operating systems to access the information on a CD-ROM.	Windows 9x, Windows NT, Windows 2000, Windows XP

 Windows ME supports both FAT and FAT32.

NTFS Permissions

With NTFS, you have the ability to set permissions on files and folders to grant or deny users access. If you set permissions at the folder level, those permissions are automatically applied to the files within the folder. In some situations, you might find it necessary to set permissions on an individual file. In this scenario, the permissions you set on an individual file override the permissions set at the folder level. You can either allow or deny a specific permission. In Table 4-7, you see a list of the folder permissions you can set, and in Table 4-8 you find a list of the file permissions.

Table 4-7: *Folder Permissions*

Permission	Permits Users To
Full Control	Perform any action on the folder.
Modify	Change files in the folder, change attributes of the folder, see the contents of the folder and the contents of its files, and run program files in the folder.
Read & Execute	See the contents of the folder and the contents of its files, and run program files in the folder.
List Folder Contents	See the contents of the folder and the contents of its files, and run program files in the folder.
Read	See the contents of the folder and the contents of its files.
Write	Change files in the folder.

Table 4-8: *File Permissions*

Permission	Permits Users To
Full Control	Perform any action on the file.
Modify	Change the file and its attributes; run a program file.
Read & Execute	See the contents of the file; run a program file.
Read	See the contents of the file.
Write	Change the file and its attributes.

The NTFS permissions you assign for a file or folder are cumulative. If you assign NTFS permissions to two groups for a folder, and a user is a member of both groups, the user will receive the permissions you assigned to both groups. For example, let's say that you assigned the Read & Execute permission to the Users group for a folder. You then assigned the Modify permission to the Administrators group for the same folder. If a user is a member of both the Users and Administrators group, the user's permissions for the folder will be Read & Execute and Modify.

Attributes

Regardless of which file system a computer is using, you can set four attributes on its files and folders. These attributes include: Archive, Hidden, Read-Only, and System. In Table 4-9, you find a description of each file attribute and how it's used.

Table 4-9: *File Attributes*

File Attribute	Used To
Archive	Indicate that a file has not been backed up. Windows automatically sets the Archive attribute on any file you create or modify. When you back up a computer, you can choose to back up only the files on which the Archive attribute is set.
Hidden	Hide a file from view in Windows Explorer or My Computer.
Read-Only	Enables users to read the contents of a file or execute it if it's a program file, and prevents users from changing the contents of a file.
System	Indicate that a file is used by the operating system.

 We talk more about the Archive attribute and how you can use it to perform a backup in Lesson 11.

How to Configure File and Folder Security

Procedure Reference: Assign File And Folder Permissions in Windows 2000

To assign file and folder permissions in Windows 2000:

1. Log on as a user with Full Control to the file or folder for which you want to assign permissions.

2. Open Windows Explorer.

3. Right-click the file or folder and choose Properties. The file or folder you select must be on an NTFS partition for you to be able to configure permissions.

4. Select the Security tab.

5. If you want to prevent users from inheriting permissions to the file or folder, uncheck Allow Inheritable Permissions From Parent To Propagate To This Object.
   - If you want to copy the previously inherited permissions to the file or folder, click Copy.
   - If you want to remove the previously inherited permissions from the file or folder, click Remove.

6. Click Add.

7. If the computer is a member of a domain and you want to assign permissions to local users or groups, from the Look In drop-down list, select the local computer.

8. In the Select Users Or Groups dialog box, select the user or group to which you want to grant permissions.

9. Click Add.

10. Click OK.

11. In the Name list, verify that the user or group you just added is selected.

12. Check or uncheck the permissions you want to assign to this user or group for the file or folder.

13. Click OK to save your changes.

14. Close Windows Explorer.

15. Test the permissions you assigned by attempting to access the file or folder as both an authorized user and an unauthorized user.

Procedure Reference: Assign File And Folder Permissions in Windows XP

To assign file and folder permissions in Windows XP:

1. Log on as a user with Full Control to the file or folder for which you want to assign permissions.

2. Open Windows Explorer.

3. Right-click the file or folder and choose Properties. The file or folder you select must be on an NTFS partition for you to be able to configure permissions.

4. Select the Security tab.

5. If you want to prevent users from inheriting permissions to the file or folder, disable inheritance.

    a.   Click Advanced.

    b.   Uncheck Inherit From Parent The Permission Entries That Apply To Child Objects.

    c.   If you want to copy the previously inherited permissions to the file or folder, click Copy.

        If you want to remove the previously inherited permissions from the file or folder, click Remove.

    d.   Click OK.

6. Click Add.

7. If the computer is a member of a domain and you want to assign permissions to local users or groups, complete the following steps:

    a.   Click Locations.

    b.   If you're prompted to log on to the domain, click Cancel.

    c.   In the Location list, select the computer name and click OK.

8. If you know the name of the user or group to which you want to assign permissions, enter it under Enter The Object Names To Select and click OK.

9. If you want to search for the user or group to which you want to assign permissions:

    a.   Click Advanced.

    b.   Click Find Now to display a list of users, groups, and computers.

    c.   Select the desired user or group and click OK.

10. Click OK to close the Select Users Or Groups dialog box.

11. In the Name list, verify that the user or group you just added is selected.

12. Check or uncheck the permissions you want to assign to this user or group for the file or folder.

13. Click OK to save your changes.

14. Close Windows Explorer.

15. Test the permissions you assigned by attempting to access the file or folder as both an authorized user and an unauthorized user.

Procedure Reference: Assign File And Folder Permissions in Windows NT

To assign file and folder permissions in Windows NT:

1. Log on as a user with Full Control to the file or folder for which you want to assign permissions.

2. Open Windows Explorer.

3. Right-click the file or folder and choose Properties. The file or folder you select must be on an NTFS partition for you to be able to configure permissions.

4. Select the Security tab.

5. Click Permissions.

6. Click Add.

7. If the computer is a member of a domain and you want to assign permissions to local users or groups, from the Look In drop-down list, select the local computer.

8. If you want to assign permissions to a group, select the group and click Add.

9. If you want to assign permissions to a user:

    a. Click Show Users.

    b. In the Names list, select the user to which you want to assign permissions.

    c. Click Add.

10. From the Type Of Access drop-down list, select the permissions you want to assign to the user or group.

11. Click OK to close the Add Users And Groups dialog box.

12. If you're assigning permissions to a folder, check the appropriate options:

    *   Check Replace Permissions On Subdirectories if you want to also grant the same permissions to the user for the subdirectories within the folder.

    *   Check Replace Permissions On Existing Files if you want to grant the permissions to the user for all files within the folder.

13. Click OK.

14. Click OK to close the file or folder Properties dialog box.

15. Close Windows Explorer.

16. Test the permissions you assigned by attempting to access the file or folder as both an authorized user and an unauthorized user.

Procedure Reference: Configure File Attributes in Windows 2000/XP/NT

To configure file attributes in Windows 2000, Windows XP, and Windows NT:

1. Log on as a user with Full Control to the file or folder for which you want to assign permissions.

2. Open Windows Explorer.

3. Right-click the file or folder for which you want to set attributes and choose Properties.

4. On the General page, check or uncheck Read-Only.

5. Check or uncheck Hidden.

6. Click OK to save your changes.

7. Close Windows Explorer.

ACTIVITY 4-5

Configuring File and Folder Security

Data Files:

- D:\Data\Personnel

- D:\Data\Proposals

Setup:

In addition to the Administrator and Admin# user accounts, you have two local user accounts: SusanH and JeffB. SusanH is a member of the built-in Administrators group. JeffB is a member of the built-in Users group.

Scenario:

Your client, Susan Hill, would like to occasionally let another user (Jeff Bernard) use her Windows 2000 computer to work on sales proposals. She has asked you to make sure that Jeff can't access any of the files and folders in the D:\Data\Personnel folder. In addition, she would like Jeff to be able to create, modify, and delete proposals in the D:\Data\Proposals folder, but she doesn't want any other users to have access to this folder. Susan doesn't want to prevent members of the Administrators group from accessing either the D:\Data\Personnel or D:\Data\ Proposals folders. The \Proposals folder contains a file named Template for New Proposals.doc. As a precaution, Susan would like this file to be read-only to prevent her or Jeff from overwriting it.

What You Do	How You Do It
1. Assign the necessary permissions for the D:\Data\Personnel folder.	a. Open Windows Explorer.
	b. Expand the D drive.
	c. Select the D:\Data folder.
	d. Right-click the D:\Data\Personnel folder and choose Properties.
	e. Select the Security tab.

f. **Uncheck Allow Inheritable Permissions From Parent To Propagate To This Object.**

g. **Click Remove** to remove the previously inherited permissions from the folder.

h. **Click Add.**

i. **From the Look In drop-down list, select WIN2000-#** to look for users and groups defined on the local computer.

Look in: WIN2000-1

⚠ Make sure you select the Administrators group, not the Administrator user.

j. In the Name list, **select Administrators.**

k. **Hold down the Control key and select JeffB.**

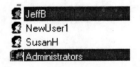

JeffB
NewUser1
SusanH
Administrators

l. **Click Add.**

m. **Click OK.**

n. In the Name list, **select the Administrators group.**

o. In the Permissions list, **check Allow next to Full Control** to assign Full Control permissions to members of the Administrators group.

p. In the Name list, **select Jeff Bernard.**

q. In the Permissions list, **check Deny next to Full Control** to deny all permissions to this user.

Permissions:	Allow	Deny
Full Control	☐	☑

r. **Click OK** to save your permissions assignments.

s. **Click Yes** to confirm that you want to deny permissions to JeffB.

2. Assign the necessary permissions for the D:\Data\Proposals folder.

a. Right-click the D:\Data\Proposals folder and choose Properties.

b. Select the Security tab.

c. Uncheck Allow Inheritable Permissions From Parent To Propagate To This Object.

d. Click Remove to remove the previously inherited permissions from the folder.

e. Click Add.

f. From the Look In drop-down list, select WIN2000-#.

⚠ Make sure you select the Administrators group, not the Administrator user.

g. In the Name list, select Administrators.

h. Hold down the Control key and select JeffB.

i. Click Add.

j. Click OK.

k. In the Name list, select the Administrators group.

l. In the Permissions list, check Allow next to Full Control.

m. In the Name list, select Jeff Bernard.

n. In the Permissions list, check Allow next to Modify (which will also assign the Write permission to the user).

Permissions:	Allow	Deny
Full Control	☐	☐
Modify	☑	☐

o. Click OK to save your permissions assignments.

3. Assign the Read-Only attribute to Template for New Proposals.doc.

   a. In Windows Explorer, **select the D:\Data\ Proposals folder.**

   b. In the right pane, **right-click Template for New Proposals.doc and choose Properties.**

   c. **Check Read-Only.**

   ☑ Read-only

   d. **Click OK** to save your changes.

   e. **Close Windows Explorer.**

4. **Test the permissions assignments.**

   a. **Log off and log back on to your computer as SusanH,** not the domain.

   b. **Open Windows Explorer.**

   c. **Verify that you can open and change the files within the D:\Data\Personnel and D:\Data\Proposals folders.**

   d. **Close Windows Explorer.**

   e. **Log off and log back on as JeffB.**

   f. **Verify that you can open and change all files but the Template for New Proposals file within the D\Data\Proposals folder.**

   g. **Attempt to make changes to the Template for New Proposals file.**

   h. **Verify that you can't access the D\Data\ Personnel folder.**

TOPIC E

Encrypt Files and Folders

Another technique you can use to further secure Windows 2000 and Windows XP computers is file and folder encryption. As an A+ technician, you might be expected to implement encryption for clients and users that work with sensitive data and thus require high security on their computers. So, in this topic, you'll learn how to implement encryption of both files and folders in Windows 2000 and Windows XP.

It's possible that a user might share a folder with his workgroup and not want those users to have access to some of the files within that folder. In this scenario, using encryption is one way that you can prevent the users from accessing those files. As an A+ technician, by encrypting users' sensitive files and folders, you'll be able to protect the intellectual assets of your company.

Encryption

Windows 2000 and Windows XP use *encryption* to translate data into a coded version for increased security. These operating systems use an encryption rule (also called a key) to determine how to encrypt the data. Windows 2000 and Windows XP use a key that's associated with your user account to encrypt or decrypt a file. Because each user's key is different, you can't open a file that another user has encrypted. Likewise, another user can't open a file that you have encrypted. In an emergency, the domain Administrator user account can decrypt an encrypted file.

 The domain Administrator user can also designate other user accounts as authorized to recover encrypted files.

How to Encrypt Files and Folders

Procedure Reference: Encrypt Files and Folders in Windows 2000 and Windows XP

To encrypt files and folders in Windows 2000 and Windows XP:

1. Log on as a user with Full Control to the file or folder for which you want to enable encryption.

2. Open Windows Explorer.

3. Right-click the folder or file you want to encrypt and choose Properties.

4. On the General page, click Advanced.

5. Check Encrypt Contents To Secure Data and click OK.

6. Click OK to close the Properties dialog box.

7. If you chose to encrypt a folder, in the Confirm Attribute Changes dialog box, make the appropriate selection:

    -   If you want to encrypt all files in the folder, as well as its subfolders and their files, select Apply Changes To This Folder, Subfolders, And Files and click OK.

- If you want to encrypt only the files in the folder and not its subfolders or their files, select Apply Changes To This Folder Only and click OK.

8. If you chose to encrypt a file, in the Encryption Warning dialog box, make the appropriate selection:

   - If you want to encrypt the file and its parent folder, select Encrypt The File And The Parent Folder and click OK.

   - If you want to encrypt only the file, select Encrypt The File Only and click OK.

9. Close Windows Explorer.

Procedure Reference: Decrypt Files and Folders in Windows 2000 and Windows XP

To decrypt files and folders in Windows 2000 and Windows XP:

1. Log on as the user who encrypted the file or folder for which you want to disable encryption.

2. Open Windows Explorer.

3. Right-click the folder or file you want to modify and choose Properties.

4. On the General page, click Advanced.

5. Uncheck Encrypt Contents To Secure Data and click OK.

6. Click OK to close the Properties dialog box.

7. If you chose to decrypt a folder, in the Confirm Attribute Changes dialog box, make the appropriate selection:

   - If you want to remove encryption from all files in the folder, as well as its subfolders and their files, select Apply Changes To This Folder, Subfolders, And Files and click OK.

   - If you want to remove encryption from only the files in the folder and not its subfolders or their files, select Apply Changes To This Folder Only and click OK.

8. If you chose to encrypt a file, in the Encryption Warning dialog box, make the appropriate selection:

   - If you want to encrypt the file and its parent folder, select Encrypt The File And The Parent Folder and click OK.

   - If you want to encrypt only the file, select Encrypt The File Only and click OK.

9. Close Windows Explorer.

ACTIVITY 4-6

Encrypting Files and Folders

Data Files:

- Salary.doc

Scenario:

Your client, Susan Hill, occasionally permits other users at her company to use her computer to access the Internet or look at reports. Because she is the accountant for the company, she keeps many of the confidential records for the company. For example, she has a document listing employee names and their salaries. This file is named Salary.doc and it's stored in the D\Data\Personnel folder. She has asked you to make sure that no user (not even an administrator) other than herself can open the file, even if she accidentally copies the file to a folder in which other users have permissions.

What You Do	How You Do It
1. Encrypt the Salary.doc file.	a. **Log on as SusanH.**
	b. **Open Windows Explorer.**
	c. **Select the D\Data\Personnel folder.**
	d. In the right pane, **right-click Salary and choose Properties.**
	e. On the General page, **click Advanced.**
	f. **Check Encrypt Contents To Secure Data.**
	☑ Encrypt contents to secure data
	g. **Click OK** to close the Advanced Attributes dialog box.
	h. **Click OK.**

i. In the Encryption Warning dialog box, **select Encrypt The File Only.**

⦿ Encrypt the file only

j. **Click OK.**

k. **Close Windows Explorer.**

---

2. **Test the encryption.**

a. **Log on as Admin#.**

b. In Windows Explorer, **attempt to open the D\Data\Personnel\Salary.doc file.**

c. **Click OK** to close the error message.

⚠ Access to E:\Data\PERSON~1\Salary.doc was denied.

OK

d. **Close Windows Explorer.**

Lesson 4 Follow-up

In this lesson, you learned how to implement local security in Windows 2000, Windows NT, and Windows XP. Knowing how to properly configure these operating systems' security enables you to protect the computers' data. In addition, these skills help you avoid having to spend time recovering data in the event of a data loss.

1. **In your company, or the companies you support, will you be working in a domain or workgroup environment? Why was this environment chosen?**

2. **Describe a scenario in which you would configure NTFS permissions on a folder.**

LESSON 5

Managing File and Print Resources in Windows 2000/NT/XP

Lesson Time
1 hour(s), 30 minutes

Lesson Objectives:

In this lesson, you will manage file and print resources in Windows 2000/NT/XP.

You will:

- Share folders.
- Connect to a network printer.
- Capture a printer port.
- Install a local printer.
- Troubleshoot printing.

Introduction

Earlier in this course you learned how to connect Windows-based computers to a network, and you learned how to create user accounts. Well, the point of connecting a computer to a network and creating user accounts is to enable users to access the resources on your network. The most common network resources users want to access are files and printers. For this reason, in this lesson, you'll learn the skills you need to provide users with access to file and print resources in Windows 2000, Windows NT, and Windows XP.

The ability to retrieve, store, and print data is the mainstay of users completing tasks and functioning in their job. As an A+ technician, it is your responsibility to make sure that users have access to the file and print resources they need to be effective.

The following CompTIA A+ Operating System Technologies (2003) Examination objectives are covered in this lesson:

- Topic A:
  - 4.1 Share resources (Understand the capabilities/limitations with each OS version), Setting permissions to shared resources.
- Topic E:
  - 3.2 Diagnostic tools, utilities and resources: Device Manager.
  - 3.3 Troubleshooting Windows-specific printing problems: Print spool is stalled, Incorrect/incompatible driver for print, Incorrect parameter.

TOPIC A

Share Folders

Earlier in this course, you learned how to configure permissions for users to access files on the local computer. But in a network environment, your users can access files on other computers as well. In this topic, you'll learn how to share folders so that users can access these folders across the network.

Without a network, if your users want to share files, they'll have to copy them to some form of removable media (such as a floppy disk or CD-ROM) and walk them over to whoever needs access to those files (you'll sometimes hear this process of walking from one computer to the next to transfer files called "sneaker-netting"). Because copying files to removable media and manually moving them from one computer to the next takes time, your users won't be as productive. And because any loss of productivity costs your company money, it's important that you know how to share folders so that your users can take full advantage of the network.

Share Permissions

When you share a folder, you can assign permissions to users or groups to control their access to that shared folder. Windows 2000 and Windows NT support three share permissions: Read, Change, and Full Control. You can configure these same three share permissions in Windows XP as long as the computer is a member of a domain. If the Windows XP computer is a member of a workgroup, you must configure it to use the Classic security model before you can configure shared folders with share permissions. Windows NT supports an additional share permission: No Access. This permission prevents the specified user or group from accessing the shared folder. Table 5-1 contains a description of each of these share permissions.

Table 5-1: *Share Permissions*

Permission	Enables Users To
Read	Connect to the folder, open the folder, open files, and run programs.
Change	Connect to the folder, open the folder, open files, run programs, and create, delete, and modify files and subfolders.
Full Control	Perform any action on files and folders within the shared folder.

The Effective Permissions Process

When a user attempts to connect to a shared folder, Windows 2000, Windows XP, and Windows NT must determine the user's effective permissions for that folder before granting (or denying) access. These operating systems use the following steps to determine the user's effective permissions:

1. The operating system examines the share permissions on the folder to see if the user has been granted share permissions directly to the folder or is a member of a group to which share permissions have been granted.

2. If the shared folder is on an NTFS partition, the operating system determines if the user (or a group of which the user is a member) has been granted NTFS permissions for that same folder.

3. If the user has been given both share permissions and NTFS permissions for the same folder, the operating system grants the user the *most restrictive* permissions of the two.

For example, as you see in Figure 5-1, a user named Sarah is attempting to access a shared folder named Reports. You have given the Users group (of which Sarah is a member) the Change share permission for this shared folder. But, you have assigned the Read NTFS permission to Sarah for this same folder. Because the operating system will apply only the most restrictive permission in this scenario, Sarah's effective permissions are Read.

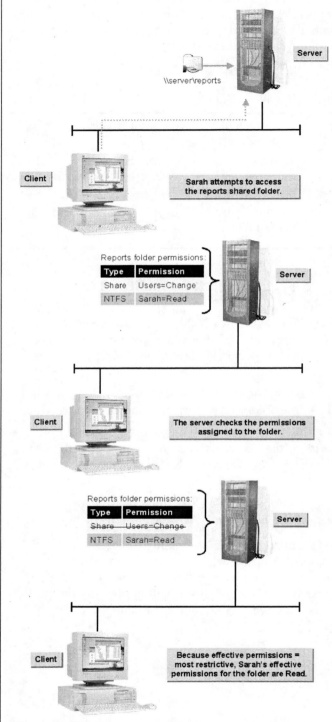

Figure 5-1: *The effective permissions process.*

How to Share Folders

Procedure Reference: Share a Folder

To share a folder in a Windows 2000, Windows NT, or Windows XP computer that is a member of a domain:

1. Log on as a local computer administrator.

2. Open Windows Explorer.

3. Right-click the folder you want to share and choose Sharing.

4. If you're using Windows 2000 or Windows XP, select Share This Folder.

5. If you're using Windows NT, select Shared As.

6. The default share name will match the folder name. If necessary, edit the default share name.

7. If you're using Windows 2000 or Windows NT and you want to limit the number of users who can connect to the share, complete the following steps:

    a. By User Limit, select Allow.

    b. In the Allow text box, type the maximum number of users you want to connect to the share simultaneously.

8. If you're using Windows XP and you want to limit the number of users who can connect to the share, complete the following steps:

    a. Select Allow This Number Of Users.

    b. In the Allow text box, type the maximum number of users you want to connect to the share simultaneously.

    If the computer is a member of a domain, you can assign permissions to either local or domain accounts.

9. Set the desired share permissions.

    a. Click Permissions.

    b. Add the necessary users, groups, or both.

    c. Assign the appropriate share permissions to these accounts.

    d. Click OK to close the Permissions dialog box.

10. Click OK. The appearance of the folder's icon changes to indicate that it is shared.

    Once you have shared the folder, you can share it again under more than one name. On the Sharing tab of the Properties dialog box, click Add New Share to add a second share name. You can set different permissions on each share name.

11. Test access to the share to verify that it is available to users and that you have set the permissions correctly.

ACTIVITY 5-1

Sharing a Folder

Setup:

Your computer is a member of the class.com domain. You have an Admin# and a DomainUser# account in the domain. The password for all user accounts is password. The Admin# user account is a member of Domain Admins.

Setup:

You will work with a partner in this exercise. You will each create and secure a shared folder for your partner to access.

Scenario:

As a member of your company's Help Desk, you find that you frequently need to share some of your report files with other members of the department. You would like this folder to be accessible by other Help Desk staffers plus the domain administrators, but no other users in the Active Directory domain. When the other Help Desk staffers and the administrators access the files on your computer, they will need to be able to make any changes required to the files. The manager of the IT department has asked that department members name shares with names that correspond to their computer names (for example, WIN2000–1 should use \SharedDocs1).

What You Do	How You Do It
1. As the Admin# user, **create an D:\SharedDocs# folder.**	a. **Log on to the class.com domain as Admin#.**
	b. **Open Windows Explorer.**
	c. **Select the D drive.**
	d. **Choose File→New→Folder.**
	e. **Type *SharedDocs#* and press Enter.**
2. **Share the folder with the desired permissions.**	a. **Right-click SharedDocs# and choose Sharing.**

b. **Select Share This Folder.** The default share name is SharedDocs#.

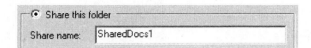

c. **Click Permissions.**

d. **Add the Administrators group from the local computer to the permissions list.**

e. In the Name list, **verify that the Administrators group is selected.**

f. In the Permissions list, **check the Allow box for Full Control.**

g. In the Name list, **select Everyone and click Remove.**

h. **Click OK twice.**

3. Test access to the shared folder on your partner's computer as an authorized and an unauthorized user.

a. From the Start menu, **choose Run.**

b. **Enter the UNC path to your partner's SharedDocs# folder.**

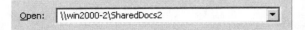

Open: \\win2000-2\SharedDocs2

c. **Click OK.** The shared folder window on your partner's computer opens.

d. **Log off and log back on as your User# account.** This account doesn't have permission to use the SharedDocs folder.

e. From the Start menu, **choose Run.**

f. **Enter the UNC path to your partner's SharedDocs# folder.**

g. **Click OK.** You should receive an Access is Denied message.

h. **Click OK** in the message box.

TOPIC B

Connect to a Network Printer

As we mentioned in Topic 5A, implementing a network makes it possible for users to access resources located throughout the network instead of only the resources on their own computers. In fact, one of the big advantages to a network is that it enables users to share expensive resources such as printers. So, in this topic, you'll learn how to connect your users' computers to network printers.

Unfortunately, there's no such thing as a paperless office—yet. Until the paperless office becomes a reality, users will need the ability to print in order to perform their jobs. Connecting users to shared printers enables you to keep your company's hardware costs low because each user won't need his or her own printer. As an A+ technician, you'll be expected to configure users' computers to take advantage of shared printers so that users can print and your company can minimize its printer hardware investment.

Network Printer

Windows 2000, Windows XP, and Windows NT support two types of network printers: a shared printer on a workstation or server, and a printer with a network card that's connected directly to the network. You access a printer with a network card through its IP address. A printer with a network card is also called a *network-attached printer*.

Print Driver

Before the Windows operating systems can print to printers, you must install the printer's driver. This driver provides Windows with the exact commands for printing to the printer. Without this driver, Windows will not be able to print successfully to the printer.

Device Settings

When you connect to a network printer, you'll find that there are several settings you can configure for the printer. These settings vary depending on the printer model. In Table 5-2, we list the most common printer device settings you can expect to encounter.

Table 5-2: *Common Printer Device Settings*

Device Setting	Use To
Form To Tray Assignment	Specify which size paper is stored in each of the printer's paper trays.
Installed Font Cartridge(s)	Configure any font cartridges you have installed in the printer.
Installable Options	Configure any additional options supported by the printer. For example, you might use this option to configure optional paper trays for the printer or to specify any additional RAM installed in the printer.

How to Connect to a Network Printer

Procedure Reference: Connect to a Network Printer in Windows 2000

To connect to a printer that is shared on the network in Windows 2000:

1. Log on with a user account and password that is valid for the print server. For example, if the network printer is shared on a domain controller, log on with a domain user account and password.

2. From the Start menu, choose Settings→Printers to open the Printers dialog box.

3. Double-click the Add Printer icon to start the Add Printer Wizard.

4. Click Next.

5. Select Network Printer.

6. Click Next.

7. On the Locate Your Printer page, make the appropriate selection:

- If the printer is shared in an Active Directory domain, select Find A Printer In The Directory.

- If the printer is shared in a workgroup, select Type The Printer Name, Or Click Next To Browse For A Printer. If you know the printer name, type it in the Name text box.

- If the printer is on the Internet or an intranet, select Connect To A Printer On The Internet Or On Your Intranet. In the URL text box, type the URL for the printer.

8. Click Next.

9. If you already have other printers installed on the computer, you'll be prompted to choose which printer you want as the default printer. Under Do You Want Your Windows-based Programs To Use This Printer As The Default Printer, select one of the following:

- Yes, if you want all Windows programs to use this printer as their default printer.

- No, if you want this printer available to Windows programs to use, but it is not their default printer.

10. Click Next and then click Finish.

11. Close the Printers window.

Procedure Reference: Connect to a Network-attached Printer in Windows 2000

To connect to a printer with a network card in Windows 2000:

1. Log on as a local administrator.

2. From the Start menu, choose Settings→Printers to open the Printers window.

3. Double-click the Add Printer icon to start the Add Printer Wizard.

4. Click Next.

5. Select Local Printer.

6. If you want Windows 2000 to use Plug and Play to attempt to detect the printer, check Automatically Detect And Install My Plug And Play Printer.

7. If you want to manually specify the printer manufacturer and type, uncheck Automatically Detect And Install My Plug And Play Printer.

8. Click Next.

9. On the Select The Printer Port page, complete the following steps:

   a. Select Create A New Port.

   b. From the Type drop-down list, select Standard TCP/IP Port.

   c. Click Next. The Add Standard TCP/IP Printer Port Wizard opens.

   d. Click Next.

   e. In the Printer Name Or IP Address text box, type the IP address of the printer.

   f. Click Next.

   g. Click Finish.

10. If you specified that you did not want Windows 2000 to use Plug and Play to attempt to detect your printer, or Plug and Play was unsuccessful, complete the following steps:

    a. Below Manufacturers, select the manufacturer of the printer.

    b. Below Printers, select the printer model.

    c. Click Next.

11. In the Printer Name text box, type a name for your printer.

12. If you already have other printers installed on the computer, you'll be prompted to choose which printer you want as the default printer. Under Do You Want Your Windows-based Programs To Use This Printer As The Default Printer, select one of the following:

    • Yes, if you want all Windows programs to use this printer as their default printer.

    • No, if you want this printer available to Windows programs to use, but it is not their default printer.

13. Click Next.

14. On the Printer Sharing page, select one of the following:

    • If you want to share the printer with other users, select Share As:. In the text box, type a share name for the printer.

    • If you do not want to share the printer with other users, select Do Not Share This Printer.

15. Click Next.

16. Under Would You Like To Print A Test Page, select one of the following:

    • Yes, if you want to print a test page to verify the printer is set up properly.

    • No, if you want to skip printing the test page.

17. Click Finish.

18. If you are prompted for the Windows 2000 installation files, insert the disk in the CD-ROM drive and click OK.

19. If you selected Yes to print a test page, click one of the following:

    • Yes, if the test page printed properly at the printer.

    • No, if the test page did not print properly at the printer.

20. Close the Printers window.

Procedure Reference: Connect to a Network Printer in Windows XP

To connect to a printer that is shared on the network in Windows XP:

1. Log on with a user account and password that is valid for the print server. For example, if the network printer is shared on a domain controller, log on with a domain user account and password.

2. From the Start menu, choose Settings→Printers And Faxes to open the Printers dialog box.

3. Click the Add Printer link to start the Add Printer Wizard.

4. Click Next.

5. Select A Network Printer, Or A Printer Attached To Another Computer.

6. Click Next.

7. On the Specify A Printer page, select the appropriate option.

   - If the computer is a member of a workgroup:

     - If you want to search for the printer name, select Browse For A Printer.

     - If you know the printer name, select Connect To This Printer and type the printer name in the Name text box.

     - If the printer is on the Internet or a home or office network, select Connect To A Printer On The Internet Or On A Home Or Office Network. In the URL text box, type the URL for the printer.

   - If the computer is a member of a domain:

     - If you want to search for the printer in the Active Directory, select Find A Printer In The Directory.

     - If you want to search for the printer or know the printer name, select Connect To This Printer (Or To Browse For A Printer).

     - If the printer is on the Internet or a home or office network, select Connect To A Printer On The Internet Or On A Home Or Office Network. In the URL text box, type the URL for the printer.

8. Click Next.

9. If you already have other printers installed on the computer, you'll be prompted to choose which printer you want as the default printer. Under Do You Want To Use This Printer As The Default Printer, select one of the following:

   - Yes, if you want all Windows programs to use this printer as their default printer.

   - No, if you want this printer available to Windows programs to use, but it is not their default printer.

10. Click Next and then click Finish.

11. Close the Printers window.

Procedure Reference: Connect to a Network-attached Printer in Windows XP

To connect to a printer with a network card in Windows XP:

1. Log on as a local administrator.

2. From the Start menu, choose Printers And Faxes to open the Printers And Faxes window.

3. Click the Add A Printer link to start the Add Printer Wizard.

4. Click Next.

5. Select Local Printer Attached To This Computer.

6. If you want Windows 2000 to use Plug and Play to attempt to detect the printer, check Automatically Detect And Install My Plug And Play Printer.

7. If you want to manually specify the printer manufacturer and type, uncheck Automatically Detect And Install My Plug And Play Printer.

8. Click Next.

9. On the Select A Printer Port page, complete the following steps:

   a. Select Create A New Port.

   b. From the Type Of Port drop-down list, select Standard TCP/IP Port.

   c. Click Next. The Add Standard TCP/IP Printer Port Wizard opens.

   d. Click Next.

   e. In the Printer Name Or IP Address text box, type the IP address of the printer.

   f. Click Next.

   g. Click Finish.

10. If you specified that you did not want Windows 2000 to use Plug and Play to attempt to detect your printer, or Plug and Play was unsuccessful, complete the following steps:

    a. Below Manufacturer, select the manufacturer of the printer.

    b. Below Printers, select the printer model.

    c. Click Next.

11. In the Printer Name text box, type a name for your printer.

12. If you already have other printers installed on the computer, you'll be prompted to choose which printer you want as the default printer. Under Do You Want To Use This Printer As The Default Printer, select one of the following:

    - Yes, if you want all Windows programs to use this printer as their default printer.

    - No, if you want this printer available to Windows programs to use, but it is not their default printer.

13. Click Next.

14. On the Printer Sharing page, select one of the following:

    - If you want to share the printer with other users, select Share Name. In the text box, type a share name for the printer.

    - If you do not want to share the printer with other users, select Do Not Share This Printer.

15. Click Next.

16. Under Do You Want To Print A Test Page, select one of the following:

    - Yes, if you want to print a test page to verify the printer is set up properly.

    - No, if you want to skip printing the test page.

17. Click Next.

18. Click Finish.

19. If you are prompted for the Windows XP installation files, insert the disk in the CD-ROM drive and click OK.

20. If you selected Yes to print a test page, click one of the following:

    - Yes, if the test page printed properly at the printer.

    - No, if the test page did not print properly at the printer.

21. Close the Printers And Faxes window.

Procedure Reference: Connect to a Network Printer in Windows NT

To connect to a printer that is shared on the network in Windows NT:

1. Log on with a user account and password that is valid for the print server. For example, if the network printer is shared on a domain controller, log on with a domain user account and password.

2. From the Start menu, choose Settings→Printers to open the Printers dialog box.

3. Double-click the Add Printer icon to start the Add Printer Wizard.

4. Select Network Printer Server.

5. Click Next.

6. In the Connect To Printer dialog box, expand the print server and select the printer.

7. Click OK to close the Connect To Printer dialog box.

8. If the print server doesn't have a suitable Windows NT driver for the printer, you'll see a message box informing you of such. Complete the following steps:

   a. Click OK to close the message box.

   b. In the File Needed dialog box, enter the path to the Windows NT installation files. If necessary, insert the Windows NT installation CD-ROM.

   c. Click OK.

9. If you already have other printers installed on the computer, you'll be prompted to choose which printer you want as the default printer. Under Do You Want Your Windows-based Programs To Use This Printer As The Default Printer, select one of the following:

   - Yes, if you want all Windows programs to use this printer as their default printer.

   - No, if you want this printer available to Windows programs to use, but it is not their default printer.

   - Click Next.

10. Click Finish.

11. Close the Printers window.

ACTIVITY 5-2

Connecting to a Network Printer

Scenario:

You're working with another technician from your company to install an HP Laser Jet 5si MX printer on the print server for one of your clients. The print server and all client computers are members of an Active Directory domain. The other technician shared the printer as NetPrint. Your job is to set up the Windows 2000 computers on the client's network so that the computers' users can print to this printer. The IT director for the company would like this printer to be the default printer for all users. Because this company has mostly temporary workers, your client configured each user to use a user name of User#, where # is the unique number assigned to the user's computer.

What You Do	How You Do It
1. Install the network printer.	a. Log on to the class.com domain as User#.
	b. From the Start menu, **choose Settings→ Printers.**
	c. **Double-click Add Printer.**
	d. **Click Next.**
	e. On the Local Or Network Printer page, **select Network Printer.**

○ Local printer
☐ Automatically detect and install my Plug and Play printer
● Network printer

f. **Click Next.**

g. On the Locate Your Printer page, **verify that Find A Printer In The Directory is selected and click Next.**

● Find a printer in the Directory

h. In the Find Printers dialog box, **click Find Now.**

i.   In the Name list, **select the HP Laser Jet 5si MX printer and click OK.**

j.   **Click Finish.** The printer object appears in the Printers folder. The check mark indicates that this is the default printer for the computer.

 Because this is the first printer installed on the computer, you are not prompted as to whether you want to make this printer the default printer.

k.   **Close the Printers window.**

TOPIC C

Capture a Printer Port

Topic 5B showed you how you can configure a computer to print to a network printer. Unfortunately, only Windows-based applications recognize network printers and permit you to print to them. If your users are using any non-Windows applications, you'll need to capture a printer port in order to print from these applications. So, in this topic, you'll learn the steps for configuring access to printers so that your users can print within their non-Windows applications.

Most non-Windows applications are custom applications that companies have had developed for them. Such applications typically cost quite a bit of money and perform a specific function for the company that isn't available in commercial, off-the-shelf applications. As an A+ technician, you're bound to encounter a non-Windows application on a computer, and you'll be expected to configure that computer so that the user can print from the custom application. Knowing how to configure printing from non-Windows applications will help you to keep your users working productively in such applications.

Printer Ports

When you connect a printer to a computer, you connect it to a printer port. Windows 2000, Windows XP, and Windows NT support the following printer ports:

- Line Printer 1 (LPT1), Line Printer 2 (LPT2), and Line Printer 3 (LPT3). These ports are also referred to as parallel ports.

- COM1, COM2, COM3, and COM4. These ports are also referred to as serial ports.

Most computers contain a single parallel port (LPT1) and two serial ports (COM1 and COM2).

In addition to the LPT and COM ports, Windows 2000 and Windows XP also support printers connected to USB ports.

 You very rarely see serial ports used for printers because their throughput is significantly slower than that of parallel or USB ports.

Port Capture

MS-DOS applications cannot print directly to the network printers you define in the Printers folder on a Windows computer. Instead, to print from these applications, you must first execute the `net print` command to capture the print jobs sent to an LPT printer port (such as LPT1 or LPT2) so that those jobs are sent to your network printer. Next, configure the application to print to whichever port you captured. The print jobs you create within the MS-DOS application will thus be "captured" and sent to the network printer.

How to Capture a Printer Port

Procedure Reference: Capture a Printer Port

To capture a printer port:

1. Log on as a local administrator.

2. From the Start menu, choose Programs→Accessories→Command Prompt.

    The net use command is persistent, which means that the port will still be captured even after the computer reboots.

3. Enter `net use lpt# \\computer_name\shared printer name`.

    If the computer has its own local printer on lpt1, use a different port such as lpt2.

4. Enter `exit` to close the Command Prompt window.

5. In each non-Windows application on the computer, complete the following steps:
   a. Install the printer driver for the shared printer.
   b. Configure the printer driver to use the port you specified in Step 3 (for example, lpt1).

6. Verify that you can print from each application.

Procedure Reference: View Captured Print Jobs

To view captured print jobs:

1. Open a Command Prompt window.

2. Enter `net print \\computer_name\shared printer name` to display a list of the print jobs redirected to the network printer.

3. Close the Command Prompt window.

Procedure Reference: Disconnect a Captured Printer Port

To disconnect a captured printer port:

1. Log on as a local administrator.

2. Open a Command Prompt window.

3. Enter `net use lpt# /delete`.

4. Close the Command Prompt window.

ACTIVITY 5-3

Capturing a Printer Port

Data Files:

- D:\Data\MyReport.txt

Scenario:

A client calls to report that she has just upgraded her computer to Windows 2000. She still runs the Edit MS-DOS application that was developed for her company. Your client reports that she's unable to print whenever she uses Edit, but she's able to print to the network printer named \\2000srv\NetPrint whenever she uses any of her Windows applications. She doesn't have a local printer attached to her computer.

What You Do	How You Do It
1. Capture the printer port.	a. If neccessary, **log in as Admin#.**
	b. From the Start menu, **choose Programs→ Accessories→Command Prompt.**
	c. Enter **`net use lpt1 \\2000srv\netprint`**
	You should see a message stating that the command completes successfully.

2. **Test the capture of the printer port.**

a. In the Command Prompt window, **enter `edit D:\Data\MyReport.txt`** to open the Edit MS-DOS application. You can use the Edit program to verify that you're able to print.

b. **Press Alt+F** to display the File menu.

c. **Press P** to print to the captured printer port.

d. **Press Enter** to confirm that you want to print the complete document.

e. **Press Alt+F.**

f. **Press X** to exit the Edit program.

g. **Enter `net print \\2000srv\netprint`** to view the accumulated print jobs.

h. **Close the Command Prompt window.**

TOPIC D

Install a Local Printer

In Topic 5B, you learned how to connect users' computers to shared network printers. Another printing scenario you might encounter, though, is setting up a locally attached printer. In this topic, you'll learn how to install and configure a local printer in Windows 2000, Windows NT, and Windows XP.

There are valid reasons why a user might need his or her own printer. For example, think about the accounts payable clerk who's responsible for printing checks on a daily basis. Because printing checks requires that the clerk load the printer with expensive pre-printed check forms instead of plain paper, you typically wouldn't want the clerk to print checks on a shared printer. Having the clerk use a shared printer might lead to other users accidentally printing letters or reports on the pre-printed checks. Likewise, you might not want other users to be able to read the check information. In some situations, the checks the clerk prints might contain sensitive information that your company wouldn't want other users to access. As an A+ technician, knowing how to configure a local printer will enable you to respond to users' requests for local printers whether these requests are for convenience or security reasons (or both).

Print Permissions

When you share a printer in Windows 2000, Windows XP, and Windows NT, there are three print permissions you can assign: Print, Manage Printers, and Manage Documents. In Table 5-3, you find a description of each of these print permissions along with who these permissions are assigned to by default when you share a printer.

Table 5-3: *Print Permissions*

Permission	Enables Users To	Assigned By Default To
Print	Print to the shared printer.	Everyone
Manage Printers	Print to the printer and fully administer the printer.	Administrators, Power Users
Manage Documents	Manage other users' documents. This permission does not include the ability to print to the printer.	Creator Owner

 Creator Owner is a special group that refers to the creator (and thus, owner) of a print job.

How to Install a Local Printer

Procedure Reference: Install a Local Printer in Windows 2000

To install a printer that is attached to the local computer in Windows 2000:

1. Log on as a local administrator.

2. From the Start menu, choose Settings→Printers to open the Printers window.

3. Double-click the Add Printer icon to start the Add Printer Wizard.

4. Click Next.

5. Select Local Printer.

6. If you want Windows 2000 to use Plug and Play to attempt to detect the printer, check Automatically Detect And Install My Plug And Play Printer.

7. If you want to manually specify the printer manufacturer and type, uncheck Automatically Detect And Install My Plug And Play Printer.

8. Click Next.

9. From the Use The Following Port list, select the port to which your printer is connected.

   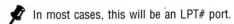 In most cases, this will be an LPT# port.

10. Click Next.

11. If you specified that you did not want Windows 2000 to use Plug and Play to attempt to detect your printer, or Plug and Play was unsuccessful, complete the following steps:

    a. Below Manufacturers, select the manufacturer of the printer.

    b. Below Printers, select the printer model.

c.   Click Next.

12. In the Printer Name text box, type a name for your printer.

13. If you already have other printers installed on the computer, you'll be prompted to choose which printer you want as the default printer. Under Do You Want Your Windows-based Programs To Use This Printer As The Default Printer, select one of the following:

   • Yes, if you want all Windows programs to use this printer as their default printer.

   • No, if you want this printer available to Windows programs to use, but it is not their default printer.

14. Click Next.

15. On the Printer Sharing page, select one of the following:

   • If you want to share the printer with other users, select Share As:. In the text box, type a share name for the printer.

   • If you do not want to share the printer with other users, select Do Not Share This Printer.

16. Click Next.

17. Under Would You Like To Print A Test Page, select one of the following:

   • Yes, if you want to print a test page to verify the printer is set up properly.

   • No, if you want to skip printing the test page.

18. Click Finish.

19. If you are prompted for the Windows 2000 installation files, insert the disk in the CD-ROM drive and click OK.

20. If you selected Yes to print a test page, click one of the following:

   • Yes, if the test page printed properly at the printer.

   • No, if the test page did not print properly at the printer.

21. Close the Printers window.

Procedure Reference: Install a Local Printer in Windows XP

To install a printer that is attached to the local computer in Windows XP:

1. Log on as a local administrator.

2. From the Start menu, choose Printers And Faxes to open the Printers And Faxes window.

3. Click the Add A Printer link to start the Add Printer Wizard.

4. Click Next.

5. Select Local Printer Attached To This Computer.

6. If you want Windows XP to use Plug and Play to attempt to detect the printer, check Automatically Detect And Install My Plug And Play Printer.

7. If you want to manually specify the printer manufacturer and type, uncheck Automatically Detect And Install My Plug And Play Printer.

8. Click Next.

9. From the Use The Following Port drop-down list, select the port to which your printer is connected.

In most cases, this will be an LPT# port.

10. Click Next.

11. If you specified that you did not want Windows XP to use Plug and Play to attempt to detect your printer, or Plug and Play was unsuccessful, complete the following steps:

    a. Below Manufacturer, select the manufacturer of the printer.

    b. Below Printers, select the printer model.

    c. Click Next.

12. In the Printer Name text box, type a name for your printer.

13. If you already have other printers installed on the computer, you'll be prompted to choose which printer you want as the default printer. Under Do You Want Your Windows-based Programs To Use This Printer As The Default Printer, select one of the following:

    - Yes, if you want all Windows programs to use this printer as their default printer.

    - No, if you want this printer available to Windows programs to use, but it is not their default printer.

14. Click Next.

15. On the Printer Sharing page, select one of the following:

    - If you want to share the printer with other users, select Share Name. In the text box, type a share name for the printer.

    - If you do not want to share the printer with other users, select Do Not Share This Printer.

16. Click Next.

17. Under Do You Want To Print A Test Page, select one of the following:

    - Yes, if you want to print a test page to verify the printer is set up properly.

    - No, if you want to skip printing the test page.

18. Click Finish.

19. If you are prompted for the Windows XP installation files, insert the disk in the CD-ROM drive and click OK.

20. If you selected Yes to print a test page, click one of the following:

    - Yes, if the test page printed properly at the printer.

    - No, if the test page did not print properly at the printer.

21. Close the Printers And Faxes window.

Procedure Reference: Install a Local Printer in Windows NT

To install a printer that is attached to the local computer in Windows NT:

1. Log on as a local administrator.

2. From the Start menu, choose Settings→Printers to open the Printers window.

3. Double-click the Add Printer icon to start the Add Printer Wizard.

4. Select My Computer.

5. From the Use The Following Port list, select the port to which your printer is connected.

    In most cases, this will be an LPT# port.

6. Click Next.

7. Below Manufacturers, select the manufacturer of the printer.

8. Below Printers, select the printer model.

9. Click Next.

10. In the Printer Name text box, type a name for your printer.

11. On the Printer Sharing page, select one of the following:
    - If you want to share the printer with other users, select Shared. In the Share Name text box, type a share name for the printer.
    - If you do not want to share the printer with other users, select Not Shared.

12. Click Next.

13. If you already have other printers installed on the computer, you'll be prompted to choose which printer you want as the default printer. Under Do You Want Your Windows-based Programs To Use This Printer As The Default Printer, select one of the following:
    - Yes, if you want all Windows programs to use this printer as their default printer.
    - No, if you want this printer available to Windows programs to use, but it is not their default printer.

14. Click Next.

15. Under Would You Like To Print A Test Page select one of the following:
    - Yes (Recommended), if you want to print a test page to verify the printer is set up properly.
    - No, if you want to skip printing the test page.

16. Click Finish.

17. If you are prompted for the Windows NT installation files, insert the disk in the CD-ROM drive and click OK.

18. If you selected Yes to print a test page, click one of the following:
    - Yes, if the test page printed properly at the printer.
    - No, if the test page did not print properly at the printer.

19. Close the Printers window.

ACTIVITY 5-4

Installing a Local Printer

Scenario:

One of your clients has just ordered a new Hewlett-Packard Color Laserjet 5. He would like to use this printer on his Windows 2000 computer as his default printer. Your client's computer has a single parallel port. He has also asked that you make the printer available to other users in the company. Even though your client hasn't yet received the printer, he would like you to configure his computer so that all he will need to do is plug in the printer when it arrives.

What You Do	How You Do It
1. **Install and share the printer.**	a. From the Start menu, **choose Settings→ Printers.**
	b. **Double-click the Add Printer icon.**
	c. **Choose Local Printer.**
	d. **Uncheck Automatically Detect And Install My Plug And Play Printer.**
	e. **Click Next.**
	f. Below Use The Following Port, **verify that LPT1 is selected.**

g. **Click Next.**

h. Below Manufacturers, **select HP.**

i. Below Printers, **select HP Color Laserjet 5.**

j. **Click Next.**

k. **Accept the default printer name of HP Color Laserjet 5.**

l. Below Do You Want Your Windows-based Programs To Use This Printer As The Default Printer, **verify that Yes is selected.**

m. **Click Next.**

n. **Select Share As.**

o. **Accept the default share name of HPColorL.**

p. **Click Next.**

q. Optionally, **enter a Location and Comment.**

r. **Click Next.**

s. Below Do You Want To Print A Test Page, **select No.**

t. **Click Next.**

u. **Click Finish.** You now see the HP Color Laserjet 5 in the Printers folder; the hand icon underneath the printer indicates that it's shared.

HP Color
LaserJet 5

v. **Close the Printers window.**

TOPIC E

Troubleshoot Printing

So far in this lesson you've seen how to configure a Windows 2000, Windows NT, or Windows XP computer to print to both local and networked computers from Windows and non-Windows applications. But what should you do if a user is still unable to print? In this topic, you'll learn about the printing process and then use this process to troubleshoot printing problems.

As an A+ technician, you can expect to be called immediately whenever a user can't print. Users use printers to perform their jobs, and they won't be able to complete their work if they can't print. Some printing problems might be caused by a hardware failure; still others arise from improperly configured software or printers. Knowing the printing process and the steps for troubleshooting printing will enable you to quickly isolate any problems that occur so that you can fix them quickly. Fixing printing problems quickly gets your users back to work performing the necessary tasks for their jobs.

Print Components

There are two major components that comprise printing: the *print driver* and the *print spooler*.

- The print driver is responsible for setting up the print job for the specific printer destination. Windows 2000, Windows XP, and Windows NT include a system service, the Graphics Device Interface (GDI), which provides a standardized communication mechanism between applications and print drivers.

- The print spooler is a collection of dynamic link library files (DLLs) that manages the rest of the printing process. It accepts the print job from the print driver and stores it until the printer can produce it. In Table 5-4, we list the components that make up the print spooler.

Table 5-4: *Print Spooler Components*

Component	What it Does
Client Spooler	Receives the print job from the print driver; returns system control to the operating system.
Server Spooler	Inserts the print job into the printing stream.
Print Router	Determines the correct print provider.
Print Provider	Handles communication between the computer and the print device.
Print Processor	Makes sure a print job is fully ready for printing. Inserts a separator page if specified.
Separator Page Processor (part of the Print Processor)	Creates a page or printer code instructions that can be sent to the printer ahead of the print job.

Print Process

The Windows 2000, Windows XP, and Windows NT print processes consist of the following steps:

1. A user prints a document in an application.
2. The GDI calls the printer driver.
3. The printer driver creates a job in printer language for the target printer. (This process is called *rendering*.)
4. The client side of the print spooler returns control of the computer system to the application.
5. The server side of the print spooler inserts the job into the printing stream.
6. The print router determines whether the job is for a local or remote printer.
    *   If the job is for a local printer, the print router routes it to the local print provider.
    *   If the job is for a remote printer:
        a. The print router routes it to the correct remote print provider for the print server.
        b. The remote print provider passes the job over the network to the spooler service at the print server, and the process resumes, at the print server, at step 5.
7. The local print provider *spools* the print job or writes it from memory to disk. By default, print jobs spool to the \Winnt\System32\Spool\Printers folder in Windows 2000, \Windows\System32\Spool\Printers folder in Windows XP, and \Winnt\System32\Spool\ Printers in Windows NT. The local print provider also locates a print processor that can render the job's data type.
8. The print processor completes any rendering needed for the job's data type.
9. The separator page processor inserts a separator page, if indicated.
10. The port monitor software for the printer's port handles the physical data communication between the computer and the printer.
11. The printer produces the output.

Common Print Problems

In Table 5-5, you find a list of common problems you can encounter with printers. For each problem listed in this table, you'll find a step in the following procedure that helps you troubleshoot that problem.

Table 5-5: *Common Print Problems*

For These Symptoms	Suspect Problems With The
Jobs accumulate in the print queue but do not print.	Printer's hardware; Spooler service; print spool stalled.
Print output is garbled.	Incorrect or incompatible print driver; application; incorrect parameter (improperly configured application or hardware).
Print jobs do not reach the print queue.	Application; user permissions; printer share name; network connectivity.

How to Troubleshoot a Printer

Procedure Reference: Troubleshoot a Printer

The troubleshooting steps below are in order of basic to complex. As you gain experience, you may be able to recognize symptoms of a particular problem and immediately go to the step that solves that particular problem. In general, to troubleshoot a printing problem in Windows 2000, Windows XP, or Windows NT:

 While troubleshooting printers, you should consult the manufacturer's documentation and user manuals and any relevant training materials.

1. Check your printer's hardware:
    - Verify that the printer is connected to a working power source.
    - Verify that the printer is online.

         Some printers have an online-offline button.

    - Verify that the printer is not out of paper or the paper is not jammed.
    - Verify that the printer is not low or out of ink or toner.
    - Reset the printer by turning it off for 5 to 10 seconds to purge the printer's memory.

         Full printer memory can cause printing problems.

    - Verify that the printer is properly connected to the computer's printer port.
    - If available, perform a self-test on the printer.

         Many printers come with self-diagnostic programs that can resolve basic hardware issues. Refer to the printer's manual on the specific steps required to perform the diagnostics.

2. Print a test document from Notepad.
    a. Restart your computer.

b.   From the Start menu, choose Programs→Accessories→Notepad.

c.   Enter some text.

d.   Print the page. If the page prints successfully, your printing issue may be specific to one program. You will need to troubleshoot that particular application.

3.   If you have a non-USB printer, print from a Command Prompt:

a.   Verify that no printer-sharing devices (such as printer switch boxes) or daisy-chained devices (such as Zip drives) are connected between the computer and the printer.

b.   Open a Command Prompt window. (From the Start menu, choose Programs→Accessories→Command Prompt.)

c.   At the command prompt, enter one of the following:

For a standard printer: `copy c:\windows\mouse.txt lpt1`

For a laser printer: `copy c:\windows\mouse.txt lpt1 /b`

For a postscript printer: `copy c:\windows\system\testps.txt lpt1`

 You can substitute another .txt file for mouse.txt if it doesn't exist on your system. You can also specify a different port if the printer is not connected to the default printer port—LPT1.

 On some inkjet and laser printers, you might need to press the Form Feed or Resume button after the printer has received the job.

If the page prints successfully, you can rule out hardware or physical connection problems. The problem might be caused by incorrect spool settings or a stalled Print Server service.

4.   If print jobs do not accumulate in the print queue, and you're printing to a shared printer, verify that you have the necessary permissions:

a.   Open the Printers folder.

b.   Right-click the shared printer and choose Properties.

c.   Select the Security tab.

d.   Verify that the user account that's attempting to print has at least the Print permission for the printer. (Keep in mind that permissions can be assigned either to the user account or to a group of which the user is a member.)

e.   If necessary, assign permissions to the user account.

f.   Close the printer's properties and the Printers folder.

5.   If print jobs do not accumulate in the print queue, verify that the computer on which the printer is defined has enough available disk space to spool the print jobs.

•   If the printer is defined on a Windows 2000 or Windows NT computer, make sure that the drive containing the \Winnt\System32\Spool\Printers folder has free disk space.

•   If the printer is defined on a Windows XP computer, make sure that the drive containing the \Windows\System32\Spool\Printers folder has free disk space.

6. If print jobs are accumulating in the print queue but not printing, and if you're using Windows 2000 or Windows XP, stop and restart the Print Spooler service:

    a.   Open Computer Management.

    b.   Below Services And Applications, select the Services object.

    c.   In the details pane, right-click the Print Spooler service and choose Stop.

    d.   Right-click the Print Spooler service and choose Start.

    e.   Close Computer Management.

7. If print jobs are accumulating in the print queue but not printing, and if you're using Windows NT, stop and restart the Spooler service:

    a.   In Control Panel, double-click Services.

    b.   In the Services list, select the Spooler service.

    c.   Click Stop.

    d.   Click Yes to confirm that you want to stop the service.

    e.   Verify that the Spooler service is still selected and click Start.

    f.   Close Services and Control Panel.

8. If stopping and restarting the Print Spooler service doesn't resolve the problem, test the spool settings:

    a.   If you're using Windows 2000 or Windows NT, from the Start menu, choose Settings→Printers.

    b.   If you're using Windows XP, from the Start menu, choose Printers And Faxes.

    c.   Right-click the printer and choose Properties.

    d.   Select the Advanced tab.

    e.   Select Print Directly To The Printer.

    f.   Click OK twice.

    g.   Print a test page from Notepad. If the page prints successfully, try different combinations of spool settings until you can print from all Windows programs.

9. Confirm the printer's properties are set correctly:

    a.   If you're using Windows 2000 or Windows NT, from the Start menu, choose Settings→Printers.

    b.   If you're using Windows XP, from the Start menu, choose Printers And Faxes.

    c.   Right-click the printer you are troubleshooting and choose Properties.

    d.   Verify that the settings correspond to those specified in the printer's manual.

10. Remove and re-install the printer driver. If you are using a printer driver installed from the Windows 2000/XP/NT CD-ROM:

    a.   If you're using Windows 2000 or Windows NT, from the Start menu, choose Settings→Printers.

    b.   If you're using Windows XP, from the Start menu, choose Printers And Faxes.

    c.   Right-click the printer and choose Delete.

    d.   Click Yes to remove all files associated with the printer.

    e.   Use the Add Printer Wizard to re-install the printer.

f. Print a test page from Notepad.

g. If the test page is not successful, use the Add Printer Wizard to install the Generic/Text Only printer driver.

h. Print a test page from Notepad.

i. If the second test page is successful, contact your printer's manufacturer for an updated printer driver.

11. Make sure that the user hasn't executed the `net use` command to redirect output from a local printer port to a shared network printer.

a. In a Command Prompt window, execute the command `net use` to determine what if any local printer ports have been captured.

b. To disconnect a captured printer port, execute the command `net use lpt# /delete`.

12. Verify the printer port is working properly.

a. If you're using Windows 2000 or Windows NT, right-click My Computer and choose Properties.

b. If you're using Windows XP, from the Start menu, right-click My Computer and choose Properties.

c. If you're using Windows NT, select the Device Manager tab.

d. If you're using Windows 2000 or Windows XP, select the Hardware tab and then click Device Manager.

e. Expand Ports (COM & LPT) by clicking the plus sign (+).

f. Select your printer port.

g. Click Properties.

h. Verify the Device Status reads This Device Is Working Properly.

i. Select the Resources tab.

j. Verify the Conflicting Devices List reads No Conflicts. If the port is not working correctly, try removing and re-installing the port. If another device is conflicting with the printer port, you need to correct the device conflict.

13. If the port is not working correctly, remove and re-install your printer port:

a. If you're using Windows 2000 or Windows NT, right-click My Computer and choose Properties.

b. If you're using Windows XP, from the Start menu, right-click My Computer and choose Properties.

c. If you're using Windows NT, select the Device Manager tab.

d. If you're using Windows 2000 or Windows XP, select the Hardware tab and then click Device Manager.

e. Click the Device Manager tab.

f. Expand Ports (COM & LPT) by clicking the plus sign (+).

g. Select your printer port.

h. Click Remove.

i. Click OK.

j.   Restart your computer. The printer port should automatically be detected by Windows when it restarts. Follow the prompts to re-install the printer port. If Windows does not automatically detect the printer port, manually add the port using the Add New Hardware wizard.

ACTIVITY 5-5

Troubleshooting Printing Problems

Scenario:

You're contracted as an A+ technician to work on-site at one of your client's locations. The client has asked you to manage all of the printers on the network. You're responsible for responding to any problems that arise with printing. While you were out at lunch, you received three trouble tickets relating to printing problems.

What You Do	How You Do It

Trouble Ticket #1

1.   Mary reports that she's unable to print from Microsoft Excel. After talking with her on the phone, you've determined that everything is okay with the printer hardware.

     When you get to her desk, what step should you take next to troubleshoot the problem?

Trouble Ticket #2

2.   Andy reports that he's attempting to print to his local printer, but none of the print jobs are printing. When you arrive at his desk, you check out the printer hardware and everything seems to be fine. When you double-click the printer in the Printers folder, you see Andy's jobs listed.

     What should you try next?

Trouble Ticket #3

3. Suzanne's computer is configured to print to both a local and a network printer. She just installed a non-Windows application and executed the command `net use lpt1` `\\2000srv\netprint` so that she can print from the non-Windows application. Suzanne reports that all her print jobs now print to the network printer.

What might be the problem and how can you fix it?

Lesson 5 Follow-up

In this lesson, you learned how to manage file and print resources in Windows 2000, Windows XP, and Windows NT. Knowing how to manage these resources will enable you to quickly respond to technical support calls. By correctly configuring access to file and print resources, and quickly resolving any problems that arise, you'll be able to keep users working productively on the network.

1. **In your company, or the companies you support, how will you implement file sharing?**

2. **In your company, or the companies you support, how will you implement printer sharing?**

LESSON 6

Managing File and Print Resources in Windows 9x

Lesson Time
1 hour(s), 30 minutes

Lesson Objectives:

In this lesson, you will manage file and print resources in Windows 9x.

You will:

- Set workgroup or domain membership.
- Configure the security level.
- Share folders.
- Install a printer.
- Troubleshoot a printer.
- Enable user profiles.

Introduction

In the last lesson, you learned how to manage file and print resources in Windows 2000, Windows XP, and Windows NT computers. Because you might be called upon to perform these same tasks on Windows 9x computers, in this lesson, you'll learn the procedures for managing file and print resources in Windows 9x.

As an A+ technician, you may encounter older yet still viable hardware and operating system technology such as Windows 9x. Your ability to manage file and print resources in these older systems will enable you to support a wider variety of systems and users.

The following CompTIA A+ Operating System Technologies (2003) Examination objectives are covered in this lesson:

- Topic C:
  - 4.1 Share resources (Understand the capabilities/limitations with each OS version), Setting permissions to share resources.
- Topic E:
  - 3.3 Troubleshooting Windows-specific printing problems: Print spool is stalled, Incorrect/incompatible driver for print, Incorrect parameter.

TOPIC A

Set Workgroup or Domain Membership

Because it affects how you configure folder and printer security in Windows 9x, the first task you should complete when managing security is to configure the computer's workgroup or domain membership. In this topic, you'll learn how to configure a Windows 9x computer as a member of either a workgroup or a domain.

Configuring the computer as a member of a domain has an impact on how you go about securing the computer's local resources such as folders and printers. If you don't configure a Windows 9x computer as a member of a domain first before you secure its local resources, you'll have to reconfigure these security settings again if you later add the computer as a member of a domain. To avoid having to redo work, you should always set the computer's workgroup or domain membership first before securing its local resources.

NetBIOS Names

Microsoft designed Windows to be user-friendly. As such, they designed Windows so that you could assign names to computers and then access them by name. In earlier versions of Windows such as Windows 9x and Windows NT, this computer name is called a NetBIOS name. In more recent versions of Windows (such as Windows 2000 and Windows XP), Microsoft replaced the NetBIOS name with a DNS name. A DNS name consists of the computer's name plus the name of the DNS domain. For example, you might have a Windows 2000 server with a DNS name of 2000srv.company.com.

In some situations when you're configuring Windows 9x, you'll find that you will need to enter the NetBIOS-equivalent name for a DNS name. The NetBIOS-equivalent name is the first part of the DNS name without the DNS domain name. Continuing with our example, the NetBIOS-equivalent name for the DNS name of 2000srv.company.com is 2000srv.

How to Set Workgroup or Domain Membership

Procedure Reference: Set Workgroup or Domain Membership

To set your computer's workgroup or domain membership:

1. Choose Start→Settings→Control Panel.

 Instead of going through Control Panel, on the Desktop, you can right-click Network Neighborhood and choose Properties to open the Network dialog box.

2. Open Network.

3. Select the Identification tab.

4. In the Workgroup text box, type the name of your workgroup or domain.

5. Click OK.

6. Click Yes to restart the computer.

7. Log back on to the computer.

 Because Windows 9x computers cannot have computer accounts in a Windows domain, they aren't truly members of the domain. When you set their workgroup membership to a domain, they are simply grouped with other domain resources for browsing purposes.

Logging on to a Domain

You can configure Windows 9x to request that a domain controller authenticate a user name and password at log on. The authenticated user would then be able to access shared domain resources from within Windows 9x. However, it is important to remember that Windows 9x itself is not a secure operating system. Even without an authenticated user name and password, a user can access the Windows 9x desktop and use the local operating system and resources.

To configure a Windows 9x computer to request user account authentication by a domain controller:

1. Choose Start→Settings→Control Panel.

2. Open Network.

3. In the The Following Network Components Are Installed list box, select Client For Microsoft Networks.

4. Click Properties.

5. In the Logon Validation box, check Log On To Windows NT Domain.

6. In the Windows NT Domain text box, type the name of your domain.

7. In the Network Logon Options box, select either:

  • Quick Logon to validate your user account and password with the domain controller, but not automatically reconnect any network drives.

- Logon And Restore Network Connections to validate your user account and password with the domain controller and connect to and verify each network drive mapping.

8. Click OK.

9. Click OK to close the Network dialog box.

10. Click Yes to restart the computer.

11. In the logon dialog box, which automatically displays the domain name, enter your user name and password.

12. Click OK to logon.

ACTIVITY 6-1

Setting the Domain Membership to the Class.com Domain

Scenario:

Your company has many Windows 9x computers connected to its network. To enable your users to easily browse other company computers for shared resources, you want all computers to be a member of your company's Class.com domain. In addition, you want all users to log on by using a domain user account.

What You Do	How You Do It
1. **Set the membership of your computer to the Class.com domain.**	a. **Reboot the computer to Windows 98 and log on as Admin#.**
	b. **Choose Start→Settings→Control Panel.**
	c. **Double-click Network.**
	d. **Select the Identification tab.**
	e. In the Workgroup text box, **type** *Class*
	f. **Click OK.**
	g. In the Copy Files From text box, **type** *C:\Win98* **and click OK.**
	h. **Click Yes** to restart the computer.
	i. **Log back on to the computer.**

TOPIC B

Configure the Security Level

Because it controls how you share resources, the first task you'll need to complete before sharing files and printers on a Windows 9x computer is to configure its security level. So, in this topic, you'll learn about the different security levels you can implement on a Windows 9x computer and how to configure your chosen security level.

Setting the security level on a Windows 9x computer properly accomplishes two goals: First, it enables you to secure the computer appropriately for its environment. Second, because changing the computer's security level removes all shares on the computer, setting the security level properly in the first place enables you to avoid having to redo the work of establishing shares on the computer.

Security Levels

There are two security levels that can be set on a Windows 9x computer then used to secure shared resources: share-level and user-level. The *share-level security* setting enables you to set a password on each individual shared resource. Anyone connecting to the shared resource who enters the correct password is granted access. The *user-level security* setting enables you to specify which users and groups have access to each individual shared resource. You grant access using the user and group accounts list from the local user accounts database or from a Windows domain. Anyone connecting to the shared resource must have their user name and password validated by the designated user accounts database before they are granted access to the resource.

How to Configure the Security Level

Procedure Reference: Configure the Security Level of a Windows 9x Computer

To configure the security level of a Windows 9x computer:

1. If you plan to implement User-level Access Control, log on to Windows 9x with a user name and password that exists on the computer from which you want to obtain the master list of users. For example, if you plan to obtain the master list from an Active Directory domain, log on as a user within that domain.

2. Choose Start→Settings→Control Panel to open Control Panel.

3. Double-click Network to open the Network applet.

4. Click the Access Control tab to switch to the Access Control page.

5. In the Control Access To Shared Resources Using box, select either of the following:

    - Share-level Access Control to apply security where you set a password on each individual shared resource.

    - User-level Access Control to apply security where you specify which users and groups have access to each individual shared resource.

6. If you selected User-level Access Control, in the Obtain List Of Users And Groups From text box, type in the name of the computer or network domain where the master list of users is stored.

If you configure Windows 9x to obtain its list of users from an Active Directory domain, type in the NetBIOS name of the domain instead of the DNS domain name. For example, if the DNS domain name for the domain is "company.com," type "company" in the Obtain List Of Users And Groups From text box.

7. Click OK to close the Network applet.

8. Close the Control Panel window.

9. Click Yes to restart your computer.

 You will be prompted to restart your computer each time you change the security level on your computer.

Once the computer restarts, the new security level is applied to your computer. Any resources that were shared with the previous security level will need to be reshared.

ACTIVITY 6-2

Configuring User-level Security

Setup:
The Admin# account is a domain user account in the Active Directory domain. The Windows 98 installation files are in C:\Win98.

Scenario:
Your company has many Windows 9x computers connected to its network. The users of these computers need to share computer resources such as folders and local printers with other network users. You want to make sure that these shares are as secure as possible. All the users of these computers have an individual user account with the company's Windows domain, class.com.

What You Do	How You Do It
1. Set the security level of your computer to user-level.	a. Choose Start→Settings→Control Panel.
	b. Double-click Network.
	c. Click the Access Control tab.
	d. In the Control Access To Shared Resources Using box, select User-level Access Control.

e. In the Obtain List Of Users And Groups From text box, **type *class***

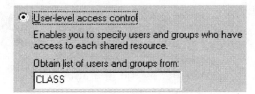

f. **Click OK.**

g. In the Copy Files From text box, **type *C:\Win98* and click OK.**

h. **Close the Control Panel window.**

i. **Click Yes** to restart the computer.

j. When prompted, **log back on to the computer.**

TOPIC C

Share Folders

Earlier in this course, you saw how to share folders in the Windows 2000, Windows NT, and Windows XP networked environments. Now, we want to show you how to perform those same tasks with Windows 9x-based computers. In this topic, you'll learn the steps for implementing shared folders in Windows 9x.

Just as you saw with the Windows 2000, Windows NT, and Windows XP operating systems, Windows 9x users also want to be able to share files without using a sneaker net. Providing your Windows 9x users with access to shared folders will help you avoid the loss of productivity that comes with manually copying files between non-networked computers.

Share Permissions in Windows 9x

Definition:

A *Windows 9x share permission* is a collection of defined rights that allow access to a shared resource. A Windows 9x share permission specifies the functions a user can perform using the shared resource. A Windows 9x share permission may include preassigned rights by the operating system or may be customized by the user.

Example: Windows 9x Share Permissions

Windows 9x includes three share permissions:

- The Read-Only access permission allows the user to view the contents of the shared resource, but not save changes. Its rights are preassigned by Windows 9x.

- The Full access permission allows the user to fully control the shared resource and its functionality. Its rights are preassigned by Windows 9x.

- The Custom access permission allows the user setting the permission to decide which rights to allow. This share permission is available only with user-level security.

How to Share Folders

Procedure Reference: Share a Folder Using Share-level Security

To share a folder on a Windows 9x computer where the security level is set to share-level:

1. If necessary, enable file sharing.
    a. Open the Network dialog box (right-click Network Neighborhood and choose Properties).
    b. Click File And Print Sharing.
    c. Check I Want To Be Able To Give Others Access To My Files.
    d. Click OK.
    e. Click OK to close the Network dialog box.
    f. If prompted, click Yes to restart the computer.
    g. Log back on to Windows 98.

2. Locate the folder you want to share using Windows Explorer, My Computer, or another local browsing tool.

3. Right-click the folder.

4. From the shortcut menu, choose Sharing.

5. On the Sharing page, select Shared As:

6. In the Share Name text box, type a maximum of 12 characters as the name for your share. This is the name other users will see when they browse for and access the share.

7. In the Comments text box, type any comments you want to display about the share. Comments are optional.

8. In Access Type, select one of the following:

- Read-Only to allow other users to view, but not make changes to the contents of the folder.

- Full to allow users to view and make changes to the contents of the folder.

- Depends On Password to set users' abilities to read-only or full depending on the password they enter when accessing the share.

9. In Passwords, enter one of the following:

   - If you selected the Read-Only access type, in the Read-Only Password text box, type your desired password.

   - If you selected the Full access type, in the Full Access Password text box, type your desired password.

   - If you selected the Depends On Password access type, in the Read-Only Password text box, type your desired password for read-only access and in the Full Access Password text box, type your desired password for full access.

10. Click OK.

11. In the Password Confirmation dialog box, re-enter the passwords you typed in the appropriate text boxes.

12. Click OK.

13. Verify that users can access the shared folder.

Procedure Reference: Share a Folder Using User-level Security

To share a folder on a Windows 9x computer where the security level is set to user-level:

1. If necessary, enable file sharing.

   a. Open the Network dialog box (right-click Network Neighborhood and choose Properties).

   b. Click File And Print Sharing.

   c. Check I Want To Be Able To Give Others Access To My Files.

   d. Click OK.

   e. Click OK to close the Network dialog box.

   f. If prompted, click Yes to restart the computer.

   g. Log back on to Windows 98.

2. Locate the folder you want to share using Windows Explorer, My Computer, or another local browsing tool.

3. Right-click the folder.

4. From the shortcut menu, choose Sharing.

5. On the Sharing page, select Shared As:

6. In the Share Name text box, type a maximum of 12 characters as the name for your share. This is the name other users will see when they browse for and access the share.

7. In the Comments text box, type any comments you want to display about the share. Comments are optional.

8. Click Add.

9. From the Name list box, select the users or groups you want to grant similar access to.

✏ You can hold down the Ctrl key to select multiple users and groups.

10. For the users or groups selected, click one of the following:
    - Read-Only to allow other users to view, but not make changes to, the contents of the folder.
    - Full Access to allow users to view and make changes to the contents of the folder.
    - Custom to select the individual rights assigned to the selected users or groups.

11. Repeat steps 8 and 9 for each set of users and groups you want to grant similar access to.

12. Click OK.

13. If you granted custom access to any users or groups, check the desired rights:
    - Read Files
    - Write to Files
    - Create Files and Folders
    - Delete Files
    - Change File Attributes
    - List Files
    - Change Access Control

    Then click OK.

14. Click OK to close the folder's Properties dialog box.

15. Verify that users can access the shared folder.

ACTIVITY 6-3

Sharing a Folder with User-level Security

Scenario:

An employee in the Human Resources Department wants you to create a folder on her computer in which all users in your company can read, but not change, the files contained in the folder. The employee has stated that it is important that no one but company employees be able to read the files. The user has a Windows 98 computer and per company policy, it is configured with user-level security using the company's domain, class.com, to obtain its user list.

What You Do	How You Do It
1. **Create and share the folder with the desired permissions.**	a. If necessary, **log on as Admin#.**
	b. Using Windows Explorer, **create a folder named C:\HRDocs.**
	c. **Right-click C:\HRDocs.**
	d. **Choose Sharing.**
	e. **Select Shared As.**
	f. In the Share Name text box, **type *HR Documents***

	g. **Click Add.**
	h. In the Name list box, **select Domain Users.**

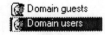

i. **Click Read Only.**

```
[ Read Only -> ]   [🔒] Domain users        [▲]
                                            [▓]
```

j. **Click OK.**

k. **Click OK.**

l. **Look at the folder.** Windows 98 displays a hand under the folder to indicate that the folder is shared.

📁 HRDocs

m. **Close Windows Explorer.**

2. **Verify that your partner can access your shared folder.**

a. From the Start menu, **choose Run.**

b. In the Open text box, **enter the UNC path to your partner's HR Documents shared folder.**

```
Open:  \\win98-2\hr documents                 [▼]
```

c. **Click OK** to connect to your partner's shared folder. Because the folder is currently empty, you will not see any files.

d. **Close the window.**

TOPIC D

Install a Printer

Earlier in this course, you saw how to install both a local printer and a network printer on Windows 2000, Windows NT, and Windows XP computers. If you encounter a company with older computers, you'll need to know how to perform these same tasks in Windows 9x. In this topic, you'll learn how to install both types of printers on Windows 9x computers.

No matter what operating system they're using, users need to print in order to perform their jobs. As an A+ technician, it will be your job to configure users' Windows 9x computers to print to either a local printer, network printer, or both. Knowing how to configure printing in Windows 9x will enable you to get users up and printing and working productively on their computers.

How to Install a Printer

Procedure Reference: Install a Local Printer

To install a printer that is attached to the local computer:

1. From the Start menu, choose Settings→Printers to open the Printers dialog box.

2. Double-click the Add Printer icon to start the Add Printer Wizard.

3. Click Next.

4. Select Local Printer.

5. Click Next.

6. From the Manufacturers list box, select the manufacturer of your printer.

7. From the Printers list box, select the model of your printer.

8. Click Next.

9. From the Available Ports list box, select the port your printer is connected on.

     In most cases, this will be an LPT# port.

10. Click Next.

11. In the Printer Name text box, type a name for your printer.

12. Under Do You Want Your Windows-based Programs To Use This Printer As The Default Printer, select one of the following:

     You'll be prompted as to whether you want to make this printer the default printer only if you have other printers defined in the Printers folder. If this is the first printer in the Printers folder, Windows 9x automatically makes the printer the default printer.

    - Yes, if you want all Windows programs to use this printer as their default printer.

    - No, if you want this printer available to Windows programs to use, but it is not their default printer.

13. Click Next.

14. Under Would You Like To Print A Test Page select one of the following:

    • Yes (Recommended), if you want to print a test page to verify the printer is set up properly.

    • No, if you want to skip printing the test page.

15. Click Finish.

16. If you are prompted for the Windows 9x setup disk, insert the disk in the CD-ROM drive and click OK.

17. If you selected Yes (Recommended) to print a test page, click one of the following:

    • Yes, if the test page printed properly at the printer.

    • No, if the test page did not print properly at the printer.

18. Close the Printers window.

Procedure Reference: Install a Network Printer

To install a printer that is shared on the network:

1. Log on to Windows 9x with a user account and password that is valid for the print server. For example, if the network printer is shared on a domain controller, log on to Windows 9x with a domain user account and password.

2. From the Start menu, choose Settings→Printers to open the Printers dialog box.

3. Double-click the Add Printer icon to start the Add Printer Wizard.

4. Click Next.

5. Select Network Printer.

6. Click Next.

7. In the Network Path Or Queue Name text box, type or browse to find the name of the printer.

8. Under Do You Print From MS-DOS-based Programs select one of the following:

    • Yes, if you will be printing from programs that run under MS-DOS.

    • No, if you will be printing from only Windows-based programs.

9. Click Next.

10. If the drivers for your version of Windows 9x are not installed on the print server, you are prompted to select the manufacturer and type of printer:

    a. From the Manufacturers list box, select the manufacturer of your printer.

    b. From the Printers list box, select the model of your printer.

    c. Click Next.

11. In the Printer Name text box, type a name for your printer.

12. If you have installed other printers on this computer, you'll be prompted to choose which printer you want as the default printer. Under Do You Want Your Windows-based Programs To Use This Printer As The Default Printer, select one of the following:

- Yes, if you want all Windows programs to use this printer as their default printer.

- No, if you want this printer available to Windows programs to use, but it is not their default printer.

13. Click Finish.

14. If you are prompted for the Windows 9x setup disk, insert the disk in the CD-ROM drive and click OK.

15. Close the Printers window.

ACTIVITY 6-4

Installing a Network Printer

Setup:
The company's network printer is named NetPrint. The Windows 98 installation files are stored on each computer in the C:\Win98 folder.

Scenario:
Your company recently installed an HP Laser Jet 5si MX printer, called \\2000srv\NetPrint, to service all company employees' print needs. The technician who installed the printer on the server did not install any additional drivers for legacy Windows clients. This printer will be the default printer for all company computers. All applications used in the company are Windows-based.

What You Do	How You Do It
1. Install the network printer on your computer.	a. From the Start menu, **choose Settings→ Printers.**
	b. **Double-click Add Printer.**
	c. **Click Next.**
	d. **Select Network Printer.**
	e. **Click Next.**

f. In the Network Path Or Queue Name text box, **browse to find the NetPrint printer on the classroom server.**

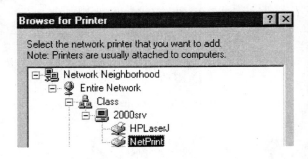

g. **Click OK** to select the printer.

h. Below Do You Print From MS-DOS-based Programs, **select No.**

i. **Click Next.**

j. In the Printer Name text box, **type *Network Printer***

k. **Click Next.**

l. Below Would You Like To Print a Test Page, **select No.**

m. **Click Finish.**

n. **Click OK** to close the Insert Disk message box.

o. In the Copy Files From text box, **type *C:\Win98* and click OK.**

p. **Close the Printers window.**

TOPIC E

Troubleshoot a Printer in Windows 9x

In Topic 6D, you learned how to install both network and local printers in the Windows 9x environment. Unfortunately, printing problems are bound to crop up. For this reason, in this topic, you'll learn how to troubleshoot printing in Windows 9x.

As we've said, nothing generates technical support phone calls faster than users who are unable to print. Your job as an A+ technician is to be able to respond to these calls quickly to diagnose and repair the printing problem. Knowing how to troubleshoot printing will enable you to get your users back printing and working productively on their Windows 9x computers.

How to Troubleshoot a Printer in Windows 9x

Procedure Reference: Troubleshoot a Printer in Windows 9x

The troubleshooting steps below are in order of basic to complex. As you gain experience, you may be able to recognize symptoms of a particular problem and immediately go to the step that solves that particular problem. In general, to troubleshoot a printing problem in Windows 9x:

 While troubleshooting printers, you should consult the manufacturer's documentation and user manuals and any relevant training materials.

1. Check your printer's hardware:
    *   Verify that the printer is connected to a working power source.
    *   Verify that the printer is online (some printers have an online-offline button).
    *   Verify that the printer is not out of paper or the paper is not jammed.
    *   Verify that the printer is not low or out of ink or toner.
    *   Reset the printer by turning it off for 5 to 10 seconds to purge the printer's memory (full printer memory can cause printing problems).
    *   Verify that the printer is properly connected to the computer's printer port.
    *   If available, perform a self-test on the printer (many printers come with self-diagnostic programs that can resolve basic hardware issues. Refer to the printer's manual on the specific steps required to perform the diagnostics).

2. Print a test document from Notepad.
    a. Restart your computer to clear all programs out of memory.
    b. From the Start menu, choose Programs→Accessories→Notepad.
    c. Enter some text.
    d. Print the page.

    If the page prints successfully, your printing issue may be specific to one program. You will need to troubleshoot that particular application.

3. If you have a non-USB printer, print from a Command Prompt:

a. Verify that no printer-sharing devices (such as printer switch boxes) or daisy-chained devices (such as Zip drives) are connected between the computer and the printer.

b. Restart your computer in SafeMode Command Prompt Only.

c. At the command prompt, enter one of the following:

For a standard printer: `copy c:\windows\mouse.txt lpt1`

For a laser printer: `copy c:\windows\mouse.txt lpt1 /b`

For a postscript printer: `copy c:\windows\system\testps.txt lpt1`

You can substitute another .txt file for mouse.txt if it doesn't exist on your system. You can also specify a different port if the printer is not connected to the default printer port—LPT1.

On some inkjet and laser printers, you might need to press the Form Feed or Resume button after the printer has received the job. If the page prints successfully, you can rule out hardware or physical connection problems. The problem might be caused by incorrect spool or bi-directional printer settings. Go to Step 4.

If the page does not print successfully, check the printer's properties. Go to Step 6.

4. Test the spool settings:

a. From the Start menu, choose Settings→Printers.

b. Right-click the printer and choose Properties.

c. Click the Details tab.

d. Click Spool Settings.

e. Select Print Directly To The Printer (if the local printer is being shared, Print Directly To The Printer will be grayed out. Stop sharing the printer to enable the choice).

f. Click OK twice.

g. Print a test page from Notepad.

If the page prints successfully, try different combinations of spool settings until you can print from all Windows programs.

5. If your printer cable does not conform to the 1284 IEEE specification bi-directional printing will not work in Windows 9x. Disable bi-directional support.

a. From the Start menu, choose Settings→Printers.

b. Right-click the printer and choose Properties.

c. Click the Details tab.

d. Click Spool Settings.

e. Select Disable Bi-Directional Support For This Printer.

f. Click OK twice.

g. Print a test page from Notepad.

If the page prints successfully, replace the printer cable with one that conforms with the 1284 IEEE specification.

6. Confirm the printer's properties are set correctly:

 a. From the Start menu, choose Settings→Printers.

 b. Right-click the printer you are troubleshooting and choose Properties.

 c. Verify that the settings correspond with those specified in the printer's manual.

7. Remove and re-install the printer driver. If you are using a printer driver installed from the Windows 9x CD-ROM:

 a. From the Start menu, choose Settings→Printers.

 b. Right-click the printer and choose Delete.

 c. Click Yes to remove all files associated with the printer.

 d. Use the Add Printer Wizard to re-install the printer.

 e. Print a test page from Notepad.

 f. If the test page is not successful, use the Add Printer Wizard to install the Generic/Text Only printer driver.

 g. Print a test page from Notepad.

 h. If the second test page is successful, contact your printer's manufacturer for an updated printer driver.

8. Verify the printer port is working properly.

 a. Right-click My Computer and choose Properties.

 b. Click the Device Manager tab.

 c. Expand Ports (COM & LPT) by clicking the plus sign (+).

 d. Select your printer port.

 e. Click Properties.

 f. Verify the Device Status reads This Device Is Working Properly.

 g. Select the Resources tab.

 h. Verify the Conflicting Devices List reads No Conflicts. If the port is not working correctly, try removing and re-installing the port. If another device is conflicting with the printer port, you need to correct the device conflict.

9. If the port is not working correctly, remove and re-install your printer port:

 a. Right-click My Computer and choose Properties.

 b. Click the Device Manager tab.

 c. Expand Ports (COM & LPT) by clicking the plus sign (+).

 d. Select your printer port.

 e. Click Remove.

 f. Click OK.

 g. Restart your computer.

The printer port should automatically be detected by Windows when it restarts. Follow the prompts to re-install the printer port. If Windows does not automatically detect the printer port, manually add the port using the Add New Hardware wizard.

Print Troubleshooter

Windows 9x has a Print Troubleshooter within the Help system that can guide you in diagnosing common problems and solutions.

To run the Print Troubleshooter in Windows 95:

a.   From the Start menu, choose Help.

b.   On the Contents page, double-click Troubleshooting.

c.   Double-click the If You Have Trouble Printing topic.

d.   Respond to the prompts.

To run the Print Troubleshooter in Windows 98:

a.   From the Start menu, choose Help.

b.   On the Contents page, select Troubleshooting.

c.   Select Windows 98 Troubleshooters.

d.   Select Print.

e.   Respond to the prompts.

 The Windows 95 Resource Kit includes a more detailed Print Troubleshooter tool called Epts.exe.

ACTIVITY 6-5

Troubleshooting Printing Problems in Windows 9x

Scenario:

You have been placed in charge of the printers for your company. This job includes not only printer installations, but troubleshooting problems as well. You've received three trouble tickets relating to printing problems.

Trouble Ticket #1

1. John has a local printer attached to his computer. He calls to say that he can't print documents from any of his Microsoft Office applications. You arrive at John's desk and check the hardware and everything seems fine. You try printing a test page from Notepad, but it also fails to print. You restart the computer in Safe Mode Command Prompt Only and enter the command `copy c:\windows\mouse.txt lpt1`. The mouse.txt file prints successfully.

    What do you suspect the problem is and how would you correct it?

Trouble Ticket #2

2. Sarah has both a local printer and a connection to a network printer, an HP LaserJet 5si. She calls to say that she can print to her local printer but not to the network printer. Sarah tells you that the IT support person recently came by and installed a Windows 9x update on her computer. You stop by the network printer and see that it is online and printing jobs from other users. You try printing a test page from Notepad, but it fails to print. You restart the computer in Safe Mode Command Prompt Only and enter the command `copy c:\windows\mouse.txt lpt1`. The mouse.txt file also fails to print. You check the printer's properties and they are set per the manufacturer's specifications.

    What do you suspect the problem might be and how do you fix it?

Trouble Ticket #3

3. Gail has both a local printer and a connection to a network printer. She calls to say that she can print to the network printer, but not to her local printer. You arrive at Gail's desk and check the local printer's hardware and everything seems fine. You try printing a test page from Notepad, but it fails to print. You restart the computer in Safe Mode Command Prompt Only and enter the command `copy c:\windows\mouse.txt lpt1`. The mouse.txt file also fails to print. You check the printer's properties and they are set per the manufacturer's specifications. You then remove and re-install the printer's driver, but still local print jobs fail to print.

What do you suspect the problem might be and how do you fix it?

TOPIC F

Enable User Profiles

Earlier in this course, you learned about user profiles in the Windows 2000, Windows NT, and Windows XP environments. Windows 9x also supports user profiles. In this topic, you'll learn how to enable user profiles in Windows 9x.

Enabling user profiles in Windows 9x makes it possible for each user of the computer to have his or her own desktop and Start menu. If you don't enable user profiles, users of the same Windows 9x computer won't be able to have unique desktops and Start menus. If your users aren't very sophisticated, sharing a desktop can lead to a lot of support phone calls with questions such as: "Why did my icons move around on the desktop?" and "How come the wallpaper has changed?" and "Where did my files go?" Configuring Windows 9x so that each user maintains their own profile will help you avoid spending a lot of time answering such questions and reconfiguring computers.

Windows 9x User Profile Folders

On Windows 9x computers where user profiles have been enabled, in the \Windows\Profiles directory, the operating system creates a folder for each user who logs on. This folder is named with the user's logon name. Be aware that the Desktop, Favorites, My Documents, Start Menu, and Temporary Internet folders are only available if they have been enabled in the Personalized Item Settings in the Users option of Control Panel. The NetHood folder is only available if it has been enabled by a system policy. This folder can contain the subfolders listed in the following table.

Folder	Stores
Application Data	Information specifying the installed application settings for this user. This might include items such as an Outlook address book (User.wab) file and list of recently opened Microsoft Office documents.
Cookies	Cookie files for Microsoft Internet Explorer.
Desktop	Contents of the Active Desktop.
Favorites	Channels for Microsoft Internet Explorer.
History	History list for Microsoft Internet Explorer.
My Documents	Contents of the My Documents folder on the user's desktop. Unlike the other folders, this folder is stored in C:\. All users of the computer share the same My Documents folder.
NetHood	Shortcuts available in Network Neighborhood.
Recent	Contents of the Start→Documents menu.
Start Menu	Contents of the Start menu, including the Programs menu.
Temporary Internet Files	Contents of the \Temporary Internet Files directory.

Windows 9x Users

Because Windows 9x is not a secure operating system, you can enter any user name and password when you log on to a Windows 9x-based computer. If you have configured Windows 9x to maintain separate profiles for each user, Windows 9x will then create a series of folders in which to store the profile for the new user name you specified.

How to Enable User Profiles

Procedure Reference: Enable User Profiles

To enable user profiles on a Windows 9x computer:

1. From the Start menu, choose Settings→Control Panel.

2. Double-click Passwords.

3. Select the User Profiles tab.

4. Select Users Can Customize Their Preferences And Desktop Settings.

5. In the User Profile Settings box, check any of the following options:
    *   Include Desktop Icons And Network Neighborhood Contents In User Settings if you want the current desktop icons and contents of Network Neighborhood to be copied to any new user profiles.
    *   Include Start Menu And Program Groups In User Settings if you want the current Start menu items and program groups to be copied to any new user profiles.

    > At the time you enable user profiles, the configuration of the computer becomes the default for all subsequent user profiles.

6. Click OK.

7. Click Yes to restart the computer.

Logging On as a New User

When a new user logs on to a computer where user profiles are enabled, the system prompts them to decide whether or not they want the computer to retain their individual settings. If they click Yes, a new user profile is created for their user name. If they click No, they log on with the default user profile.

ACTIVITY 6-6

Enabling User Profiles on a Windows 98 Computer

Scenario:

You work for a company that runs three different 8-hour shifts. Each Windows 98 computer is used by three different users during a 24-hour period. Each user has a unique user account that they log in with to connect to network resources. Many of the users have complained that when they come in for their shift, their work environment isn't as they left it; documents on the Start→Documents menu aren't the ones they opened, items have been added or deleted from their Start menu, Active Desktop items have been changed and someone keeps changing the wallpaper! They ask you to make sure "their stuff" isn't changed during the other shifts.

What You Do	How You Do It
1. Enable user profiles.	a. From the Start menu, **choose Settings→ Control Panel.**
	b. **Double-click Passwords.**
	c. **Select the User Profiles tab.**
	d. **Select Users Can Customize Their Preferences And Desktop Settings.**

⊙ Users can customize their preferences and desktop settings. Windows switches to your personal settings when you log on.

	e. In the User Profile Settings box, **check Include Desktop Icons And Network Neighborhood Contents In User Settings and Include Start Menu And Program Groups In User Settings.**

User profile settings

☑ Include desktop icons and Network Neighborhood contents in user settings.

	f. **Click OK.**
	g. **Close Control Panel.**
	h. **Click Yes** to restart Windows 98.

2. Test to verify user profiles are working correctly.

   a. Log on to the computer as TestUser.

   b. **Click Yes** to confirm that you want the computer to retain your individual settings.

   ✎ The user profile for your TestUser is created.

   c. **Make a change to the display properties of the desktop.**

   d. **Log off as TestUser.**

   e. **Log on as Admin#.**

   f. **Click Yes** to confirm that you want the computer to retain your individual settings.

   g. **Log on as TestUser.** The Windows 98 Desktop display changes from the default were retained for the TestUser.

   h. **Log off TestUser.**

   i. **Log on as Admin#.**

Lesson 6 Follow-up

In this lesson, you learned how to manage file and print resources in Windows 9x. Many companies have computers with older operating systems such as Windows 9x. Knowing how to configure file and print resources in Windows 9x expands your marketability because you are able to configure and support a wider variety of computers beyond just the latest technology.

1. **In your organization, or the organizations you support, how will you implement shared file resources?**

2. **In your organization, or the organizations you support, how will you implement printer sharing?**

LESSON 7
Managing Disk Resources in Windows 2000/NT/XP

Lesson Time
1 hour(s), 30 minutes

Lesson Objectives:

In this lesson, you will manage disk resources in Windows 2000/NT/XP.

You will:

- Create or delete a partition.
- Convert a partition to NTFS.
- Compress files and folders.
- Defragment a hard disk.

Introduction

So far in this course, you've managed applications, implemented network connectivity, and configured file and print resources in the Windows 2000, Windows NT, Windows XP, and Windows 9x operating systems. You might think of these tasks as basic configuration tasks—the tasks you must perform to get users up and working. Now, it's time to turn your attention to managing the computer's disk resources. In this lesson, you'll learn how to manage disk resources in Windows 2000, Windows NT, and Windows XP.

The hard drive is a computer's key storage resource. At best, if it isn't configured properly, disk performance and data security will be compromised. At worst, users will be unable to access the data and applications they need. As an A+ technician, you will be responsible for managing critical disk resources.

The following CompTIA A+ Operating System Technologies (2003) Examination objectives are covered in this lesson:

- Topic A:
  — 1.4 Partitions: Active Partition, Primary Partition, Extended Partition.
- Topic C:
  — 1.4 Files: File Compression.
- Topic D:
  — 1.5 Disk Management Tools: DEFRAG.EXE.
  — 2.4 Disk Defragmentation.

TOPIC A

Create or Delete a Partition

An important part of managing partitions is knowing how to create or delete a partition. As an A+ technician, you need the skills to create the appropriate disk configuration for each user. To do so, you'll need to be able to create or delete partitions whenever necessary. So, in this topic, you'll learn the steps for creating and deleting partitions in the Windows 2000, Windows NT, and Windows XP environments.

There are a lot of reasons why you might need to create or delete the partitions on a hard disk. For example, you might encounter a situation in which you're asked to configure a user's old computer for a new user's use. In this scenario, you won't want the new user to have access to the old user's data, so the best solution is to delete the computer's existing partitions and create the partitions the new user will need. Another scenario in which you might be called upon to create a partition is if you encounter a hard disk with unused free space. Creating a partition in this free space will enable the user to take advantage of otherwise unusable disk space.

Partitions

Definition:

A *partition* is an area of a hard disk that is treated logically as a single unit of storage. A partition can use some or all of the available disk space on a hard disk. In order for a partition to be accessible, you must format it and assign a drive letter to it. A partition can be either primary or extended. A *primary partition* can be used to boot the computer; an *extended partition* cannot. You must mark a primary partition as active in order for it to be used to boot the computer. In the disk management utilities, Windows 2000 and Windows XP indicate which partition is active by displaying (System) for that partition. In the disk management utility for Windows NT, the active partition is indicated with an asterisk (*). The MS-DOS, Windows 9x, Windows NT, Windows 2000, and Windows XP operating systems all use partitions to access disk space.

When you format a disk, you assign a file system to it. Windows 2000 and Windows XP support the following file systems:

- FAT
- FAT32
- NTFS

Windows NT supports the following file systems:

- FAT
- HPFS
- NTFS

Example:

In Figure 7-1, you see the disk information for a drive with three primary partitions. Notice that each partition is assigned its own drive letter.

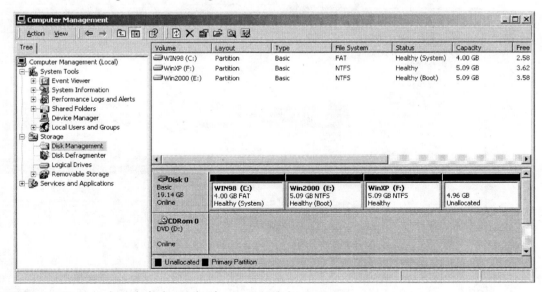

Figure 7-1: *A hard disk with three partitions.*

Other Names for Partitions

You'll find that you often hear different names used for partitions. Although the names differ, they all refer to some or all of the disk space on a particular hard disk. These synonymous names include:

- Disk
- Drive
- Volume

Basic Disks

Definition:

A *basic disk* is a physical hard disk that is divided logically into partitions. Windows NT, Windows 2000, and Windows XP support basic disks. You can create a maximum of four partitions on a basic disk. If you create four partitions, you can either create all four as primary partitions or one extended partition and three primary partitions (you can have a maximum of one extended partition on a hard disk).

 Windows 9x and MS-DOS do not support basic disks. Instead, you can configure a maximum of one primary and one extended partition on these operating systems.

Example:

In Figure 7-2, you see a computer with two basic disks. Each basic disk contains a single primary partition.

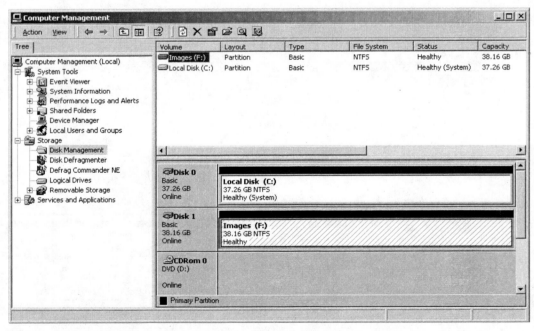

Figure 7-2: *A computer with two basic disks, each containing a single partition.*

Dynamic Disks

Definition:

A *dynamic disk* is a physical hard disk that is divided logically into volumes. Only Windows 2000 and Windows XP support dynamic disks. You create a dynamic disk by converting an existing basic disk to a dynamic disk. Once converted, you cannot convert a dynamic disk back to a basic disk. There is no limit to the number of volumes you can create and format on a physical hard disk. The types of volumes you can create include:

- A simple volume, which is an area of a single dynamic disk that you format and to which you assign a drive letter. (A basic volume is essentially the same as a partition.) If you format the basic volume to use the NTFS file system, you can increase the volume's size by extending it to unformatted free space on the same disk.

- A striped volume, which is multiple areas of space from two or more dynamic disks that you treat as a single logical volume. Windows 2000 and Windows XP write to all disks in the volume simultaneously for improved disk performance.

- A spanned volume, which is multiple areas of space from two or more dynamic disks that you treat as a single logical volume. Windows 2000 and Windows XP write to each disk in sequence. You typically use a spanned volume when you want to increase the amount of disk space in an existing volume.

 Windows Server 2003 also supports dynamic disks.

See Appendix C for more information on how to convert a basic disk to a dynamic disk.

Example:

In Figure 7-3, you see a computer with two basic disks and a dynamic disk. The dynamic disk contains two simple volumes.

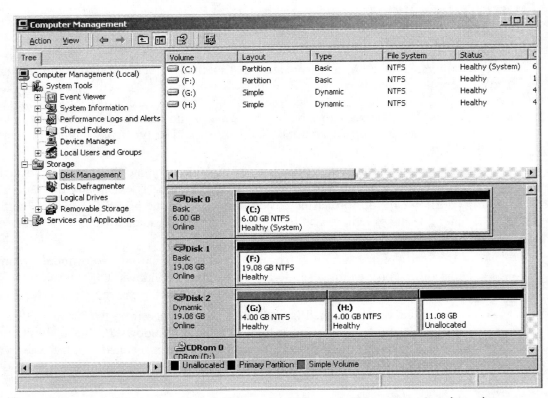

Figure 7-3: *A computer with a dynamic disk containing two simple volumes.*

How to Create or Delete a Partition

Procedure Reference: Create a Primary Partition in Windows 2000 and Windows XP

To create a primary partition in Windows 2000 and Windows XP:

1. Log on as a local administrator.

2. Open Computer Management (right-click My Computer and choose Manage).

3. In the console pane, select the Disk Management folder.

4. If you're using Windows 2000, right-click the available free space in the disk on which you want to create a new partition and choose Create Partition. The Create Partition Wizard starts.

5. If you're using Windows XP, right-click the available free space in the disk on which you want to create a new partition and choose New Partition. The New Partition Wizard starts.

6. Click Next.

7. On the Select Partition Type page, select Primary Partition.

8. Click Next.

9. If you're using Windows 2000, in the Amount Of Disk Space To Use text box, type the size of the partition you want to create.

10. If you're using Windows XP, in the Partition Size In MB text box, type the size of the partition you want to create.

11. Click Next.

12. On the Assign Drive Letter Or Path page, select one of the following:

    - If you want to assign a permanent drive letter to the new partition, choose a drive letter from the drop-down list.

    - If you want to mount the partition into an empty NTFS folder, enter the path to the folder or click Browse to select a folder.

    - If you do not want to assign a drive letter or mount path, select Do Not Assign A Drive Letter Or Drive Path.

13. Click Next.

14. Select whether or not to format this partition. If you choose to format the partition, you can select from the following options:

    - The file system to use (FAT, FAT32, or NTFS).

    - The allocation unit size. This is the size of the smallest available file-storage unit on the disk, and determines the size of the file clusters.

    - The volume label, a name that's assigned to the partition.

    - Check Perform A Quick Format if you want to perform a quick format instead of a full format.

    - Check Enable File And Folder Compression to enable compression on the entire partition.

15. Click Next.

16. Click Finish.

17. Close Computer Management.

18. Verify that the new partition is accessible by using a utility such as Windows Explorer or My Computer.

Procedure Reference: Create a Primary Partition in Windows NT

To create a primary partition in Windows NT:

1. Log on as a local administrator.

2. From the Start menu, choose Programs→Administrative Tools→Disk Administrator.

3. If this is the first time you have run Disk Administrator, click OK in the message box stating that your system configuration will be updated.

4. Right-click the available free space in the disk on which you want to create a new partition and choose Create.

5. In the Confirm message box stating that this partition will not be accessible if you boot the computer under MS-DOS, click Yes.

6. In the Create Partition Of Size text box, type the size of the partition you want to create.

7. Click OK to create the partition.

    Until you commit the changes in Disk Administrator, Windows NT does not actually create or delete partitions on the drive.

8. Choose Partition→Commit Changes Now.

9. Click Yes to confirm that you want to commit your changes.

10. Click OK to close the Disk Administrator message box.

11. Format the partition by completing the following steps:

   a. Right-click the new partition and choose Format.

   b. From the File System drop-down list, select the file system (FAT or NTFS).

   c. From the Allocation Unit drop-down list, select the allocation unit size.

   d. Optionally, in the Volume Label text box, assign a name to the partition.

   e. Check Quick Format to perform a quick format.

   f. Check Enable Compression to enable compression on the new partition.

   g. Click Start.

   h. Click OK to confirm that you want to format the new partition.

   i. Click OK to close the Format Complete message box.

   j. Click Close to close the Format dialog box.

12. Close Disk Administrator.

13. Verify that the new partition is accessible by using a utility such as Windows Explorer or My Computer.

Procedure Reference: Create an Extended Partition in Windows 2000 and Windows XP

To create an extended partition in Windows 2000 and Windows XP:

1. Log on as a local administrator.

2. Open Computer Management (right-click My Computer and choose Manage).

3. In the console pane, select the Disk Management folder.

4. If you're using Windows 2000, right-click the available free space in the disk on which you want to create a new partition and choose Create Partition. The Create Partition Wizard starts.

5. If you're using Windows XP, right-click the available free space in the disk on which you want to create a new partition and choose New Partition. The New Partition Wizard starts.

6. Click Next.

7. On the Select Partition Type page, select Extended Partition.

8. Click Next.

9. In the Amount Of Disk Space To Use text box, type the size of the partition you want to create.

10. Click Next.

11. Click Finish.

12. Create at least one logical drive within the extended partition:

   a. If you're using Windows 2000, right-click an extended partition with free space and choose Create Logical Drive. The Create Partition Wizard starts.

b. If you're using Windows XP, right-click an extended partition with free space and choose New Logical Drive. The New Partition Wizard starts.

c. Click Next.

d. On the Select Partition Type page, click Next.

e. In the Amount Of Disk Space To Use text box, type the size of the logical drive you want to create.

f. Click Next.

g. On the Assign Drive Letter Or Path page, select one of the following:

- If you want to assign a permanent drive letter to the new logical drive, choose a drive letter from the drop-down list.

- If you want to mount the logical drive into an empty folder, enter the path to the folder or click Browse to select a folder.

- If you do not want to assign a drive letter or mount path, select Do Not Assign A Drive Letter Or Drive Path.

h. Click Next.

i. Select whether or not to format the logical drive. If you choose to format the logical drive, you can select from the following options:

- The file system to use (FAT, FAT32, or NTFS).

- The allocation unit size. This is the size of the smallest available file-storage unit on the disk, and determines the size of the file clusters.

- The volume label, a name that's assigned to the partition.

- Check Perform A Quick Format if you want to perform a quick format instead of a full format.

- Check Enable File And Folder Compression to enable compression on the entire partition.

j. Click Next.

k. Click Finish.

13. Close Computer Management.

14. Verify that the new partition is accessible by using a utility such as Windows Explorer or My Computer.

Procedure Reference: Create an Extended Partition in Windows NT

To create an extended partition in Windows NT:

1. Log on as a local administrator.

2. From the Start menu, choose Programs→Administrative Tools→Disk Administrator.

3. If this is the first time you have run Disk Administrator, click OK in the message box stating that your system configuration will be updated.

4. Right-click the available free space in the disk on which you want to create a new partition and choose Create Extended.

5. In the Create Partition Of Size text box, type the size of the partition you want to create.

6. Click OK to create the partition.

📌 Until you commit the changes in Disk Administrator, Windows NT does not actually create or delete partitions on the drive.

7. Choose Partition→Commit Changes Now.

8. Click Yes to confirm that you want to commit your changes.

9. Click OK to close the Disk Administrator message box.

10. Create at least one logical drive within the extended partition by completing the following steps:

    a. Right-click the free space in the extended partition and choose Create.

    b. In the Create Logical Drive Of Size text box, type the size of the logical drive you want to create.

    c. Click OK to create the logical drive.

11. Choose Partition→Commit Changes Now.

12. Click Yes to confirm that you want to commit your changes.

13. Click OK to close the Disk Administrator message box.

14. Format the partition by completing the following steps:

    a. Right-click the new logical drive and choose Format.

    b. From the File System drop-down list, select the file system (FAT or NTFS).

    c. From the Allocation Unit drop-down list, select the allocation unit size.

    d. Optionally, in the Volume Label text box, assign a name to the logical drive.

    e. Check Quick Format to perform a quick format.

    f. Check Enable Compression to enable compression on the new logical drive.

    g. Click Start.

    h. Click OK to confirm that you want to format the new logical drive.

    i. Click OK to close the Format Complete message box.

    j. Click Close to close the Format dialog box.

15. Close Disk Administrator.

16. Verify that the new partition is accessible by using a utility such as Windows Explorer or My Computer.

Procedure Reference: Delete a Primary Partition in Windows 2000 and Windows XP

To delete a primary partition in Windows 2000 and Windows XP:

1. Log on as a local administrator.

2. Open Computer Management (right-click My Computer and choose Manage).

3. In the console pane, select the Disk Management folder.

4. Right-click the partition you want to delete and choose Delete Partition.

5. Click Yes to confirm that you want to delete the primary partition.

6. Close Computer Management.

7.   Verify that the partition is no longer accessible by using a utility such as Windows Explorer or My Computer.

Procedure Reference: Delete a Primary Partition in Windows NT

To delete a primary partition in Windows NT:

1.   Log on as a local administrator.

2.   From the Start menu, choose Programs→Administrative Tools→Disk Administrator.

3.   Right-click the partition you want to delete and choose Delete.

4.   Click Yes to confirm that you want to delete the primary partition.

5.   Choose Partition→Commit Changes Now.

6.   Click Yes to confirm that you want to commit your changes.

7.   Click OK to close the Disk Administrator message box.

8.   Close Computer Management.

9.   Verify that the partition is no longer accessible by using a utility such as Windows Explorer or My Computer.

Procedure Reference: Delete an Extended Partition in Windows 2000 and Windows XP

To delete an extended partition in Windows 2000 and Windows XP:

1.   Log on as a local administrator.

2.   Open Computer Management (right-click My Computer and choose Manage).

3.   In the console pane, select the Disk Management folder.

4.   Delete any logical drives within the extended partition first:
     a.   Right-click a logical drive and choose Delete Logical Drive.
     b.   Click Yes to confirm that you want to delete the logical drive.
     c.   Repeat these steps for each logical drive within the extended partition.

5.   Right-click the extended partition you want to delete and choose Delete Partition.

6.   Click Yes to confirm that you want to delete the extended partition.

7.   Close Computer Management.

8.   Verify that the partition is no longer accessible by using a utility such as Windows Explorer or My Computer.

Procedure Reference: Delete an Extended Partition in Windows NT

To delete an extended partition in Windows NT:

1.   Log on as a local administrator.

2.   Open Disk Administrator.

3.   Delete any logical drives within the extended partition first:
     a.   Right-click a logical drive and choose Delete.
     b.   Click Yes to confirm that you want to delete the logical drive.

c.   Repeat these steps for each logical drive within the extended partition.

d.   Choose Partition→Commit Changes Now.

e.   Click Yes to confirm that you want to commit your changes.

f.   Click OK to close the Disk Administrator message box.

4.   Right-click the extended partition you want to delete and choose Delete.

5.   Choose Partition→Commit Changes Now.

6.   Click Yes to confirm that you want to commit your changes.

7.   Click OK to close the Disk Administrator message box.

8.   Close Computer Management.

9.   Verify that the partition is no longer accessible by using a utility such as Windows Explorer or My Computer.

ACTIVITY 7-1

Creating an Extended Partition

Setup:
Restart the computer and choose Windows 2000 Professional from the boot menu.

Scenario:
One of your clients has a computer configured to boot Windows 98, Windows 2000, and Linux; the client uses this computer to test custom applications he develops. The computer has a single hard disk, and each operating system is configured with its own primary partition. The client has asked you to make the 1 GB of free space remaining on the disk available to both Windows 98 and Windows 2000. Your client would like you to assign the drive letter of S (for "shared") to this partition.

What You Do	How You Do It
1. Given that your client wants the partition to be accessible to both Windows 98 and Windows 2000, what type of partition must you create (given the current configuration of the hard disk)? Why?	
2. What file system(s) can you use on this partition? Why?	

3. Create an extended partition.

    a. **Log on to the Local computer as Admin#.**

    b. **Open Computer Management and select Disk Management** (right-click My Computer and choose Manage to open Computer Management).

    c. On Disk 0, **right-click the available free space and choose Create Partition.**

    d. **Click Next.**

    e. **Select Extended Partition and click Next.**

    f. In the Amount Of Disk Space To Use text box, **type 1024** to create an extended partition that is 1 GB in size.

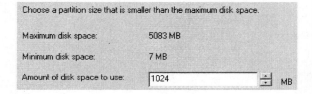

    g. **Click Next.**

    h. **Click Finish.**

4. Create and format a logical drive within the extended partition.

    a. **Right-click the extended partition and choose Create Logical Drive.**

    b. **Click Next.**

    c. On the Select Partition Type page, **click Next** to accept the default of Logical Drive.

    d. **Click Next** to create the logical drive to use all the available space within the extended partition.

e. From the Assign A Drive Letter drop-down list, **select S:.**

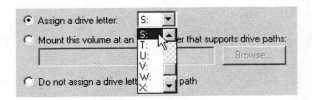

f. **Click Next.**

g. From the File System To Use drop-down list, **select FAT32.**

h. **Check Perform A Quick Format.**

i. **Click Next.**

j. **Click Finish.**

k. When the format is complete, **close Computer Management.**

---

5. **Verify that the new drive is accessible.**

a. **Open Windows Explorer.**

b. **Access the S drive.**

c. **Close Windows Explorer.**

ACTIVITY 7-2

Deleting a Partition

Scenario:

A client calls to ask for your help with her Windows 2000 computer. She has installed a hard disk given to her by a friend into the Windows 2000 computer. When she accesses this hard disk, she finds that it has an S: partition on it. She would like to get rid of the S: partition and create a new one so that she can be sure that all her friend's old data is no longer on the disk.

What You Do	How You Do It
1. Delete the S: partition.	a. **Open Computer Management and select the Disk Management folder.**
	b. **Right-click the S: partition and choose Delete Logical Drive.**

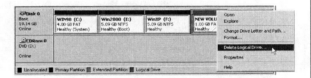

	c. **Click Yes** to confirm that you want to delete the logical drive.
	d. **Right-click the extended partition and choose Delete Partition.**

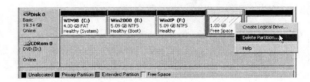

	e. **Click Yes** to confirm that you want to delete the extended partition.
	f. **Close Computer Management.**

2. Verify that the S: partition is no longer accessible.

   a. Open Windows Explorer.

   b. Check the list of drives.

   c. Close Windows Explorer.

ACTIVITY 7-3

Creating a Primary Partition

Scenario:

One of your clients reports that she's running out of disk space on her computer. After examining her computer, you've determined that she has two partitions, one primary and one extended. Your client also has free space left over on the hard disk. She uses her computer to run both Windows and non-Windows applications. One of her non-Windows applications cannot access the NTFS file system. All hard disk space must be accessible by all applications. Your client has asked you to assign the letter Z to the partition if possible.

What You Do	How You Do It
1. Create a primary partition in the free space.	a. Open Computer Management and select Disk Management.
	b. Right-click the free space on Disk 0 and choose Create Partition.
	c. Click Next.
	d. Verify that Primary Partition is selected.

Select the type of partition you want to create:

   ⦿ Primary partition

   ○ Extended partition

   e. Click Next.

   f. In the Amount Of Disk Space To Use text box, **type 100** to configure the new partition with 100 MB of disk space.

   g. Click Next.

h. From the Assign A Drive Letter drop-down list, **select Z:** to assign Z as the drive letter for the new partition.

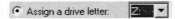

i. **Click Next.**

j. **Verify that Format This Partition With The Following Settings is selected.**

k. From the File System To Use drop-down list, **select FAT.**

l. **Check Perform A Quick Format.**

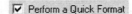

m. **Click Next.**

n. **Click Finish.**

o. **Close Computer Management.**

2. **Verify that the new drive is accessible.**

   a. **Open Windows Explorer.**

   b. **Access the Z drive.**

   c. **Close Windows Explorer.**

TOPIC B

Convert a FAT Partition to NTFS

In Topic 7A, you learned how to create a partition and format it with the FAT or FAT32 file systems. Now, for extra security, the network administrator has asked that you change all FAT partitions to use the NTFS file system instead. As you know, re-formatting the partition to use the NTFS file system will destroy the data that's currently stored on it. So in this topic, you'll learn exactly the steps you need to convert a FAT or FAT32 partition to use the NTFS file system without destroying the data that's currently stored on the partition.

To appreciate the ease of converting a partition to NTFS, let's take a look at a scenario: Imagine you're working the Help Desk when the CEO of the company calls in and tells you he's concerned about the security of his computer. "No problem," you say. "I can easily help you to lock down your computer." But when you arrive at his desk, you find that his computer's partitions are using the FAT file system. The CEO is breathing down your neck because he doesn't want you to lose any of his sensitive and valuable data. In this situation, knowing how to convert a FAT-based partition to NTFS will really make you a hero. You'll be able to quickly convert the CEO's partitions to the NTFS file system, which means he'll be able to take advantage of NTFS's advanced security features such as encryption and file- and folder-level security. And, you'll be able to make this change without any risk of losing the CEO's data!

File System Conversion

In Windows 2000, Windows XP, and Windows NT, if you decide that you want to take advantage of the enhanced capabilities of the NTFS file system, you can convert a FAT partition to the NTFS file system without the risk of losing any data on the partition. This conversion is a one-way process. In other words, once you have converted a FAT partition to NTFS, you can't later convert the NTFS partition back to the FAT file system.

How to Convert a FAT Partition to NTFS

Procedure Reference: Convert a FAT Partition to NTFS in Windows 2000/XP/NT

To convert a FAT partition to NTFS in Windows 2000, Windows XP, and Windows NT:

1. Log on as a local administrator.

2. Determine the drive letter or mount path and the volume label of the partition you want to convert (use Computer Management in Windows 2000 and Windows XP, or Disk Administrator in Windows NT).

3. Open a Command Prompt window.

4. Enter `convert drive /fs:ntfs`. You can use the drive letter, mount path, or volume label for the `drive` variable. If you use the drive letter in Windows 2000 or Windows XP, you'll need to enter the volume label of the drive to confirm the conversion.

5. If prompted, enter the volume label for the drive.

6. If you're converting the boot partition or an active partition, you'll be prompted to restart the computer to complete the conversion.

ACTIVITY 7-4

Converting a FAT Partition to NTFS

Scenario:

A client just called to ask you how to set folder permissions on her hard disk. She is sharing her computer temporarily, and would like to prevent other users from accessing her confidential files. The confidential files are all stored on the Z drive.

What You Do	How You Do It
Do not convert the C drive to NTFS.	
1. **Verify the volume label and file system on the Z drive.**	a. In Windows Explorer, **display the properties for the Z drive.**
	b. **Record the volume label:** _____
	c. **Record the file system:** _____
	d. **Close Windows Explorer.**
2. **Convert the Z drive to NTFS.**	a. **Open a Command Prompt window** (from the Start menu, choose Programs→ Accessories→Command Prompt).
	b. **Enter convert z: /fs:ntfs**

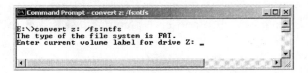

c. When prompted, **enter the volume label.**

```
The type of the file system is FAT.
Enter current volume label for drive Z: NEW VOLUME
```

d. **Close the Command Prompt window.**

3. **Verify that the Z drive is using the NTFS file system.**

    a. In Computer Management, **display the properties for the Z drive.**

    b. **Verify that the file system is now NTFS.**

    c. **Close Computer Management.**

TOPIC C

Compress Files and Folders

Up to this point in the lesson, we've talked about the strategies you can use to create, manage, and delete partitions on your users' computers. But what happens if your users run out of disk space? In this topic, you'll learn how you can optimize the available disk space on users' computers by implementing compression.

As an A+ technician, it's likely that you'll encounter a situation where a user is running out of disk space and upgrading to a larger hard disk (or adding a second hard disk) isn't an option that's available to you. In this scenario, your best solution to keep the user's computer functioning productively is to implement file and folder compression. Using compression will enable you to conserve precious disk space so that the user can continue to work on the computer.

Compression

In Windows 2000, Windows NT, and Windows XP, you can use compression on NTFS partitions to reduce the amount of space required to store files on the hard disk. Compression reduces the amount of disk space used by files by changing the way the characters in a file are written to disk. For example, when you compress a file, the operating system removes any blank or null characters from the file. When you open the file, the operating system adds these characters back in.

How to Compress Files and Folders

Procedure Reference: Compress a File or Folder

To compress a file or folder:

1. Log on as a user with full control over the file or folder you want to compress.

2. Open Windows Explorer.

3. Right-click the file or folder you want to compress and choose Properties.

4. On the General page, make a note of the amount of disk space in use by the file or folder by recording the value you see next to Size On Disk.

5. If you're using Windows 2000 or Windows XP, complete the following steps:

   a. On the General page, click Advanced.

   b. Check Compress Contents To Save Disk Space.

   c. Click OK.

6. If you're using Windows NT, on the General page, click Compress.

7. Click OK to close the Properties dialog box for the file or folder.

8. If you're using Windows 2000 or Windows XP and you selected a folder to compress, select one of the following:

   - If you want to compress the folder and its files only (and not any subfolders), select Apply Changes To This Folder Only and click OK.

   - If you want to compress the folder and its files, along with any subfolders and their files, select Apply Changes To This Folder, Subfolders And Files and click OK.

9. If you're using Windows NT and you selected a folder to compress, check Also Compress Subfolders if you want to compress the subfolders and click OK.

10. Right-click the file or folder to display its properties. Verify that the disk space used is reduced.

    If you want, you can configure Windows Explorer to display compressed files and folders in a different color. For more information, see the Configuring Windows Explorer procedure below.

11. Close Windows Explorer.

Procedure Reference: Compress a Drive

To compress a drive:

1. Log on as a user with at least the Modify NTFS permission for the file or folder you want to compress.

2. Open Windows Explorer.

3. Right-click the drive you want to compress and choose Properties.

4. If you're using Windows 2000 or Windows XP, check Compress Drive To Save Disk Space.

5. If you're using Windows NT, check Compress *drive letter*.

6. Click OK to close the Properties dialog box for the drive.

7. If you're using Windows 2000 or Windows XP, select one of the following:

   - If you want to compress the drive only, select Apply Changes To *drive letter* Only.

   - If you want to compress the drive, its subfolders, and files, select Apply Changes To *drive letter*, Subfolders And Files and click OK.

8. If you're using Windows NT, check Also Compress Subfolders if you want to compress the subfolders and click OK.

9. Close Windows Explorer.

Procedure Reference: Configure Windows Explorer to Display Compressed Files

To configure Windows Explorer to display compressed files in an alternate color:

1. In Windows Explorer, choose Tools→Folder Options.

2. Select the View tab.

3. Below Files And Folders, check Display Compressed Files And Folders With Alternate Color.

4. Click OK.

ACTIVITY 7-5

Compressing Files

Data Files:

- D:\Data\NASA

Scenario:

One of your clients, a contractor with the Stennis Space Center, is responsible for downloading and presenting space-related images. Because these images are so large, they are using up much of her computer's disk space. She would like you to take whatever steps you can to minimize the amount of disk space required for these images. Your client downloads these images to the D:\Data\NASA folder.

What You Do	How You Do It
1. Compress the D:\Data\NASA folder.	a. Open Windows Explorer.
	b. Right-click the D:\Data\NASA folder and choose Properties.
	c. Record the value for Size On Disk: _____
	Size on disk: 9.85 MB (10,334,208 bytes)
	d. Click Advanced.

e. **Check Compress Contents To Save Disk Space.**

☑ Compress contents to save disk space

f. **Click OK.**

g. **Click OK** to close the Properties dialog box.

h. **Select Apply Changes To This Folder, Subfolders And Files.**

⦿ Apply changes to this folder, subfolders and files

i. **Click OK.**

j. **Right-click the D:\Data\NASA folder and choose Properties.**

k. **Compare the Size On Disk to what you recorded in step C.** You should see that compressing the D:\Data\NASA folder reduced the amount of disk required for the folder.

Size on disk: 5.92 MB (6,211,326 bytes)

l. **Click Cancel** to close the Properties dialog box.

2. **Configure Windows Explorer to display compressed files in a different color.**

a. In Windows Explorer, **choose Tools→ Folder Options.**

b. **Select the View tab.**

c. **Check Display Compressed Files And Folders With Alternate Color.**

☑ Display compressed files and folders with alternate color

d. **Click OK.**

e. **Examine the folder list in Windows Explorer.** You can now easily see which files are compressed and which are not.

f. **Close Windows Explorer.**

3. **What will happen if your client downloads a new file to the D:\Data\NASA folder?**

4. **What will happen if your client moves one of the files from the D:\Data\NASA folder to another folder on the same partition?**

5. **What will happen if your client copies one of the files from the D:\Data\NASA folder to another uncompressed folder on the same partition?**

TOPIC D

Defragment a Hard Disk in Windows 2000/XP

Part of managing disk resources in Windows 2000 and Windows XP is to keep the disks performing optimally. You can accomplish this task by defragmenting the hard disk on a consistent basis. In this topic, you'll learn the steps for defragmenting a hard disk in Windows 2000 and Windows XP.

Defragmenting your disks improves the performance and life expectancy of your disks by allowing for more efficient storage of files. More efficient storage of files means less physical wear and tear on the heads of the disks themselves, quicker operating system and application startup times, faster application performance, and more rapid retrieval of files.

Fragmentation

The Windows operating systems do not write a file to disk as a single large block. Instead, they break up the file into smaller pieces. When Windows writes these smaller pieces to the disk, it tries to write them close together so that the disk can retrieve the file quickly whenever a user opens it. As a disk fills up and files are added and removed, it becomes harder for Windows to find enough contiguous space to write all the pieces of a file. As a result, Windows ends up writing the file wherever it can find free space on a disk. The end result is that files can become fragmented, meaning their pieces can be spread out all over the disk. The greater the amount of *fragmentation*, the more work the operating system must perform to retrieve and write files. You can counteract fragmentation by defragmenting a computer's hard disk.

How to Defragment a Hard Disk in Windows 2000/XP

Procedure Reference: Defragment a Hard Disk in Windows 2000 and Windows XP

To defragment a hard disk in Windows 2000 and Windows XP:

1. Log on as a local administrator.

2. From the Start menu, choose Programs→Accessories→System Tools→Disk Defragmenter.

3. In the top pane of the Disk Defragmenter window, select the disk you want to defragment.

4. If you want to analyze the fragmentation state of the disk before defragmenting, click Analyze.

5. After the analysis, you will see a message box with a recommendation as to whether you should defragment or not. This recommendation is made based on a Disk Defragmenter algorithm, rather than a specific fragmentation level, but it is common practice to defragment disks that are more than five percent fragmented.

   Click View Report to see details of the fragmentation state of the disk.

6. To begin the defragmentation, click Defragment in the analysis message box, in the Analysis Report dialog box, or in the Disk Defragmenter window itself. Disk Defragmenter will re-analyze the disk and begin the defragmentation. You can view the progress in the progress bar.

✏ Defragmentation of a large, highly fragmented, and very full disk can take several hours.

7. When the defragmentation is complete, you can click View Report to see detailed information about the defragmentation.

ACTIVITY 7-6

Defragmenting a Hard Disk

Scenario:

One of your clients is complaining that his hard disk in his Windows 2000 computer is very slow. He says that he can hear the hard disk "crunching away" whenever he attempts to save a file to the D drive. He's asked you to do what you can to resolve the problem.

What You Do	How You Do It
1. **Analyze the fragmentation on the hard disk.**	a. From the Start menu, **choose Programs→ Accessories→System Tools→Disk Defragmenter.**
	b. In the Volume list, **select the D drive.**
	c. **Click Analyze.**
	d. In the Disk Defragmenter message box, **click View Report.**
	e. In the Volume Information area, **scroll to the Volume Fragmentation statistics.** You can determine the overall fragmentation percentage here.

Volume fragmentation
   Total fragmentation   = 7 %
   File fragmentation   = 14 %
   Free space fragmentation   = 0 %

	f. In the Most Fragmented Files list, **click the Fragments column heading** to sort by this column. The larger files have the greatest amount of fragmentation.
	g. **Click Close.**

2. Based on the analysis you see in the report, should you defragment this disk?

_____

3. **Defragment the disk.**

    a. **Click Defragment.** The information displayed in Disk Defragmenter and the status bar changes as the defragmentation progresses.

         If you don't want to take the time for defragmentation to complete, click Stop.

    b. **Close Disk Defragmenter.**

Lesson 7 Follow-up

In this lesson, you learned how to create, manage, and delete partitions in the Windows 2000, Windows NT, and Windows XP environments. By properly configuring the partitions in your computers, your users will be able to access the hard disk resources they need to do their jobs.

1. **In your organization, or the organizations you support, what disk management tasks are you expected to perform? Why?**

2. **In your organization, or the organizations you support, what is the configuration of the hard disk partitions on your Windows 2000 computers? Why?**

LESSON 8

Managing Disk Resources in Windows 9x

Lesson Time
2 hour(s)

Lesson Objectives:

In this lesson, you will manage disk resources in Windows 9x.

You will:

*   Create or delete a partition.
*   Compress a hard disk.
*   Convert a FAT partition to FAT32.
*   Defragment a hard disk.

Introduction

Earlier in this course you learned how to manage the disk resources in the Windows 2000, Windows NT, and Windows XP environments. Because many companies have quite an investment in Windows 9x-based computers, odds are that as an A+ technician you'll also be called on to perform the same management tasks on Windows 9x computers. In this lesson, you'll learn how to create, manage, and delete partitions in the Windows 9x environment.

Hard drives and their associated partitions are critical resources in any computer, and a 9x-based system is no exception. Without properly configured disk resources, your users won't be able to access the files they need. Since you may encounter these older but still viable systems, your ability to manage disk resources is critical.

The following CompTIA A+ Operating System Technologies (2003) Examination objectives are covered in this lesson:

- Topic A:
  — 1.5 Disk Management Tools: FDISK.EXE.
- Topic D:
  — 1.5 Disk Management Tools: DEFRAG.EXE.
  — 2.5 Disk Defragmentation.

TOPIC A

Create or Delete a Partition

Just as in Windows 2000, Windows NT, and Windows XP, creating and deleting partitions is an important part of managing partitions in the Windows 9x environment. If your company or clients have Windows 9x computers, as an A+ technician, you'll be expected to know how to configure such computers' hard disks. For this reason, you'll learn the steps to create and delete partitions in this topic.

One of the most common reasons why you'll be asked to create a partition on a computer is when a new hard disk has been installed. A computer (and thus the computer's user) won't be able to use the new hard disk unless it has at least one partition. To enable a user to take advantage of the new hard disk, you'll need to know how to create partitions on that disk. On the other hand, you might encounter a situation where a user no longer needs a hard disk and you want to move that hard disk to a different computer. Because that hard disk might have sensitive data stored on it, you should always delete the disk's partitions before moving the disk to a new computer. Knowing how to delete the old partitions will enable you to protect against the new user accessing the old user's data.

Large Disk Support

Windows 95 OSR2 and Windows 98 provide support for EIDE hard disks larger than 2 gigabytes (GB) when using the FAT32 file system. With the *FAT32 file system*:

- Hard disk space is used 10 to 15 percent more efficiently than FAT or FAT16 drives due to the smaller cluster size used.
- Your hard disks can be from 512 megabytes up to 2 terabytes in size. However, some system BIOS will not accept more than a 7.8 GB bootable partition.

Windows ME also provides support for FAT32.

On a dual-boot system, FAT32 partitions can be accessed only by the Windows 95 OSR2, Windows 98, Windows ME, Windows 2000, and Windows XP operating systems.

MS-DOS Mode

In Windows 9x, you can simulate the MS-DOS environment by starting the operating system in MS-DOS mode. You typically use MS-DOS mode when troubleshooting an application that won't run in Windows 9x. In addition, you use MS-DOS mode to run the programs that enable you to create, format, and delete partitions. In Figure 8-1, you see the option for restarting in MS-DOS mode on the Shut Down Windows menu.

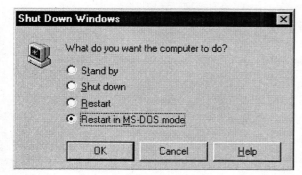

Figure 8-1: *Restarting a Windows 9x computer in MS-DOS mode.*

How to Create or Delete a Partition

Procedure Reference: Create Partitions on a Windows 9x Computer

To create a partition on a Windows 9x computer using Fdisk.exe:

1.   Restart the computer in MS-DOS mode.

    a.   Choose Start→Shut Down.

    b.   In the Shut Down Windows dialog box, select Restart In MS-DOS Mode.

    c.   Click OK.

2.   At the C:\Windows prompt, type `fdisk` and press Enter.

3.   If you have a Windows 98 computer with a hard disk larger than 512 MB, type one of the following and press Enter:

    • Y to enable large disk support and use 32-bit FAT as the file system on your computer. Do not choose this option if you plan to configure the computer to dual-boot between Windows 9x and Windows 2000, Windows NT, or Windows XP.

    • N to bypass enabling large disk support and use 16-bit FAT as the file system on your computer.

4.   If the computer is configured to dual-boot with Windows 2000, Windows NT, or Windows XP, and your computer has an NTFS partition, you will be asked if you want to treat NTFS partitions as large. Type N and press Enter.

5.   Type 1 and press Enter to create a DOS partition or logical DOS drive.

6. Type one of the following and press Enter:
   - 1 to create a primary DOS partition.
   - 2 to create an extended DOS partition.

   📌 Fdisk allows you to create one primary and one extended partition per hard disk. You must create the primary partition before you can create the extended partition.

7. If you are creating a primary DOS partition, type one of the following and press Enter:
   - Y to specify that you want Fdisk to create a primary partition from the maximum space available and mark the partition active.
   - N to specify you want to manually enter a size for your primary partition and manually mark it active.

8. If you are creating a primary DOS partition and you entered N to specify you want to manually enter a size for your primary partition and manually mark it active, type the size for your primary partition in percentage or megabytes and press Enter. You might see that Fdisk adjusts the size you enter.

9. If you are creating a primary DOS partition and you manually entered a size for your primary partition, set the primary partition as active:
   1. Type 2 and press Enter.
   2. Use the arrow keys to highlight the partition you want to be marked active.
   3. Press Enter.

10. If you are creating an extended DOS partition, type the size for your extended partition in percentage or megabytes and press Enter.

11. Press Esc to return to the Fdisk main menu.

12. If you are creating an extended DOS partition, press Enter to confirm that you want to create a logical drive within your computer's extended partition.

13. If you are creating an extended DOS partition, the logical drive information is displayed. Press Esc to return to the Fdisk main menu. You might see that Fdisk adjusted the size you entered for the partition.

14. Press Esc to exit out of Fdisk.

15. Press Esc to exit from the message prompting you to shut down Windows.

16. Press Ctrl+Alt+Delete to restart your computer.

17. If the computer is configured to dual-boot, from the boot menu, choose Microsoft Windows.

18. Format the newly created partition so that it is usable within Windows 9x:
    - Using the `format` command line utility:
      a. At the C:\Windows prompt, type `format drive_letter:`.

      📌 The drive letter is the letter assigned to the partition by Fdisk.

      b. Press Enter.
      c. Type Y and press Enter to confirm you want to format your drive.

    d.   When the format is complete, either type a label for your drive and press Enter, or press Enter to leave the label blank.

- Using Windows Explorer:

    a.   Open Windows Explorer.

    b.   Right-click the new partition's drive letter and choose Format.

    c.   Click Start.

    d.   Click OK to confirm that you want to format the partition.

    e.   Click OK again to confirm formatting the partition.

    f.   Click Close to close the Format Results dialog box.

    g.   Click OK to close the message box prompting you to run ScanDisk.

    h.   Close Windows Help.

    i.   Close the Format dialog box.

    j.   Close Windows Explorer.

19. In Windows Explorer, verify that you can access the new drive.

Procedure Reference: Delete Partitions on a Windows 9x Computer

To delete a partition on a Windows 9x computer using Fdisk.exe:

1.   Restart the computer in MS-DOS mode.

    a.   Choose Start→Shut Down.

    b.   In the Shut Down Windows dialog box, select Restart In MS-DOS Mode.

    c.   Click OK.

2.   At the C:\Windows prompt, type `fdisk` and press Enter.

3.   If you have a Windows 98 computer with a hard disk larger than 512 MB, type one of the following and press Enter:

- Y to enable large disk support and use 32-bit FAT as the file system on your computer.

- N to bypass enabling large disk support and use 16-bit FAT as the file system on your computer.

4.   If the computer is configured to dual boot with Windows 2000, Windows NT, or Windows XP, and your computer has an NTFS partition, you will be asked if you want to treat NTFS partitions as large. Type N and press Enter.

5.   Type 3 and press Enter to delete a DOS partition or logical DOS drive.

6.   Type one of the following and press Enter:

- 1 to delete a primary DOS partition.

- 2 to delete an extended DOS partition.

- 3 to delete a logical drive within an extended DOS partition.

- 4 to delete a non-DOS partition, such as NTFS partitions created by Windows 2000.

When you are deleting partitions, you must delete any existing partitions in the following order:

A.   Any logical drives within the extended MS-DOS partition.

B.   The extended partition.

C.   The primary MS-DOS partition.

7.   Type the number of the partition or the letter of the logical drive you want to delete and press Enter.

8.   If prompted, enter the volume label and press Enter.

9.   Type Y and press Enter to verify you want to delete the entered partition or drive.

10. Press Esc to return to the Fdisk main menu.

11. Press Esc to exit out of Fdisk.

12. Press Esc to exit from the message prompting you to shut down Windows.

13. Press Ctrl+Alt+Delete to restart your computer.

If you deleted your primary partition, you will need an MS-DOS boot disk to restart the computer.

ACTIVITY 8-1

Creating an Extended Partition on a Windows 98 Computer

Setup:
In Windows 2000, open Computer Management and delete the Z drive.

Scenario:
When the Windows 98 computers in AlphaBeta Company were set up, the primary partition that Windows 98 was installed on didn't take up the entire space available on the hard disk—1 GB of free space was left. Over the years, users have utilized much of the space on the existing primary partition. The Administrative Assistant at AlphaBeta has asked you to make the extra space on her computer usable for storing additional files.

What You Do	How You Do It
1. **Restart Windows 98 in MS-DOS mode.**	a. **Restart the computer and choose Microsoft Windows from the boot menu to load Windows 98.**
	b. **Log on as Admin#.**
	c. **Choose Start→Shut Down.**
	d. **In the Shut Down Windows dialog box, select Restart In MS-DOS Mode.**
	e. **Click OK.**

2. **Create a 1 GB extended partition on the computer.**

a. At the C:\Windows prompt, **enter fdisk**

b. **Enter N** to bypass enabling large disk support and use 16-bit FAT as the file system on your computer.

c. **Enter N** to bypass treating all NTFS partitions as large disks (you see this message only because you have NTFS partitions on the computer).

d. **Enter 1** to select Create A DOS Partition Or Logical DOS Drive.

e. **Enter 2** to select Create An Extended DOS Partition.

f. **Enter 1024.**

```
Enter partition size in Mbytes or percent of disk space (%) to
create an Extended DOS Partition.............................:[ 1024]
```

g. **Press Esc.**

h. **Press Enter** to confirm that you want to create a logical drive within your computer's extended partition. The logical drive information is displayed. You might see that Fdisk adjusted the size of the partition slightly.

```
Enter logical drive size in Mbytes or percent of disk space (%)...[ 1028]
```

i. **Press Esc** to return to the Fdisk main menu.

j. **Press Esc** to exit out of Fdisk.

k. **Press Esc again.**

l. **Press Ctrl+Alt+Delete** to reboot the computer.

m. **Choose Microsoft Windows from the boot menu** to load Windows 98.

---

3. Format the D drive.

a. Log on as Admin#.

b. Open Windows Explorer.

c. Right-click on D: and choose Format.

d. In the Format - (D:) dialog box, verify that Quick (Erase) is selected for the Format Type.

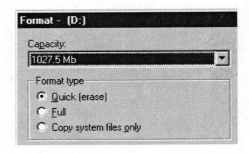

e. Click Start to begin the format.

f. Click OK to confirm that you want to format this drive.

g. Click OK again to confirm the format.

h. Click Close to close the Format Results dialog box.

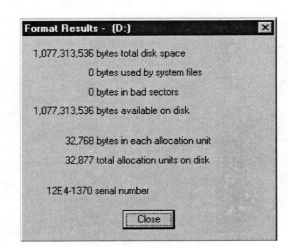

i. Click OK to close the ScanDisk message box.

j. Close Windows Help.

k. **Click Close.**

4. **Verify that you can access the D drive.**	a. In Windows Explorer, **select D:**. You don't see any files because the drive is empty.

TOPIC B

Compress a Hard Disk

An important part of managing a Windows 9x-based computer's hard disk resources is optimizing its disk space usage. If disk space on a computer is tight, you'll want to take any steps you can to maximize the available disk space. Compressing the hard disk is one technique you can use to increase available disk space, and that's what you'll learn in this topic.

Although hard disks these days are becoming bigger and bigger while their prices are steadily dropping, as an A+ technician, you're bound to encounter a situation where a company or client just can't afford to upgrade a computer's hard disk. Or, you might encounter a computer with BIOS that doesn't support the large hard disks available today. In either case, if such a computer is running out of available disk space, your best solution is to compress the hard disk. Compressing the hard disk will enable you to increase the available disk space on the computer without your having to upgrade the computer's hard disk or add a second disk to the computer.

How to Compress a Hard Disk

Procedure Reference: Compress a Drive

To compress a drive in Windows 9x:

 Do not compress the C drive if you dual-boot the computer between Windows 98 and Windows 2000, Windows XP, or Windows NT.

1. If necessary, install DriveSpace 3.

    a. In Control Panel, double-click Add/Remove Programs.

    b. Select the Windows Setup tab.

    c. In the Components list, select System Tools and click Details.

    d. Check Disk Compression Tools and click OK.

    e. In the Add/Remove Programs Properties dialog box, click OK.

    f. When prompted, insert the Windows 98 installation CD-ROM into the CD-ROM drive.

    g. Click OK.

    h. Close Control Panel.

2. Choose Start→Programs→Accessories→System Tools→DriveSpace.

3. In the DriveSpace dialog box, select the drive you want to compress.

4. Choose Drive→Compress.

5. If desired, click Options to change the drive letter of the host drive by selecting a letter from the drop-down list box and change the default free space available on the host drive. Click OK.

6. Click Start.

7. Click Yes if you want to update or create a Windows 98 startup disk. Otherwise, click No.

8. If you're compressing a drive on a dual-boot computer, click OK to close the message stating that a Windows 98 compressed drive isn't accessible by Windows NT, Windows 2000, and Windows XP.

9. If you want to back up your files before compressing the disk, click Back Up Files.

10. Click Compress Now to compress the disk.

11. Click Close to close the Compress A Drive dialog box.

12. If you see a message stating that the hard drive is full, click Cancel.

13. Close DriveSpace.

14. Click Yes to restart the computer.

⚠ You cannot compress drives that are formatted to FAT32.

Procedure Reference: Uncompress a Drive

To uncompress a compressed drive in Windows 9x:

1. Choose Start→Programs→Accessories→System Tools→DriveSpace.

2. In the DriveSpace dialog box, select the drive you want to uncompress.

3. Choose Drive→Uncompress.

4. Click Start.

5. Click Uncompress Now.

6. If you are uncompressing the last compressed drive, click Yes to remove the compression driver from memory.

7. Click Close to close the Uncompress A Drive dialog box.

8. Close DriveSpace.

9. Click Yes to restart the computer.

ACTIVITY 8-2

Compressing a Drive on a Windows 98 Computer

Setup:

You have created a D drive that is 1 GB in size. The Windows 98 installation files are in C:\Win98.

Scenario:

Your client, AlphaBeta Company, has many older Windows 98 computers with small hard disks. Users are complaining that they don't have enough room on their computers to store their files. They often have to do a bit of cleanup by deleting files or moving them to other media before they can save new ones on their D drives. With the downturn in the economy, AlphaBeta can't afford to replace the hard disks with larger ones. They've asked you to try to gain them more space on the hard disks without replacing them.

What You Do	How You Do It
1. Determine how much free space is on the D drive of your computer.	a. Open Win98-#.
	b. Select the D drive.
	c. Record the free space listed in the left pane:_____
	(D:) Local Disk Capacity: 1.00 GB ▨ Used: 0 bytes ▢ Free: 1.00 GB 
	d. Close Win98-#.
2. If necessary, **install DriveSpace 3.**	a. In Control Panel, **double-click Add/Remove Programs.**
	b. Select the Windows Setup tab.
	c. In the Components list, **select System Tools and click Details.**

d. **Check Disk Compression Tools and click OK.**

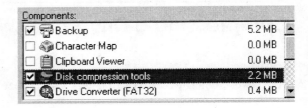

e. **Click OK.**

f. In the Insert Disk message box, **click OK.**

g. In the Copying Files dialog box, **enter c:\win98 and click OK.**

h. **Click OK.**

i. **Close Control Panel.**

3. **Compress the D drive on your computer.**

⚠ Do not compress the C drive.

a. **Choose Start→Programs→Accessories→ System Tools→DriveSpace.**

b. In the DriveSpace dialog box, **select Drive D.**

c. **Choose Drive→Compress.** Notice that you will nearly double the size of the D drive by compressing it.

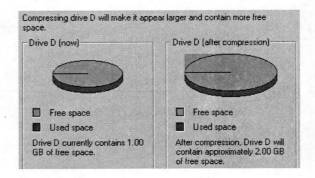

d. **Click Options.**

e. **Click OK** to accept the default host drive letter and free space size.

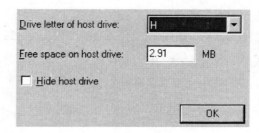

f. **Click Start.**

g. **Click No** to skip creating a Windows 98 Startup disk.

📌 A Windows 98 compressed drive is also not accessible in Windows 2000 or Windows XP.

h. **Click OK** to close the message box stating that a Windows 98 compressed drive is not accessible in Windows NT.

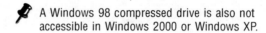

Windows NT, OS/2, or another operating system may be installed on your computer. If you compress drive D, you may not be able to access its contents while using another operating system.

OK   Cancel

i. If neccessary, **click Compress Now.**

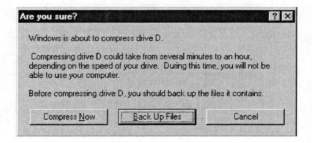

Are you sure?

Windows is about to compress drive D.

Compressing drive D could take from several minutes to an hour, depending on the speed of your drive. During this time, you will not be able to use your computer.

Before compressing drive D, you should back up the files it contains.

Compress Now   Back Up Files   Cancel

📌 Compressing the D drive will take several minutes.

j. **Click Cancel** to close the message stating that the hard disk is full (you receive this error message because the host file created on the D drive uses almost all of the available disk space).

k. **Click Close** to close the Compress A Drive dialog box.

l. **Close DriveSpace.**

m. When prompted, **click Yes** to restart the computer.

---

4. **Verify the free space on D.**

a. When the computer restarts, **choose Microsoft Windows** from the boot menu.

b. **Log on as Admin#.**

c. In Win98-#, **check the free space on D.** You should see that you now have 2 GB of free space (instead of 1 GB).

d. **Close My Computer.**

ACTIVITY 8-3

Uncompressing a Drive on a Windows 98 Computer

Scenario:

Your client, AlphaBeta Company, has many older Windows 98 computers with small hard disks. Users complained that they didn't have enough room on their computers to store their files, so their D drives were compressed using DriveSpace. The company has decided to replace the hard disks with larger ones and wants to make sure when they transfer the data to the new drive no compression information gets copied.

What You Do	How You Do It
1. **Uncompress the D drive on your computer.**	a. **Choose Start→Programs→Accessories→ System Tools→DriveSpace.**
	b. In the DriveSpace dialog box, **select the D drive.**

c. **Choose Drive→Uncompress.**

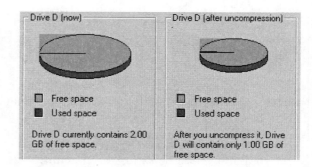

d. **Click Start.**

e. If neccessary, **click Uncompress Now.**

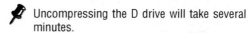 Uncompressing the D drive will take several minutes.

f. **Click Yes** to remove the compression driver from memory.

g. **Click Close.**

h. **Close DriveSpace.**

i. When prompted, **click Yes** to restart the computer.

2. **Verify that the D drive is no longer compressed.**

a. From the boot menu, **choose Microsoft Windows.**

b. **Log on as Admin#.**

c. In Win98-1, **check the free space on D.** You should see that you now have only 1 GB of free space.

d. **Close Win98-1.**

TOPIC C

Convert a FAT Partition to FAT32

In Topic 8A, you learned the steps for creating and formatting a FAT partition. However, for large hard disks on Windows 98-based computers, Microsoft recommends that you use the FAT32 file system instead. That's why you'll learn the steps for converting a FAT partition to the FAT32 file system in this topic.

As you know, hard disks just keep getting bigger and bigger in size. Using the FAT32 file system for a partition instead of the FAT file system improves the performance of the hard disk. Because the slowest hardware component in any computer is its hard disk, anything you can do to optimize the performance of the hard disk will improve the overall performance of the computer itself. And converting a FAT partition to FAT32 instead of deleting the partition and creating a new one means that you won't have to worry about losing the user's data. By converting from FAT to FAT32, you can easily switch a computer's hard disk to the optimized FAT32 file system without any loss of data.

The Conversion Process

When you convert a partition from FAT to FAT32, the conversion process:

1. Boots the computer into MS-DOS.
2. Runs ScanDisk to check the integrity of your disk and correct problems it detects.
3. Runs the converter to:
    a. Check your drives.
    b. Remove uninstall, multi-boot, and extended attribute files.
    c. Convert directories.
    d. Create space for the 32-bit file allocation table.
    e. Convert the file allocation table to 32 bits.
    f. Remove any unused clusters.
    g. Update the partition type.
    h. Update the master boot record.
    i. Update the copy of the file allocation table.
    j. Move the root directory to the beginning of the drive.
4. Boots back into Windows.
5. Runs the Disk Defragmenter.

Cluster Size

All operating systems read from and write to hard disks in chunks of bytes rather than byte by byte. These chunks are called *clusters*. Windows automatically selects the cluster size based on the size of the partition and the file system with which it's formatted. In Table 8-1 and Table 8-2, you see the cluster sizes for different partition sizes and the FAT and FAT32 file systems.

The cluster size determines the smallest unit of disk space the Windows operating system can use when writing to disk. For example, if you save a 1 KB file to a FAT partition that is 1,024 MB in size, Windows uses a 32 KB cluster to store that file; Windows cannot use the remaining 31 KB within that cluster. As you can see, the cluster size can affect the amount of available disk space dramatically. On the other hand, if you save that same 1 KB file to a 1,024 MB FAT32 partition, you see that Windows would use only a 4 KB cluster to store that same file. By using a smaller cluster size, the FAT32 partition is more efficient with using disk space.

Table 8-1: *FAT Cluster Sizes*

Partition Size	Cluster Size
0 – 15 MB	512 bytes
16 – 127 MB	2 KB
128 – 255 MB	4 KB
256 – 511 MB	8 KB
512 – 1,023 MB	16 KB
1,024 – 2,047 MB	32 KB
2,048 – 4,096 MB	64 KB (This cluster size is supported only on FAT partitions in Windows 2000, Windows NT, or Windows XP.)

Table 8-2: *FAT32 Cluster Sizes*

Partition Size	Cluster Size
0.256 – 8.01 GB	4 KB
8.02 – 16.02 GB	8 KB
16.03 – 32.04 GB	16 KB
> 32.04 GB	32 KB

How to Convert a FAT Partition to FAT32

Procedure Reference: Convert a FAT Partition to FAT32

To convert an existing FAT partition on a Windows 98 or Windows 95 OSR-2 computer to FAT32:

1. Choose Start→Programs→Accessories→System Tools→Drive Converter (FAT32). This menu shortcut runs the Drive Converter utility, cvt1.exe.

     If you would like information on the Drive Converter (FAT32) utility and limitations of the FAT32 file system, click Details.

2. Click Next.

3. In the Drives list box, select the FAT16 drive you want to convert.

4. Click Next.

5. Click OK to verify you understand the warning regarding OS limitations with FAT32 while dual-booting a computer.

Drive Converter scans your computer for anti-virus programs and disk utilities that will not work with FAT32.

6. If Drive Converter finds any incompatible programs or utilities, select them and choose Details.

7. Click Next.

8. If you have backup hardware installed on your computer and you want to back up your files before converting your drive to FAT32, click Create Backup.

9. Click Next.

10. Click Next to restart your computer in MS-DOS mode and begin the conversion.

> Depending on the size of the drive, the conversion could take several hours.

> The Drive Converter (FAT32) file, Cvt1.exe, is installed in the Windows folder by default.

ACTIVITY 8-4

Converting an Existing Windows 98 FAT Partition to FAT32

Scenario:

The AlphaBeta Company has many Windows 98 computers where space has become an issue. As a consultant, you interviewed many of the users and found that while they store a lot of files on the D drives of their hard disks, the size of the files they typically store is fairly small. You believe the cluster size being used on the FAT16 partition may be increasing the amount of space each file consumes. You want to reduce the cluster size in hopes of regaining quite a bit of unused space on each computer for your client.

What You Do	How You Do It
1. Convert the D drive to FAT32. ⚠ Do not convert the C drive to FAT32.	a. Choose Start→Programs→Accessories→ System Tools→Drive Converter (FAT32). b. Click Next.

c. In the Drives list box, **select the D drive.**

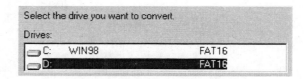

d. **Click Next.**

e. If necessary, **click OK** to close any anti-virus messages.

f. **Click OK** to verify you understand the warning regarding OS limitations with FAT32 while dual-booting a computer.

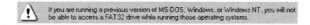

If you are running a previous version of MS-DOS, Windows, or Windows NT, you will not be able to access a FAT32 drive while running those operating systems.

g. **Click Next twice** to advance the Disk Converter wizard.

h. **Click Next** to restart your computer in MS-DOS mode and begin the conversion.

i. From the boot menu, **choose Microsoft Windows.**

j. **Log on as Admin#.**

k. **Click Finish** to close the Drive Converter (FAT32) wizard.

The conversion was successful.

2. **Verify the drive has been converted to FAT32.**

a. **Open Windows Explorer.**

b. **Right-click the D drive and choose Properties.** The File System reads FAT32.

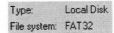

| Type: | Local Disk |
| File system: | FAT32 |

c. **Click OK.**

d. **Close Windows Explorer.**

TOPIC D

Defragment a Hard Disk

Part of managing disk resources in Windows 9x is to keep the disks performing optimally. This can be accomplished by defragmenting the hard disk on a consistent basis. In this topic, you'll learn the steps for defragmenting a hard disk in Windows 9x.

Defragmenting your disks improves their performance and life expectancy by allowing for more efficient storage of files. More efficient storage of files means less physical wear and tear on the heads of the disks themselves, quicker operating system and application startup times, faster application performance, and more rapid retrieval of files.

How to Defragment a Hard Disk

Procedure Reference: Defragment a Hard Disk

To defragment a drive in Windows 9x:

1. Choose Start→Programs→Accessories→System Tools→Disk Defragmenter.

2. In the Select Drive dialog box, select the drive you want to defragment.

3. In Windows 95, click the Advanced button if you want to change the settings of the defragmentation utility from the default.

   In Windows 98, click the Settings button if you want to change the settings of the defragmentation utility from the default.

   Click OK to close the Settings dialog box.

4. Click OK.

5. If you want to see the details of the defragmentation process on your hard disk, click Show Details.

   Click Hide Details to show only the summary information.

6. Click Yes to close Disk Defragmenter when the defragmentation process is complete.

ACTIVITY 8-5

Defragmenting a Hard Disk in Windows 98

Scenario:

Some of the users at your client, AlphaBeta Company, have been complaining that their Windows 98 computers have slowed down to a crawl. They say that it takes forever to load the operating system at startup. Some application startup times are much slower than others, and the computer takes a long time to respond to their input. After interviewing the users, you discover that the computers get passed from an exiting employee to their replacement. Preparation of the computer for the new employee only includes deleting personal files of the exiting employee and removing any unnecessary or unauthorized programs applications. You suspect that the hard disks are very fragmented causing inefficient storage of files. Each computer has a single C partition on its hard disk.

What You Do	How You Do It
1. Defragment your computer.	a. Choose Start→Programs→Accessories→System Tools→Disk Defragmenter.
	b. In the Select Drive dialog box, the C drive is selected by default. **Click OK** to start the defragmentation process.
	c. **Click Show Details** to graphically display the defragmentation process.
	d. **Click Legend** to display the legend for the various graphics you see in the Show Details window.

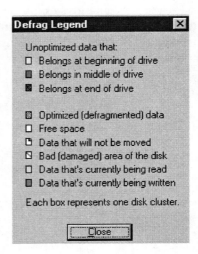

e. **Click Close** to close the Defrag Legend dialog box.

f. **Click Yes** to close Disk Defragmenter when defragmentation is finished.

Lesson 8 Follow-up

In this lesson, you learned how to create, manage, and delete partitions in the Windows 9x environment. By properly configuring the partitions in your Windows 9x computers, your users will be able to access the hard disk resources they need to do their jobs.

1. **In your organization, or the organizations you support, what disk management tasks are you expected to perform? Why?**

2. **In your organization or the organizations you support, what is the configuration of the hard disk partitions on your Windows 9x computers? Why?**

LESSON 9

Connecting to Internet and Intranet Resources

Lesson Time
2 hour(s)

Lesson Objectives:

In this lesson, you will connect to Internet and intranet resources.

You will:

*   Create a dial-up connection.

*   Create a VPN connection.

*   Configure a Web browser.

*   Configure an email client.

*   Troubleshoot Internet and intranet connections.

Introduction

Earlier in this course you worked through a number of tasks you'll be expected to perform to connect Windows-based computers to a network. In this lesson, you'll learn about the additional steps you'll need to take to connect computers to the Internet and how to connect remote computers to your corporate intranet. You'll also learn how to configure the software your users will most commonly use when accessing the Internet or intranet: a Web browser and an email client.

The ability for users to access information on the Internet and share information on company intranets is vital to organizations. It is your responsibility, as an A+ technician, to maintain and support these crucial connections so that users have the access they need.

The following CompTIA A+ Operating System Technologies (2003) Examination objectives are covered in this lesson:

- Topic A:
  — 4.2 Connectivity technologies: Dial-up networking, DSL networking, ISDN networking, Cable, Satellite, Wireless, LAN.
  — 4.2 Installing and configuring browsers: Configure security settings.
- Topic C:
  — 4.2 Protocols and terminologies: HTML, HTTP, SSL, Telnet, FTP.
  — 4.2 Installing and configuring browsers: Enable/disable script support, Configure proxy settings.
- Topic D:
  — 4.2 Protocols and terminologies: E-mail (POP, SMTP, IMAP).
- Topic E:
  — 2.5 Caches, Temporary File Management.
  — 3.3 Other Common Problems: Option (Sound card, modem, input device) or will not function.

TOPIC A

Create a Dial-up Connection

Earlier in this course, you configured all of the network components necessary for your users to make local connections to your company's network, including installing a LAN driver, installing and configuring network protocols, and optionally installing a network client. But in today's environment, more and more users telecommute—which means they'll need to be able to access your company's intranet via a remote connection. Likewise, these same users might also need access to the Internet. In order to accommodate remote users, in this topic, you'll learn how to create dial-up connections that your users can use to access your company's intranet and the Internet.

As you know, providing users with reliable access to network resources enables them to perform the tasks they need to accomplish their jobs. This situation is no different when users connect to your network from a remote location: Users still need to be able to access network resources (including the Internet) reliably. By mastering the skills necessary to configure remote users with dial-up connections, you'll be able to keep your company's users working productively regardless of where they are. In addition, properly configuring users' dial-up connections will help minimize the amount of time you must spend troubleshooting their connections.

Outbound Connection

Definition:

An outbound connection, also referred to as a remote connection or remote-access connection, is a network connection that connects clients on one physical network to resources on a remote network. Outbound connections use:

- LAN or WAN media to carry the data from the client to the remote network.

- Remote access protocols, to transmit packets on a variety of WAN media types.

- A server running remote-access software (RAS) on the remote network to act as a gateway between the client and the remote network's resources.

- Remote client adapter hardware.

- Authentication methods to establish secure communications between the client and the RAS server.

The WAN media can be Public Switched Telephone Network (PSTN), Digital Subscriber Line (DSL), Integrated Services Digital Network (ISDN), or X.25 (a technology that breaks transmissions up into packets and transmits them over a worldwide telecommunications network). Client hardware can be a specialized modem, adapter, or packet assembler/disassembler (PAD). The data within the communication might be encrypted. Table 9-1 gives a brief description of each of these media types and the typical client adapter hardware you need for the connection.

Table 9-1: *WAN Media Types*

WAN Media Type	Description	Typical Client Adapter Hardware
qPSTN	Standard analog telephone lines. Also referred to as Plain Old Telephone Service (POTS).	Modem
DSL	High-speed (broadband) network access from telephone service providers that piggybacks over analog phone lines.	DSL modem
Cable	Broadband network access that piggybacks on existing cable TV infrastructure.	Cable modem
ISDN	A network of leased digital phone lines.	ISDN adapter
X.25	A worldwide packet-switching telecommunications network.	Packet Assembler/ Disassembler (PAD)
Satellite	Network transmissions are bounced off satellites orbiting above the Earth.	Satellite dish and decoder

WAN Media Type	Description	Typical Client Adapter Hardware
Wireless	Devices can communicate without physical connection through the use of wireless transmissions that use cellular telephone networks.	Wireless network adapter and antenna

 Individual clients rarely connect directly to ISDN and X.25 networks. The connectivity is usually provided by a dedicated server that the client connects to through other means.

Example: Example: Dial-up Connection

A dial-up connection is an example of an outbound connection. In a dial-up connection, a user at the remote client uses a modem attached to their computer to dial in across phone lines to a modem connected to remote access server on the remote network. The client communicates with the server using the most common Windows dial-up RAS protocol Point-to-Point Protocol (PPP).

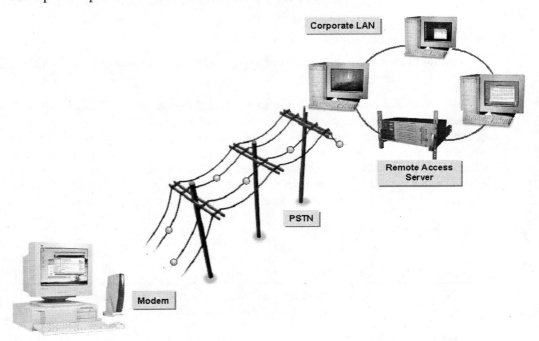

Figure 9-1: *A dial-up connection.*

Example: Example: Virtual Private Network Connection

A Virtual Private Network (VPN) connection is an example of an outbound connection. In a VPN connection, a user dials up to their Internet service provider. The client then establishes a connection with the company's Internet gateway server. The client uses the Internet gateway at that company's LAN to connect to through the Internet to their own company's VPN server. The client communicates with the VPN server using Point-to-Point Tunneling Protocol (PPTP), a Microsoft proprietary VPN protocol.

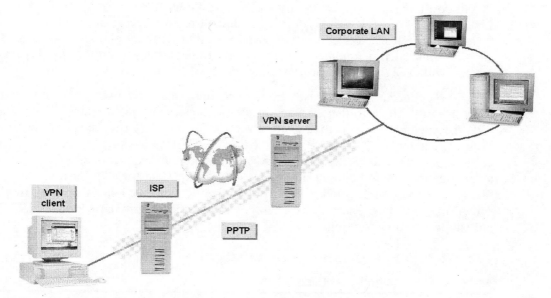

Figure 9-2: *A Virtual Private Network connection.*

Non-Example: Non-example: Cable Modems

Cable modems, another popular method for broadband connectivity from homes to the Internet, operate through the coaxial cable television network, not the phone system. These connections generally appear to the user as local area connections and use LAN protocols to communicate with the remote network.

Dial-Up Connection

Definition:

A dial-up connection is an outbound connection that uses WAN transmission media such as modems and phone lines to connect a client on one physical network to a Remote Access Server (RAS) on a remote network. The client communicates over the connection using a remote access protocol designed for communication over phone lines.

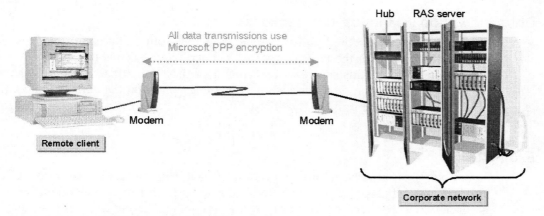

Figure 9-3: *A detailed dial-up connection.*

In Windows, the remote access protocol can be Point-to-Point Protocol (PPP) or Serial Line Internet Protocol (SLIP). PPP is the default remote access protocol in Windows that can transmit packets created with various different LAN protocols such as TCP/IP and NWLink. SLIP is another remote access protocol that can only transmit packets created with TCP/IP and must transmit over serial lines.

A dial-up connection always uses an authentication method to secure the communications from the client to the RAS server as it moves across phone lines. When using PPP, the authentication method can be Microsoft Challenge Handshake Authentication Protocol version 2 (MS-CHAP v2), MS-CHAP, CHAP, Password Authentication Protocol (PAP)/Clear Text, Shiva PAP (SPAP), or Smart Card Authentication. The authentication method chosen might also encrypt the data for additional security. Table 9-2 gives a brief description of each PPP authentication method. To connect to a SLIP server, the user must enter user credentials in a separate terminal window. SLIP does not support data encryption.

Table 9-2: *RAS PPP Authentication Methods*

Authentication Method	Description
MS-CHAP v2	A Microsoft encrypted-password authentication protocol. Supports mutual client-server authentication and data encryption.
MS-CHAP	The original version of MS-CHAP. It does not support mutual authentication.
CHAP	An encrypted-password protocol that supports connection to some third-party PPP servers. It does not support data encryption.
PAP/Clear Text	Sends clear-text passwords. PAP/Clear text should only be used to connect to servers that don't support password encryption.
SPAP	A proprietary version of PAP used to connect to RAS servers manufactured by the Shiva Corporation.
Smart Card Authentication	Uses authentication information encoded on a smart card. The user must insert the smart card into a reader device connected to the client in order to establish the remote connection. Smart Card and other external authentication methods are supported by the Extensible Authentication Protocol (EAP).

Data Encryption for Dial-up Connections

The authentication method you choose ensures that your client can establish secure communications with the target server. Data encryption ensures that the content of your communication remains secure as it travels over the phone lines. If you use MS-CHAP or EAP authentication, you can also use data encryption on the connection. Outbound PPP connections use proprietary Microsoft Point-to-Point Encryption (MPPE) to encrypt data.

Example:

A remote client uses a dial-up connection to establish communication through their modem and public phone lines to their company's RAS server. The client sends the information to the server using PPP. The PPP communication is secured using MS-CHAP v2. As the data travels to the RAS server over the phone lines it is encrypted using Microsoft Point-to-Point Encryption. The client validates the identity of the server. The server validates the identity of the client and sends data back using PPP as well.

How to Create a Dial-up Connection

Procedure Reference: Create a Dial-up Connection in Windows 2000

To create a dial-up connection on a Windows 2000 computer:

1. Log on as a local administrator.

2. If necessary, install a modem.

   a. Open Control Panel.

   b. Double-click Phone And Modem Options.

   c. In the Location Information dialog box, enter your area code or city code.

   d. If necessary, enter the number you dial to access an outside line.

   e. Select tone or pulse dialing.

   f. Click OK.

   g. Select the Modems tab.

   h. Click Add to add a new modem.

   i. If you have a Plug and Play modem, click Next to have Windows 2000 detect your modem.

      If you have a non-Plug and Play modem, check Don't Detect My Modem, I Will Select It From A List.

      Click Next.

   j. If you are installing a non-Plug and Play modem, below Manufacturers, select the name of your modem's manufacturer. Below Models, select the model of your modem.

      If your modem is not in the list, you will need an installation disk from the manufacturer. Insert it in your floppy disk drive and click Have Disk. Select your modem and click OK.

      Click Next.

   k. In the Select The Port To Use With This Modem list box, select the port your modem will communicate through.

   l. Click Next.

   m. Click Finish.

   n. Click OK to close the Phone And Modems dialog box.

   o. Close Control Panel.

3. Create a new connection object.

   a. Choose Start→Settings→Network and Dial-Up Connections→Make New Connection.

   b. Click Next.

   c. Select Dial-Up To Private Network.

   d. Click Next.

   e. If you have more than one communications device installed on your computer, check the device(s) you want the connection to use.

   f. Click Next.

g.   Check Use Dialing Rules.

h.   Enter the area code for the remote access server.

i.   Enter the telephone number for the remote access server.

j.   Select your country or region code.

k.   Click Next.

l.   Select Create This Connection For All Users or Only For Myself.

m.   Click Next.

n.   Enter a name for your connection.

o.   Click Finish.

4.   If necessary, make changes to the default configuration information for the connection.

a.   Choose Start→Settings→Network and Dial-Up Connections.

b.   Right-click your connection object and choose Properties.

c.   On the General page, you can change the following configuration information:

- The modem or device the connection uses.
- Click the Configure button to make configuration changes to the modem hardware.
- Enable or disable all devices using the same phone number.
- Enable or disable using dialing rules.
- Area code.
- Telephone number.
- Country code.
- Enabling or disabling the display of an icon on the taskbar when you're using this connection.

d.   On the Options page, you can change the following configuration information:

- Enable or disable dialing options.
- Enable or disable redialing option.
- Configuring multiple devices assigned to the connection.
- Configuring X.25 logon configuration settings.

e.   On the Security page, you can change the following configuration information:

- Validation type for passwords.
- Data encryption and logon security.
- Interactive logon and scripting.

f.   On the Networking page, you can change the following configuration information:

- Type of dial-up server and its settings.
- The networking components used by the connection and their properties.

g.   On the Sharing page, you can specify whether or not the connection will be shared. Along with whether or not you want on-demand dialing for the connection.

h.   Click OK.

Procedure Reference: Create a Dial-up Connection to a Private Server in Windows XP

To create a dial-up connection to a private server in Windows XP:

1.   Log on as a local administrator.

2.   If necessary, install a modem.

   a.   Open Control Panel.

   b.   Click Printers And Other Hardware.

   c.   Click Phone And Modem Options.

   d.   Select the Modems tab.

   e.   Click Add to add a new modem.

   f.   If you have a Plug and Play modem, click Next to have Windows XP detect your modem.

   If you have a non-Plug and Play modem, check Don't Detect My Modem, I Will Select It From A List.

   Click Next.

   g.   If you are installing a non-Plug and Play modem, below Manufacturer, select the name of your modem's manufacturer. Below Models, select the model of your modem.

   If your modem is not in the list, you will need an installation disk from the manufacturer. Insert it in your floppy disk drive and click Have Disk. Select your modem and click OK.

   Click Next.

   h.   Select the port your modem will communicate through.

   i.   Click Next.

   j.   Click Finish.

   k.   Click OK to close the Phone and Modem Options dialog box.

3.   Create a new connection object.

   a.   In Control Panel, click Network And Internet Connections.

   b.   Click Network Connections.

   c.   Click Create A New Connection.

   d.   Click Next.

   e.   On the Network Connection Type page, select Connect To The Network At My Workplace.

   f.   Click Next.

   g.   Verify that Dial-Up Connection is selected and click Next.

   h.   In the Company Name text box, type a name for the connection.

   i.   Click Next.

j. In the Phone Number text box, type the phone number for the server to which the computer will connect.

k. Click Next.

l. Select Create This Connection For Anyone's Use or My Use Only.

m. Click Next.

n. If you want to create a shortcut to this connection on the desktop, check Add A Shortcut To This Connection To My Desktop.

o. Click Finish.

4. In the Connect dialog box for the new dial-up connection, complete the following tasks:

a. In the User Name text box, type the user name you must use to connect to the remote server.

b. In the Password text box, type this user account's password.

c. If you want to save the user account information with the connection, check Save This User Name And Password For The Following Users and select one of the following:

- Me Only, if you want to save the user account information for only your user.

- Anyone Who Uses This Computer, if you want all users of the computer to use the same user account information when connecting to the remote server.

d. Click Dial to connect to the server, or click Cancel to close the Connect dialog box.

5. If necessary, make changes to the default configuration information for the connection.

a. In Control Panel, click Network And Internet Connections.

b. Click Network Connections.

c. Right-click your connection object and choose Properties.

d. On the General page, you can change the following configuration information:

- The modem or device the connection uses.

- Click the Configure button to make configuration changes to the modem hardware.

- Enable or disable all devices using the same phone number.

- Enable or disable using dialing rules.

- Area code.

- Telephone number.

- Alternate phone numbers.

- Enabling or disabling the display of an icon on the taskbar when you're using this connection.

e. On the Options page, you can change the following configuration information:

- Enable or disable dialing options.

- Enable or disable redialing option.

- Configuring X.25 logon configuration settings.

f. On the Security page, you can change the following configuration information:

- Validation type for passwords.

- Data encryption and logon security.

- Interactive logon and scripting.

g. On the Networking page, you can change the following configuration information:

- Type of dial-up server and its settings.

- The networking components used by the connection and their properties.

h. On the Advanced page, you can specify the following configuration information:

- Whether or not you want to implement an Internet Connection Firewall.

- Whether or not the connection will be shared, along with whether or not you want on-demand dialing for the connection.

i. Click OK to close the dial-up connection's Properties dialog box.

6. Test the connection.

Procedure Reference: Create a Dial-up Connection in Windows NT

To create a dial-up connection on a Windows NT computer:

1. Log on as a local administrator.

2. If necessary, install a modem.

a. Open Control Panel.

b. Double-click Modems.

c. If you want to have Windows NT attempt to detect your modem for you, click Next.

d. If you want to manually add your modem, select Don't Detect My Modem; I Will Select It From A List and click Next.

e. If you are manually adding your modem, or if Windows NT did not correctly locate your modem, below Manufacturers, select the name of your modem's manufacturer. Below Models, select the model of your modem.

If your modem is not in the list, you will need an installation disk from the manufacturer. Insert it in the floppy disk drive or CD-ROM drive and click Have Disk. Select your modem and click OK.

f. Click Next.

g. In the On Which Ports Do You Want To Install It list, select the ports your modem will communicate through.

h. Click Next.

i. Click Finish.

j. Click Close to close the Modems Properties dialog box.

k. Close Control Panel.

3. From the Start menu, choose Programs→Accessories→Dial-Up Networking.

4. If necessary, click Install to install the Dial-Up Networking components.

   a. If prompted, insert the Windows NT installation CD-ROM or enter a path to the Windows NT installation files.

   b. In the Add RAS Device dialog box, select your modem and click OK.

   c. Click Continue.

   d. When prompted, click Restart to restart your computer.

   e. Log back on as a local administrator.

   f. From the Start menu, choose Programs→Accessories→Dial-Up Networking.

5. In the What Area (Or City) Code Are You In Now text box, type your area code and click Close.

6. Click OK to begin adding a phonebook entry to the phonebook.

   a. In the Name The New Phonebook Entry text box, type a name for the new connection.

   b. If you are familiar with creating phonebook entries, select I Know All About Phonebook Entries And Would Rather Edit The Properties Directly, or click Next to use the New Phonebook Entry Wizard.

   c. In the Server dialog box, click Next.

   d. Check Use Telephony Dialing Properties.

   e. In the Phone Number text box, type the area code and telephone number of the server you will call. If you have multiple numbers for the same server, click Alternates to add the additional numbers.

   f. Click Next.

   g. Click Finish.

7. If necessary, make changes to the default configuration information for the phonebook entry.

   a. Open Dial-Up Networking.

   b. Select an entry from the Phonebook Entry To Dial drop-down list.

   c. Click More.

   d. Click Edit Entry And Modem Properties.

   e. On the Basic page, you can change the following configuration information:

      • Entry name

      • Comment

      • Country code

      • Area code

      • Phone numbers

      • Whether to use Telephony dialing properties

      • Which modem(s) to use for the entry

   f. On the Server page, you can change the following configuration information:

      • Dial-up server type

      • Network protocols

      • Compression

      • PPP LCP extensions

g. On the Script page, you can change login script information.

h. On the Security page, you can change authentication and encryption settings.

i. On the X.25 page, you can change X.25 network logon options.

j. Click OK to save your changes.

Procedure Reference: Create a Dial-up Connection in Windows 98

To create a dial-up connection on a Windows 98 computer:

1. Install the Dial-Up Networking Windows Setup component.

   a. Choose Start→Settings→Control Panel.

   b. Double-click Add/Remove Programs.

   c. Select the Windows Setup tab.

   d. Select (don't uncheck!) Communications.

   e. Click Details.

   f. Check Dial-Up Networking.

   g. Click OK.

   h. Click OK.

   i. If prompted, enter the path to the Windows 9x setup files and click OK.

   j. Reboot the computer when prompted.

   ✐ If you have a modem already installed on the computer that you want to use for the dial-up connection, you can skip step #1.

2. If you don't have a modem already installed, install a modem.

   a. Open Control Panel.

   b. Double-click Modems.

   c. If a modem is already installed on the computer, click Add to add a new modem.

   d. If you have a plug and play modem, click Next to have Windows 9x detect your modem.

      If you have a non-plug and play modem, check Don't Detect My Modem, I Will Select It From A List.

      Click Next.

   e. If you are installing a non-plug and play modem, in the Manufacturers list box, select the name of your modem's manufacturer. In the Models list box, select the model of your modem.

      If your modem is not in the list, you will need an installation disk from the manufacturer. Insert it in your floppy disk drive and click Have Disk. Select your modem and click OK.

      Click Next.

   f. In the Select The Port To Use With This Modem list box, select the port your modem will communicate through.

   g. Click Next.

   h. Click Finish.

3. If you just installed a modem, configure telephony dialing properties.

    a. After you install the first modem on your computer, the Location dialog box opens. Select your country.

    b. Enter your area code or city code.

    c. If necessary, enter the number you dial to access an outside line.

    d. Select tone or pulse dialing.

    e. Click OK.

4. Create a new connection object.

    a. Open My Computer.

    b. Double-click Dial-Up Networking.

    c. Double-click Make New Connection.

    d. Enter a name for your connection.

    e. If you have more than one modem installed on your computer, select the modem you want the connection to use.

    f. Click Next.

    g. Enter the area code for the remote access server.

    h. Enter the telephone number for the remote access server.

    i. Select your country or region code.

    j. Click Next.

    k. Click Finish.

5. If necessary, make changes to the default configuration information for the connection.

    a. In the Dial-Up Networking folder, right-click your connection and choose Properties.

    b. On the General page, you can change the following configuration information:

        • Area code.

        • Telephone number.

        • Country code.

        • Enable or disable Use Area Code and Dialing Properties.

        • The modem the connection uses.

        • Click the Configure button to make configuration changes to the modem hardware.

    c. On the Server Types page, you can change the following configuration information:

        • Type of dial-up server.

        • Enabling or disabling logging on to the network.

        • Enabling or disabling software compression.

        • Enabling or disabling password encryption.

        • Enabling or disabling data encryption.

        • Enabling or disabling recording a log file for the connection.

        • Selecting the protocols that will be used by the connection.

- Click the TCP/IP Settings button to make changes to the TCP/IP protocol for the connection.

d. On the Scripting page, you can specify a script assigned to the connection for manual logon.

e. On the Multilink page, you can specify two or more devices to increase the bandwidth of your dial-up connection.

ACTIVITY 9-1

Creating a Dial-up Connection on a Windows 2000 Computer

Setup:

Restart the computer to Windows 2000.

Setup:

Smith Sales and Service's remote access server is running the TCP/IP protocol exclusively. The phone number for access is (585)555–5555.

Scenario:

You work for Smith Sales and Service in the IT department. Many of Smith's employees work from their homes across the United States and dial in to the company's Remote Access Server (RAS) for access to company email and network resources. Jane is a new employee who needs her desktop computer configured for dial-in access from her home in the 315 area code to the company's RAS server. A Cirrus Logic Cirrus Data Fax Voice MDK1414EC2 modem has been installed in her computer, but Windows 2000 did not recognize it and the drivers aren't installed yet. Jane tells you that her phone service is tone and she doesn't dial anything special to dial out.

What You Do	How You Do It
1. Install the Cirrus Logic MDK1414EC2 modem's drivers on your computer.	a. Log on as Admin#.
	b. Open Control Panel.
	c. Double-click Phone And Modem Options.
	d. In the Location Information dialog box, enter *315* as the area code.
	e. Verify that Tone Dialing is selected.
	f. Click OK.
	g. Select the Modems tab.
	h. Click Add.
	i. Check Don't Detect My Modem, I Will Select It From A List.

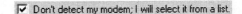

j. Click Next.

k. In the Manufacturers list box, **select Cirrus Logic.**

l. In the Models list box, **select Cirrus Data Fax Voice MDK1414EC2.**

m. Click Next.

n. In the Select The Port To Use With This Modem list box, **select one of the available COM ports.**

> You have selected the following modem:
>
> Cirrus Data Fax Voice MDK1414EC2
>
> On which ports do you want to install it?
>
> ○ All ports
> ● Selected ports
>
> **COM1**

o. **Click Next.**

p. **Click Finish.**

q. **Click OK** to close the Phone and Modem Options dialog box.

r. **Close Control Panel.**

---

2. **Create a new connection object to the RAS server.**

a. **Choose Start→Settings→Network and Dial-Up Connections. Double-click Make New Connection.**

b. **Click Next.**

c. **Select Dial-Up To Private Network.**

> ● **Dial-up to private network**
> Connect using my phone line (modem or ISDN).

d. **Click Next.**

e. If necessary, on the Select A Device page, **check the modem you want this connection to use and click Next.**

f. **Check Use Dialing Rules.**

g. **Enter** *585* **for the area code of the** remote access server.

h. **Enter** *555-5555* **as the telephone number** for the remote access server.

i. Select the Unites States of America (1).

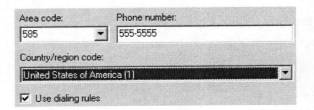

j. Click Next.

k. Verify that Create This Connection For All Users is selected.

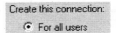

l. Click Next.

m. Enter *Smith Remote Access* as the name for your connection.

n. Click Finish.

o. Click **Cancel** to close the Connect Smith Remote Access dialog box.

3. **Configure the Smith Remote Access connection to use only the TCP/IP protocol.**

a. **Right-click your connection object and choose Properties.**

b. **Select the Networking tab.**

c. In the Components Checked Are Used By This Connection box, **verify that only Internet Protocol (TCP/IP) and Client For Microsoft Networks are checked. Uncheck any other protocols.**

d. **Click OK** to save your changes.

TOPIC B

Create a VPN Connection

In Topic 9A, you learned how to connect a remote computer to your corporate intranet by defining a dial-up connection. Another and even faster technique you can use to connect users to your intranet is to create a VPN connection. In this topic, you'll learn the steps for creating a VPN connection.

In many cases, users who telecommute will have faster connections to the Internet than a dial-up connection. For example, the typical speed of a DSL connection is up to 1.5 Mbps, whereas the fastest speed of a modem is only 56 Kbps. Because so many users have such fast connections to the Internet, they'll see significantly faster performance if they can connect to your company's intranet via the Internet instead of a dial-up modem. By configuring VPN connections, you'll enable your users to take advantage of their fast Internet connections—which means they'll be able to work more productively when telecommuting.

Virtual Private Network Connection

Definition:

A Virtual Private Network (VPN) connection is an outbound connection that uses existing local or outbound connection objects to connect a client on one physical network, through a private connection over a public network, to a VPN server on a remote network.

The client communicates over the connection using a VPN protocol designed for secure communication over public networks such as the Internet.

In Windows, the VPN protocol can be Point-to-Point Tunneling Protocol (PPTP) or Layer Two Tunneling Protocol (L2TP). PPTP is a Microsoft proprietary VPN protocol for connecting to Microsoft Routing and Remote Access Service (RRAS) servers running PPP. L2TP is an Internet standard VPN protocol for connecting a variety of VPN servers, including RRAS servers running L2TP.

A VPN connection always uses data encryption to keep the connection secure. PPP uses MPPE for data encryption. L2TP requires IP Security (IPSec), an industry-standard set of specification for creating end-to-end security on IP networks.

Example: Example: VPN Connection

A corporate sales representative attaches her laptop to a LAN network port at a client's office to connect to the Internet. Her computer then uses the Internet to connect to a private VPN server at her home office. The communication across the Internet is transmitted using PPTP and is encrypted using MPPE.

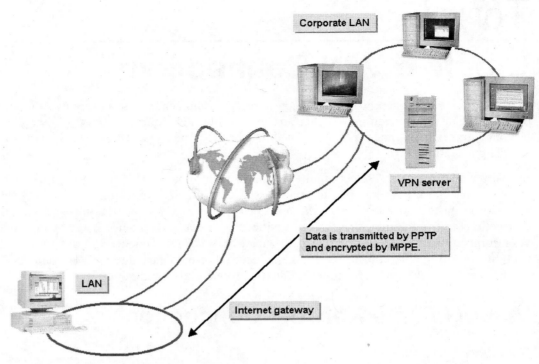

Figure 9-4: *A detailed VPN connection.*

How to Create a VPN Connection

Procedure Reference: Create a VPN Connection in Windows 2000

To create a VPN connection on a Windows 2000 computer:

1. Log on as a local administrator.

2. Create a new connection object.

   a. Choose Start→Settings→Network and Dial-Up Connections→Make New Connection.

   b. Click Next.

   c. Select Connect To A Private Network Through The Internet.

   d. Click Next.

   e. Select one of the following:

      - Do Not Dial This Initial Connection.

      - Automatically Dial This Initial Connection and then select an existing dial-up connection from the drop-down list.

   f. Click Next.

   g. Enter the host name or IP Address for the remote access server.

   h. Click Next.

   i. Select Create This Connection For All Users or Only For Myself.

   j. Click Next.

   k. Enter a name for your connection.

   l. Click Finish.

3.   If necessary, make changes to the default configuration information for the connection (in Network Connections, right-click the connection and choose Properties).

4.   Click Dial to test the connection.

Procedure Reference: Create a VPN Connection in Windows XP

To create a VPN connection in Windows XP:

1.   Log on as a local administrator.

2.   If necessary, create a connection to the Internet.

3.   Create a new connection object.

   a.   In Control Panel, click Network And Internet Connections.

   b.   Click Network Connections.

   c.   Click Create A New Connection.

   d.   Click Next.

   e.   On the Network Connection Type page, select Connect To The Network At My Workplace.

   f.   Click Next.

   g.   Select Virtual Private Network Connection and click Next.

   h.   In the Company Name text box, type a name for the connection.

   i.   Click Next.

   j.   On the Public Network page, select one of the following:

   •   Do Not Dial The Initial Connection, if you do not need to dial in to the Internet before you connect to the VPN server.

   •   Automatically Dial This Initial Connection, if you need to dial in to the Internet before you connect to the VPN server. From the drop-down list, select the dial-up connection you want to use.

   k.   Click Next.

   l.   In the Host Name Or IP Address text box, type the host name or IP address for the server to which the computer will connect.

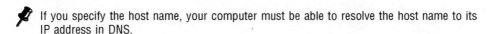 If you specify the host name, your computer must be able to resolve the host name to its IP address in DNS.

   m.   Click Next.

   n.   Select Create This Connection For Anyone's Use or My Use Only.

   o.   Click Next.

   p.   If you want to create a shortcut to this connection on the desktop, check Add A Shortcut To This Connection To My Desktop.

   q.   Click Finish.

4.   In the Connect dialog box for the new dial-up connection, complete the following tasks:

   a.   In the User Name text box, type the user name you must use to connect to the remote server.

   b.   In the Password text box, type this user account's password.

c. If you want to save the user account information with the connection, check Save This User Name And Password For The Following Users and select one of the following:

- Me Only, if you want to save the user account information for only your user.

- Anyone Who Uses This Computer, if you want all users of the computer to use the same user account information when connecting to the remote server.

d. Click Connect to connect to the server, or click Cancel to close the Connect dialog box.

5. If necessary, make changes to the default configuration information for the connection (in Network Connections, right-click the connection and choose Properties).

6. Click Dial to test the connection.

Procedure Reference: Create a VPN Connection in Windows NT

To create a VPN connection on a Windows NT computer:

1. Log on as a local administrator.

2. If necessary, create a connection to the Internet.

3. Install the Point-To-Point Tunneling Protocol.

a. Open Control Panel.

b. Double-click Network.

c. Select the Protocols tab and click Add.

d. Select Point-To-Point Tunneling Protocol and click OK.

e. If prompted, insert the Windows NT installation CD-ROM and click OK.

f. In the PPTP Configuration dialog box, enter the number of concurrent VPN connections you need to create and click OK.

g. Click OK to start Remote Access Setup.

h. In the Remote Access Setup dialog box, click Add.

i. Select a VPN connection from the list of RAS capable devices and click OK.

j. Repeat steps h and i for each VPN connection object.

k. Click Continue.

l. Click Close to close the Network Properties dialog box.

m. When prompted, click Yes to restart the computer.

4. Create a new connection object.

a. Open Dial-Up Networking.

b. Click New.

c. Type a name for the new connection and click Next.

d. Click Next.

e. On the Modem Or Adapter page, select a VPN entry and click Next.

f. On the Phone Number page, uncheck Use Telephony Dialing Properties.

g. In the Phone Number text box, type the host name or IP address of your VPN server and click Next.

h. Click Finish to save the new connection.

5. Click Dial to test the connection.

Procedure Reference: Create a VPN Connection in Windows 9x

To create a VPN connection on a Windows 9x computer:

1. Install the Dial-Up Networking Windows Setup component.

2. Install the Virtual Private Networking Windows Setup component.

    a. Choose Start→Settings→Control Panel.

    b. Double-click Add/Remove Programs.

    c. Select the Windows Setup tab.

    d. Select (don't uncheck!) Communications.

    e. Click Details.

    f. Check Virtual Private Networking.

    g. Click OK.

    h. Click OK.

    i. If prompted, enter the path to the Windows 9x setup files and click OK.

    j. Reboot the computer when prompted.

3. Create a new VPN connection object.

    a. Open My Computer.

    b. Double-click Dial-Up Networking.

    c. Double-click Make New Connection.

    d. Enter a name for your connection.

    e. From the Select A Device drop-down list, select the Microsoft VPN Adapter.

    f. Click Next.

    g. Enter the host name or IP Address for the remote access server.

    h. Click Next.

    i. Click Finish.

4. Click Dial to test the connection.

ACTIVITY 9-2

Creating a Virtual Private Networking Connection on a Windows 2000 Computer

Setup:

The company's VPN Server's IP address is 192.168.200.200.

Scenario:

You work for Smith Sales and Service in the IT department. Many of Smith's employees work from their homes across the United States and connect to company email and network resources through their Internet Service Providers using a cable modem. Jane is a new employee who needs her desktop computer configured for VPN access from her home to the company's VPN server. Her Internet Service Provider has installed a network card and a cable modem on her desktop.

What You Do	How You Do It
1. Create a new VPN connection object.	a. Double-click Make New Connection.
	b. Click Next.
	c. Select Connect To A Private Network Through The Internet.

> ⊙ **Connect to a private network through the Internet**
> Create a Virtual Private Network (VPN) connection or 'tunnel' through the Internet.

	d. Click Next.
	e. Select Do Not Dial This Initial Connection.
	f. Click Next.
	g. Enter *192.168.200.200* as the host name or IP Address for the VPN server.

> Host name or IP address (such as microsoft.com or 123.45.6.78):
> | 198.168.200.200 |

	h. Click Next.
	i. Verify that Create This Connection For All Users is selected.
	j. Click Next.
	k. Enter *Smith VPN Connection* as the name for your connection.
	l. Click Finish.

2. **Test the VPN connection.**

    a. In the Connect Smith VPN Connection dialog box, in the User Name text box, **enter *Admin#***

    b. In the Password dialog box, **enter *password***

    c. **Click Connect.**

    d. **Click OK** to close the Connection Complete message box.

    e. In the taskbar, **right-click the Smith VPN Connection and choose Disconnect.**

TOPIC C

Configure a Web Browser

So far in this lesson, you've seen only the steps for connecting a user to the Internet and your corporate intranet. But once you've established these connections, your next task is to configure the software they'll use to access both Internet and intranet resources—their Web browser. In this topic, you'll learn about the options you can configure in a Web browser to tailor it to your company's requirements.

Some companies want all users to access the Internet through a standard home page that requires them to agree to the company's Internet access policy before continuing on to surfing the Internet. Other companies will want you to minimize the amount of disk space that can be eaten up on users' computers with temporary Internet files and cookies. As an A+ technician, it's your job to configure users' Web browsers properly so that users have access to the resources they need while conforming to the company's rules and standards for Internet and intranet access.

Web Browser

Definition:

A Web browser is a software application used to locate and display Web pages. A Web browser can be a text-only browser or a graphical browser, which means it can display graphics and text. In addition, a Web browser may be able to present multimedia elements of sound and video. To present some formats of sound and video, an additional piece of software (called a plug-in) is needed. Web browsers use Internet protocols to establish communication between the client and the Web server. Web browsers contain a field in which you can enter the address of the Web page you wish to display. In addition, your Web browser may contain graphical buttons that you can use for navigation purposes and a menu structure to provide additional functionality.

Example:

Internet Explorer is an example of a graphical Web browser that you can use to locate and display Web pages.

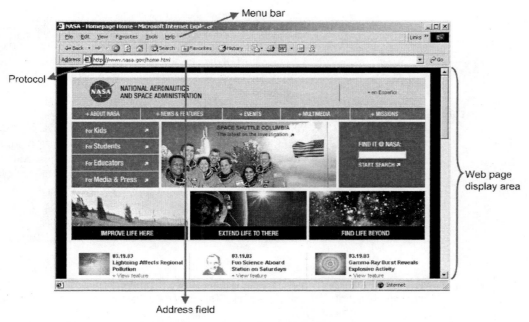

Figure 9-5: *Internet Explorer is a graphical Web browser.*

Web Protocols

Definition:

A Web protocol is a communication protocol that formats data for transmission from a Web client to a Web server. A Web protocol defines how messages are formatted and transmitted, and what actions Web servers and browsers should take in response to various commands. The protocol may or may not provide security for its communications.

Example: Web Protocols

Table 9-3 describes the protocols commonly used with Internet Explorer and Netscape Navigator to communicate between Web clients and Web servers.

Table 9-3: *Web Protocols*

Web Protocol	Description
Hypertext Transfer Protocol (HTTP)	With HTTP, communication is in one direction—only downloading Web page files written in the HyperText Markup Language (HTML) from the Web server to the client browser for viewing. HTTP is the most common protocol used to make Web requests.
File Transfer Protocol (FTP)	A protocol used to upload files to or download files from an FTP file server. With FTP communication is in two directions—allowing both the client to download files from the server or upload files from the server. Most FTP servers require users to log on.

Web Protocol	Description
Telnet	Telnet is a terminal emulation protocol that enables a user at one site to simulate a session on a remote host. It does this by translating keystrokes from the user's terminal to instructions recognized by the remote host, then carrying the output back to the user's terminal and displaying it in a format native to the remote host. This service is transparent (it gives users the impression that their terminals are directly attached to the remote host).
Secure Socket Layer (SSL)	A security protocol that uses certificates for authentication and encryption to protect Web communication. SSL is widely deployed on Web sites and the Internet because it's a server-driven process. The client simply has to support SSL; it doesn't need a registered certificate. This means that any of 60 million Internet users can connect to a Web site through a secure connection, as long as their clients can support SSL. Web sites that begin with **https://** are sites that require SSL.

 HyperText Markup Language (HTML) is the authoring language used to create documents on the Web. HTML defines the structure and layout of a Web document as it should present itself in a Web browser.

How to Configure a Web Browser

Procedure Reference: Set up an Internet Connection in Windows 2000

To set up an Internet Connection on a Windows 2000 computer for Internet or intranet access:

1. Choose Start→Programs→Accessories→Communications→Internet Connection Wizard.

2. Select one of the following connection types:
   - I want to sign up for a new Internet account (My telephone line is connected to my modem.)
   - I want to transfer my existing Internet account to this computer. (My telephone line is connected to my modem.)
   - I want to set up my Internet connection manually, or I want to connect through a local area network (LAN).

    Most businesses will use the last choice—they will either manually set up the connection or connect to the Internet through their LANs. The steps in this procedure document this scenario.

3. Click Next.

4. Select one of the following connection options:
   - I connect through a phone line and a modem.
   - I connect through a local area network (LAN).

5. Click Next.

6. If you selected to connect through a phone line and modem:

a. Enter the telephone number to connect to the Internet Service Provider.

b. Use the Advanced button to change the connection type from PPP to SLIP or C-SLIP; change the logon procedure from none to manual logon or use a script; or change the IP address of the computer or the DNS server from automatic to manual. Click OK.

c. Click Next.

d. Enter the User Name and Password that will be authenticated by the ISP.

e. Enter a name for your connection.

f. Click Next.

7. If you selected to connect through a local area network (LAN):

a. If you use a proxy server, check the appropriate check box to either automatically discover proxy server settings or manually enter the settings.

b. Click Next.

c. If you chose to manually enter the settings, enter your proxy and port information for each service your ISP supports.

d. Click Next.

e. If you chose to manually enter the settings, enter any Internet addresses you do not want to use a proxy server and click Next.

8. Select Yes if you want to set up an Internet mail account. Select No if you want to skip the step because you have an existing mail account or you don't want to use mail.

9. Click Next.

10. If desired, uncheck the To Connect To The Internet Immediately check box, so that Windows 9x won't attempt to connect to the Internet immediately.

11. Click Finish.

12. Test the connection.

Procedure Reference: Set Up an Internet Connection in Windows XP

To create an Internet connection in Windows XP:

1. Log on as a local administrator.

2. If necessary, install a modem.

3. Create a new connection object.

a. In Control Panel, click Network And Internet Connections.

b. Click Network Connections.

c. Click Create A New Connection and click Next.

d. On the Network Connection Type page, select Connect To The Internet and click Next.

e. Below How Do You Want To Connect To The Internet, select one of the following:

- Choose From A List Of Internet Service Providers (ISPs), if you want to select from a list of pre-configured connections to ISPs.

- Set Up My Connection Manually, if you want to manually define your connection to the ISP.

- Use The CD I Got From An ISP, if you want to use an ISP's installation CD to set up the connection.

f. Click Next.

g. If you choose to set up the connection manually, complete the following steps:

1. On the Internet Connection page, select one of the following:

Connect Using A Dial-Up Modem.

Connect Using A Broadband Connection That Requires A User Name And Password, if you have a cable or DSL modem.

Connect Using A Broadband Connection That Is Always On, if you have a cable modem or DSL connection, or a LAN connection that is always on.

2. Click Next.

3. In the ISP Name text box, type the name of your ISP and click Next.

4. If you selected to connect to the ISP via a dial-up connection, in the Phone Number text box, type the phone number and click Next.

5. Select Create This Connection For Anyone's Use or My Use Only.

6. Click Next.

7. On the Internet Account Information page, complete the following information:

The user name you selected with the ISP.

The user account's password.

Confirm the user account's password.

You can also select any or all of the following:

Whether you want to use this same user account and password whenever anyone uses this computer to connect to the Internet.

Whether you want this connection to be the default Internet connection.

Whether you want to turn on the Internet Connection Firewall for this connection.

8. Click Next.

9. If you want to create a shortcut to this connection on the desktop, check Add A Shortcut To This Connection To My Desktop.

10. Click Finish.

4. If necessary, make changes to the default configuration information for the connection (in Network Connections, right-click the connection and choose Properties).

5. Test the connection.

Procedure Reference: Set up an Internet Connection in Windows NT

To set up an Internet Connection on a Windows NT computer for Internet or intranet access:

1. Log on as a local administrator.

2. If necessary, install a modem.

3. Open Dial-Up Networking.

4. Click New.

5. In the Name text box, type a name for the connection and click Next.

6. In the Server dialog box, check I Am Calling The Internet and click Next.

7. In the modem or adapter list, select the modem you will use to dial your ISP and click Next.

8. Check Use Telephony Dialing Properties.

9. Type the area code and telephone number of your ISP and click Next.

10. Click Finish.

Procedure Reference: Set up an Internet Connection in Windows 9x

To set up an Internet Connection on a Windows 9x computer for Internet or intranet access:

1. Choose Start→Programs→Accessories→Internet Tools→Internet Connection Wizard.

2. Select one of the following connection types:

   - I want to sign up for a new Internet account (My telephone line is connected to my modem.)

   - I want to transfer my existing Internet account to this computer. (My telephone line is connected to my modem.)

   - I want to set up my Internet connection manually, or I want to connect through a local area network (LAN).

   > Most businesses will use the last choice—they will either manually set up the connection or connect to the Internet through their LANs. The steps in this procedure document this scenario.

3. Click Next.

4. Select one of the following connection options:

   - I connect through a phone line and a modem.

   - I connect through a local area network (LAN).

5. Click Next.

6. If you selected to connect through a phone line and modem:

   a. Enter the telephone to connect to the Internet Service Provider.

   b. Use the Advanced button to change the connection type from PPP to SLIP; change the logon procedure from none to manual logon or use a script; or change the IP address of the computer or the DNS server from automatic to manual. Click OK.

   c. Click Next.

   d. Enter the User Name and Password that will be authenticated by the ISP.

   e. Enter a name for your connection.

   f. Click Next.

7. If you selected to connect through a local area network (LAN):

   a. If you use a proxy server, check the appropriate check box to either automatically discover proxy server settings or manually enter the settings.

   b. Click Next.

   c. If you chose to manually enter the settings, enter your proxy and port information for each service your ISP supports.

   d. Click Next.

   e. If you chose to manually enter the settings, enter any Internet addresses you do not want to use a proxy server and click Next.

8. If desired, uncheck the To Connect To The Internet Immediately check box, so that Windows 9x won't attempt to connect to the Internet immediately.

9. Click Finish.

Procedure Reference: Configure the Internet Explorer Web Browser

To configure Internet Explorer on a Windows 2000, Windows XP, Windows NT, or Windows 9x computer:

1. If you're using Windows 2000, Windows NT, or Windows 9x, right-click Internet Explorer on the desktop and choose Properties.

   If you're using Windows XP, on the Start menu, right-click Internet Explorer on the desktop and choose Internet Properties.

   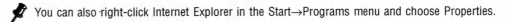 You can also right-click Internet Explorer in the Start→Programs menu and choose Properties.

2. Configure the desired General properties. On the General page you can configure:
   - Your home page.
   - Settings for handling temporary Internet files and refreshing stored pages.
   - Settings for your history list.
   - Colors used in Internet Explorer.
   - Fonts used on Web pages that have no specified text font.
   - The languages displayed on Web sites offering content in several languages.
   - Accessibility options.

3. Configure the desired Security properties. On the Security page, you can configure:
   - The placement of Web sites in local intranet, trusted sites, and restricted sites zones.
   - The security level for each zone. By default, scripts and ActiveX controls are handled differently for each security level. To customize support for scripts and ActiveX controls, select the security level you want to configure and click Customize to open the Security Settings dialog box, where you can also configure how Internet Explorer handles cookies, downloads, Java, and user authentication.

4. Configure the desired Content properties. On the Content page, you can:
   - Enable content ratings to control the Internet content that can be viewed on the computer.

- Enable certificates that can be used for identification purposes.

- Enable the AutoComplete feature which lists possible matches for what you are typing from items you've entered previously.

- On Windows 98, enable the Wallet feature to store personal information for ease of Internet shopping.

- Configure a personal profile.

5. Configure the desired Connections properties. On the Connections page, you can configure:

- Select a dial-up or VPN connection to automatically connect when Internet Explorer runs.

- On Windows 98, you can enable the system to perform a security check before dialing a connection.

- Your LAN settings, where you can enable the use of scripts for LAN configuration and a proxy server for your Internet connection. To use a proxy server, check Use A Proxy Server, and then enter the server's IP address and the port to which you want to connect.

You can also start the Internet Connection Wizard by clicking the Setup button.

6. Configure the Programs properties. On the Programs page, you can configure the default programs Internet Explorer will use for:

- An HTML editor.

- An email program.

- A newsgroup server.

- An Internet meeting program.

- A calendar program.

- A contact list.

You can reset the Internet Explorer programs to their defaults by clicking the Reset Web Settings button.

7. Configure the Advanced properties. On the Advanced page, you can configure the functionality of Internet Explorer by checking (enabling) and unchecking (disabling) features.

8. Click OK.

Procedure Reference: Install the Netscape Navigator 7.01 Web Browser

To install Netscape Navigator 7.01 on a Windows 2000, Windows XP, Windows NT, or Windows 9x computer:

1. Run the NSSetup.exe file.

 The NSSetup.exe file is available for download from the Netscape site at http://channels.netscape.com/ns/borwsers/download.asp or by ordering the CD-ROM.

2. Click Next to begin the Wizard.

3. Click Accept to accept the license agreement.

4. Select the type of setup you prefer.

   The choices available are:
   - Recommended: Installs the most common options. Quickest to download; recommended for most users.
   - Full: Installs a range of options, including Java and several media players.
   - Custom: Recommended for advanced users.

   ⚠ The remaining steps assume the setup type selected was Recommended.

5. If prompted, click Yes to create a *root_drive:*\Program Files\Netscape\Netscape folder.

6. Select or clear the additional components you want to install.

   Additional components include: SunJava2 and Winamp.

7. Click Next.

8. Enable or disable Quick Launch which keeps portions of the Netscape in memory at all times for quicker launch times.

9. Click Next.

10. Enable or disable Additional Options.

    The additional options available are: Make Netscape.com my home page and, if you are downloading Netscape from the Web site, Save installer files locally.

11. Click Next.

12. Click Install.

13. If you have an existing Netscape or AOL Instant Messenger screen name, enter it along with your password and follow the prompts to log on to the Netscape network.

    If not, click Cancel.

14. Click Finished.

Procedure Reference: Configure the Netscape Navigator 7.01 Browser

To configure Netscape Navigator 7.01 on a Windows 2000, Windows XP, Windows NT, or Windows 9x computer:

1. Run Netscape Navigator.

2. Choose Edit→Preferences.

3. In the Category list box, select Navigator.

4. On the Navigator page, set your general navigator options.

   The options available from the Navigator page are:
   - The page to display when Navigator starts up. The choices are Blank page, Home page, or Last page visited.
   - Enable or disable Netscape as your default browser.
   - Enter the address of a Web page for your home page.

- Select the buttons you want to see in the toolbars.

5. In the Category list box, select History.

6. On the History page, set your history options.

   The options available from the History page are:
   - The number of days in your History list.
   - The location of your History bar in the Netscape Navigator window.
   - The number of pages in your session history list.

7. Select Languages.

8. On the Languages page, add or remove the languages you would like to view Web pages in.

9. Select Helper Applications.

10. On the Helper Applications page, set your file type association settings.

    The options available on the Helper Applications page are:
    - Adding file type associations.
    - Enabling or disabling the Plug-in Finder Service.
    - Reset your file-opening preferences to the default.

11. Select Smart Browsing.

12. On the Smart Browsing page, set your smart browsing options.

    The options available on the Smart Browsing page are:
    - Enabling or disabling Internet keywords, which enables quick access to services such as stock quotes and Internet searching from the Location bar.
    - Enabling or disabling the Location bar autocomplete feature.

13. Select the Internet Search page.

14. On the Internet Search page, set your Internet search options.

    The options available on the Internet Search page are:
    - Setting your default Internet search engine.
    - Enabling or disabling the auto-open feature of the Search bar.
    - Setting your sidebar search tab preference as a basic or advanced search.

15. Select Tabbed Browsing.

16. Set your Tabbed Browsing options.

    The options available on the Tabbed Browsing page are:
    - Set your tab display options.
    - Set tab versus window settings.

17. Select Downloads.

18. Set your Downloads options.

    The options on the Downloads page specify what behavior Netscape Navigator should display when downloading files.

19. Select Privacy & Security. You can use the pages under Privacy & Security to configure how Navigator handles cookies, manage stored passwords, and configure SSL.

20. Select Advanced. You can use these pages to configure script support and configure proxy servers for your Internet connection.

ACTIVITY 9-3

Configuring a Web Browser on a Windows 2000 Computer

Data Files:

- C:\Data\Internet Security Policy.htm

Scenario:

The management at AlphaBeta Company has recently realized that the value of allowing their employees to access critical business information located on the Internet outweighs the risks of personal Web browsing on company time. They have hired you to configure all their Windows 2000 computers for Internet access on their company LAN. However, they have created an Internet policy statement that they want presented to the user each time they run Internet Explorer, so all employees are aware of the company's Internet access policy. They have provided the file, Internet Security Policy.htm, to you. The network does not have a proxy server, and the company does not currently have any email accounts.

What You Do	How You Do It
1. Set up an Internet Connection on your computer.	a. Choose Start→Programs→Accessories→ Communications→Internet Connection Wizard.
	b. Select I Want To Set Up My Internet Connection Manually, or I Want To Connect Through A Local Area Network (LAN).
	c. Click Next.
	d. Select I Connect Through A Local Area Network (LAN).

How do you connect to the Internet?

○ I connect through a phone line and a modem

◉ I connect through a local area network (LAN)

	e. Click Next.
	f. Uncheck Automatic Discovery Of Proxy Server (Recommended) to bypass using a proxy server.
	g. Click Next.
	h. Click No to bypass setting up an Internet Mail account.
	i. Click Next.
	j. Uncheck the To Connect To The Internet Immediately check box, so that Windows 2000 won't attempt to connect to the Internet immediately.
	k. Click Finish.

2. **Set the home page of Internet Explorer to Internet Security Policy.htm**

a. **Right-click Internet Explorer on the desktop and choose Properties.**

b. **On the General page, in the Home Page box, in the Address text box, type** *C:\Data\Internet Security Policy.htm*

c. **Click OK.**

d. **Open Internet Explorer.** The home page is set to the Internet Security Policy.htm file.

e. **Close Internet Explorer.**

TOPIC D

Configure an Email Client

In Topic 9C, you learned how to configure users' Web browsers to access Internet and intranet resources. Now, you need to configure users with an email client so that they can send and receive email messages. In this topic, you'll learn the exact steps for configuring users' email clients.

In today's business world, email is considered an essential part of doing business. Without email, many companies just can't compete. Imagine if your company used "snail" mail to deliver its marketing materials to customers (which could take several days) while your competitors deliver the same information via email (which takes only a few seconds). Obviously, the company that uses email will have a competitive edge because it will be able to reach its customers faster. For this reason, your job as an A+ technician is to be prepared to configure users' email clients so that they can access their email. Further, nothing will generate a technical support call quicker than a user who's unable to send or receive email! You need to be prepared to handle such calls so that you can get the user back up and running as quickly as possible.

Email Protocol

Definition:

An email protocol is a communications protocol that enables the transmission of electronic messages over communications networks. The message that is sent can be text entered directly in an email software package or can be electronic files stored on a disk. An email protocol can be used to retrieve email from a server or to send email.

Example: Example: Email Protocols

Table 9-4 describes the protocols commonly used with email software packages.

Table 9-4: *Email Protocols*

Email Protocol	Description
Post Office Protocol (POP) and POP2	Communications protocols used to retrieve email from a mail server. Each must be used in conjunction with the SMTP protocol that can send email to a mail server.
POP3	A newer version of POP that can be used with or without SMTP.
Internet Message Access Protocol (IMAP)	A communications protocol used to retrieve messages from an email server.
IMAP4	A newer version of IMAP that, like POP, can be used with or without SMTP. It has additional features that allow you to search through your email by keyword and then retrieve just the emails that meet your search criteria.
Simple Mail Transfer Protocol (SMTP)	A communications protocol used to send email to a mail server. It must be used with a communications protocol such as a POP or IMAP protocol to retrieve messages from the mail server.

Email Clients

Definition:

An email client is a software application that runs on a client computer and enables the user to send, receive, and organize email messages.

Example: Email Client

Email clients are used to send, receive, and organize email.

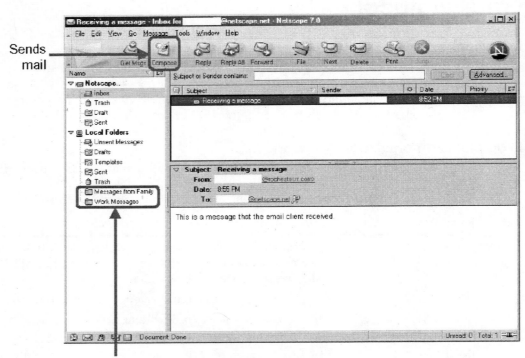

Sends mail

Folders for organizing mail

Figure 9-6: *An email client.*

Common Email Client Packages

Common email client packages include:

- Microsoft Outlook—Part of Microsoft Office.
- Microsoft Outlook Express—Free with Windows products.
- Netscape Mail—Free with Netscape Navigator.
- Microsoft Hotmail—Free from MSN.
- Lotus Notes—Must be purchased.
- Qualcomm Eudora—Free for download.
- Novell Groupwise—Must be purchased.

How to Configure an Email Client

Procedure Reference: Configure Outlook Express

To configure Outlook Express to send and receive email:

1. Obtain the necessary email account information.
   - Full name.
   - Email address.
   - Incoming mail server type: POP3, IMAP, or HTTP.
   - Incoming mail server name (required for POP3 and IMAP accounts, but not for HTTP).
   - Outgoing mail server name (required for POP3 and IMAP accounts, but not for HTTP).

2. In Windows 2000 and Windows 9x, choose Start→Programs→Outlook Express.

    In Windows XP, choose Start→All Programs→Outlook Express.

    In Windows NT, download and install the latest version of Internet Explorer from Microsoft's Web site at **www.microsoft.com/ie** (Outlook Express will be automatically installed as part of the installation of Internet Explorer). When the installation is complete, choose Start→Programs→Outlook Express.

> If there is an Outlook Express shortcut on your desktop or system tool bar, you can use it to access Outlook Express.

3. In the Display Name text box, type your full name and click Next.

4. In the E-Mail Address text box, type your email address. Click Next.

5. From the My Incoming Mail Server Is A _____ Server drop-down list, select the type of email server (POP3, IMAP, or HTTP).

6. In the Incoming Mail (POP3, IMAP Or HTTP) Server text box, type the fully qualified domain name for this server (for example, pop3.earthlink.net).

7. In the Outgoing Mail (SMTP) Server text box, type the fully qualified domain name for this server.

8. Click Next.

9. On the Internet Mail Logon page, in the Account Name text box, type your user account.

10. In the Password text box, type your user account's password.

11. If you want Outlook Express to save your password, leave Remember Password checked.

    If you want Outlook Express to prompt you for your password before retrieving your email, uncheck Remember Password.

12. Click Next.

13. Click Finish.

14. Test to see that you can send and receive email.

Procedure Reference: Add a New Account to Outlook Express

To add a new email account to Outlook Express:

1. Obtain the necessary email account information.
    - Full name.
    - Email address.
    - Incoming mail server type: POP3, IMAP, or HTTP.
    - Incoming mail server name (required for POP3 and IMAP accounts, but not for HTTP).
    - Outgoing mail server name (required for POP3 and IMAP accounts, but not for HTTP).

2. Open Outlook Express.

3. Choose Tools→Accounts.

4. Select the Mail tab.

5. Click Add and choose Mail.

6. Enter a display name for the person who will be using the account.

7. Click Next.

8. Select one of the following:
   - I Already Have An E-mail Address That I'd Like To Use. Then enter the email address in the text box.
   - I'd Like To Sign Up For A New Account From. Then select an Internet mail provider from the drop-down list box.

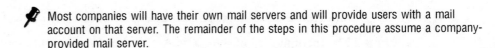 Most companies will have their own mail servers and will provide users with a mail account on that server. The remainder of the steps in this procedure assume a company-provided mail server.

9. Click Next.

10. From the My Incoming Mail Server Is A _____ Server drop-down list box, select the type of mail server Outlook Express will be connecting to.

11. In the Incoming Mail (POP3, IMAP, or HTTP) Server: text box, enter the name of your incoming mail server.

12. In the Outgoing Mail (SMTP) Server: text box, enter the name of your outgoing mail server.

13. Click Next.

14. In the Account Name text box, enter your mail account name.

15. In the Password text box, enter the password for your mail account.

16. To have Outlook Express automatically remember your password, check Remember Password. To enter your password each time you start Outlook Express, uncheck Remember Password.

17. If your mail server requires Secure Password Authentication, check Log On Using Secure Password Authentication (SPA).

18. Click Next.

19. Click Finish.

ACTIVITY 9-4

Configuring Outlook Express on a Windows 2000 Computer

Scenario:

The AlphaBeta Company has grown to a large enough size that it is critical for them to have email capabilities for all their employees. They feel this will allow them to respond much quicker to each other and their customers. They have hired you to install and configure Outlook Express on all their Windows 2000 computers so that all employees can send and receive email.

What You Do	How You Do It
1. **Obtain the email account information.**	

Full name:

_____

Email address:

_____

Incoming mail server type:

_____

Incoming mail server name (if necessary):

_____

Outgoing mail server name (if necessary):

_____

Account password:

_____

---

2. **Configure Outlook Express to send and receive email.**

    a. **Choose Start→Programs→Outlook Express.** Outlook Express prompts you to set up an email account.

    b. In the Display Name text box, **type the name for the email account.**

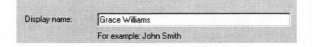

Display name: Grace Williams
For example: John Smith

    c. **Click Next.**

d. In the E-Mail Address text box, **type the user's email address.**

E-mail address: | Grace_Williams1@hotmail.com
For example: someone@microsoft.com

e. **Click Next.**

f. From the My Incoming Mail Server Is A _____ Server drop-down list box, **select the incoming mail server type.**

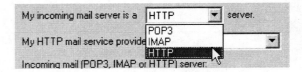

My incoming mail server is a | HTTP ▼ | server.
POP3
My HTTP mail service provide IMAP
HTTP
Incoming mail (POP3, IMAP or HTTP) server:

g. If necessary, in the Incoming Mail (POP3, IMAP, or HTTP) Server: text box, **type the name of the incoming server.**

h. If necessary, in the Outgoing Mail (SMTP) Server: text box, **type the name of the outgoing server.**

i. **Click Next.**

j. In the Account Name text box, **enter the user's email address.**

k. In the Password text box, **enter the user's password.**

Account name: | Grace_Williams1@hotmail.com
For example: someone@microsoft.com

Password: | ********
☑ Remember password

l. **Click Next.**

m. **Click Finish.**

3. **Test that you can send and receive mail.**

   ✎ Work with a partner.

a. **Click the New Mail button.**

b. In the To: text box, **type your partner's email address.**

c. In the Subject text box, **type** *Test Email*

d. **Click Send.** When the email from your partner arrives in your inbox, you have verified you can both send and receive emails.

e. **Close Outlook Express.**

TOPIC E

Troubleshoot Internet and Intranet Connections

As you've seen in this lesson, most companies consider Internet and intranet access a critical part of their business. Without such access, many companies are unable to compete against their competitors. As an A+ technician, you'll need to be prepared to quickly identify and resolve any problems with Internet and intranet connections, and that's just what you'll learn in this topic.

Nothing will make you a hero faster than repairing a user's Internet connection. Likewise, nothing will make you more unpopular than if you're unable to resolve a user's Internet or intranet access problem. Many companies rely on the research they can perform on the Internet to make critical business decisions. Without such access, a company will be unable to get the information it needs. As an A+ technician, your job is to make sure that companies are able to access the information superhighway without hitting any potholes or experiencing a breakdown altogether. Knowing how to diagnose and repair Internet/intranet connection problems quickly will enable your users to get back to working productively on their computers.

Common Internet/Intranet Problems

Table 9-5 describes common Internet/intranet connection problems.

Table 9-5: *Common Internet/Intranet Connection Problems*

Symptoms	Possible Causes
Can't establish a dial-up connection	The problem could be with the client hardware (check the modem.log file), the client RAS protocol (check the ppp.log file), or with the dial-up connection settings (verify the phone number, server type, and protocol settings). The RAS server could also be down.

Symptoms	Possible Causes
Can't establish a VPN connection	A VPN connection problem could be caused by the same things as a dial-up connection or network connection problem. In addition, you need to verify with the network administrator that the VPN server is up and that the user has permissions to access the network through the VPN server.
Can't send email	The SMTP server is not configured correctly, the SMTP server is down, or you have a problem communicating with the DNS server.
Page Cannot Be Displayed message in browser	Whenever your browser cannot display a Web page, either the browser can't reach the page or the browser's configuration is set so that it is preventing the Web page from being displayed. On the client end, the cause could be with the Web page address, the connection, or proxy server settings. Check simple things first—verify the Web address is typed correctly in the Address bar. If it is, you'll want to check your connection to your DNS server and that your proxy server settings are correct in your browser.
Not Authorized to View Web Page	The Web page you are attempting to access is private. Contact the Web master of the site or your network administrator to obtain a user name and password for the site.
Browser crashes	If you get an error message when you try to open a Web page, your browser crashes, or your browser won't display a full page, the cause could be that your browser cache or History list contains a bad file, you need updated software to display graphics, an old cookie is causing a problem, or the TCP/IP protocol is corrupt.

How to Troubleshoot Internet/Intranet Connection Problems

Procedure Reference: Troubleshoot Internet/Intranet Connection Problems

An Internet/intranet connectivity problem could range from problems with the actual physical connection to a problem with the application that is trying to use the Internet/intranet connection. To troubleshoot Intranet/intranet connectivity problems:

1. Define the symptoms. Ask questions such as:

    *   When did the problem arise?

    *   Was there a change in the system at that time? For example, were other applications or operating system patches installed?

    *   Does the problem exist within one application that uses Internet access or all applications?

        If it exists in one application, but not others, you can rule out problems with the physical connection and the software for the connection object.

        If it exists in all applications, the problem most likely exists with the physical connection or the software for the connection object.

2. Close all programs, except the one you are trying to connect with. This eliminates the variable of other programs affecting your connectivity and assists in isolating the problem to a particular component or piece of software.

3. Test physical connectivity.

- Verify modems are properly installed and connected to the computer and turned on.

- If you have a VPN connection utilizing a network card and cable, verify the network card is functioning and the cable is connected.

- Try pinging another computer to test the physical link.

- If you have multilinked devices in your connection object, test the physical connectivity of each device.

4. If the problem is physical, once you narrow the problem to a specific physical component:

   - Review any log files.

   - Check all physical components for hardware failure.

   - Look for patches on the manufacturer's Web site.

   - Re-install the device's driver.

5. If the problem is not physical, based on the symptoms, isolate the problem to either the application you are attempting to access the Internet with (Internet Explorer or Outlook Express), or the connection object (the dial-up or VPN connection software).

   Review any log files of the software components to gather symptoms.

6. Test your connection to your DNS server.

   a. At a command prompt, enter ipconfig /all or use winipcfg to obtain your DNS server address.

   b. At a command prompt, ping the DNS server's IP address. If you receive a response, the problem is not with the DNS server.

7. Verify your proxy server settings.

   a. Choose Start→Settings→Control Panel.

   b. Open Internet Options.

   c. Select the Connections tab.

   d. Verify the Access The Internet Using A Proxy Service check box is checked and the proxy server address and port are entered as given to you by your Internet Service Provider or company's network administrator.

   e. Click OK.

   f. If you are using a dial-up connection, in the Dial-Up Settings list box, select your connection object and click Settings. In the Settings dialog box, select Use A Proxy Server and enter the proxy server address and port as given to you by your Internet Service Provider or company's network administrator.

   g. If you are connected to a LAN that provides Internet access check LAN Settings.

8. If you can't send email:

   a. Verify the email client's SMTP server is set correctly.

   b. Ping the SMTP server to verify it is running.

   c. Check your DNS connection.

9. If your Web browser is crashing, complete the following steps. After each step, stop to see if the problem is resolved. If not, go on to the next step.

a. Clear your History and delete your temporary files.

1. Choose Start→Settings→Control Panel.

2. Open Internet Options.

3. On the General page, click Delete Files and click OK.

4. Click Clear History and click Yes.

b. Enable IE to launch browser windows in a separate process.

1. In the Internet Options dialog box, select the Advanced page.

2. Under Browsing, check Launch Browser Windows In A Separate Process.

c. Install the latest version of DirectX.

d. Verify TCP/IP is working by pinging your loopback address 127.0.0.1.

e. If TCP/IP is not working, uninstall and re-install TCP/IP.

f. Check your cookies:

1. In Windows Explorer, display the *root_drive*\Windows\Cookies folder.

2. Select all files in the Cookies folder except index.dat.

3. Move all the files to a new folder.

4. Open your browser.

5. Move each cookie one at a time back into the Windows\Cookie folder. After each move, open your browser to see if it crashes. Continue until you've found the cookie that is causing the crash.

10. On a computer that has Internet connectivity, search Microsoft Knowledge-base articles for known issues and their resolutions based on your defined symptoms.

a. Go to **www.microsoft.com/technet/default.asp**.

b. Click Advanced Search.

c. Uncheck all items except Knowledge Base.

d. In the Search For text box, enter a word or few words that describe your symptoms.

e. Click Submit Query.

f. Review the articles returned for pertinence.

11. Make one suggested change at a time. If the change does not solve the problem, reverse the change before you attempt another suggested change.

ACTIVITY 9-5

Troubleshooting Internet/Intranet Connection Problems

Scenario:

AlphaBeta Company has recently implemented Internet/intranet connectivity on all their Windows 2000 computers. Each computer is running Outlook Express as its default mail client and Internet Explorer as its default Web browser. Because this is a new implementation, several problems have cropped up. You receive your first trouble ticket submitted by John.

What You Do	How You Do It

1. John has called to complain that he can't access the cnn.com site from Internet Explorer.

   What questions would you ask to define the problem?

2. John tells you that last night before he left he could access Internet sites through Internet Explorer. Today he can't access any sites. When he tries to send email, that fails as well. No one has made any changes to the configuration of his computer between last night and this morning.

   You arrive at John's desk and attempt to ping an external Internet site by name. You receive an unknown host message. You attempt to ping an external site by IP address. You receive three request timed out messages.

   What do you suspect is the problem?

3. What are your next steps for troubleshooting John's computer?

4. Ken is working in email. He has several items in his Outbox. When he clicks the Send/Receive mail button in his email client, Ken gets new messages from the mail server, but the messages in his Outbox won't transfer to the mail server. Karen, who sits next to Ken, sends Ken an email and it arrives in his Inbox just fine.

    What do you suspect is the problem?

5. Carolyn, who works for Human Resources, has been accessing payroll data on the HR department's intranet Web server. She clicks a link entitled Performance Reviews and receives a message "You Are Not Authorized To View This Page."

    What do you suspect is the problem?

Lesson 9 Follow-up

In this lesson you learned how to configure software to connect users' networked PCs to the Internet or an intranet. By properly configuring a Web browser, your users will be able to more effectively use information available to them internally via an intranet server and globally via the Internet. When you configure email access for your users, communication becomes quicker and more effective.

1. **In your organization, or the organizations you support, what types of intranet or Internet resources do your users access?**

2. **In your organization, or the organizations you support, what is the effect on communication using email?**

LESSON 10

Implementing Virus Protection

Lesson Time
2 hour(s)

Lesson Objectives:

In this lesson, you will implement virus protection.

You will:

*   Install virus protection software.
*   Configure virus protection software.
*   Create a clean boot disk.
*   Manually update virus definitions.
*   Remove a virus.

LESSON 10

Introduction

Unfortunately, one of the skills you'll need as an A+ technician is how to handle viruses. For this reason, it's important that you learn how to both protect computers from viruses as well as to repair a computer in the event it becomes infected, and that's what we'll do in this lesson.

Viruses create costly corruption of data and user downtime. As an A+ technician you will be expected to prevent virus infections and to repair infected computers quickly.

The following CompTIA A+ Operating System Technologies (2003) Examination objectives are covered in this lesson:

- Topic A:
  — 3.1 Using the correct Utilities: Boot Disk.
  — 3.3 Viruses and virus types: What they are, TSR (Terminate Stay Resident) programs and viruses, Sources (floppy, emails, etc.), How to determine presence.
- Topic C:
  — 2.3 Creating Emergency Disks with OS Utilities.

TOPIC A

Install Virus Protection Software

Your first task in implementing virus protection is to know the types of viruses you can run into and how to install software to protect a computer from these viruses. Because viruses are so prevalent, you need the skills to handle them. In this topic, you'll learn about the types of viruses that can potentially infect a computer. You'll then learn how to install virus protection software so that you can prevent a computer from becoming infected.

Knowing how to install virus protection software enables you to respond to your users' requests to protect their computers from viruses. If you don't know how to install virus protection software, you won't be able to respond to these requests—which can lead to unhappy users or clients (or both!). In addition, knowing how to install virus protection software enables you to protect your users' computers and data from viruses. By installing virus software, you can be proactive by protecting computers against viruses instead of having to be reactive by repairing computers after they've been infected.

Malicious Code Attacks

Definition:

A *malicious code attack* is a software-based attack in which an attacker inserts malicious code into a user's system to disrupt or disable the operating system or an application. A malicious code attack might:

- Make the operating system or application take action to disrupt or disable other systems on the same network or on a remote network.
- Use an unsuspecting user to spread the code by making the executable file that launches the malicious code appear as if it is from a trusted or safe source.
- Exploit the data stored in the user's own system to spread the code to other remote systems.

Example: Example: Virus

A *virus* is a piece of malicious code that spreads from one computer to another by attaching itself to other files. The code in the virus might corrupt or erase files (including executable files), the boot sector, or partition information on a user's computer, when an unsuspecting user opens or executes the file to which the virus is attached.

 An example of a destructive virus is the Melissa virus, which spread throughout the world attached to Microsoft Word documents that were sent as email attachments.

 In DOS environments, a Terminate and Stay Resident (TSR) virus will attach itself to a computer's memory once it has been loaded by way of an infected executable file.

Example: Example: Worm

A *worm* is a piece of malicious code that spreads from one computer to another on its own, not by attaching itself to another file. The code in a worm might corrupt or erase files on a user's computer, compromise the security of the system, or use up the computer's resources to the point where the system shuts down.

 An example of a destructive worm is the W32.Klez.A@mm worm. The worm spreads through email and network shares.

 A worm that sits dormant on a user's computer until it is triggered by a specific event, such as a specific date, can also be referred to as a logical bomb.

Example: Example: Trojan Horse

A *Trojan Horse* is a piece of malicious code that masquerades as a harmless file. When a user executes it (thinking that it is a harmless application), it can destroy and corrupt data on the user's hard drive, take over your computer and control it remotely, or use your computer to perform attacks that disrupt Web sites.

 An example of a Trojan Horse is the Love Bug which users receive in an email attachment and open, thinking it is a non-threatening letter from someone they know.

Non-Example: Hoaxes

A *hoax* is used to trick users into believing there is a malicious code threat to their systems. Hoaxes typically contain warnings, the purpose of which is to frighten or mislead users and entice them to spread the hoax further by warning others. Hoaxes typically arrive in the form of an email and do little more than clog mail servers and take up network bandwidth when spread by uneducated users.

 An example of a hoax is the Virtual Card for You which is an email warning users to not open any virtual cards sent to them with the subject of Virtual Card for You or it will freeze your computer so that you must reboot the computer and the virus destroys sector zero permanently destroying the hard disk. The email encourages users to pass the word on.

Before passing on any warnings, check out the validity of the warning at one of the following Web sites:

- The United States government Web site at **hoaxbusters.ciac.org.**
- Symantec's Web site at **www.symantec.com/avcenter/hoax.html.**

- McAfee's Web site at **vil.mcafee.com/hoax.asp.**

Virus Protection Software

Definition:

Virus protection software is a software package that is designed to detect and remove viruses. Virus protection software consists of two components: the software engine and the virus definition files. Virus definition files are updated continuously to include protection against newly discovered threats and must be downloaded to the software engine to be effective in protecting against the latest malicious code threats. In some instances, the virus protection software may be able to repair damage done by a malicious piece of code.

Example:

Symantec Norton AntiVirus and McAfee VirusScan are two popular virus protection software packages. Each program has an engine which runs on your computer and definition files that are downloaded from the manufacturers' Web sites.

System Requirements

To install Symantec Norton AntiVirus 2003 or McAfee VirusScan Professional 7.0, your system must meet the minimum requirements for virus protection application. Table 10-1 lists the system requirements for Symantec Norton AntiVirus 2003. Table 10-2 lists the system requirements for McAfee VirusScan Professional 7.0.

Table 10-1: *System Requirements for Symantec Norton AntiVirus 2003*

Operating System	Requirements
Windows XP Home Edition/ Professional	<ul><li>Intel Pentium (or compatible) 300 MHz or higher processor.</li><li>128 MB of RAM.</li><li>70 MB of hard disk space.</li><li>Internet Explorer 5.0 or later (5.5 recommended).</li><li>CD-ROM or DVD-ROM drive.</li><li>A user account with administrative rights.</li></ul>
Windows 2000 Professional	<ul><li>Intel Pentium (or compatible) 133 MHz or higher processor.</li><li>64 MB of RAM.</li><li>70 MB of hard disk space.</li><li>Internet Explorer 5.0 or later (5.5 recommended).</li><li>CD-ROM or DVD-ROM drive.</li><li>A user account with administrative rights.</li></ul>
Windows 98	<ul><li>Intel Pentium (or compatible) 133 MHz or higher processor.</li><li>32 MB of RAM.</li><li>70 MB of hard disk space.</li><li>Internet Explorer 5.0 or later (5.5 recommended).</li><li>CD-ROM or DVD-ROM drive.</li></ul>

Table 10-2: *System Requirements for McAfee VirusScan Professional Version 7.0*

Operating System	Requirements
Windows 98, Windows 2000 Professional, Windows XP Home Edition/Professional	• Intel Pentium (or compatible) 100 MHz or higher processor. • 32 MB of RAM. • 65 MB of hard disk space. • Internet Explorer 4.01 or later, with Service Pack 2 or higher (5.1 or later recommended). • CD-ROM drive. • On Windows 2000 Professional, Windows XP Home Edition/Professional, a user account with administrative rights.

How to Install Virus Protection Software

Procedure Reference: Install Symantec Norton AntiVirus 2003

To install Symantec Norton AntiVirus 2000 in Windows XP, Windows 2000, Windows NT, or Windows 98:

 If you have a 2000 to 2002 version of Norton AntiVirus, the 2003 version will automatically remove the older version. If you have a version prior to version 2000, you must uninstall it before you install version 2003.

1. On Windows 2000, Windows NT, or Windows XP systems, log on to the system using a user account with administrative rights.

2. Start the installation program.
    - Insert the Norton AntiVirus CD into the CD-ROM drive and, in the Norton AntiVirus 2003 window, click Install Norton AntiVirus 2003.

         If you are using the Norton AntiVirus CD and the Norton AntiVirus 2003 window does not open when you insert the CD into the CD-ROM drive, browse the CD and double-click Cdplay.exe.

    - Access the Norton AntiVirus installation files and double-click Setup.exe.

3. If Setup updates any system files, you are prompted to restart your computer. Click OK.

     On Windows 98, Norton AntiVirus scans your computer's memory for viruses before installing. If a virus is found, you will be prompted to use your Emergency Repair Disk to remove the virus before continuing with the installation.

4. In the Norton AntiVirus 2003 Setup wizard, click Next.

5. Click I Accept The License Agreement.

6. Click Next.

7. If you are upgrading from Norton AntiVirus version 2000 to 2002, click Yes to keep your option settings or click No to reset the option settings to the program defaults. Click Next.

8. If desired, use the Browse button to specify a different destination folder for the program.

9. Click Next.

10. Click Next to begin the installation.

11. Read the text of the Readme Information and click Next.

12. Click Finish.

13. If prompted to restart the computer, click Yes.

> To uninstall Norton AntiVirus, use the Add/Remove Programs applet in Control Panel.

14. Log back on to Windows 98.

15. Register your copy of Norton AntiVirus 2003 by filling in the prompts of the Norton AntiVirus Information Wizard.

16. Your displayed subscription service expiration date is one year from your installation date. Click Next.

17. Enable or disable the desired post-installation tasks you wish to complete by checking and unchecking the task boxes.

18. Click Next.

19. Click Finish.

20. If you enabled LiveUpdates, follow the prompts in the wizard to connect to the LiveUpdate site and install any new updates. Click Finish.

21. If you are running Windows 98 and you enabled Rescue Disks, select a destination drive and click Create. If you are using floppy disks, replace the disks when prompted.

22. Click OK and Close to close the Rescue Disk program.

23. If you enabled VirusScan, the scan starts.

24. In the Scan: Summary dialog box, click Details to see specific information on the scan, or Finished to close the scan window.

25. The Norton AntiVirus System Status dialog box opens. Identify any items that need your immediate attention (they are marked in red).

26. To process any items that need your attention, click the link and follow the prompts.

27. When finished, close the Norton AntiVirus window.

Procedure Reference: Install McAfee Security VirusScan Professional 7.0

To install McAfee Security Virus Scan 7.0 in Windows XP, Windows 2000, Windows NT, or Windows 98:

1. On Windows 2000, Windows NT, or Windows XP systems, log on to the system using a user account with administrative rights.

2. Start the installation program by either:
   - Inserting the McAfee VirusScan CD into the CD-ROM drive and, in the Installation Wizard window, clicking Install VirusScan Professional.

If you are using the McAfee VirusScan CD and the Installation Wizard window does not open when you insert the CD into the CD-ROM drive, browse the CD and double-click setup.exe.

- Accessing the McAfee VirusScan installation files and double-clicking Setup.exe.

3. In the McAfee Consumer Products Installation dialog box, click Install VirusScan Professional.

4. In the McAfee VirusScan Professional Edition dialog box, click Next.

5. In the McAfee End User License Agreement dialog box, select your country from the drop-down list box. Read the license agreement.

6. Click Accept.

7. Select the Setup Type: Typical Installation or Custom Installation. Choose Custom Installation if you want to specify the installation features you want to install or change the default installation path. (See Step 9.)

8. Click Next.

9. If you chose Custom Installation:

    a. Click Change to modify the destination directory for the McAfee VirusScan files.

    b. Enable or disable Safe & Sound.

    c. Click Next.

    d. Click Change to modify the destination directory for the McAfee Firewall files.

    e. Enable or disable installing McAfee Firewall.

    f. Click Next.

    g. Enable or Disable Create Emergency Disk, Run Default Scan After Installation, and Scan Boot Record.

    h. Click Next.

10. Click Install.

11. Enable or disable checking for an available McAfee VirusScan Professional update after the installation is complete.

12. Click Next.

13. Enable or Disable Starting McAfee VirusScan Professional Edition immediately.

14. Click Next.

15. Register the software.

    a. On the Product Registration page, click Next.

    b. Complete the required user information (email address, name, address, and so on). Click Next.

    c. Choose any additional options you want to specify.

        - Check I Want To Receive Product Announcements if you want to receive emails from McAfee about new enhancements to the VirusScan software.

- Check I Want To Receive Special Offers if you want to receive emails from McAfee about any new products they release.
- Use the drop-down list to specify where you bought McAfee VirusScan.

d. Click Finish. The McAfee Instant Updater sends your registration information via the Internet. It also checks for any new updates.

e. If new updates were found, click Update.

f. If necessary, click Yes to confirm installing the updates.

g. Click Finish.

h. Click Yes to restart your computer.

ACTIVITY 10-1

Installing Norton AntiVirus 2003 on a Windows 98 Computer

 You'll be keying either the Norton AntiVirus or the McAfee VirusScan activities depending on your classroom setup.

Setup:

The installation files for Norton AntiVirus 2003 reside on the company's corporate server, 2000SRV, in the share called AntiVirus.

Scenario:

The company you work for, Jake's Snack Shack, recently implemented Internet connectivity on the few Windows 98 computers it has. Prior to this point, the owner, Jake, wasn't concerned about virus protection on his computers because the threat was so minimal. However, employees now have the ability to download information from the Internet, as well as send and receive email—all of which increases the susceptibility of Jake's company computers. He would like you to protect his computers against this threat and has purchased licenses for Symantec's Norton AntiVirus 2003 for all his company's computers. There is no need to register the individual copies due to the license agreement Jake has signed with Symantec. You do not need to create a rescue disk set at this time, but you do need to scan for viruses when the installation is complete.

What You Do	How You Do It
1. **Install Norton AntiVirus 2003 on your computer.**	a. **Restart the computer and choose Microsoft Windows from the boot menu.**
	b. If necessary, **log on as Admin#.**
	c. **Access the \\2000SRV\AntiVirus share.**
	d. **Double-click Setup.exe.** Setup updates the operating system files.
	e. If prompted, **restart your computer.** From the boot menu, **choose Microsoft Windows.**
	f. In the Norton AntiVirus 2003 Setup wizard, **click Next.**
	g. **Click I Accept The License Agreement.**

⦿ I accept the license agreement

	h. **Click Next.**
	i. **Click Next** to accept the default destination folder.
	j. **Click Next** to begin the installation.
	k. **Read the text of the Readme Information and click Next.**

```
Norton AntiVirus 2003 for Windows 98/ME/2000/XP
Copyright 2002 Symantec Corporation.
All rights reserved.
README.TXT                                 August 2002
```

	l. **Click Finish.**
	m. **Click Yes** to restart your computer.
	n. **Log on as Admin#.** The Norton AntiVirus Information Wizard automatically starts.

2. **Scan for viruses.**

a. In the Norton AntiVirus Information Wizard, **click Next.**

b. **Click Skip** to skip registering your product.

c. **Click Yes** to confirm that you want to skip registering Norton AntiVirus.

d. Your displayed subscription service expiration date is one year from your installation date. **Click Next.**

Start Date: 1/14/03

Expiration Date: **1/15/04**

e. **Uncheck Run LiveUpdate and Create A Rescue Disk Set.**

☐ Run LiveUpdate
Uses your Internet connection to download the latest virus protection and program updates.

☐ Create a Rescue Disk Set
Copies your computer's critical setup data and startup files to a set of removable disks.

f. **Click Next.**

g. **Click Finish.** The virus scan begins.

h. In the Scan: Summary dialog box, **click Finished.**

Summary	No Infection found
Scan time	9 minute(s) 33 second(s)

Action:	Files	Master Boot Record	Boot Record
Scanned:	20035	1	2
Infected:	0	0	0
Repaired:	0	0	0
Quarantined:	0	-	-
Deleted:	0	-	-

More Info

[Finished]   [More Details]

i. The Norton AntiVirus System Status dialog box opens. **Identify any items that need your immediate attention** (they are marked in red).

System Status: Attention ⚠

Security Scanning Features

✓	Auto-Protect	On
✓	Email Scanning	On
✓	Script Blocking	On
✓	Full System Scan	1/14/03

Virus Definition Service

⚠	Virus Definitions	8/19/02
✓	Subscription Service	1/15/04
✓	Automatic LiveUpdate	On

j. **Close the Norton AntiVirus window.**

ACTIVITY 10-2

Installing McAfee VirusScan version 7.0 on a Windows 2000 Computer

Setup:

The installation files for McAfee VirusScan version 7.0 reside on the company's corporate server, 2000SRV, in the share called VirusScan.

Scenario:

The company you work for, Jake's Snack Shack, recently implemented Internet connectivity on all its Windows 2000 computers. Prior to this point, the owner, Jake, wasn't concerned about virus protection on his computers because the threat was so minimal. However, employees now have the ability to download information from the Internet, as well as send and receive email—all of which increase the susceptibility of Jake's company computers. He would like you to protect his computers against this threat and has purchased licenses for McAfee VirusScan Professional for all his company's computers. He does not feel that the personal firewall program is necessary, however, because he has a network firewall installed.

What You Do	How You Do It
1. Install McAfee VirusScan Professional on your computer.	a. Access the \\2000SRV\VirusScan share.
	b. Double-click Setup.
	c. In the McAfee Consumer Products Installation dialog box, **click Install VirusScan Professional.**
	d. In the McAfee VirusScan Professional Edition dialog box, **click Next.**
	e. In the McAfee End User License Agreement dialog box, from the drop-down list box, **select your country.**

	f. **Click Accept.**
	g. **Select Custom Installation.**
	h. **Click Next.**
	i. **Click Next** to accept the default destination directory for McAfee VirusScan program files.
	j. **Uncheck Install McAfee Firewall.**

	k. **Click Next twice.**

l.   **Click Install.**

Click Install to begin.

If you want to review or change any of your installation
settings, click Back. Click Cancel to exit the wizard.

m.   **Click Next.**

n.   On the Product Registration page, **click Cancel** to skip registering McAfee VirusScan.

o.   **Click Finish** to complete the installation and start McAfee VirusScan.

p.   If the Emergency Disk Wizard starts, **click Cancel.**

q.   After the initial scan is done, **click OK** to close the McAfee Virus Scan window.

TOPIC B

Configure Virus Protection Software

You have a lot of choices to make after you install virus protection software. For example, do you want the software to scan the computer periodically for viruses? Do you want it to scan all incoming email messages? In this topic, you'll learn the options you can configure in virus protection software that enable you to increase a computer's defenses against viruses.

In some situations, the default configuration of virus protection software won't meet your users' or clients' needs. For example, you might have a client whose work is so critical that he wants his virus protection software to scan for viruses on a daily basis but the default setting is to scan only weekly. As an A+ technician, you must be prepared to configure your users' virus protection software so that it's tailored to their needs.

Common Virus Protection Software Configuration Properties

Many virus protection software packages allow you to set configuration parameters to customize the performance of the product to meet your needs. This customization includes specifying:

- Automatic and manual scans.
- Specific file types to include or exclude in a scan.
- Email scans.
- Automatically and manually obtaining virus definition updates.

Norton AntiVirus configuration options are listed in Table 10-3, Table 10-4, and Table 10-5. The McAfee VirusScan configuration options are listed in Table 10-6, Table 10-7, and Table 10-8.

Table 10-3: *Norton AntiVirus System Options*

Option	Description
Auto-Protect	Checks your computer's programs for viruses as you run them and monitors your computer for activity that is typical of a virus. You can:
	• Enable or disable auto-protect.
	• Enable or disable automatic start-up of auto-protect when Windows starts.
	• Enable or disable an icon in the system tray for auto-protect.
	• Select how Norton AntiVirus deals with found viruses. You can have Norton AntiVirus automatically repair the infected file, try to repair then quarantine if unsuccessful, deny access to the infected file, or prompt you for a decision each time a virus is found.
	• Select which types of files to scan for viruses. You choose between a comprehensive file scan or customize the types scanned by file extension or specific file name.
Script Blocking	Monitors Visual Basic and JavaScript scripts for virus-like activities to identify viruses without the need for specific virus definitions. You can:
	• Enable or disable ScriptBlocking.
	• Select how Norton AntiVirus deals with found malicious scripts. You can have Norton AntiVirus prompt you for a decision each time a malicious script is found or stop all suspicious activities without prompting you.
Manual Scan	Specifies what items to scan in addition to files when you request a manual scan—memory, boot records, and master boot records. You can:
	• Select how Norton AntiVirus deals with found viruses. You can have Norton AntiVirus automatically repair the infected file, try to repair then quarantine if unsuccessful, deny access to the infected file, or prompt you for a decision each time a virus is found.
	• Select which types of files to scan for viruses. You choose between a comprehensive file scan or customize the types scanned by file extension or specific file name. You can also enable or disable the scanning of compressed files.

Option	Description
Bloodhound	Uses scanning technology to identify new and unknown viruses based on the file's structure, its behavior, programming logic, computer instructions, and any data included in the file. You can: • Enable or disable the bloodhound feature. • Select the level of protection—highest, default, or lowest.
Exclusions	Specifies the files or folders to be excluded from scans. You can exclude the individual items selected from virus detection, low level format of the hard disk, write to hard disk boot records, or write to floppy disk boot records.

Table 10-4: *Norton AntiVirus 2003 Internet Options*

Option	Description
Email	Checks your email for viruses and worms. You can: • Enable or disable scanning of incoming email. • Enable or disable scanning of outgoing email. • Select how Norton AntiVirus deals with found viruses or worms. You can have Norton AntiVirus automatically repair the infected file, prompt you for a decision each time a virus is found, try to repair then quarantine if unsuccessful, try to repair then silently quarantine if unsuccessful, or try to repair then quietly delete if unsuccessful. • Enable or disable worm blocking. • Enable or disable alert when scanning email attachments.
Advanced Email	Specifies the default behavior when scanning email. You can: • Enable or disable protection against timeouts. • Enable or disable an icon in the system tray for auto-protect. • Enable or disable progress indicator when sending email.
Instant Messenger	Specifies which instant messenger programs will be protected by Norton AntiVirus 2003. You can: • Select AOL Instant Messenger, MSN Instant Messenger, and Yahoo Messenger to protect. • Select how Norton AntiVirus deals with found viruses. You can have Norton AntiVirus automatically repair the infected file, prompt you for a decision each time a virus is found, or try to repair then quarantine if unsuccessful. • Enable notification of received infected files for MSN.
LiveUpdate	Specify how updates will be applied to the system. You can: • Enable or disable automatic LiveUpdate. • Enable or disable virus protection updates by applying updates without interrupting the user or notification when updates are available. • Enable or disable notification of available program updates.

Table 10-5: *Norton AntiVirus 2003 Other Options*

Option	Description
Inoculation	Available on Windows 98 systems only, monitors changes to system files. You can: • Enable or disable inoculate boot record. • Select how Norton AntiVirus deals with a change in an inoculated boot record. You can have Norton AntiVirus prompt you for a decision each time a virus is found, or just notify you about the change.
Miscellaneous	Specify miscellaneous settings for Norton AntiVirus protection. You can: • Enable or disable creating a backup file in quarantine before attempting to repair a file. • Enable or disable the Office plug-in to scan and protect Microsoft Office documents. • Enable or disable an alert when virus protection is out-of-date. • Enable or disable a system file scan at Windows startup. • Enable or disable password protection to make changes to the configuration of Norton AntiVirus 2003.

Table 10-6: *McAfee VirusScan System Scan Options*

Option	Description
Detection	Used to specify the types of events that cause scanning to occur and the types of files you want to scan. The Advanced button can be used to enable heuristics scanning, which uses scanning technology to identify new and unknown viruses based on the file's structure, its behavior, programming logic, computer instructions, and any data included in the file.
Action	Used to specify how the VShield program will handle viruses that it detects in a file on either a local or network drive.
Report	Used to specify if VirusScan activity will be logged and what types of information will be included in the log. You can use the Browse button to select a new location for the log file.
Exclusion	Used to specify what drives, folders, subfolders, and individual files to exclude from the virus scans.

Table 10-7: *McAfee VirusScan Email Scan Options*

Option	Description
Detection	Enables or disables scanning your email attachments. Specifies the types of attachments to scan. The Advanced button can be used to enable heuristics scanning.
Action	Used to specify how the VShield program will handle viruses that it detects in an email attachment.
Alert	Used to specify warnings that happen if a virus is found in an email.
Report	Used to specify if VirusScan activity will be logged and what types of information will be included in the log. You can use the Browse button to select a new location for the log file.

Table 10-8: *McAfee VirusScan HAWK Options*

Option	Description
Email	Enables or disables HAWK for your email and specifies the settings HAWK will use.
Script Stopper	Enables or disables the Script Stopper feature of HAWK and allows you to add a list of trusted scripts to circumvent the Script Stopper feature.

How to Configure Virus Protection Software

Procedure Reference: Configure Norton AntiVirus 2003

To make changes to the default configuration settings of Norton AntiVirus 2003 in Windows XP, Windows 2000, or Windows 98:

1. From the Start menu, choose Programs→Norton AntiVirus→Norton AntiVirus 2003.

2. Click Options.

3. Make any desired changes to the System options. The System options are listed in Table 10-3.

4. Make any desired changes to the Internet options. The Internet options are listed in Table 10-4.

5. Make any desired changes to the Other options. The Other options are listed in Table 10-5.

6. Click OK.

Procedure Reference: Configure McAfee VirusScan Version 7.0

To make changes to the default configuration settings of McAfee VirusScan version 7.0 in Windows XP, Windows 2000, or Windows 98:

1. From the Start menu, choose Programs→McAfee→VirusScan Professional Edition.

2. Under Tasks, click Configure Automatic Protection Settings.

3. Enable or disable the following protection settings:

   - System Scanning
   - Microsoft Outlook E-Mail Scanning
   - HAWK for E-Mail
   - HAWK for Script Stopper

    HAWK stands for Hostile Activity Watch Kernel which monitors your computer for suspicious activity that might be the work of a virus.

4. Click Advanced.

5. Click System Scan.

6. Make any desired changes to the System Scan settings. The System Scan options are shown in Table 10-6. You can set various detection, action, reporting, and exclusion settings for system scans.

7. Click E-Mail Scan.

8. Make any desired changes to the E-mail Scan settings. The E-mail Scan options are shown in Table 10-7.

9. Click HAWK.

10. Make any desired changes to the HAWK settings. The HAWK options are shown in Table 10-8.

11. Click OK.

12. Close the VirusScan Professional Edition dialog box.

ACTIVITY 10-3

Configuring Norton AntiVirus 2003 on a Windows 98 Computer

Scenario:

You have installed Norton AntiVirus 2003 software on all the Windows 98 computers at Jake's Snack Shack. Users have noticed that since you have installed Norton AntiVirus 2003 on their computers, the computers' performance has slowed down considerably. After researching the configuration options, the IT Director has decided that setting protection to a lower level and disabling the options users do not need will improve performance. The IT Director would like you to make the following changes:

- Disable the Auto-Protect system tray icon.
- Disable Scan Floppy Disk In A: For Boot Viruses When Shutting Down.
- Disable outgoing mail scans.
- Disable the alert when scanning email attachments for worms.
- Change the setting for automatic virus protection updates to notification.

What You Do	How You Do It
1. **Make the desired System option changes to Norton AntiVirus on your computer.**	a. From the Start menu, **choose Programs→ Norton AntiVirus→Norton AntiVirus 2003.**
	b. **Click Options.**
	c. Under System, **click Auto-Protect.**

d. Under How To Stay Protected, **uncheck Show The Auto-Protect Icon In The Tray.**

How to stay protected

☑ Enable Auto-Protect (recommended)

☑ Start Auto-Protect when Windows starts up (recommended)

☐ Show the Auto-Protect icon in the tray

e. Under System, **click Advanced.**

f. Under What Activities To Monitor When Using Floppy Disks, **uncheck Scan Floppy Disk In A: For Boot Viruses When Shutting Down.**

What activities to monitor when using floppy disks

☑ Scan floppy disk for boot viruses every time it is mounted

☐ Scan floppy disk in A: for boot viruses when shutting down

☐ Scan all additional floppies on shutdown

2. **Make the desired Internet option changes to Norton AntiVirus on your computer.**

a. Under Internet, **click Email.**

b. Under What To Scan, **uncheck Scan Outgoing Email (Recommended).**

c. Under Internet, **click LiveUpdate.**

d. Under How To Keep Your Virus Protection Updated, **select Notify Me When Updates Are Available.**

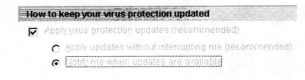

e. **Click OK** to save your configuration changes.

f. **Close Norton AntiVirus.**

ACTIVITY 10-4

Configuring McAfee VirusScan on a Windows 2000 Computer

Scenario:

You have installed McAfee VirusScan software on all the Windows 2000 computers at Jake's Snack Shack. Users have noticed that since you have installed McAfee VirusScan Professional on their computers, the computers' performance has slowed down considerably. After researching the configuration options, the IT Director has decided that setting protection to a lower level and disabling the options users do not need will improve performance. The IT Director would like you to make the following changes:

- Disable scan on outbound files.
- Disable scan floppies: for viruses when shutting down.

In addition, the IT Director is concerned about email. He wants you to make sure that the email system won't carry in any viruses.

What You Do	How You Do It
1. **Make the desired System Scan option changes to McAfee Virus Scan on your computer.**	a. From the Start menu, **choose Programs→ McAfee→VirusScan Professional Edition.**
	b. Under Tasks, **click Configure Automatic Protection Settings.**

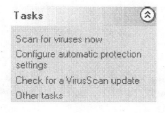

	c. **Click Advanced.**
	d. On the Detection page for System Scan, in the Scan box, **uncheck Outbound Files.**

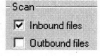

e. On the Detection page for System Scan, in the Scan Floppies On box, **uncheck Shutdown.**

2. **Make the desired E-Mail Scan option changes to McAfee Virus Scan on your computer.**

a. On the left side of the System Scan Properties dialog box, **click E-Mail Scan.**

b. **Check Enable Scanning of E-mail Attachments In Microsoft Outlook.**

> ☑ Enable Scanning of e-mail attachments

c. **Click OK.**

d. **Close the VirusScan Professional Edition dialog box.**

TOPIC C
Create a Clean Boot Disk

As you saw in Topic 10A, one of the types of malicious code you can encounter is a virus that affects your boot sector. Depending on the virus protection software you install, you will need a clean (non-infected) boot disk to be able to remove such a virus. In this topic, you'll learn the steps you must take to create a clean boot disk.

Some boot sector viruses can be removed only by first booting the computer with a clean boot disk. You can create this disk only on a computer that isn't already infected with a virus. For this reason, it's essential that you create a clean boot disk before the computer becomes infected. Without a clean boot disk, you might not be able to remove a boot sector virus from a computer, and the user's data and program files can be destroyed.

Boot Disk

Definition:

A boot disk is a diskette that you can use to boot a computer when the operating system installed on the hard disk will not boot. A boot disk contains a minimal set of system files required to boot the computer to a base operating system such as MS-DOS or a Windows product. A boot disk allows you access to the base operating system to make repairs.

A boot disk may be created using your operating system or your virus protection software. A boot disk must be created before there is a problem on the computer. A boot disk created by your virus protection software may contain additional files used to scan your computer for malicious code.

Example: AntiVirus Software Boot Disks

Virus Protection Boot Disks	Contains
Norton Rescue Disk Set	The Norton AntiVirus Rescue Disk set contains backup copies of partition information, CMOS information, master boot record information, and system startup files needed to boot your computer into Windows 98. In addition, it contains a virus scanner and virus definition files. It might contain Norton Utilities if it is installed on your computer.
Norton Emergency Disk Set	In addition to containing the system file needed to boot your particular operating system (Windows XP, Windows 2000, Windows 98, or Windows NT), the Norton AntiVirus Emergency Disk set contains a scanning utility that scans your computer and removes viruses.
McAfee Emergency Disk Set	In addition to containing the system files needed to boot your particular operating system, the Norton Emergency Disk set includes BOOTSCAN.EXE, a specialized, small-footprint command-line scanner that can scan your hard disk boot sectors and master boot record allowing you to boot into a virus-free environment to make repairs.

How to Create a Clean Boot Disk

Procedure Reference: Create a Norton AntiVirus Rescue Disk Set in Windows 98

If you are running Windows 98, you can create a rescue disk set. To create a rescue disk set after you have initially installed the product and run the Norton AntiVirus Information wizard:

1. Open Norton AntiVirus.

2. In the Norton AntiVirus windows, click the Rescue icon at the top of the window.

3. Select drive A.

4. Click Create.

5. If necessary, click Yes to disable virus scanning.

6. Label the disks as prompted and click OK.

7. Insert the disks as prompted.

8. Close Norton AntiVirus.

9. Test your rescue disk set:

   a. Close all open programs.

   b. Insert the rescue disk labeled Basic Rescue Boot Floppy Disk into the A drive.

   c. Shut down and power off your computer.

   d. Turn on your computer.

   e. The computer should restart using the rescue boot floppy and display the Rescue Disk screen. Press Esc to exit to MS-DOS.

   f. Remove your Basic Rescue Boot Floppy Disk from the A drive.

   g. Restart your computer.

Procedure Reference: Updating a Norton AntiVirus 2003 Rescue Disk Set in Windows 98

You can update your existing Rescue Disk set instead of creating a new set:

1. Open Norton AntiVirus.

2. In the Norton AntiVirus window, click the Rescue icon at the top of the window.

3. Select drive A.

4. Click Update.

5. Insert the rescue disk labeled Basic Rescue Boot Floppy Disk into the A drive.

6. Click OK.

7. Insert the disks as prompted.

8. Close Norton AntiVirus.

Procedure Reference: Creating a Norton AntiVirus Emergency Disk Set

To create a Norton AntiVirus Emergency Disk set in Windows XP, Windows 2000, Windows NT, or Windows 98:

1. Insert the Norton AntiVirus CD in the CD-ROM drive.

2. Click Browse CD.

3. Double-click the Support folder.

4. Double-click the Edisk folder.

5. Double-click the Ned.exe file.

6. In the Welcome window, click OK.

7. Label the disk as instructed and insert it in drive A.

8. Click Yes.

9. Repeat labeling, inserting the disk in drive A and clicking OK for all prompted disks.

10. Remove the final disk from the A drive.

11. Click OK.

12. Close all open windows.

13. Remove the Norton AntiVirus CD-ROM from the CD-ROM drive.

14. Test the emergency disk set:

    a. Insert the first disk in the set into the A drive.

    b. Shut down and power off Windows.

    c. Turn on the computer.

    d. In the Norton AntiVirus window, press Enter to scan the C drive.

    e. When prompted, insert the second disk in the set and press Enter.

    f. When prompted, insert the third disk and press Enter.

    g. If you don't want to wait for the scan to complete, turn off the computer, remove the emergency disk, and turn the computer back on.

    h. When the scan is complete, reinsert the first emergency disk and press any key to continue.

    i. Turn off the computer, remove the emergency disk, and turn the computer back on.

Procedure Reference: Creating a McAfee VirusScan version 7.0 Emergency Disk

To create a McAfee VirusScan emergency disk in Windows XP, Windows 2000, Windows NT, or Windows 98:

1. Open McAfee VirusScan Professional.

2. Under Tasks, click Other Tasks.

3. Click McAfee Emergency Disk.

4. In the Emergency Disk Wizard, click Next.

5. If your computer contains one or more FAT32 or NTFS partitions, McAfee VirusScan automatically formats the disk to use the NAI-OS file system. Click Next.

    If your computer contains only a FAT partition, select a format for your disk and click Next.

    • Format using the installed operating system.

    • Create an NAI-OS emergency disk.

6. Insert a blank high-density disk in drive A.

7. Click Next.

8. If you chose to format your disk, complete the following steps:

    a. Click OK to verify you understand you must check Copy System Files in the Format Dialog box.

    b. If you chose to format your disk, check Copy System Files in the Format dialog box and click Start.

    c. Click Close twice.

9. Click Finish.

10. Remove the disk, label it, and write-protect it.

11. Close the VirusScan Professional window.

12. Test the emergency disk.

    a. Close all open programs.

    b. Insert the emergency disk into the A drive.

    c. Shut down and power off the computer.

    d. Turn on the computer.

    e. Enter Y to confirm that you performed a cold boot of the computer.

    f. Press any key to continue.

    g. After a few minutes, virus scanning begins, which means that the emergency disk works properly. When the scanning completes, remove the emergency disk and restart the computer.

       If you don't want to wait for the virus scanning to complete, turn off the computer, remove the emergency disk, and then restart the computer.

ACTIVITY 10-5

Creating a Norton AntiVirus Rescue Disk Set in Windows 98

Setup:

To create a rescue disk set, you will need 8 floppy disks.

Scenario:

You have installed and configured Norton AntiVirus 2003 on all the Windows 98 computers at Jake's Snack Shack. Unfortunately, you've had a problem already with a master boot record virus on one of the computers. You were forced to re-install Windows 98 because you didn't have a set of rescue disks for the computer. You've decided to create a set of rescue disks for each computer.

What You Do	How You Do It
1. Create a rescue disk set for your computer.	a. Open Norton AntiVirus.
	b. In the Norton AntiVirus window, click Rescue.

c. **Select drive A.**

Select Destination Drive

◉ ▭ A: Floppy

d. **Click Create.**

e. If necessary, **click Yes** to disable virus scanning.

f. From the Basic Rescue Disk List, **select Basic Rescue Boot Floppy Disk and click OK.**

g. **Label the disks as prompted and click OK.**

h. **Insert the disks as prompted.**

i. When finished, **remove the final disk.**

2. Test your rescue disk set.

    a. **Insert the rescue disk labeled Basic Rescue Boot Floppy Disk into the A drive.**

    b. **Click Restart.** The computer should restart using the rescue boot floppy and display the Rescue Disk screen.

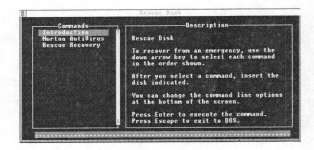

    c. **Press Esc to exit to MS-DOS.**

    d. **Remove your Basic Rescue Boot Floppy Disk from the A drive.**

    e. **Restart your computer.** From the boot menu, **choose Microsoft Windows.**

    f. **Log on as Admin#.**

ACTIVITY 10-6

Creating a McAfee Virus Scan Emergency Disk in Windows 2000

Setup:

To create an emergency disk, you will need a floppy disk.

Scenario:

You have installed and configured McAfee VirusScan on all the Windows 2000 computers at Jake's Snack Shack. Unfortunately, you've had a problem already with a virus on one of the computers that prevented you from booting into Windows 2000. You were forced to re-install Windows 2000 because you didn't have an emergency disk for the computer. You've decided to create an emergency disk for each computer.

What You Do	How You Do It
1. Create an emergency disk for the computer.	a. Open McAfee VirusScan Professional.
	b. Under Tasks, click Other Tasks.
	c. Click McAfee Emergency Disk.

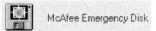

	d. In the Emergency Disk Wizard, click Next.
	e. Click Next to format your emergency disk with NAI-OS.

> Your emergency disk will be formatted using the NAI-OS. The NAI-OS will give you full protection from boot sector viruses on NTFS and FAT-32 partitions as well as file scanning capabilities on FAT-16 partitions.

	f. Click Next.
	g. Insert a blank high-density disk in drive A.
	h. Click Next.

i.   When the disk is created, **click Finish.**

> **An Emergency Disk has been created.**
>
> - Label it -"*McAfee Emergency Boot Disk*".
>
> - Write protect it. To write protect the disk, open the write-protect notch in the upper corner of the disk.
>
> - To test your Emergency Disk, restart your computer with the disk in the A: drive. When you get to the A: prompt, type C: and press the ENTER key to access your hard drive. If you can access your hard drive in this test your Emergency Disk is functioning properly.
>
> - Store the disk in a safe place.

j.   **Remove the disk, label it, and write-protect it.**

k.   **Close the VirusScan Professional window.**

2. **Test your emergency disk.**

    a. **Close all open programs.**

    b. **Insert the emergency disk into the A drive.**

    c. **Shut down and power off the computer.**

    d. **Turn on your computer.** The computer restarts using the emergency disk and the McAfee Virus Removal Tool opens.

    e. **Enter Y** to confirm that you performed a cold boot of the computer.

```
[=============================================]
|             NETWORK ASSOCIATES VIRUS REMOVAL TOOL              |
|                                                               |
|   THIS DISKETTE IS USED TO SIMPLIFY THE TASK OF REMOVING A    |
|   VIRUS FROM YOUR COMPUTER.  IT IS IMPORTANT TO ENSURE THAT   |
|   YOU COLD BOOTED YOUR MACHINE BEFORE USING THIS DISKETTE.    |
|   A COLD BOOT MEANS THAT THE POWER TO THE COMPUTER IS TURNED  |
|   OFF AND THEN TURNED ON WITH THIS DISKETTE IN THE A: DRIVE.  |
[=============================================]
Did you cycle the power off and on (Y/N)?
```

    f. **Press any key** to continue. When virus scanning begins, the disk is working properly.

    g. **Turn off the computer** to stop the virus scanning.

    h. **Remove your emergency disk from the A drive.**

    i. **Restart your computer.**

    j. From the boot menu, **choose Windows 2000 Professional.**

    k. **Log on as Admin#.**

TOPIC D

Manually Update Virus Definitions

A computer's virus protection software is only as good as its most recent list of viruses. As an A+ technician, if you're called out to work on a computer that you suspect might be infected with a virus, one of the first steps you should take is to make sure that the computer's virus definitions are current. In this topic, you'll learn how to manually update the virus definitions within a computer's virus protection software.

Because hackers are releasing new viruses every day, it's possible for the virus definitions in your users' virus protection software to become out of date. If a computer's virus protection software doesn't have a particular virus' definition, it's possible for that computer to become infected with the new virus. You can avoid leaving your users' computers vulnerable to new viruses by manually updating their virus definitions whenever you hear about new viruses. If you don't act proactively by manually updating a computer's virus definitions, your users' computers won't be protected from new viruses, which leaves them vulnerable to losing their data and applications. Failing to remove a virus may mean the loss of valuable data and productivity by the users, which might mean your job.

How to Manually Update Virus Definitions

Procedure Reference: Manually Update Virus Definitions in Norton AntiVirus 2003

To manually update Norton AntiVirus definition files in Windows XP, Windows 2000, Windows NT, and Windows 98:

1. Open Norton AntiVirus 2003.

2. In the Norton AntiVirus window, click the LiveUpdate icon at the top of the window.

3. Click Next to scan for updates.

4. Click Next to download and install updates.

5. Click Finish.

6. Click OK to reboot the computer.

Procedure Reference: Manually Update Virus Definitions in McAfee AntiVirus Professional

To manually update McAfee AntiVirus definition files in Windows XP, Windows 2000, Windows NT, and Windows 98:

1. Open McAfee VirusScan Professional Edition.

2. Under Tasks, click Check For A VirusScan Update.

3. If updates are found, check the items you want to download and click Update.

4. If prompted, click OK to verify you understand a reboot of your system is necessary.

5. Click Finish.

6. If prompted, click Yes to restart your computer.

    If you installed updates, an automatic scan begins.

7. Close the McAfee Instant Updater dialog box.

ACTIVITY 10-7

Manually Updating Norton AntiVirus Definition Files on a Windows 98 Computer

Scenario:

You've just read about a new virus threat on Symantec's Web site at http://securityresponse.symantec.com. Symantec has updated their virus definition files to scan for this virus. You want to make sure that all the Windows 98 computers at Jake's Snack Shack are protected from this nasty virus immediately.

What You Do	How You Do It
1. Manually update your Norton AntiVirus definition files.	a. **Open Norton AntiVirus.**
	b. In the Norton AntiVirus window, **click the LiveUpdate icon** (at the top of the window).
	c. **Click Next** to check for updates.

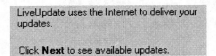

LiveUpdate uses the Internet to deliver your updates.

Click **Next** to see available updates.

d. **Click Next** to download and install updates.

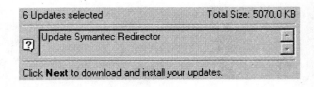

6 Updates selected   Total Size: 5070.0 KB

Update Symantec Redirector

Click **Next** to download and install your updates.

e. **Close the Norton AntiVirus window.**

f. **Click Finish.**

g. **Click OK** to reboot the computer.

INSTRUCTOR ACTIVITY 10-8

Manually Updating McAfee VirusScan Definition Files on a Windows 2000 Computer

Scenario:

You've just read about a new virus threat on McAfee's Web site at **http://www.webimmune.net**. McAfee has updated their virus definition files to scan for this virus. You want to make sure that all the Windows 2000 computers at Jake's Snack Shack are protected from this nasty virus immediately.

What You Do	How You Do It
1. **Manually update your McAfee VirusScan definition files.**	a. **Open McAfee VirusScan Professional Edition.**
	b. **Under Tasks, click Check For A VirusScan Update.** The McAfee Instant Updater dialog box opens.

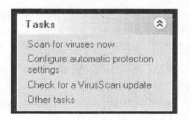

c. If any updates are found, **click Update** to download and install the available updates.

d. **Click Finish.**

e. When the automatic scan is complete, **close the McAfee Instant Updater dialog box.**

TOPIC E

Remove a Virus

So far in this lesson, you've seen the techniques you can use to help avoid a virus infection on a computer. But despite your best efforts to avoid viruses on the computers you support, you're bound to encounter a virus sooner or later. As an A+ technician, it's essential that you know how to remove a virus. For this reason, this topic discusses the techniques you can use to remove a virus from an infected computer.

You can expect to hear immediately when any of your users' computers become infected with a virus. As an A+ technician, your job will often depend on your ability to either talk a user through removing the virus or removing it yourself. It's important for you to master the skills necessary to remove a virus so that you are seen as both able to quickly respond to your users' requests and successful in removing the virus.

Virus Removal Options

If your virus protection software package discovers a piece of malicious code, you will typically have three choices in dealing with the code—attempt to repair the infected file, quarantine the infected file, or delete the infected file. When you quarantine an infected file, the software package will isolate the file so that it cannot be opened or executed. Each software package will have its own way of stating these options, but in general you will be allowed to choose from these three functions.

With a known piece of malicious code, you will want to try to repair or delete the infected file. With a piece of malicious code that you suspect is not yet known, you will want to quarantine it and then submit it to your virus protection software manufacturer for analysis. Both Symantec and McAfee have procedures posted on their security Web sites for submitting malicious code.

How to Remove a Virus

Procedure Reference: Remove a Virus Using Norton AntiVirus 2003

If the virus is found during a scan, the affected files may be automatically repaired or deleted. In some cases, you will need to take action to remove a virus using Norton AntiVirus 2003:

1. You may be prompted to fix the file using the Repair wizard.

    a. Uncheck any files you don't want Norton AntiVirus to fix.

    b. Click Fix.

    Any files that Norton AntiVirus can't fix or delete are added to the Quarantine window.

    c. In the Quarantine window, uncheck any files you don't want to quarantine.

    d. Click Quarantine.

    Any files that Norton AntiVirus can't quarantine are added to the Delete pane.

    e. Uncheck any files you do not want to delete.

⚠ Any infected files that you do not delete remain on your computer and can cause damage or be transferred to other computers.

    f.   Click Delete.

    g.   Review the details of the summary pane and click Finished.

2.   You may be issued an alert that a virus was found and repaired by the Auto-Protect feature.

- In Windows 98, click Finish to close the alert.
- In Windows 2000 or Windows XP, click OK to close the alert.

If you have set your options so that the Auto-Protect feature prompts you to decide what to do with the file, you need to select one of the following:

- Repair the infected file.
- Quarantine the infected file.
- Delete the infected file.
- Do not open the file, but leave the problem alone.
- Ignore the problem and do not scan this file in the future.
- Ignore the problem and continue with the infected file.

The recommended choice will be selected in the alert dialog box.

3.   You may be issued an alert that a virus was found in a script. You must select one of the presented options to remove the threat. The recommended option is to stop running the script.

4.   You may be issued an alert that a worm was found in an outgoing email attachment. You must select one of the presented options to remove the worm. The recommended action is to quarantine the file.

5.   On Windows 98 systems, you may be alerted to a change in your system files. You must select one of the following options to respond to the inoculation alert:

- Update the saved copy of your master boot record—select this option if you know there has been a legitimate change to the system files such as applying an operating system patch or repartitioning the hard disk.
- Restore your master boot record—select this option if you are sure there has not been a legitimate change to the system files.

6.   You may be prompted that Norton AntiVirus can't repair a file.

- If an .exe, .doc, .dot., or .xls file is infected, use the Repair Wizard to fix the problem.
- If the master boot record, boot record, or a system file is infected, replace the file using the Rescue Disks or your operating system installation disk.

7.   If the computer won't boot normally, use the Rescue Disk set to repair or replace infected files.

    a.   Insert the basic rescue boot floppy disk in drive A and restart your computer.

    b.   Use the arrow keys to select one of the following programs:

- Norton AntiVirus to scan your computer for viruses and repair any infected files.
- Rescue Recovery to check and restore boot and partition information.

    c.   Press Enter to run the selected program.

    d.   Respond to the prompts for inserting and removing disks from the rescue disk set.

    e.   When the rescue recovery is complete, remove the rescue disk from the A drive.

    f.   Restart your computer.

8.   After any alert, you should manually run LiveUpdate to obtain the latest definition files.

9.   After you have the most up-to-date virus definition files installed, you should scan your system.

Procedure Reference: Remove a Virus Using McAfee VirusScan Professional

If the virus is found during a scan, the affected files may be automatically repaired or deleted. In some cases, you will need to take action to remove a virus using McAfee VirusScan Professional:

1.   You may be prompted to fix the file by selecting one of the following options:

   - *Continue:* This option directs VirusScan to continue with the present scan and not take any other action on the infected file. If you have reporting enabled, the incident will be recorded in the log file.

   - *Stop:* This option directs VirusScan to stop the present scan immediately. To continue the scan, you need to click Scan For Viruses Now.

   - *Clean Infection or Clean File:* One of these options will be presented depending on the type of problem found. These options direct VirusScan to attempt to remove the virus code from the infected file. If you have reporting enabled, the incident and its resolution will be recorded in the log file. Review the log file to verify the virus.

   - *Delete:* This option directs VirusScan to first attempt to remove the virus code from the file and then to delete the infected file if it cannot repair the file.

   - *Quarantine:* This option directs VirusScan to move the infected file to the default quarantine folder and continue with the scan.

   - *Info:* This option directs VirusScan to run Internet Explorer and go to the AVERT Web site at **www.webimmune.net** where you can research the suspected file or virus.

2.   If an infected file is quarantined:

   a.   Open McAfee VirusScan Professional.

   b.   Click the down arrow for Advanced Tasks.

   c.   Click Manage Quarantined Files.

You will need to manage the file by selecting one of the following options:

- *Add:* This option allows you to browse for and quarantine a file that VirusScan did not automatically quarantine.

- *Clean:* This option directs VirusScan to attempt to remove the virus code from the infected file. If the virus cannot be removed, VirusScan notifies you.

- *Restore:* This option directs VirusScan to restore a file to its original location. It does not clean the file—you should click Clean and verify the virus is removed before restoring a file.

- *Delete:* This option directs VirusScan to delete the infected file.

⚠ Make sure you have a backup copy of the file before you delete.

- *Submit quarantined files to AVERT via WebImmune:* If you suspect the file is infected with a new, unknown virus, this option directs VirusScan to submit the file to McAfee's investigative labs via the **www.webimmune.net** site.

3. If the computer won't boot normally, use the Emergency Disk to perform an emergency scan that examines your hard disk boot sectors, your Master Boot Record, your system directories, program files, and other common sources of infection on your hard disk.

   a. Insert the Emergency Disk in drive A and restart your computer.

   b. Press Enter to select Next.

   c. Press N to use the DAT files from the Emergency Disk or press L to select another location.

   d. Press F to begin the scan.

   e. When the rescue recovery is complete, remove the rescue disk from the A drive.

   f. Restart your computer.

   a. Insert the NAI-OS Emergency Disk in drive A and turn off the power to your computer.

   b. Restart your computer.

   c. Press Y to indicate that you cycled the power off.

   d. When the rescue recovery is complete, remove the rescue disk from the A drive.

   e. Restart your computer.

🔖 The Emergency Disk does not scan for macro viruses, script viruses, or Trojan Horse programs.

4. After any alert, you should manually run McAfee's Instant Updater to obtain the latest definition files.

5. After you have the most up-to-date virus definition files installed, you should scan your system.

ACTIVITY 10-9

Removing Viruses from Your Computer

Scenario:

You've installed virus protection software on all the computers at Jake's Snack Shack. You feel confident that the computers are protected. However, support calls have come in reporting viruses. You need to respond and get the users back up and working.

What You Do	How You Do It

1. Naomi calls the Help Desk to tell you that she was trying to read an email attachment she received. She now has a Norton AntiVirus alert on her Windows 98 system telling her there has been a change in her system files.

    What is your response?

2. Steve calls the Help Desk to tell you he downloaded a program from an Internet site and now his Windows 2000 computer won't boot. He assures you he was running his Norton AntiVirus program all along.

    What is your response?

3. Hank calls the Help Desk to tell you that McAfee VirusScan found a virus on his computer and he chose to clean the file. His Windows 2000 computer is functioning just fine.

    What is your response?

4. Pat calls the Help Desk to report he's getting a McAfee VirusScan alert. You get to Pat's Windows XP computer and choose to clean the infected file. VirusScan reports that the file cannot be cleaned, so you quarantine the file. You look on McAfee's **www.webimmune.net** site, but you can't find any information on this virus. What is your response?

Lesson 10 Follow-up

In this lesson, you learned how to implement virus protection. With properly installed and configured virus protection software, you can both prevent viruses from causing problems on your computer systems and repair computers should they become infected.

1. In your organization, or the organizations you support, what steps have you taken to protect against viruses?

2. In your organization, or the organizations you support, what additional steps do you need to take to protect against viruses?

NOTES

LESSON 11

Preparing for Disaster Recovery

Lesson Objectives:

In this lesson, you will prepare for disaster recovery.

You will:

*   Create a boot disk.

*   Create an emergency repair disk.

*   Install the Recovery Console.

*   Back up data.

*   Back up system state data.

*   Back up the Registry.

*   Prepare for an Automated System Recovery.

Introduction

Throughout this course, you've built, step-by-step, completely configured computers. You've configured users' applications, implemented network connectivity, secured the computers, shared folders and printers, managed the computers' hard disks, configured Internet and intranet connectivity, and even installed and configured virus protection software. At this point, your computers are ready for users to begin working productively on them. But what would happen if your computer crashed? Do you have what you need to recover from the problem? To make sure you're prepared for just such an emergency, in this lesson you'll learn how to prepare for disaster recovery so that you can repair a computer as quickly as possible.

It is inevitable that users' computers will crash. It is your responsibility as an A+ technician to prepare for disaster recovery and minimize the down time and cost to your company.

The following CompTIA A+ Operating System Technologies (2003) Examination objectives are covered in this lesson:

- Topic A:
  - 1.2 Windows 9x-specific files: IO.SYS, MSDOS.SYS, AUTOEXEC.BAT, COMMAND.COM, CONFIG.SYS, WIN.COM, SYSTEM.INI, WIN.INI.
  - 1.2 Windows NT-based specific files: BOOT.INI, NTLDR, NTDETECT.COM, NTBOOTDD.SYS.
  - 1.5 File Management Tools: ATTRIB.EXE
  - 2.3 Boot Sequence: Files required to boot, Boot steps (9.x, NT-based).
  - 2.3 Alternative Boot Methods: Command Prompt mode.
  - 2.5 Caches.
  - 3.2 Startup disks: Required files for a boot disk.
- Topic B:
  - 2.3 Creating emergency repair disk (ERD).
- Topic C:
  - 2.3 Alternative Boot Methods: Recovery Console.
- Topic D:
  - 1.4 Files: File attributes – Read Only, Hidden, System and Archive attributes.
- Topic E:
  - 1.3 Command line functions and utilities include: SCANREG.
  - 1.5 System Management Tools: SCANREG.

TOPIC A

Create a Boot Disk

The first task you should perform in preparing for disaster recovery is to create a boot disk for each user's computer. Creating a boot disk is a quick and easy task, but one that will pay off tenfold in the event you encounter a computer that won't boot. In this topic, you'll learn the steps for creating a boot disk for each operating system you might encounter, including DOS, Windows 9x, Windows 2000, Windows NT, and Windows XP.

If you're unable to boot a computer, you won't be able to perform any other diagnostics or access any of the operating system's tools for troubleshooting the computer. Having a boot disk handy will enable you to at least boot the computer so that you can begin to troubleshoot and fix the problem that prevented it from booting. By booting the computer successfully, you'll be able to begin the work of repairing the computer.

DOS Boot Files

In order to boot a computer using the MS-DOS operating system, your computer must have the necessary files for booting MS-DOS. In Table 11-1, you see a list of the files used to boot a computer with the MS-DOS operating system. These files must be located wherever the computer is booting from, whether it be the computer's hard disk or a floppy boot disk.

Table 11-1: *MS-DOS Boot Files*

File	Used To
Io.sys	Provide MS-DOS and any programs you run access to the computer's hardware. Io.sys includes drivers for hardware devices such as the keyboard, printer ports, serial ports, floppy drives, and hard drives.
Msdos.sys	Manage input and output to and from the computer's disks.
Command.com	Provide the command prompt interface (C:\>). It also provides you with access to certain DOS commands such as `dir`, `copy`, and `cd`. These commands are called internal DOS commands because they are built into the Command.com file. You'll also hear Command.com referred to as the DOS shell or the command interpreter.
Config.sys	Load device drivers, configure the operating system environment, and optimize memory management. For example, you might use the Config.sys file to load the driver for a computer's CD-ROM drive.
Autoexec.bat	Set the initial configuration of MS-DOS and to run any programs you want to run each time the computer boots.

DOS Boot Process

When you turn on an MS-DOS-based computer, it performs the following steps to boot the computer:

1. The computer performs a power-on self test (POST) to test RAM, disk drives, peripheral devices (such as printers), and other hardware components to verify that they are working.

2. Next, the computer looks for the instructions for loading an operating system. These instructions are called the *Master Boot Record (MBR)*; the computer looks for them on a floppy disk, CD-ROM, or the first hard disk in the computer. (The order in which it looks for boot disks depends on how you configure the computer; by default, computers check for the MBR on the floppy disk drive first, then the CD-ROM drive, followed by the first hard disk.) When the computer finds the MBR, it loads it into RAM.

3. The MBR locates the *boot sector* on the boot disk. The boot sector contains the information that enables the computer to locate the Io.sys file.

4. The computer loads the Io.sys file into RAM.

5. The Io.sys file runs a special routine (called Sysinit) that loads the Msdos.sys file into RAM.

6. The Msdos.sys file then processes the commands in the Config.sys file.

7. The Command.com file is loaded into RAM.

8. The Command.com file calls and processes the commands in the Autoexec.bat file.

9. You now see a system command prompt (typically C:\>).

Windows 9x Boot Files

In order to boot a computer using the Windows 9x operating systems, your computer must have the necessary files for booting Windows 9x. Because Windows 9x is actually integrated with MS-DOS, you'll find that it uses many of the same DOS boot files plus several Windows files to boot the computer. In Table 1–2, you see a list of the files used to boot a computer with Windows 9x. These files are located on the hard disk that's used to boot the computer.

Table 11-2: *Windows 9x Boot Files*

File	Used To
Io.sys	Provide MS-DOS and any programs you run to access the computer's hardware. Io.sys includes drivers for hardware devices such as the keyboard, printer ports, serial ports, floppy drives, and hard drives.
Msdos.sys	Manage input and output to and from the computer's disks.
Config.sys	Load device drivers. The Config.sys file is replaced by the Registry in the Windows 9x environment.
Autoexec.bat	Set the initial configuration of Windows 9x to run programs you want to run each time the computer boots. The Autoexec.bat file is replaced by the Registry and the Startup group in Windows 9x.
Win.ini	Configure specific parameters in the Windows environment. In Windows 9x, this file is typically used to set environment parameters for applications written to run on Windows 3.1; these applications are called 16-bit applications. (Newer applications written for the Windows 9x environment, also called 32-bit applications, use the Registry instead of the Win.ini file.)
Win.com	Load Windows 9x.

File	Used To
System.ini	Configure specific parameters used by DOS and the Windows 9x operating system. For example, you can configure the cache size using System.ini by adding the minfilecache and maxfilecache parameters to [vcache] (maxfilecache shouldn't be more than 25% of total memory). Like the Win.ini file, the System.ini file is used primarily by older Windows applications.
Registry	Identify and load the necessary device drivers for the computer's hardware, software, and the operating system itself.
Virtual Device Driver	Initialize the computer's hardware.

Windows 9x Boot Process

When you turn on a Windows 9x-based computer, it performs the following steps to boot the computer:

1. The computer performs a power-on self test (POST) to test its hardware.
2. The computer locates the Master Boot Record (MBR) and loads it into RAM.
3. The MBR locates the boot sector on the boot disk. The boot sector contains the information that enables the computer to locate the Io.sys file.
4. The computer loads the Io.sys file into RAM.
5. The Io.sys file runs a special routine (called Sysinit) that loads the Msdos.sys file into RAM.
6. The Io.sys file loads the System.dat Registry file into RAM but does not process it at this time.
7. If you have configured multiple hardware profiles, Io.sys prompts the user to select a hardware profile.
8. Io.sys processes the Config.sys and Autoexec.bat files (if they exist).
9. When these tasks are complete, Io.sys executes Win.com.
10. Win.com loads the drivers specified within the Registry.
11. Win.com processes the System.ini and Win.ini files.
12. Win.com loads the necessary virtual device drivers, the basic Windows 9x operating system (called the kernel), and the graphical display interface (GDI).
13. The Windows kernel loads the Explorer user interface, including the Desktop, Start menu, and taskbar.
14. The Windows kernel processes any programs in the Startup folder and restores any network connections.
15. The Windows operating system is now ready for the user to use.

Windows 2000/NT/XP Boot Files

When you attempt to boot a computer using Windows 2000, Windows NT, or Windows XP, your computer must have the necessary files for booting Windows. In Table 11-3, you see a list of the files used to boot a computer with Windows 2000, Windows NT, or Windows XP. The boot files are located on the disk you want the computer to boot from.

Table 11-3: *The Windows 2000/NT/XP Boot Files*

File	Used To
Ntldr	Load the Windows 2000, Windows NT, or Windows XP operating system.
Boot.ini	Point the computer to the disk location where the Windows 2000, Windows NT, or Windows XP files are stored. In a dual-boot environment, the contents of the Boot.ini file are used to build the boot menu so that you can choose which operating system you want to load.
Bootsect.dos	Load any non-Windows 2000, Windows NT, or Windows XP operating system you choose from the menu. For example, if you have configured a computer to dual-boot between Windows 98 and Windows 2000, the boot.ini file loads the bootsect.dos file when you choose Windows 98 from the boot menu.
Ntdetect.com	Examine the hardware, build a hardware list, and pass the list to Ntldr. Ntldr adds this information to the computer's Registry.
Ntbootdd.sys	Initialize SCSI hard disks on which the BIOS is disabled.
Ntoskrnl.exe	Load the basic Windows 2000, Windows NT, or Windows XP operating system kernel.
Hal.dll	Isolate the computer's hardware and its device drivers from the Windows 2000, Windows NT, or Windows XP operating system. Isolating the hardware from the operating system enables Microsoft to use the same basic operating system for different types of hardware (such as different processors).
System	Store the system configuration settings that control how devices and services are loaded during the boot process. System is one of the files that makes up the Windows 2000, Windows NT, and Windows XP Registries.

Windows 2000/NT/XP Boot Process

The Windows 2000, Windows NT, and Windows XP operating systems all use the same boot process. This boot process consists of two main phases: the *boot sequence* and the *load phases*. The Windows 2000/NT/XP boot sequence consists of the following steps:

1. The computer runs its power-on self test (POST) to check the hardware.

2. The computer locates the boot device and loads the Master Boot Record into RAM.

3. The MBR finds the active partition on the boot device and loads the boot sector into RAM.

4. The boot sector loads and initializes the Ntldr file, which takes over control of the rest of the boot process.

5. Ntldr configures the computer's processor to address all of the computer's memory; this mode is called the 32-bit flat memory mode.

6. Ntldr starts the file system that corresponds to the formatting of the disk that Windows 2000, Windows NT, or Windows XP will load from. This could be the FAT file system, or Microsoft's NTFS file system.

7. Ntldr reads the Boot.ini file to locate the Windows 2000/NT/XP operating system, and to build the boot menu on dual-boot computers.

8. Ntldr loads Windows 2000, Windows NT, or Windows XP, or, in a dual-boot environment, whatever operating system the user selects from the boot menu.

9. If the operating system selected is Windows 2000, Windows NT, or Windows XP, Ntldr runs Ntdectect.com to build the hardware list. Ntldr loads Ntoskrnl.exe and the Windows 2000/NT/XP load phases start.

   If the operating system selected is anything other than Windows 2000, Windows NT, or Windows XP, Ntldr passes control of the computer to Bootsect.dos.

There are four load phases in the second stage of the Windows 2000/NT/XP boot sequence. These phases include:

1. Kernel Load Phase: The kernel load phase begins when Ntldr loads Ntoskrnl.exe at the end of the boot sequence. You can identify this phase by the Starting Windows progress bar that shows up across the bottom of the screen.

2. Kernel Initialization Phase: In this phase, Ntoskrnl.exe is initialized and takes control of the computer. In Windows 2000 and Windows XP, the computer switches to graphical mode, and you can see a window with an animated Starting Up progress bar. In Windows NT, you can identify this phase when the computer screen turns blue.

3. Service Startup: Ntoskrnl.exe continues by loading the Session Manager (Smss.exe) program. In Windows 2000 and Windows XP, you'll see a window with Please Wait in the title bar during this phase. In Windows NT, you'll see the logon dialog box. During this time, Session Manager loads the high-order services—those necessary for a user to log on.

4. Logon Phase: A Windows 2000/NT/XP boot isn't considered complete until a user logs on successfully. During the logon phase, you can initiate logon. However, Windows 2000/NT/XP will continue to load lower-level services in the background. For this reason, the computer's response time will seem slow to users during the logon phase.

Windows 2000/NT/XP Partition Terminology

In Windows 2000, Windows NT, and Windows XP, Microsoft uses two distinct terms for the computer's partitions. The *system partition* is the partition that contains the files necessary for booting the operating system. In almost all cases, the system partition is the C drive on a computer. The system partition contains the following files:

- Boot.ini
- Bootsect.dos
- Ntldr
- Ntdetect.com

Microsoft refers to the partition that contains all the Windows 2000, Windows NT, or Windows 2000 operating system files as the *boot partition*. The boot partition contains the \Windows folder in the case of Windows 2000 or Windows XP, and the \Winnt folder in Windows NT.

If you have configured the computer with only a single C partition, in this scenario, the system and boot partitions are the same. In contrast, if you have configured the computer with a C partition and a D partition, and installed the operating system into the D partition, the C partition is then the system partition, and the D partition is the boot partition.

The Boot.ini File

Windows 2000, Windows NT, and Windows XP use the Boot.ini file to locate the boot partition (the partition containing the \Windows or \Winnt folder). The Boot.ini file consists of two sections, [Boot Loader] and [Operating Systems], as shown in Figure 11-1. The [Boot Loader] section identifies which operating system you want the computer to default to if no selection is made from the boot menu during the boot process. The timeout parameter specifies how long (in seconds) the computer will display the boot menu before booting the default operating system.

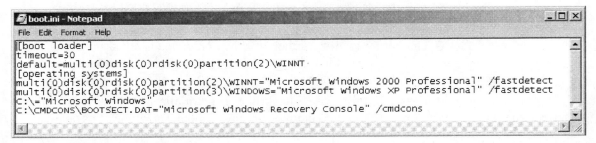

Figure 11-1: *The Boot.ini file.*

The [Operating Systems] section lists the paths to each operating system's files (these are the files stored on the boot partition). Microsoft uses the Advanced RISC Computing (ARC) naming syntax to identify the path to the boot partition. The syntax for ARC path naming is:

- scsi | multi(x)disk(y)rdisk(z)partition(a)\path

In Table 11-4, you find a description of each of the elements that make up the ARC naming syntax.

Table 11-4: *ARC Naming Syntax*

Element	Description
scsi	multi	Indicates the type of hard disk controller in the computer. Uses scsi for SCSI disks with the BIOS disabled; uses multi for all other disks.
(x)	The ordinal number of the disk controller adapter. Ordinal numbering starts with 0. So, if your computer has only one IDE disk controller, the ARC naming syntax would be multi(0).
disk(y)	The SCSI ID of the target disk. If the ARC path starts with multi, (y) is always 0.
rdisk(z)	The disk device's logical unit number. If the ARC path starts with scsi, (z) is always 0. If the ARC path starts with multi, (z) is the ordinal number of the disk on the adapter (usually 0 or 1).
partition(a)	The cardinal number of the Windows 2000/NT/XP boot partition. (Cardinal numbering starts with 1.)

Element	Description
\path	The name of the folder in which the Windows 2000/NT/XP files are stored (typically either \Windows or \Winnt).

How to Create a Boot Disk

Procedure Reference: Create an MS-DOS Boot Disk in Windows 98

You can create a floppy disk to boot a computer using the MS-DOS operating system. To create an MS-DOS boot disk:

1. Start Windows 98.

2. Open Windows Explorer.

3. Format the boot disk using the following steps:

    a.   Insert a floppy disk into the floppy disk drive.

    b.   In Windows Explorer, right-click 3 1/2 Floppy (A:) and choose Format.

    c.   Below Other Options, check Copy System Files.

    d.   Click Start.

    e.   When the format is complete, click Close to close the Format Results dialog box.

    f.   Click Close to close the Format – 3 1/2 Floppy (A:) dialog box.

4. Configure Windows Explorer to display file extensions and hidden files for the C:\Windows\Command folder.

    a.   Select the C:\Windows\Command folder.

    b.   Choose View→Folder Options.

    c.   Select the View tab.

    d.   Below Hidden Files, select Show All Files.

    e.   Uncheck Hide File Extensions For Known File Types.

    f.   Click OK.

5. If you want to use the boot disk to perform such tasks as creating or deleting partitions, correcting boot problems, changing file attributes, or formatting partitions, copy the following program files from C:\Windows\Command to the boot disk.

    *   Attrib.exe
    *   Edit.com
    *   Edit.hlp
    *   Fdisk.exe
    *   Format.com
    *   Scandisk.exe
    *   Scandisk.ini
    *   Sys.com

    To copy the files, complete the following steps:

a. In Windows Explorer, select the C:\Windows\Command folder.

b. Select the first file you want to copy.

c. Hold down the Control key and select all other files you want to copy.

d. Right-click the selected files and choose Send To→3 1/2 Floppy (A).

6. Close Windows Explorer.

7. Test the boot disk to verify that it works.

a. Restart the computer with the floppy disk in the disk drive to verify that you can boot successfully.

b. If necessary, run the computer's System Setup utility to configure it to boot from floppy first.

c. The computer boots successfully if you see an MS-DOS prompt displayed.

8. Remove the MS-DOS boot disk, label it, and store it in a safe location. You might also want to write-protect the disk.

Procedure Reference: Create a Startup Disk for Windows 98

You can create a startup disk in Windows 98 that enables you to boot the computer to DOS with support for the computer's CD-ROM. You might create such a disk if you want to re-install Windows 98 on a computer, or if you want to perform diagnostic tests. To create a startup disk for Windows 98:

1. From the Start menu, choose Settings→Control Panel.

2. Double-click Add/Remove Programs.

3. Select the Startup Disk tab.

4. Click Create Disk.

5. When prompted, insert the Windows 98 installation CD-ROM and click OK.

> You do not have to format the floppy disk before creating the startup disk. Windows 98 automatically formats the disk for you.

6. Insert a floppy disk into the floppy disk drive.

7. Click OK.

> It will take several minutes for Windows 98 to create the startup disk.

8. Click OK to close the Add/Remove Programs Properties dialog box.

9. Close Control Panel.

10. Test the startup disk to verify that it works.

a. Restart the computer with the floppy disk in the disk drive to verify that you can boot successfully.

b. If necessary, run the computer's System Setup utility to configure it to boot from floppy first.

c. From the Startup menu, choose from one of the following options:

• Start Computer With CD-ROM Support.

• Start Computer Without CD-ROM Support.

- View The Help File.

Alternatively, you can press the following key combinations:

- F5, to start in Safe Mode.
- Shift+F5, to start in Command Prompt mode.
- Shift+F8, to start Windows 98 in Step-By-Step Confirmation Mode.

11. Remove the startup disk, label it, and store it in a safe location. You might also want to write-protect the disk.

Procedure Reference: Create a Boot Disk for Windows 2000/XP/NT

To create a boot disk for Windows 2000, Windows XP, and Windows NT:

1. Log on as a user with permissions to the system partition.

2. Open Windows Explorer.

   You must format the disk in the appropriate operating system for the disk to be bootable.

3. Format the boot disk using the following steps:

   a. Insert a floppy disk into the floppy disk drive.

   b. In Windows Explorer, right-click 3 1/2 Floppy (A:) and choose Format.

   c. Optionally, check Quick Format to reduce the amount of time required to format the disk.

   d. Click Start.

   e. Click OK to confirm that you want to format the disk.

   f. When the format is complete, click OK.

   g. Click Close to close the Format A:\ dialog box.

4. If necessary, if you're using Windows 2000 or Windows XP, configure Windows Explorer to display system and hidden files on the C drive using the following steps:

   a. Select the C drive.

   b. In Windows Explorer, choose Tools→Folder Options.

   c. Select the View tab.

   d. Below Hidden Files And Folders, select Show Hidden Files And Folders.

   e. Uncheck Hide File Extensions For Known File Types.

   f. Uncheck Hide Protected Operating System Files (Recommended).

   g. Click OK.

5. If necessary, if you're using Windows NT, configure Windows Explorer to display system and hidden files on the C drive using the following steps:

   a. Select the C drive.

   b. In Windows Explorer, choose View→Options.

   c. Below Hidden Files, choose Show All Files.

   d. Uncheck Hide File Extensions For Known File Types.

   e. Click OK.

6. Copy the following files to the boot disk:

- Boot.ini.

- Bootsect.dos (if it exists). This file will be present only if you dual-boot the computer between Windows 9x and Windows 2000, Windows XP, or Windows NT.

- Ntbootdd.sys (if it exists). This file will be present only if the computer contains BIOS-disabled SCSI disk drives.

- Ntdetect.com.

- Ntldr.

To copy the files, complete the following steps:

a. Select the boot.ini file.

b. Hold down the Control key and select each additional file.

c. Right-click the selected files and choose Send To→3 1/2 Floppy (A:).

7. Close Windows Explorer.

8. Test the boot disk to verify that it works.

a. Restart the computer with the floppy disk in the disk drive to verify that you can boot successfully.

b. If necessary, run the computer's System Setup utility to configure it to boot from floppy first.

c. If the computer has multiple operating systems, verify that you can start each operating system from the boot disk.

9. Remove the boot disk, label it, and store it in a safe location. You might also want to write-protect the disk.

Procedure Reference: Create an MS-DOS Boot Disk in Windows XP

To create an MS-DOS boot disk in Windows XP:

1. Start Windows XP.

2. Log on as a user.

3. Open Windows Explorer.

4. Format the boot disk using the following steps:

a. Insert a floppy disk into the floppy disk drive.

b. In Windows Explorer, right-click 3 1/2 Floppy (A:) and choose Format.

c. Check Create An MS-DOS Startup Disk.

d. Click Start.

e. Click OK to confirm that you want to erase all data on the disk.

f. When the format is complete, click OK.

g. Click Close to close the Format 3 1/2 Floppy (A:) dialog box.

5. Close Windows Explorer.

6. Test the boot disk to verify that it works.

a. Restart the computer with the floppy disk in the disk drive to verify that you can boot successfully.

b.   If necessary, run the computer's System Setup utility to configure it to boot from floppy first.

c.   The computer boots successfully if you see an MS-DOS prompt displayed.

7.   Remove the MS-DOS boot disk, label it, and store it in a safe location. You might also want to write-protect the disk.

ACTIVITY 11-1

Creating Boot Disks

Setup:

You will need three floppy disks to complete this activity.

The Windows 98 installation files are in the C:\Win98 folder on your computer's hard disk.

Scenario:

As an A+ technician, you want to be prepared for any emergency such as computers that won't boot. To be prepared, you need to have boot disks that you can use to boot any operating system, including MS-DOS, Windows 98, Windows 2000, Windows XP, or Windows NT. On the MS-DOS boot disk, you would like to include the files necessary for changing file attributes, formatting partitions, editing files, creating or deleting partitions, scanning disks for errors, and for transferring the operating system files.

What You Do	How You Do It
1. In Windows 98, **create an MS-DOS boot disk.**	a. **Restart the computer and choose Microsoft Windows from the boot menu.**
	b. **Log on as Admin#.**
	c. **Open Windows Explorer.**
	d. **Insert a floppy disk into the floppy disk drive.**
	e. **Right-click 3 1/2 Floppy (A:) and choose Format.**

f.   Below Other Options, **check Copy System Files Only.**

Other options
Label:

☐ No label
☑ Display summary when finished
☑ Copy system files

g.   **Click Start.**

h.   When the format is complete, **click Close** to close the Format Results dialog box.

i.   **Click Close** to close the Format dialog box.

j.   **Select the C:\Windows\Command folder.**

k.   **Choose View→Folder Options.**

l.   **Select the View tab.**

m.   Below Hidden Files, **choose Show All Files.**

Hidden files
   ○ Do not show hidden files
   ○ Do not show hidden or system files
   ◉ Show all files

n.   **Uncheck Hide File Extensions For Known File Types.**

☐ Hide file extensions for known file types

o.   **Click OK.**

p.   From C:\Windows\Command, **copy the following files to the boot disk:**
   • Attrib.exe
   • Edit.com
   • Edit.hlp
   • Fdisk.exe
   • Format.com

- Scandisk.exe
- Scandisk.ini
- Sys.com

    q.   **Close Windows Explorer.**

⚠ If your computer is configured to boot from hard disk before a floppy disk, you won't be able to test the boot disk. Reconfigure the computer to support booting from floppy disk before attempting to boot from a hard disk.

2.   **Test the MS-DOS boot disk.**

    a.   **Verify that you have the boot disk in the floppy drive.**

    b.   **From the Start menu, choose Shutdown.**

    c.   **Select Restart.**

    d.   **Click OK.**

    e.   **When the computer restarts, you will see an MS-DOS prompt displayed if the boot disk you created works properly.**

    f.   **Remove the boot disk from the floppy drive.**

    g.   **Label the floppy disk "MS-DOS boot disk"**

---

3.   **Create a Windows 98 Startup disk.**

    a.   **Restart the computer and choose Microsoft Windows from the boot menu.**

    b.   **Log on as Admin#.**

    c.   **In the Control Panel, double-click Add/ Remove Programs.**

    d.   **Select the Startup Disk tab.**

e. **Click Create Disk.**

If you have trouble starting Windows 98, you can use a startup disk to start your computer, run diagnostic programs, and fix many problems.

To create a startup disk, click Create Disk. You will need one floppy disk.

Create Disk...

f. When prompted to insert the Windows 98 CD-ROM, **click OK.**

g. In the Copy Files From text box, **type C:\Win98 and click OK** to install the necessary files from the copy of the Windows 98 CD-ROM on your hard disk.

Copy files from:

C:\Win98

h. **Insert a floppy disk into the floppy disk drive.**

i. **Click OK.**

j. When Windows 98 completes creating the Startup disk, **click OK** to close the Add/ Remove Programs Properties dialog box.

k. **Close Control Panel.**

4. Test the Windows 98 Startup disk.

   a. **Verify that you have the Startup disk in the floppy drive.**

   b. **Restart the computer** (from the Start menu, choose Shutdown. Select Restart and click OK).

   c. From the Startup menu, **choose Start Computer With CD-ROM Support.**

   d. **You will see an MS-DOS prompt** if the computer boots successfully with the Startup disk.

   e. **Remove the boot disk from the floppy drive.**

   f. **Label the floppy disk "Windows 98 Startup disk"**

5. Create a Windows 2000 boot disk.

    a. **Restart the computer and choose Windows 2000 Professional from the boot menu.**

    b. **Log on as Admin#.**

    c. **Open Windows Explorer.**

    d. **Insert a floppy disk into the floppy disk drive.**

    e. **Right-click 3 1/2 Floppy (A:) and choose Format.**

    f. **Check Quick Format** to reduce the amount of time required to format the floppy disk.

    Format options
    ☑ Quick Format

    g. **Click Start.**

    h. **Click OK** to confirm that you want to format the disk.

    i. When the format is complete, **click OK.**

    j. **Click Close** to close the Format A:\ dialog box.

    k. In Windows Explorer, **select the C drive.**

    l. **Choose Tools→Folder Options.**

    m. **Select the View tab.**

    n. Below Hidden Files And Folders, **select Show Hidden Files And Folders.**

    o. **Uncheck Hide File Extensions For Known File Types.**

    p. **Uncheck Hide Protected Operating System Files (Recommended).**

    q. **Click Yes** to confirm.

r. Click OK.

s. From C:\, **copy the following files to the boot disk:**
    - Boot.ini
    - Bootsect.dos (if it exists)
    - Ntbootdd.sys (if it exists)
    - Ntdetect.com
    - Ntldr

t. **Close Windows Explorer.**

---

6. **Test the Windows 2000 boot disk.**

a. **Verify that the boot disk is in the floppy disk drive.**

b. From the Start menu, **choose Shut Down.**

c. From the drop-down list, **select Restart and click OK.**

d. From the boot menu, **choose Windows 2000 Professional.** The computer boots successfully from the boot disk if Windows 2000 loads properly.

e. **Remove the boot disk from the floppy drive.**

f. **Label the boot disk "Windows 2000 boot disk"**

TOPIC B

Create an Emergency Repair Disk

In Windows 2000 and Windows NT, one of the techniques you can use to repair a computer in the event of a crash is to perform an emergency repair. But in order to perform an emergency repair, you'll need a copy of the computer's critical configuration files on a special disk called the emergency repair disk. In this topic, you'll learn how to create an emergency repair disk for both Windows 2000 and Windows NT computers.

Without an emergency repair disk, you won't be able to perform an emergency repair to attempt to correct a computer's problem. Having an emergency repair disk enables you to be prepared for just such an emergency. Further, performing an emergency repair is one of the quickest methods to get a crashed computer back up and running. By having an emergency repair disk at the ready, you'll be able to quickly repair most problems so that your users can get back to work.

Emergency Repair Disk

In Windows 2000 and Windows NT, you can create a disk that contains information about the current configuration of the operating system. You can use this disk, called an *emergency repair disk (ERD)*, to repair your computer if it will not boot up. In addition, you can use the ERD to repair damaged or lost operating system files. When you create an ERD, Windows stores the ERD's information in the \Windows\Repair or \Winnt\Repair folder. In the event you can't find your ERD, the computer can use the information in this folder to repair the computer (provided the hard disk is accessible).

The Emergency Repair Process

After you have created an emergency repair disk, you can use it to repair the computer in the event you encounter a problem. The procedures you use for repairing the computer are as follows:

1. Boot the computer from the Windows 2000 or Windows NT installation CD-ROM. If the computer doesn't support booting from the CD-ROM or the CD-ROM itself is not bootable, you can create installation boot floppies using another computer. (See the Creating Installation Boot Disks procedure.)

2. When prompted to repair the computer, press R.

3. From the Repair Options menu, press R to use the emergency repair process.

4. Choose Fast Repair to perform all repair options, or choose Manual Repair to select the repair options you want to perform.

5. Follow the prompts to repair the computer from the ERD or from the Repair folder on the hard disk.

6. Complete the process and restart the computer.

Creating Installation Boot Disks

Procedure Reference: Create Installation Boot Disks for Windows 2000

To create the installation boot disks for Windows 2000:

1. Obtain three blank floppy disks.

2. Use Windows Explorer to access the \Bootdisk folder on the Windows 2000 installation CD-ROM.

3. Double-click the appropriate program to create the disks.
   - If you're using a Windows 2000, Windows NT, or Windows XP computer to create the disks, double-click makebt32.exe.
   - If you're using Windows 9x, double-click makeboot.exe to create the disks.

4. Label and insert each floppy disk as prompted.

5. Remove the Windows 2000 installation CD-ROM.

6. Close Windows Explorer.

Procedure Reference: Create Installation Boot Disks for Windows NT

To create the installation boot disks for Windows NT:

1. Obtain three blank floppy disks.

2. Insert the Windows NT installation CD-ROM.

3. Run the appropriate program to create the disks.
   - If you're using a Windows 2000, Windows NT, or Windows XP computer to create the disks, from the Start menu, choose Run. In the Open text box, type winnt32 /ox and click OK.
   - If you're using Windows 9x to create the disks, from the Start menu, choose Run. In the Open text box, type winnt /ox and click OK.

4. Label and insert each floppy disk as prompted.

5. Remove the Windows NT installation CD-ROM.

6. Close Windows Explorer.

How to Create an Emergency Repair Disk

Procedure Reference: Create an Emergency Repair Disk in Windows 2000

To create an emergency repair disk in Windows 2000:

1. Log on as a local administrator.

2. From the Start menu, choose Programs→Accessories→System Tools→Backup.

3. Insert a blank floppy disk into the floppy disk drive.

4. Click Emergency Repair Disk.

5. Check Also Back Up The Registry To The Repair Directory to store a backup copy of the emergency repair disk information on the computer's hard disk.

6. Click OK to create the disk.

7. Click OK to close the Emergency Repair Diskette message box.

8. Close Backup.

9. Remove the floppy disk, label it, and store it in a safe place.

> 🖈 The only way to test an ERD is to perform an emergency repair. You'll learn how to perform an emergency repair in Lesson 12.

Procedure Reference: Create an Emergency Repair Disk in Windows NT

To create an emergency repair disk in Windows NT:

1. Log on as a local administrator.

2. From the Start menu, choose Run.

3. Insert a blank floppy disk into the floppy disk drive.

4. In the Open text box, type one of the following:
   - `rdisk`, if you want to create an emergency repair disk that does not contain the user accounts database.
   - `rdisk /s`, if you want to create an emergency repair disk that does contain the user accounts database.

5. Click OK.

6. If you typed `rdisk /s` to create the emergency repair disk along with a copy of the user accounts database, complete the following steps:
   a. Click Update Repair Info to store a backup copy of the emergency repair disk information on the computer's hard disk.
   b. Click Yes to confirm that you want to update the repair information.
   c. Click Yes to create the emergency repair disk.
   d. Click OK to confirm that the disk will be reformatted.
   e. Click OK to close the Repair Disk Utility message box.
   f. Click Exit to close the Repair Disk Utility.

> 🖈 Windows NT automatically backs up the emergency repair disk information to the computer's hard disk when you run `rdisk /s`.

7. If you typed `rdisk` to create the emergency repair disk, complete the following steps:
   a. Click Yes to create the emergency repair disk.
   b. Click OK to confirm that the disk will be reformatted.
   c. Click OK to close the Repair Disk Utility message box.

8. Remove the floppy disk, label it, and store it in a safe place.

> 🖈 The only way to test an ERD is to perform an emergency repair. You'll learn how to perform an emergency repair in Lesson 12.

Activity 11-2

Creating an Emergency Repair Disk

Scenario:

One of your clients is an elementary school. You're responsible for keeping all the Windows 2000 computers at the school up and running. All the computers are configured identically. You want to be prepared for any emergency, including a computer that has corrupted files that require repair.

What You Do	How You Do It
1. Create an emergency repair disk.	a. Verify that you're logged on to Windows 2000 as Admin#.
	b. From the Start menu, **choose Programs→ Accessories→System Tools→Backup.**
	c. **Insert a blank floppy disk into the floppy disk drive.**
	d. **Click Emergency Repair Disk.**
	Emergency Repair Disk This option helps you create an Emergency Repair Disk that you can use to repair and restart Windows if it is damaged. This option does not back up your files or programs, and it is not a replacement for regularly backing up your system.
	e. **Check Also Back Up The Registry To The Repair Directory** to store a backup copy of the emergency repair disk information on the computer's hard disk.
	☑ Also backup the registry to the repair directory. This backup can be used to help recover your system if the registry is damaged.
	f. **Click OK** to create the disk.
	g. **Click OK** to close the Emergency Repair Diskette message box.
	h. **Close Backup.**
	i. **Remove the floppy disk, label it, and store it in a safe place.**

TOPIC C

Install the Recovery Console

In Topic 11B, you learned how to create an emergency repair disk so that you can perform an emergency repair on Windows 2000 and Windows NT computers. In Windows XP, the equivalent tool to an emergency repair is the Recovery Console. In this topic, you'll learn how to install the Recovery Console on Windows XP computers so that it's accessible on the computer's startup menu.

The Recovery Console is like a spare tire for Windows XP and Windows 2000. If you have a flat, a spare tire will get you back up and on the road again, but only if you have a spare tire. Likewise, the Recovery Console can get your user's computer up and running again, but only if you can load the Recovery Console software. Installing the Recovery Console on a user's computer is like double-checking that you have a good spare tire in your car's trunk. By installing the Recovery Console, you can be sure that it's always available to you whenever you need it.

Recovery Console

Windows XP and Windows 2000 include a utility that you can use to perform emergency repairs on the computer; it's called the *Recovery Console*. The Recovery Console is a command-line utility that you can use to perform administrative tasks for repairing the computer. For example, you might use the Recovery Console to repair the computer's Master Boot Record. You can start the Recovery Console by booting the computer from the Windows 2000 or Windows XP installation disks, by using the Winnt32 /cmdcons command, or by adding it to the computer's boot menu.

How to Install the Recovery Console

Procedure Reference: Install the Recovery Console

To install the Recovery Console:

1. Log on as a local computer administrator.

2. Execute the `winnt32.exe /cmdcons` command from the appropriate installation CD-ROM.

   - If you're installing the Recovery Console on a Windows 2000 computer, execute this command from the Windows 2000 installation CD-ROM.

   - If you're installing the Recovery Console on a Windows XP computer, execute this command from the Windows XP installation CD-ROM.

   - If you're installing the Recovery Console on a computer configured to dual-boot both Windows 2000 and Windows XP, you MUST execute this command from the Windows XP installation CD-ROM.

   ⚠ You must install the Recovery Console from the Windows XP installation CD-ROM if the computer is configured to dual-boot between Windows 2000 and Windows XP. If you install the Recovery Console using the Windows 2000 installation CD-ROM, you will not be able to boot Windows XP on the computer.

3. Click Yes to confirm that you want to install the Recovery Console.

4. If your computer is connected to the Internet, Windows Setup will automatically connect to the Internet and download updated Windows XP or Windows 2000 installation files from the Microsoft Web site.

5. If you want to cancel the automatic updates, complete the following steps:

   a. Press Esc if you do not want to connect to the Internet.

   b. Click Yes to confirm the cancellation.

   c. Select Skip This Step And Continue Installing Windows and click Next.

6. When the Recovery Console installation is complete, click OK.

7. Test the Recovery Console installation by using the following steps:

   a. Shut down and restart the computer.

   b. From the boot menu, select Microsoft Windows Recovery Console.

   c. When prompted, enter the number of the Windows XP Professional installation you want to log on to (if the computer is a single-boot system, this will be installation number 1. If you have Windows 2000 or Windows NT on the computer, you can use the Recovery Console to repair those installations as well).

   d. Enter the Administrator password to log on to Windows XP or Windows 2000.

   e. To end the Recovery Console session and restart the computer, type exit and press Enter.

ACTIVITY 11-3

Installing the Recovery Console

Setup:

The Windows XP Professional installation files are located in the \\2000srv\WinXP share on the classroom server.

Scenario:

One of your clients is an elementary school. In addition to keeping all the Windows 2000 computers at the school up and running, you're also responsible for managing the Windows XP computers. You want to be prepared for any emergency on the Windows XP computers. Having the Recovery Console installed before you encounter problems will make it easier for you to repair the computer in the event of a problem.

What You Do	How You Do It
1. **Install the Recovery Console as a startup option.**	a. **Restart the computer and choose Windows XP Professional from the boot menu.**
	b. **Log on as Admin#.**
	c. From the Start menu, **choose Run.**
	d. In the Open text box, **type \\2000srv\WinXP\i386\Winnt32.exe#/cmdcons**
	e. **Click OK.**
	f. **Click Yes** to confirm that you want to install the Recovery Console.
	📌 If your computer is connected to the Internet, Windows Setup will automatically connect to the Internet and download updated Windows XP Professional installation files from the Microsoft Web site.
	g. When the Recovery Console installation is complete, **click OK.**
2. **Test the Recovery Console installation.**	a. **Shut down and restart the computer.**
	b. From the boot menu, **select Microsoft Windows Recovery Console.**
	c. When prompted, **enter 2** (the number assigned to the Windows XP professional installation).
	d. When you're prompted for Administrator's password, **enter password**
	e. Enter **exit** to exit the Recovery Console and restart the computer.
	f. **Select Windows 2000 Professional from the boot menu.**

TOPIC D

Back Up Data

Up to this point in the lesson, you've seen the tools you can use to prepare for disaster recovery: creating a boot disk and an emergency repair disk, and installing the Recovery Console. You'll use these tools primarily to recover from problems with a computer's operating system files or configuration. Now it's time to turn your attention to avoiding losing the data stored on a computer. In this topic, you'll learn how to back up data so that you can later restore it.

As an A+ technician, there are several situations in which you'll need a current backup of a user's data. For example, you will need a current backup of a user's data if you're moving that user to a new computer. By having a current backup, you'll be able to quickly transfer the user's data files to her new computer. Other situations you might encounter include a user who accidentally deletes some files (or even an entire folder) that he needs, or the user's hard disk could become damaged. In either scenario, you'll need to be prepared to restore the data so that your user can gain access to the files he needs to perform his job.

The Archive File Attribute

The Windows operating systems automatically assign the Archive file attribute to every file you create or modify on the computer. In Figure 11-2, you see a file with the Archive attribute enabled. You can use this attribute to assist you in performing selective backups of the data on a computer. For example, on one night you might back up all files on the computer's hard disk and remove the Archive attribute from those files. Later, you can back up only those files with the Archive attribute (which means you'll be backing up only the new files the user has created or any existing files modified). Backing up only the files that have changed enables you to reduce the amount of time required to back up the computer.

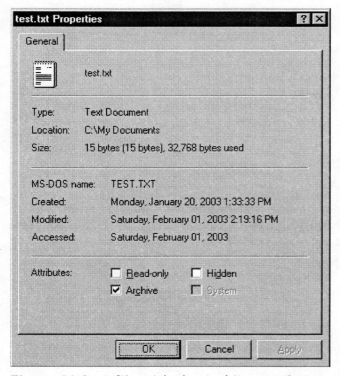

Figure 11-2: *A file with the Archive attribute enabled.*

Backup Types

Windows 2000, Windows NT, Windows XP, and Windows 9x support four backup types: full, copy, incremental, and differential. In Table 11-5, you see a description of each backup type and how it interacts with the Archive attribute. You will typically use one or more of these backup types, as follows:

- Perform a full backup on a nightly basis. Use this strategy if the computer does not contain so much data that the backup cannot complete within the necessary time frame.

- Perform a full backup on a weekly basis. Perform either an incremental or a differential backup on a nightly basis. This strategy enables you to reduce the amount of time required to back up the data on a nightly basis.

Table 11-5: *Backup Types*

Backup Type	Description
Copy	Backs up some or all files on the computer. Does not clear the Archive attribute from the files it backs up.
Full	Backs up some or all files on the computer. Clears the Archive attribute from all files. You'll sometimes hear a full backup referred to as a *normal* backup.
Incremental	Backs up all files since the last full or incremental backup. Clears the Archive attribute from all files.
Differential	Backs up all files since the last full backup. Does not clear the Archive attribute.
Daily	Backs up the files created or modified on the day the backup is performed. Does not clear the Archive attribute.

Backup Media

With the exception of Windows NT, the Windows operating systems support a variety of media to which you can back up. This media includes tape, floppy disks, shared folders on other computers, CD-ROM disks, and Zip disks. Windows NT supports backing up only to tape.

Batch/Script Files

Definition:

Batch and script files are files that contain commands for performing specific tasks on the computer. You can create a batch file or a script file by using any text editor such as Notepad. You must save a batch file with either the .bat or .cmd extensions. You execute a batch file simply by double-clicking it in Windows Explorer or by typing its name in a Command Prompt window.

You create a script file by using the Visual Basic Scripting (VBScript) or JScript languages. You must save a script file with the .wsf extension. Before you execute a script file, you must first run the Windows Script Host (wscript.exe). After you have run the Windows Script Host, you can run the script file by double-clicking it in Windows Explorer.

Example:

In Figure 11-3, you see an example of a batch file. In Figure 11-4, you see an example of a script file.

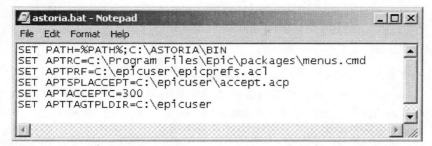

Figure 11-3: *A batch file.*

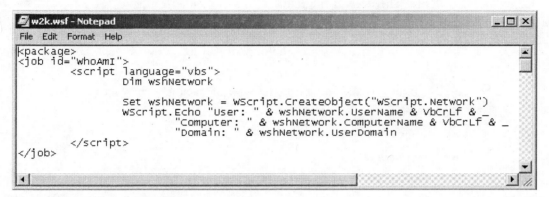

Figure 11-4: *A script file.*

How to Back Up Data

Procedure Reference: Back Up Data in Windows 2000

To back up data in Windows 2000:

1. Log on as a user who's either a member of the Backup Operators or Administrators groups, owner of a file, or a user who has at least the Read NTFS permissions to back up file data.

2. If you plan to back up to floppy disk, insert a floppy disk into the floppy disk drive.

3. If you plan to back up to tape, insert a tape into the tape drive.

4. From the Start menu, choose Programs→Accessories→System Tools→Backup.

5. Click Backup Wizard.

6. Click Next.

7. On the What To Back Up page, select one of the following:

   • Back Up Everything On My Computer, to back up all files and folders on the computer.

   • Back Up Selected Files, Drives, Or Network Data, to back up only the files you select.

   • Only Back Up The System State Data, to back up just the System State data.

8. Click Next.

9. If you chose to back up only selected files, complete the following steps:

   a. Below What To Back Up, expand the source location of the files and check the check box for each item that you want to back up.

   b. If you want to back up only selected files within a location, below Name, check the specific files you want to back up.

   c. Click Next.

10. On the Where To Store The Backup page:

    a. From the Backup Media Type drop-down list, select the type of backup you want to create (if you do not have a local tape backup device, your only choice will be File).

    b. In the Backup Media Or File Name, type a path and file name for the backup file. The default file name is Backup.bkf.

    c. Click Next.

11. To create the backup using the default settings, click Finish. Otherwise, click Advanced.

12. If you click Advanced, select the type of backup you want to perform.

    - Normal
    - Copy
    - Incremental
    - Differential
    - Daily

13. Check Backup Migrated Remote Storage Data if you want to back up files that have been migrated to removable media.

14. Click Next.

15. Check Verify Data After Backup to have Backup check that you got a valid backup of the data.

16. Click Next.

17. Below If The Archive Media Already Contains Backups, select one of the following:

    - Append This Backup To The Media
    - Replace The Data On The Media With This Backup

18. Click Next.

19. On the Backup Label page, enter a backup label and a media label.

20. Click Next.

21. On the When To Back Up page, verify that Now is selected and click Next.

    See the following procedure for scheduling backups.

22. Click Finish to begin the backup.

23. Review the Backup Progress dialog box to verify that the backup completed successfully.

24. Click Close to close the Backup Progress dialog box.

25. Close Backup.

Procedure Reference: Schedule a Backup in Windows 2000

To schedule a backup in Windows 2000:

1. Use Backup to create a backup job.

2. On the last page of the wizard, click Advanced.

3. Select any advanced options on the Type Of Backup, How To Back Up, Media Options, and Backup Label pages.

4. On the When To Back Up Page, select Later.

5. In the Set Account Information dialog box, complete the following:

   a. In the Run As text box, type the user name of a user with the permissions and rights necessary to back up the files.

   b. In the Password text box, type the password for this user.

   c. In the Confirm Password text box, re-type the password for this user.

   d. Click OK.

6. In the Job Name text box, type a name for the job.

7. Click Set Schedule.

8. Select your scheduling options. You can schedule a task to run Once, Daily, Weekly, Monthly, At System Startup, At Logon, or When Idle. For Daily, Weekly, or Monthly schedules, you can configure specific times and days.

9. If you chose a Daily, Weekly, or Monthly schedule, click Advanced, configure the properties, and then click OK. You can configure start and end dates for the task, and configure the task to run more than once at the scheduled time.

10. If you want to run this task on more than one schedule (for example, weekly and also monthly), check Show Multiple Schedules and click New to create additional schedules.

11. To configure how this task will respond to system conditions such as a low battery, select the Settings tab and configure the settings. See the Windows Backup Help system for specific information.

12. When you have finished creating and configuring all schedules, click OK.

13. On the When To Back Up page, click Next.

14. Click Finish.

Procedure Reference: Back Up Data in Windows XP

To back up data in Windows XP:

1. Log on as a user who's either a member of the Backup Operators or Administrators groups, owner of a file, or a user who has at least the Read NTFS permissions to back up file data.

2. If you plan to back up to floppy disk, insert a floppy disk into the floppy disk drive.

3. If you plan to back up to tape, insert a tape into the tape drive.

4. From the Start menu, choose All Programs→Accessories→System Tools→ Backup.

5. Click Next.

6. On the What Do You Want To Do page, select one of the following:
   - Back Up Files And Settings.
   - Restore Files And Settings.

7. Click Next.

8. On the What To Back Up page, select one of the following:
   - My Documents And Settings, to back up the current user's My Documents folder, Favorites list, desktop settings, and Internet cookie files.
   - Everyone's Documents And Settings, to back up this same information for all users of the computer.
   - All Information On This Computer, to back up everything on the computer.
   - Let Me Choose What To Back Up, to back up only the files you select.

9. Click Next.

10. If you chose the Let Me Choose What To Back Up option, complete the following steps:
    a. Below Items To Back Up, expand the source location of the files and check the check box for each item that you want to back up.
    b. If you want to back up only selected files within a location, below Name, check the specific files you want to back up.
    c. Click Next.

11. On the Backup Type, Destination, and Name page:
    a. From the Select The Backup Type drop-down list, select the type of backup you want to create (if you do not have a local tape backup device, your only choice will be File).
    b. From the Choose A Place To Save Your Backup drop-down list, select the location where you want to store your backup (if you do not have a local tape backup device, your default choice will be 3 1/2 Floppy).
    c. In the Type A Name For This Backup text box, type a name for the backup. The default file name is Backup.
    d. Click Next.

12. To create the backup using the default settings, click Finish. Otherwise, click Advanced.

13. If you click Advanced, select the type of backup you want to perform.
    - Normal
    - Copy
    - Incremental
    - Differential
    - Daily

14. Click Next.

15. On the How To Back Up page, check any of the following options:

- Check Verify Data After Backup to have Backup check that you got a valid backup of the data.

- Check Use Hardware Compression, If Available, if you're backing up to tape and your tape drive supports compression.

- Check Disable Volume Shadow Copy, if you want to disable support for backing up files even when they're being written to.

16. Click Next.

17. Below Backup Options, select one of the following:

- Append This Backup To The Existing Backups.

- Replace The Existing Backups.

18. Click Next.

19. On the When To Back Up page, verify that Now is selected and click Next.

   See the following procedure for scheduling backups.

20. Click Finish to begin the backup.

   Windows Backup closes automatically when you click Finish.

21. Review the Backup Progress dialog box to verify that the backup completed successfully.

22. Click Close to close the Backup Progress dialog box.

Procedure Reference: Schedule a Backup in Windows XP

To schedule a backup in Windows XP:

1. Use Backup to create a backup job.

2. On the last page of the wizard, click Advanced.

3. Select any advanced options on the Type Of Backup, How To Back Up, and Backup Options pages.

4. On the When To Back Up Page, select Later.

5. In the Job Name text box, type a name for the job.

6. Click Set Schedule.

7. Select your scheduling options. You can schedule a task to run Once, Daily, Weekly, Monthly, At System Startup, At Logon, or When Idle. For Daily, Weekly, or Monthly schedules, you can configure specific times and days.

8. If you chose a Daily, Weekly, or Monthly schedule, click Advanced, configure the properties, and then click OK. You can configure start and end dates for the task, and configure the task to run more than once at the scheduled time.

9. If you want to run this task on more than one schedule (for example, weekly and also monthly), check Show Multiple Schedules and click New to create additional schedules.

10. To configure how this task will respond to system conditions such as a low battery, select the Settings tab and configure the settings. See the Windows Backup Help system for specific information.

11. When you have finished creating and configuring all schedules, click OK.

12. On the When To Back Up page, click Next.

13. In the Set Account Information dialog box, complete the following:

    a. In the Run As text box, type the user name of a user with the permissions and rights necessary to back up the files.

    b. In the Password text box, type the password for this user.

    c. In the Confirm Password text box, re-type the password for this user.

    d. Click OK.

14. Click Finish.

Procedure Reference: Back Up Data in Windows NT

To back up data in Windows NT:

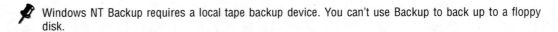 Windows NT Backup requires a local tape backup device. You can't use Backup to back up to a floppy disk.

1. Log on as a user who's either a member of the Backup Operators or Administrators groups, owner of a file, or a user who has at least the Read NTFS permissions to back up file data.

2. Insert a tape into the tape drive.

3. From the Start menu, choose Programs→Administrative Tools→Backup.

4. If you want to back up all data on the computer, in the Drives list, check all drives.

5. If you want to back up only selected files or folders, complete the following steps:

    a. In the Drives list, double-click the drive containing the files you want to back up.

    b. If you want to back up an entire folder, in the left pane, check the folder.

    c. If you want to back up only selected files, in the left pane, select the folder containing the files. In the right pane, check each file you want to back up.

6. On the toolbar, click Backup.

7. Configure any necessary backup options.

    • Check Verify After Backup if you want Windows NT Backup to verify the accuracy of the backup.

    • Check Restrict Access To Owner Or Administrator if you want to restrict restoring the files in the backup to either the owner of the files or the Administrator.

8. In the Description text box, type a description for the backup.

9. From the Backup Type drop-down list, select the type of backup you want to perform. Windows NT supports the following backup types:

- Normal
- Copy
- Differential
- Incremental
- Daily

10. Below Log Information, select how much information you want to store in the backup log file.

11. Click OK to begin the backup.

12. When the backup is complete, click OK to close the Verify Status dialog box.

13. Close Windows NT Backup.

Procedure Reference: Schedule a Backup in Windows NT

To schedule a backup in Windows NT:

1. Verify that the Task Scheduler service is started and configured to start automatically whenever Windows NT boots.

    a. From the Start menu, choose Settings→Control Panel.

    b. Double-click Services.

    c. In the list of Services, select Task Scheduler.

    d. If necessary, click Start.

    e. If the Startup column displays Manual, click Startup. Below Startup Type, select Automatic and click OK.

    f. Click Close to close Services.

    g. Close Control Panel.

2. Create a batch file that contains the commands to perform the backup.

    a. From the Start menu, choose Programs→Accessories→Notepad.

    b. Enter the command ntbackup backup *path options*. Replace *path* with the path you want to back up (see Table 11-6 for a list of the options you can use with this command). For example, to back up the entire C drive and verify the backup when it's complete, you should enter ntbackup backup C: /v.

    c. Choose File→Save As.

    d. In the Save As dialog box, select a drive and folder in which to store the batch file.

    e. From the Save As Type drop-down list, select All Files.

    f. In the File Name text box, type a name for the batch file and use the .cmd extension. (For example, backup.cmd).

    g. Click Save.

    h. Close Notepad.

Table 11-6: *NTBackup Options*

Option	Use to
/a	Append the backup to the existing backups on the tape.
/b	Back up the Registry. Note: You must also choose another file on the same partition for Windows NT Backup to be able to back up the Registry.
/d "text"	Assign a descriptive name to the backup set.
/e	Log errors that occur during the backup to a file named Backup.log. This file is stored in the \%systemroot% folder.
/l filename	Assign a different file name to the log file.
/r	Restrict access to the tape to members of Administrators or Backup Operators, and the user that created the backup.
/v	Verify that the files were backed up successfully.
/hc:on or /hc:off	Turn hardware compression on or off.

3. Open a Command Prompt window (from the Start menu, choose Programs→ Command Prompt).

4. Enter at *computer_name id time options* "*command*" to schedule the backup batch file to run automatically.

    *   Replace *computer_name* with the name of the computer you want to back up.

    *   Replace *id* with the number you want to assign to this scheduled job. You can later use this number to delete or view information about the job.

    *   Replace *time* with the time at which you want the backup job to run. Enter the time as hour: minutes using the 24-hour notation. For example, to schedule a backup at 11:00 p.m., use 23:00 as the time.

    *   For a list of available options, see Table 11-7.

    *   Replace "*command*" with the path and name of the batch file. For example, if you stored the backup.cmd batch file in C:\Winnt, the command would be "C:\Winnt\backup.cmd".

Table 11-7: *At Command Options*

Option	Use to
/interactive	Permit the job to interact with the desktop of the user who is logged on at the computer.
/every:date[,...n]	Configure at to perform the job on specific days of the week or month. Identify days by using the abbreviations M, T, W, Th, F, S, or Su. Identify days of the month by using the number date (1 to 31).

Option	Use to
/next:date[,...n]	Configure when the at command will next run the job.

5.   Review the schedule for the backup job by entering `at` at the Command Prompt. If necessary, delete the job using the `at` *id* `/delete` command and execute a different `at` command to correct any mistakes.

6.   Close the Command Prompt window.

Procedure Reference: Back Up Data in Windows 98

To back up data in Windows 98:

1.   If necessary, install Windows 98 Backup (Msbackup.exe).

   a.   In Control Panel, double-click Add/Remove Programs.

   b.   Select the Windows Setup tab.

   c.   In the Components list, select (don't check or uncheck) System Tools.

   d.   Click Details.

   e.   Check Backup and click OK.

   f.   Click OK to close the Add/Remove Programs Properties dialog box.

   g.   When prompted, insert the Windows 98 installation CD-ROM and click OK.

   h.   Click Yes to restart the computer.

   i.   If necessary, log back on to Windows 98.

   j.   Close Control Panel.

2.   If you plan to back up to floppy disk, insert a floppy disk into the floppy disk drive.

3.   If you plan to back up to tape, insert a tape into the tape drive.

4.   From the Start menu, choose Programs→Accessories→System Tools→Backup.

5.   If you don't have an attached tape drive, click No in the Microsoft Backup error message box.

6.   In the Microsoft Backup dialog box, select Create A New Backup Job.

7.   Click OK.

8.   In the Backup Wizard, select one of the following:

   •   Back Up My Computer, to back up everything on the computer.

   •   Back Up Selected Files, Folders, And Drives, to select the files or folders you want to back up.

9.   Click Next.

10.   If you chose to back up only selected files, complete the following steps:

   a.   Below What To Back Up, expand the source location of the files and check the check box for each item that you want to back up.

   b.   If you want to back up only selected files within a location, below Name, check the specific files you want to back up.

c. Click Next.

11. On the What To Back Up page, select one of the following:
- All Selected Files, to back up all files in the folder.
- New And Changed Files, to back up only the files with the Archive attribute.

12. Click Next.

13. On the Where To Back Up page, complete the following:

a. From the Where To Back Up drop-down list, select the type of backup you want to create (if you do not have a local tape backup device, your only choice will be File).

b. In the other text box, type a path and file name for the backup file. The default path and file name is C:\MyBackup.qic. If you want to store the backup on a floppy disk, use the A drive instead.

c. Click Next.

14. On the How To Back Up page, select any or all of these options:
- Check Compare Original And Backup Files, to verify that your backup was successful.
- Check Compress The Backup Data, to save space in your backup media (either tape or disk).

15. Click Next.

16. In the Type A Name For This Backup Job text box, type a name for the backup job. You can later re-use this job to perform the same backup.

17. Click Start.

18. Review the Backup Progress dialog box to verify that the backup completed successfully.

19. Click OK to close the Backup Progress dialog box.

20. Close Backup.

You can't schedule a backup in Windows 98.

User Data Files

In some situations, you might find it necessary to back up only the files that a user has created on a computer, and not the program files on that computer. In this situation, you can typically get most of the user's data by backing up the contents of the user's My Documents folder. When looking at other folders on the computer, you can typically identify the data files by their file extensions. In Table 11-8, we list some of the common user data file extensions and the programs used to create them.

Table 11-8: *Common Data File Extensions*

File Extension	Created In
.doc	Microsoft Word
.xls	Microsoft Excel
.ppt	Microsoft PowerPoint
.mdb	Microsoft Access

File Extension	Created In
.txt	Microsoft Word or Notepad

ACTIVITY 11-4

Backing Up Data in Windows 2000

Data Files:

- D:\Data\Personnel

Setup:

Restart the computer. From the boot menu, choose Windows 2000.

Scenario:

One of your clients is concerned about the personnel records she keeps on her computer. She would like you to show her how she can make backup copies of the files to floppy disk. She stores all personnel records in files and folders within the D:\Data\Personnel folder.

Lesson 11

What You Do	How You Do It
1. **Back up the D:\Data\Personnel folder** (including all files and folders within it).	a. **Log on as Admin#.**
	b. **Insert a floppy disk into the floppy disk drive.**
	c. From the Start menu, **choose Programs→ Accessories→System Tools→Backup.**
	d. **Click Backup Wizard.**
	e. **Click Next.**
	f. **Select Back Up Selected Files, Drives, Or Network Data.**

Select what you want to back up:

- ○ Back up everything on my computer
- ● Back up selected files, drives, or network data
- ○ Only back up the System State data

g. **Click Next.**

h. Below What To Back Up, **expand Win2000-# and then the D drive.**

i. **Expand the D:\Data folder.**

```
Data
    AutoShop
    NASA
    Personnel
    Proposals
```

j. **Check Personnel.**

```
Data
    AutoShop
    NASA
    Personnel
    Proposals
```

k. **Click Next.**

l. In the Backup Media Or File Name text box, **type** *A:\personnel.bkf*

> Backup media or file name:
> A:\personnel.bkf

m. **Click Next.**

n. **Click Finish.**

2. **View the Backup Report to check for any errors.**

a. When the backup completes, **click Report.**

b. **Verify that the backup completed and that four files were backed up.**

```
Backup started on 1/16/2003 at 3:34 PM.
Backup completed on 1/16/2003 at 3:34 PM.
Directories: 4
Files: 4
Bytes: 8,139
Time:  4 seconds
```

c. **Close Notepad.**

d. **Click Close** to close the Backup Progress dialog box.

e. **Close Backup.**

f. **Remove the floppy disk and label it.**

TOPIC E

Back Up System State Data

In Topic 11D, you learned how to back up user data files so that you can be prepared in the event a user accidentally deletes files or the hard disk corrupts some of the user's data files. But if a Windows 2000 or Windows XP computer crashes altogether, another type of backup you'll need is a backup of the computer's system state data. In this topic, you'll learn how to back up a computer's system state data so that it's available to you in the event of a complete computer failure.

If you must recover a computer that's failed altogether, you'll need to not only be able to restore the user's data, but also all of the operating system's configuration information as well. So how do you prepare for such a disaster? You could perform a complete backup of each user's computer on a daily basis, but such backups take a long time to complete and require a lot of room on backup media (such as tapes). By backing up only the system state data, you can create a much smaller backup with the essential information you need to get the computer back up and running. In addition, you'll find it much quicker to restore only the system state data as compared to having to select individual files from a complete backup of the user's computer. So, as you can see, backing up system state data provides you with a quick and easy way to grab a copy of the Windows 2000 or Windows XP configuration information so that you can be prepared in the event disaster strikes.

System State Data

Windows 2000 and Windows XP refer to the critical system components that contain the operating system's configuration information as *system state data*. The system state data includes the following components:

- The Windows 2000 or Windows XP boot files.
- All files installed during the installation of Windows 2000 or Windows XP that have the .sys, .dll, .ttf, .fon, .ocx, and .exe extension.
- The Registry.
- COM+ object registrations, which is a database of program components that are shared between applications.

How to Back Up System State Data

Procedure Reference: Back Up System State Data in Windows 2000

To back up System State Data in Windows 2000:

1. Log on as a user who's either a member of the Backup Operators or Administrators groups, owner of a file, or a user who has at least the Read NTFS permissions to back up file data.

   Backing up the System State Data requires approximately 400 MB of space. You must back it up to a tape, a folder on the local computer, or a shared folder on a server.

2. If you plan to back up to tape, insert a tape into the tape drive.

3. If you plan to back up to a folder, verify that you have enough available disk space. Create the folder.

4. From the Start menu, choose Programs→Accessories→System Tools→Backup.

5. Click Backup Wizard.

6. Click Next.

7. On the What To Back Up page, select Only Back Up The System State Data.

8. Click Next.

9. On the Where To Store The Backup page:

   a. From the Backup Media Type drop-down list, select the type of backup you want to create (if you do not have a local tape backup device, your only choice will be File).

   b. In the Backup Media Or File Name, type the path and name for the backup file. The default file name and path is A:\Backup.bkf.

   c. Click Next.

10. To create the backup using the default settings, click Finish (click Advanced if you want to specify any other backup options).

11. Review the Backup Progress dialog box to verify that the backup completed successfully.

12. Click Close to close the Backup Progress dialog box.

13. Close Backup.

Procedure Reference: Back Up System State Data in Windows XP

To back up System State Data in Windows XP:

1. Log on as a user who's either a member of the Backup Operators or Administrators groups, owner of a file, or a user who has at least the Read NTFS permissions to back up file data.

 Backing up the System State Data requires approximately 400 MB of space. You must back it up to a tape, a folder on the local computer, or a shared folder on a server.

2. If you plan to back up to tape, insert a tape into the tape drive.

3. If you plan to back up to a folder, verify that you have enough available disk space. Create the folder.

4. From the Start menu, choose All Programs→Accessories→System Tools→ Backup.

5. Click Next.

6. Verify that Back Up Files And Settings is selected and click Next.

7. On the What To Back Up page, select Let Me Choose What To Back Up.

8. Click Next.

9. Below Items To Back Up, expand My Computer and check System State.

10. Click Next.

11. On the Backup Type, Destination, and Name page, complete the following tasks:

   a. From the Select The Backup Type drop-down list, select the type of backup you want to create (if you do not have a local tape backup device, your only choice will be File).

   b. Next to Choose A Place To Save Your Backup, click Browse to browse for the folder in which you will store the backup. If you're backing up to file, you must store the System State Data backup on a hard disk because you will need approximately 400 MB of storage space.

   c. In the Type A Name For This Backup text box, type a name for the backup file.

   d. Click Next.

12. To create the backup using the default settings, click Finish (click Advanced if you want to specify any other backup options).

13. Review the Backup Progress dialog box to verify that the backup completed successfully.

14. Click Close to close the Backup Progress dialog box.

Windows 98 and System State Data

Windows 98 automatically uses the Windows Registry Checker (scanreg.exe) to make backup copies of the Registry, account information, protocol bindings, software program settings, and user preferences on a daily basis. If the Registry becomes corrupt, you can use the scanreg program in MS-DOS mode to restore the previous day's backup of this information.

ACTIVITY 11-5

Backing Up the System State Data

Setup:

You will need approximately 400 MB of free space on your C drive to complete the backup.

Scenario:

One of your clients uses his computer 100 percent of the time to do his job. His computer uses the Windows 2000 operating system. He is very concerned about a computer crash. He wants to make sure that you will be able to reconstruct his computer as quickly as possible in the event of an operating system failure.

What You Do	How You Do It
1. Create a folder for storing the System State Data backup.	a. Open Windows Explorer.
	b. Select the C drive.
	c. Right-click the C drive and choose Properties.
	d. Verify that you have enough free disk space to store the System State Data backup.

■ Used space:	1,395,195,904 bytes	1.29 GB
▨ Free space:	751,271,936 bytes	716 MB

e. **Click Cancel** to close the Properties dialog box.

f. **Choose File→New→Folder.**

g. **Type** *Backup* **and press Enter.**

h. **Close Windows Explorer.**

2. **Back up the System State Data.**

    a. From the Start menu, **choose Programs→ Accessories→System Tools→Backup.**

    b. **Click Backup Wizard.**

    c. **Click Next.**

    d. **Select Only Back Up The System State Data.**

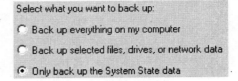

Select what you want to back up:

    ○ Back up everything on my computer

    ○ Back up selected files, drives, or network data

    ● Only back up the System State data

    e. **Click Next.**

    f. In the Backup Media Or File Name text box, **type** *C:\Backup\SystemState.bkf*

    g. **Click Next.**

    h. **Click Finish.** You can see the amount of time and size of the backup in the Backup Progress dialog box.

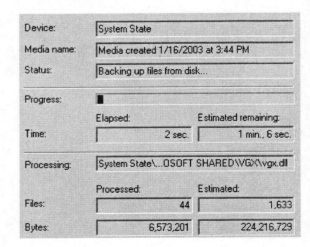

Device:	System State
Media name:	Media created 1/16/2003 at 3:44 PM
Status:	Backing up files from disk...

Progress:	▮	
	Elapsed:	Estimated remaining:
Time:	2 sec.	1 min., 6 sec.

Processing:	System State\...OSOFT SHARED\VGX\vgx.dll	
	Processed:	Estimated:
Files:	44	1,633
Bytes:	6,573,201	224,216,729

    i. When the backup is complete, **click Close.**

    j. **Close Backup.**

TOPIC F

Back Up the Registry

In Topic 11E, you learned how to perform a backup of a computer's system state data, which does include a backup of the computer's Registry. In some cases, though, you might want to back up a computer's Registry but not all of its system state data. Further, neither Windows 9x nor Windows NT include an option for backing up a computer's system state data. Instead, you'll have to manually back up these computers' Registries in order to be prepared for a disaster. In this topic, you'll learn the exact steps for backing up a computer's Registry.

There are a number of situations in which you'll need to manually back up a computer's Registry. For example, you should always perform a backup of the Registry before making any changes to it. That way, you can restore this backup if you make a mistake during the editing process. In another example, you might want to back up a Windows 9x or Windows NT computer's Registry so that you can have its configuration information at the ready in the event of a system failure.

How to Back Up the Registry

Procedure Reference: Back Up a Registry Key with Registry Editor

To back up a Registry key with Registry Editor in Windows 2000, Windows XP, Windows NT, or Windows 98:

 You also back up the Registry when you create an emergency repair disk for these operating systems or back up the system state data.

1. Log on as a local administrator.

2. From the Start menu, choose Run.

3. In the Open text box, type `regedit` and click OK. Using the 16-bit version of Registry Editor (regedit.exe) makes it easier for you to back up the entire Registry.

4. In the left pane, select My Computer.

5. In Windows 2000, Windows NT, and Windows 98, choose Registry→Export Registry File.

6. In Windows XP, choose File→Export.

7. From the Save In drop-down list, select the folder in which you want to store the backup.

8. In the File Name text box, type a name for the backup file.

9. Below Export Range, verify that All is selected.

10. Click Save.

11. Close Registry Editor.

12. In Windows Explorer, verify that the backup file was created successfully.

Procedure Reference: Back Up the Registry with Windows NT Backup

To back up the entire Registry with Windows NT Backup:

The Registry is backed up automatically in Windows 98 and Windows XP when you perform a system state data backup.

1. Log on as a user who's either a member of the Backup Operators or Administrators groups, owner of a file, or a user who has at least the Read NTFS permissions to back up file data.

2. Insert a tape into the tape drive.

3. In Backup, select at least one file on the partition on which the operating system is installed. For example, if Windows NT is on the D drive, create a job to back up a single file on that drive.

4. Click Backup.

5. In the Options dialog box, check Back Up Windows Registry.

6. Configure any necessary backup options.
    *   Check Verify After Backup if you want Windows NT Backup to verify the accuracy of the backup.
    *   Check Restrict Access To Owner Or Administrator if you want to restrict restoring the files in the backup to either the owner of the files or the Administrator.

7. In the Description text box, type a description for the backup.

8. From the Backup Type drop-down list, select the type of backup you want to perform. Windows NT supports the following backup types:
    *   Normal
    *   Copy
    *   Differential
    *   Incremental
    *   Daily

9. Below Log Information, select how much information you want to store in the backup log file.

10. Click OK to begin the backup.

11. When the backup is complete, click OK to close the Verify Status dialog box.

12. Close Windows NT Backup.

Procedure Reference: Back Up the Registry with Windows 98 Backup

To back up the Registry with Windows 98 Backup:

1. Create and save a backup job to back up at least one file on the partition on which the operating system is installed. For example, if Windows 98 is on the C drive, create a job to back up a single file on that drive.

2. In Backup, open the backup job.

3. Below How To Back Up, click Options.

4.   Select the Advanced tab.

5.   Check Back Up Windows Registry and click OK.

6.   Choose Job→Save to save the changes to your backup job.

7.   If you want to run the backup now, click Start.

8.   Close Backup.

ACTIVITY 11-6

Backing Up a Registry Key with Registry Editor

Scenario:

After researching a problem one of your clients is experiencing in Windows 2000, you have determined that the only way you can repair the problem is by editing the Registry. You need to make a change to the HKEY_LOCAL_MACHINE\Software\Microsoft key. Before you make this change, you want to back up the Registry in case anything goes wrong during the repair.

What You Do	How You Do It
1. **Back up the Registry.**	a. From the Start menu, **choose Run.**
	b. In the Open text box, **type** *regedit* **and press Enter.**
	c. In the left pane, **verify that My Computer is selected.**
	d. **Expand HKEY_LOCAL_MACHINE.**
	e. **Expand Software.**
	f. **Select the Microsoft key.**

	g. **Choose Registry→Export Registry File.**
	h. From the Save In drop-down list, **select the C drive.**
	i. **Double-click the Backup folder.**
	j. In the File Name text box, **type** *regback*
	k. **Click Save** to back up the Registry.
	l. **Close Registry Editor.**
2. **Verify the Registry backup.**	a. **Open Windows Explorer.**
	b. **Select the C:\Backup folder.**

c. In the right pane, **verify that you see the RegBack.reg file.**

regback.reg

d. **Close Windows Explorer.**

TOPIC G

Prepare for an Automated System Recovery

Up to this point in the lesson, you've been working with the various tools for preparing for disaster and creating a variety of backups that you can use to recover a computer if disaster strikes. But, despite your best efforts to protect your users' computers, you're bound to encounter a situation where your only choice is to completely re-install the computer—a true disaster! The good news is that Windows XP includes a tool called Automated System Recovery that makes it much easier for you to recover in the event of just such a failure, and that's what you'll learn about in this topic.

Take a moment to think about what you would do if you were faced with a computer that has crashed and you're unable to do anything with it. You're unable to boot the computer using a boot disk, so you can't restore any user or system state data. What would you do? Your first instinct might be to re-install Windows XP and then begin the process of restoring your backups. But wait—there's a better way! If you've prepared the computer for an Automated System Recovery, you'll be able to save yourself a lot of work and time because you'll be able to rebuild the computer to its configuration before the crash.

Automated System Recovery Process

Automated System Recovery (ASR) is a process that uses backup data and the Windows XP Professional installation source files to rebuild a failed computer system. To perform ASR, you will need:

- The Windows XP Professional installation CD-ROM.

- An ASR floppy disk, which contains files with the information Windows Setup needs to run ASR recovery.

- An ASR backup set, created with Windows Backup, that contains a complete copy of the Windows XP Professional system files and all configuration information.

You should be aware that an ASR backup set does not include any data from the computer. If you want to return the failed computer to its original state, you will also need to restore a backup of the user data.

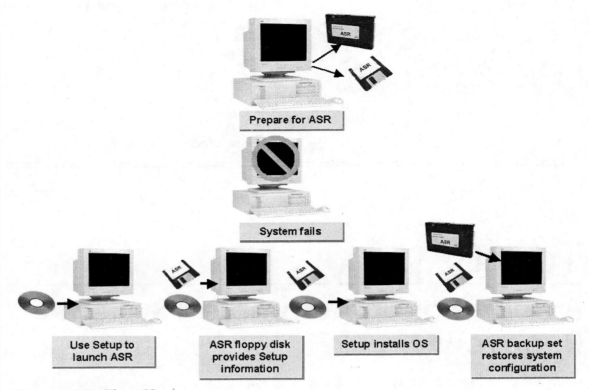

Figure 11-5: *The ASR process.*

The ASR process consists of the following phases:

1. You use Windows Backup to create an ASR backup set and ASR floppy disk.

    • The ASR backup set must be stored on local backup media, not on a network drive.

    • The ASR backup set cannot be stored on the same hard disk as the Windows XP Professional installation, as this disk can be re-initialized during the ASR process.

2. A system suffers a complete and catastrophic failure. For example, the hard disk completely fails.

3. You select a computer to use to restore the system.

4. You run Windows Setup from the Windows XP installation CD-ROM, and initiate ASR.

5. You provide the ASR floppy disk.

6. The computer passes the information in the ASR floppy disk to Windows Setup.

7. Windows Setup installs the operating system as specified on the ASR floppy disk.

8. You provide the ASR backup set.

9. ASR configures the computer according to the information in the backup set.

How to Prepare for an Automated System Recovery

Procedure Reference: Prepare for an ASR

To prepare for an ASR:

1. Log on as a local administrator.

2. Format a floppy disk, and verify that you have enough space on your backup media to hold the complete Windows XP Professional backup (between 1 and 2 GB of data).

3. Run Windows Backup.

4. On the Welcome page, click Advanced Mode.

5. Click Automated System Recovery Wizard.

6. Click Next.

7. Select a backup location and enter a name for the backup file. Click Next.

8. Click Finish. Backup creates the backup set.

9. When prompted, insert the formatted floppy disk and click OK.

10. Click OK to close the message box when the floppy disk creation is complete.

11. Click Close to close the Backup Progress dialog box.

12. Close Backup.

13. Remove the floppy disk and backup media and store them in a safe location.

Procedure Reference: Prepare for an ASR with a Complete Backup

To create an ASR backup set in addition to a complete system backup:

1. Log on as a local administrator.

2. Format a floppy disk, and verify that you have enough space on your backup media to hold the complete Windows XP Professional backup (between 1 and 2 GB of data).

3. Run Windows Backup in Wizard mode.

4. Click Next.

5. On the Backup Or Restore page, verify that Back Up Files And Settings is selected and click Next.

6. Select All Information On This Computer and click Next. You will need enough storage space on your backup media to back up the complete contents of your computer (including all data and application files).

7. Follow the prompts in the wizard to create the ASR floppy disk, ASR backup set, and a backup set with your computer's information.

8. Close Backup.

9. Remove the floppy disk and backup media and store them in a safe location.

ACTIVITY 11-7

Preparing an ASR Backup Set

Setup:

To complete this activity, you will need a blank, formatted floppy disk. You will also need either:

- approximately 2 GB of unallocated free space on your hard disk (not on your C drive); or

- a local backup device. A local backup device could be a second hard disk, a local CD-ROM burner, a compact-storage drive such as an Iomega Jaz drive, or a tape backup device, but not a network drive.

Setup:

To prepare for this activity:

1. Restart the computer and choose Windows XP Professional from the boot menu.

2. Log on as Admin#.

3. Use Computer Management to delete the G: partition.

4. Create a new 2 GB primary partition.

5. Format the new partition to use the NTFS file system.

Scenario:

One of your client's Windows XP computers is critical to the operation of her business. For this reason, she has asked you to minimize the amount of downtime she might incur in the event of a catastrophe.

What You Do	How You Do It
1. Create the ASR backup set.	a. **Run Backup** (from the Start menu, choose All Programs→Accessories→System Tools→Backup).
	b. On the Welcome page, **click Advanced Mode.**
	c. **Click Automated System Recovery Wizard.**
	d. **Click Next.**

e. In the Backup Media Or File Name text box, **type** *G:\ASR.bkf*

Backup media or file name:

G:\ASR.bkf

f. **Click Next.**

g. **Click Finish.** The Backup Progress dialog box will show you the status of the backup. This process can take up to 30 minutes to complete.

---

2. **Create the ASR floppy disk.**

 Make sure that the floppy disk you use is formatted. If it isn't, this step will fail and you will have to re-create the ASR backup set from the beginning.

a. When prompted, **insert a blank, formatted floppy disk into the floppy disk drive and click OK.**

 Insert a blank, 1.44 MB, formatted diskette in drive A:. Recovery information will be written to this diskette.

b. When the disk creation is complete, **click OK.**

Remove the diskette, and label it as shown:

Windows Automated System Recovery Disk for ASR.bkf created 1/23/2003 at 10:53 AM

Keep it in a safe place in case your system needs to be restored using Windows Automated System Recovery.

c. In the Backup Progress dialog box, **click Close.**

d. **Close Backup.**

---

3. **Store the ASR disks in a safe location.**

a. **Remove the floppy disk from the disk drive and label it.**

b. If you created the ASR backup set on removable media (such as a tape), **remove the media and label it.**

Lesson 11 Follow-up

In this lesson, you learned tasks such as creating boot disks and emergency repair disks, backing up, and preparing for an Automated System Recovery. By mastering these skills, you can be prepared for any disaster that might head your way. And by being prepared, you can get a computer up and running much quicker, which reduces the computer's downtime.

1. Which techniques presented in this lesson do you currently use in your work environment? Why?

2. What types of disasters have you encountered with computers?

LESSON 12

Recovering from Disaster

Lesson Time
*2 hour(s) to 3 hour(s),
30 minutes*

Lesson Objectives:

In this lesson, you will recover from disaster.

You will:

- Troubleshoot an application.
- Troubleshoot hard disks.
- Restore user data.
- Restore the Registry.
- Restore system state data.
- Recover boot sector files.
- Perform an automated system recovery.

Introduction

In Lesson 11, you saw all the steps you should take to prepare for disaster. In this lesson, you'll learn what to do if disaster strikes. You'll begin by troubleshooting applications and a computer that won't boot, move on to how you restore any type of backup, and then master the steps for performing an Automated System Recovery.

As an A+ technician, you can know everything possible about preparing for disaster recovery, but the true test is to actually repair the computer after the disaster strikes. You will be expected to get the computer back up and running as quickly as possible.

The following CompTIA A+ Operating System Technologies (2003) Examination objectives are covered in this lesson:

- Topic A:
    - 1.5 System Management Tools: Task Manager.
    - 3.1 Common Error Messages: Event Viewer — Event log is full.
    - 3.1 Using the correct Utilities: Dr. Watson, Event Viewer.
    - 3.2 Diagnostic tools, utilities and resources: User/installation manuals, Internet/web resources, Training materials, Task Manager, Dr. Watson, Event Viewer, Device Manager.
    - 3.3 Other Common problems: General Protection Faults, Bluescreen error (BSOD) illegal operation, Invalid working directory, System lock up, Application will not start or load.
- Topic B:
    - 2.3 Alternative Boot Methods: Using a Startup disk, Safe/VGA-only mode, Last Known Good configuration.
    - 3.1 Common Error Messages: Boot failure and errors: Invalid boot disk, Inaccessible boot device, Missing NTLDR, Bad or missing Command interpreter.
    - 3.1 Common Error Messages: Startup messages: Error in CONFIG.SYS line XX, Himem.sys not loaded, Missing or corrupt Himem.sys, Device/Service has failed to start.
    - 3.1 Common Error Messages and Codes: A device referenced in SYSTEM.INI, WIN.INI, Registry is not found.
    - 3.1 Common Error Messages and Codes: Failure to start GUI.
    - 3.2 Startup Modes: Safe mode, Safe Mode with command prompt, Safe mode with networking, Step-by-Step/Single Step mode.
    - 3.2 Diagnostic tools, utilities, and resources: Boot Disk, WinMSD, Recovery CD, CONFIGSAFE.
- Topic C:
    - 1.5 Disk Management Tools: Backup/Restore Utility (MSBackup, NTBackup, etc).
    - 2.1 Restore user data files (if applicable).
- Topic D:
    - 3.1 Common Error Messages and Codes: Registry corruption.

TOPIC A

Troubleshoot an Application

Earlier in the course, you learned how to install and configure both Windows and non-Windows applications. Most of the time, installing and configuring an application is all you need to do to get your users up and running. But no application always runs perfectly, and there will be instances in which you'll need to fix a problem. In this topic, you'll learn the skills necessary to troubleshoot an application that isn't working correctly.

An application that doesn't work properly is probably one of the most common problems users face. All too often, system lockups, lost data, and unexplained crashes have their origins in an application that is experiencing problems. Being able to diagnose and fix the problem enables you to respond quickly when an application fails, which means you'll be able to get your users back up and running as soon as possible.

Common Problems

There are many problems you can encounter when troubleshooting applications. Table 12-1 lists the symptoms of problems you can expect to encounter.

Table 12-1: *Common Application Problems*

Symptom	Suspected Problem
Application won't install	You're trying to install an application that needs to overwrite a file that is currently in use on the computer.
Application won't start or load	The application was installed incorrectly, a version conflict between the application and other applications on the computer exists, or your computer is experiencing memory access errors.
Event log is full	The application or system logs have filled up because of too many error messages.
General Protection Fault	An application is accessing RAM that another application is using or the application is attempting to access a memory address that doesn't exist.
Illegal operation	An application is attempting to perform an action that Windows does not permit. Windows forces the application to close.
Invalid working directory	The application can't find the directory for storing its temporary files (typically \Temp). This can happen if you delete the folder that an application needs for storing its temporary files.
System lock up (Windows 98), Blue screen (Windows 2000/NT/XP)	The computer has too many instructions to process at once given its available RAM and processor resources.
Windows Protection Error	Windows did not load a virtual device driver properly. This error typically occurs at startup or shutdown.

Troubleshooting Tools

The Windows operating systems contain tools and techniques you can use to assist you in troubleshooting problems with applications. In Table 12-2, you see a list of these tools, an analysis of the information they give you, and the operating systems in which they're included.

Table 12-2: *Troubleshooting Tools*

Suspected Problem	Tool/Technique	Analysis	Supported Operating Systems
Open files are keeping you from installing an application.	Close all open applications.	An open application can prevent you from installing an application. Close all applications before starting the installation.	Windows 2000, Windows XP, Windows NT, and Windows 98
Application was installed incorrectly or a version conflict between this application and other applications on the computer exists.	Add/Remove Programs	You can use Add/Remove Programs to install or remove applications. Depending on the application, you might also be able to use Add/Remove Programs to repair the installation of the application.	Windows 2000, Windows XP, Windows NT, and Windows 98
The computer is experiencing memory access errors.	Close Program dialog box	Enables you to view a list of applications currently running on your computer. You can also close any applications that aren't responding.	Windows 98
Windows did not load a device driver properly.	Device Manager	Enables you to view the status of the computer's hardware devices.	Windows 2000, Windows XP, Windows NT, and Windows 98
An application is attempting to access RAM that another application is using or an address that doesn't exist in RAM; an application is attempting to perform an action that Windows does not permit.	Dr. Watson	Provides you with detailed information when an application hangs or ends abnormally. You can run Dr. Watson by choosing Start→Run and entering drwatson in the Open text box. Dr. Watson runs in the background and displays information only if you experience a problem with an application.	Windows 2000, Windows XP, Windows NT, and Windows 98

Suspected Problem	Tool/Technique	Analysis	Supported Operating Systems
An application won't install, start, or load.	Event Viewer	Enables you to determine if an application has reported any errors in the Application or System logs.	Windows 2000, Windows XP, and Windows NT
An application won't start or load; Windows did not load a device driver properly.	Expand.exe	Manually extract files from the Windows installation CD-ROM; use these files to replace corrupted system files on the hard disk (you must use Expand.exe because the files are stored in a compressed format on the Windows CD-ROM).	Windows 2000, Windows XP, Windows NT, and Windows 98
An application won't install, start, or load.	Registry Editor	Enables you to view and modify your computer's Registry.	Windows 2000, Windows XP, Windows NT, and Windows 98
An application won't start or load.	Setver	Configure the version of DOS Windows reports to a program (use Setver to simulate an older version of DOS if an application won't run in Windows 2000/XP/NT).	Windows 2000, Windows XP, Windows NT, and Windows 98
An application won't start or load.	System Configuration Utility (MSConfig)	Edit your computer's configuration files.	Windows 98
System lock up or blue screen.	System Properties (in Control Panel)	Use to determine the version of the operating system and which Service Packs are installed.	Windows 2000, Windows XP, and Windows NT (you can use System Properties in Windows 98 to determine the version of Windows installed, but not any patches).
The computer is experiencing memory access errors.	Task Manager	Enables you to list the applications currently running on the computer. You can also use Task Manager to close an application that isn't responding.	Windows 2000, Windows XP, and Windows NT

Web Sites for Troubleshooting Information

Microsoft has several very good Web sites that you can use to research the error messages you encounter on a Windows computer. The Microsoft Help and Support Web site, as shown in Figure 12-1, provides you with access to the Knowledge Base, software downloads, and more. Most importantly, you can use the Knowledge Base to research specific error messages you see. In many cases, Microsoft will provide the solution for this error as well. You can access the Help and Support Web site by going to **support.microsoft.com**.

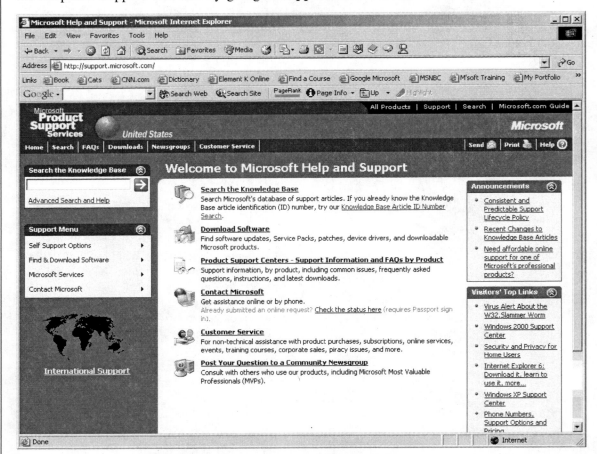

Figure 12-1: *The Microsoft Help and Support Web site.*

Another good Web site to use when troubleshooting is Microsoft Technet. You can access Microsoft Technet by going to **www.microsoft.com/technet**. This Web site also has information you can use to research error messages. In addition, it has the product manuals and Resource Kits (additional documentation) for each Windows operating system.

Finally, you should make sure that you bookmark the Microsoft Web sites for each Windows operating system. In Table 12-3, you see each Windows operating system and the URL for its associated Microsoft Web site.

Table 12-3: *Windows Web Sites*

Windows Version	Web Site
Windows 98	**www.microsoft.com/windows98**
Windows NT	**www.microsoft.com/ntworkstation**
Windows 2000	**www.microsoft.com/windows2000**
Windows XP	**www.microsoft.com/windowsxp**

How to Troubleshoot an Application

Procedure Reference: Troubleshoot an Application

To troubleshoot an application:

 While troubleshooting applications, you should consult the manufacturer's documentation and user manuals and any relevant training materials.

1. Collect information about the problem.

   - Try running Dr. Watson and then the application to see if Dr. Watson displays any information about the error.

   - If the problem is occurring on a Windows 2000, Windows NT, or Windows XP computer, check the Application and System logs in Event Viewer to see if the application reported any errors (see the Using Event Viewer to Research Errors procedure below).

   - Use System Properties to determine which version of Windows and Service Packs are installed.

   - Use Device Manager to see if any hardware devices are reporting errors.

2. Isolate the problem.

   - Ask the user if the application ever worked. If it did, find out if anything has been changed on the computer. If it didn't, suspect a configuration problem.

   - Ask the user if she's experiencing problems with all applications or only one application. If it's only one application that's experiencing problems, suspect a problem with that application. If all applications are having problems, suspect a problem with the operating system.

   - Research the problem by using the Knowledge Base on Microsoft's Help and Support Web site or the application manufacturer's Web site.

3. Correct the problem using the following steps.

   a. If you've found a solution in the Knowledge Base or the application manufacturer's Web site, implement the solution. In some cases, Microsoft recommends that you fix a problem by editing the computer's Registry using Registry Editor. Or, you might need to download and install a patch from Microsoft or the application manufacturer's Web site. Proceed to Step 4.

   b. Install the latest Service Pack for Windows 2000, Windows NT, or Windows XP. If you're using Windows 98, connect to the Windows Update Web site and install all recommended patches. Proceed to Step 4.

   c. Uninstall the application. Restart the computer. Resintall the application. Go to Step 4.

4. Test the application to verify that you've resolved the problem. If you're still experiencing the problem, return to Step 3.

5. Document the problem and its solution for future reference.

Procedure Reference: Use Windows Event Viewer to Research Errors

To use Windows Event Viewer to review the System and Application error logs in Windows 2000, Windows NT, and Windows XP:

1. Open Event Viewer.

    -   If you're using Windows 2000 and Windows XP, open Computer Management. In the console tree, select Event Viewer.

    -   If you're using Windows NT, from the Start menu, choose Programs→ Administrative Tools→Event Viewer.

2. Open the appropriate log.

    -   In Windows 2000 and Windows XP, expand Event Viewer and then select Application or System to display its contents.

    -   In Windows NT, choose Log→Application or Log→System.

3. If necessary, filter the events in the Application log.

    a. If you're using Windows 2000 or Windows XP, choose View→Filter.

    b. If you're using Windows NT, choose View→Filter Events.

    c. In the Filter dialog box, select the information on which you want to filter the log. You can filter the messages in the log by any of the following information:

        -   Event Source

        -   Category

        -   User name

        -   Computer name

        -   Event type (Information, Warning, Error, Success Audit, or Failure Audit)

        -   Date

    d. Click OK.

4. Record the details of the error message.

5. Close all open windows.

Procedure Reference: Clear a Log File

If the Application or System logs become full, complete the following steps to clear the log file:

1. Open Event Viewer.

2. Select the log that's full.

3. Back up the log file.

    a. In Windows 2000 and Windows XP, choose Action→Save Log File As.

        In Windows NT, choose Log→Save As.

    b. In the File Name text box, type a name for the log file and click Save.

4. Clear the log file.

    a. In Windows 2000 and Windows XP, choose Action→Clear All Events.

        In Windows NT, choose Log→Clear All Events.

b.   When you're prompted to save the log file, click No.

5.   Close all open windows.

DISCOVERY ACTIVITY 12-1

Troubleshooting Application Problems

Scenario:

Your company's network consists of a mix of Windows 2000 Professional and Windows 98 clients. You have installed the company's applications on all client computers. As part of your job as an A+ technician, you're responsible for troubleshooting any problems users encounter with these applications. You have several technical support calls waiting for you.

1.   A Windows 2000 user reports that he attempted to install a new application on his computer. During the installation, the power failed. When the user attempted to resume the installation, he received an error message stating that the application is already installed. But, the application won't run and the user is also unable to uninstall the application. After researching the problem on Microsoft's Help and Support Web site, you've determined that you must edit the user's Registry in order to completely remove the application from the computer. Once you've edited the Registry, the user will be able to complete the installation of the application.

What utility should you use to edit the user's Registry?

a) Registry Editor (regedt32.exe)

b) Registry Editor (regedit.exe)

c) System Configuration Editor (sysedit.exe)

d) Microsoft Configuration Utility (msconfig.exe)

2.   A user calls to tell you that when she received a low disk space error message, she attempted to free up disk space on her computer by deleting files. She's now unable to run any of the applications in Microsoft Office.

What's the most efficient way to solve this user's problem?

a) Identify which files she deleted and copy them from another computer to the user's computer.

b) Re-install Microsoft Office.

c) Determine which files the user deleted. Copy the files from the Microsoft Office installation CD-ROMs and expand them by using Expand.exe.

d) Remove Microsoft Office. Reboot the computer, and then re-install Microsoft Office.

3. One of your Windows 2000 users is experiencing intermittent problems with an application. The user is receiving the "program performed an illegal operation" error message. You want to search the application publisher's Knowledge Base to see if you can find a solution for the problem.

What utility can you use to capture detailed information about the problem?

Topic B
Troubleshoot Hard Disks

Throughout this course, we've been working under the assumption that everything's okay with your users' computers and their hard disks. But what should you do if you suspect a problem with a hard disk? In this topic, you'll learn the common problems you can encounter with hard disks and the troubleshooting tools you can use to diagnose these problems.

A computer without a functioning hard disk is essentially dead in the water. The computer's user won't be able to work on the computer, and thus can't complete her work. Because the hard disk is so critical to the computer, as an A+ technician, many of your technical support cases will involve troubleshooting computer hard disks. It's important that you know how to respond to these calls to quickly repair the hard disk problems so that you can get the computer back up and running and the user back to being productive on her computer.

Common Error Messages

During the boot/startup process, and at other times during normal operation, you're going to encounter a variety of error messages. Table 12-4 lists common boot error messages, Table 12-5 lists common startup error messages, and Table 12-6 lists some other common errors and messages you might see on your Windows computers.

Table 12-4: *Common Boot Error Messages*

Error Message Indicates	Suspect a Problem With the
Invalid boot disk	Hard disk, or the CD-ROM or floppy disk being used to boot the computer.
Inaccessible boot device	Hard disk or hard disk controller.
Missing NTLDR	Hard disk, floppy disk, or CD-ROM being used to boot computer. Also, check to see if there's a non-bootable floppy in the floppy drive on a Windows NT/2000/XP computer.
Bad or missing command interpreter	Hard disk or Command.com file.

Table 12-5: *Common Startup Error Messages*

Error Message Indicates	Suspect a Problem With the
Error in Config.sys line *xx*	Config.sys file at the specified line.
Himem.sys not loaded; Missing or corrupt Himem.sys	Config.sys file, or the Himem.sys file itself (missing or corrupt).
Device/Service has failed to start; Option will not function	Device drivers or resource conflicts.

Table 12-6: *Other Common Errors and Messages*

Error Message Indicates	Suspect a Problem With the
A device referenced in System.ini/Win.ini/Registry is not found	Virtual device driver (missing or damaged).
Failure to start GUI	Msdos.sys file or a missing or damaged virtual device driver.

Windows 2000/NT/XP Boot Troubleshooting Tools

Windows 2000, Windows NT, and Windows XP also include tools that you can use to troubleshoot problems with booting the computer. Table 12-7 lists these tools and a description of each.

Table 12-7: *Windows 2000/NT/XP Boot Troubleshooting Tools*

Tool	Purpose
Boot disk	You can use a Windows 2000, Windows NT, or Windows XP boot disk in the event the computer is unable to boot from the hard disk. Once you've booted the computer successfully, you can recopy any missing files to the hard disk from the boot disk.
Emergency Repair	You can perform an emergency repair in Windows NT and Windows 2000 to correct problems with booting the computer, missing or corrupt system files, and Registry problems.
Notepad	If you change the partitioning on your hard disk, you might find that the computer can no longer boot due to the boot.ini file incorrectly pointing to the Windows boot partition. Use Notepad to edit the boot.ini file so that it points to the correct partition.
Recovery Console	You can use the Recovery Console in Windows 2000 and Windows XP to repair problems with the system and boot partitions and copy missing files.
WinMSD	Used to access diagnostic tools and system information, including OS version, system resources, devices, and services.

Tool	Purpose
Recovery CD-ROM	Used to recover the operating system if it will no longer start, often used to boot and copy operating system files from a special partition on the hard drive. Shipped with most Windows computers.
imagineLAN ConfigSafe	Used to take a "snapshot" of the system and restore the system from the snapshot after a critical failure.

How to Troubleshoot Hard Disks

Procedure Reference: Troubleshoot a Hard Disk in Windows 2000/XP/NT

To troubleshoot a hard disk in Windows 2000, Windows XP, and Windows NT:

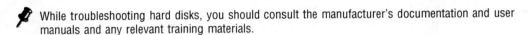 While troubleshooting hard disks, you should consult the manufacturer's documentation and user manuals and any relevant training materials.

1. If you suspect that a device driver you just installed is preventing the computer from booting, boot the computer with the Last Known Good boot option. Use these steps:

    a. Restart the computer. If necessary, turn the computer off and back on.

    b. If you're using Windows 2000 or Windows NT, select the appropriate operating system from the boot menu and press the Spacebar. From the options menu, select Last Known Good.

    c. If you're using Windows XP (or if you're using a computer configured to dual boot between Windows XP and Windows 2000 or Windows NT), press F8 after the computer completes the POST. From the Advanced Options Menu, choose Last Known Good Configuration.

    d. Start the operating system and log on. Windows automatically restores the last known good Registry information, so the problem should now be resolved.

2. Determine if it is a hardware or software failure.

    Use a Windows 2000, Windows XP, or Windows NT boot disk to attempt to boot the computer.

    - If Windows 2000, Windows XP, or Windows NT loads successfully, the failure is most likely due to one of the following:
        - An error in the ARC paths in the Boot.ini file.
        - A problem with the Windows 2000, Windows XP, or Windows NT system partition.
    - If the operating system fails to load, the failure is most likely due to one of the following:
        - A hardware problem.
        - An error in the ARC paths in the Boot.ini file.

- A problem with the Windows 2000, Windows XP, or Windows NT system partition.

3. If you suspect the hard disk problem is a hardware failure, complete the following tasks:

   a. Verify that the IDE or SCSI hard disk is on the Windows Hardware Compatibility List (HCL). You can check the HCL by going to **http://www.microsoft.com/hwdq/hcl/**.

   b. If the computer has an IDE drive:

      - Check for bad cables and connectors.

      - Verify that the driver for the disk controller is not corrupt or missing.

      - Verify that the jumpers are configured correctly.

      - Verify the hard disk's BIOS settings: Boot into the computer's CMOS setup utility and verify that the number of heads, cylinders, and sectors per track are set correctly.

   c. If the computer has a SCSI drive:

      - Check for bad cables.

      - Check for incorrect termination.

      - Verify the SCSI identifier for the hard disk is correct.

      - Disable sync negotiation in the SCSI BIOS.

   d. Try installing the hard disk in a computer that you know is not experiencing any problems:

      - If the good computer can't access the disk, the hard disk has failed. Replace the disk.

      - If the good computer can access the disk, troubleshoot other hardware in the original computer such as the hard disk controller and power supply.

4. Use an MS-DOS boot disk with the Fdisk utility to verify the partitions on the hard disk. Make sure that the appropriate primary partition is marked active.

5. If you suspect that some of the computer's boot files are missing or corrupt, or that the boot.ini file points to the wrong partition, complete the following tasks:

   a. Use the appropriate Windows 2000, Windows XP, or Windows NT boot disk to boot the computer.

   b. Log on as a local administrator.

   c. Correct the problem by replacing the corrupted file with a good copy from the boot floppy disk or by modifying the incorrect entries in the Boot.ini file.

   d. Restart the computer. It should boot normally.

6. If you suspect a problem with the Boot.ini file, edit the ARC paths in the Boot.ini file. To edit the Boot.ini file:

   Windows numbers all primary partitions on the disk first, and then any extended partitions.

   a. Use Disk Management in Windows 2000 and Windows XP or Disk Administrator in Windows NT to determine the partitions on the computer's hard disk. Identify the disk number and the partition number on which Windows 2000, Windows XP, or Windows NT is installed.

   b. Open Windows Explorer.

c.   If necessary, if you're using Windows 2000 or Windows XP, configure Windows Explorer to display system and hidden files.

   1.   Select the C drive.

   2.   In Windows Explorer, choose Tools→Folder Options.

   3.   Select the View tab.

   4.   Below Hidden Files And Folders, select Show Hidden Files And Folders.

   5.   Uncheck Hide File Extensions For Known File Types.

   6.   Uncheck Hide Protected Operating System Files (Recommended).

   7.   Click OK.

If necessary, if you're using Windows NT, configure Windows Explorer to display system and hidden files.

   1.   Select the C drive.

   2.   In Windows Explorer, choose View→Options.

   3.   Below Hidden Files, choose Show All Files.

   4.   Uncheck Hide File Extensions For Known File Types.

   5.   Click OK.

d.   Remove the Read-Only attribute from the Boot.ini file.

e.   Double-click C:\Boot.ini to open it in Notepad.

f.   Change the ARC naming paths to accurately reflect the computer's partitions.

g.   Save your changes.

h.   Restart the computer to verify that the change resolved the problem.

i.   Copy the revised Boot.ini file to the boot disk.

7.   If you suspect a problem with the system partition and the computer can boot to Windows, complete the following steps:

a.   Use Disk Management (Windows 2000/XP) or Disk Administrator (Windows NT) to verify that the C partition is marked active.

b.   Re-write the master boot record and boot sector information by using an Emergency Repair (in Windows 2000 and Windows NT) or the Recovery Console (in Windows XP).

8.   If the computer attempts to boot but hangs, use the Safe Mode boot options:

a.   Restart the computer (turn the power off and on if necessary).

b.   After the POST phase of the boot sequence, and during the display of the boot menu (if you have one), press F8.

c.   Select the desired Safe Mode boot option from the menu. Use Table 12-8 as a guide.

d.   Log on as a local administrator.

e.   Click Yes in the Safe Mode message box.

f.   Use the appropriate troubleshooting steps to correct the problem. For example, re-install or update a corrupt device driver, copy or delete files, modify a system setting, or uninstall a service or application.

g.   Reboot to normal mode.

Table 12-8: *Safe Mode Boot Options*

Option	Description	Use When
Safe Mode	Starts the computer with a minimal set of drivers and services, including the mouse, keyboard, VGA display, and hard disk.	The problem might be with the networking components.
Safe Mode with Networking	Starts the computer with the Safe Mode drivers and services, along with the networking drivers and services.	You need to access the network to repair the problem.
Safe Mode with Command Prompt	Starts the computer with the Safe Mode drivers and services, and a command prompt interface.	A problem is preventing Windows from displaying the graphical desktop.

9. Check the event logs for errors.

   a. Log on as a local administrator.

   b. If you're using Windows 2000 or Windows XP, right-click My Computer and choose Manage. Below System Tools, expand Event Viewer.

   c. If you're using Windows NT, from the Start menu, choose Programs→ Administrative Tools→Event Viewer.

   d. Review the Application, Security, and System logs for any Warning and Error messages. Look for the most recent messages (these are the messages at the beginning of the log).

   e. Look for any Information events just before the Warning or Error messages; these events might give you a clue as to what was changed on the system prior to the Warning or Error.

   f. After you identify the first event that triggered the problem, review the event's description (along with any related events) to determine the problem's cause.

   g. Research specific error messages by using Microsoft's Knowledge Base at **support.microsoft.com**.

   h. If possible, fix the problem.

10. If the computer is able to boot but the user is experiencing intermittent problems with the disk, or disk access is slow, complete the following steps:

   a. Check the System log in Event Viewer to determine if any disk errors have been recorded by Windows. Such errors could indicate that the disk is failing.

   b. If you're using Windows 2000 or Windows XP, update the driver for the hard disk.

      1. In Device Manager, expand Disk Drives.

      2. Right-click the hard disk and choose Properties.

      3. Select the Driver tab.

      4. Click Update Driver.

c. If you're using Windows 2000 or Windows XP, use Disk Cleanup to remove unnecessary files from the hard disk.

   1. In Windows Explorer, right-click the disk and choose Properties.

   2. Click Disk Cleanup.

   3. On the Disk Cleanup page, check the check boxes for any categories of files that you want to clean up. Disk Cleanup displays the number of KB in the category; if you want to see the actual files you will be deleting, click View Files.

   4. To compress old files, check Compress Old Files and click Options to set the length of the expiration window.

   5. Click OK to perform the disk cleanup.

   6. Click Yes to confirm.

d. Defragment the hard disk.

11. If you're using Windows XP and all else fails, perform an Automated System Recovery (see Topic 12G).

Procedure Reference: Troubleshoot a Hard Disk in Windows 98

To troubleshoot a hard disk in Windows 98:

1. If necessary, create an MS-DOS boot disk on another Windows 98 computer. Include the following files on this boot disk:
   - Attrib.exe
   - Edit.com
   - Edit.hlp
   - Fdisk.exe
   - Format.com
   - Scandisk.exe
   - Scandisk.ini
   - Sys.com

2. Attempt to boot the computer with the MS-DOS boot disk.

3. If the computer will not boot at all, complete the following steps:

   a. If the computer boots from the floppy disk, the problem is with the boot files for Windows 98.

   b. If the computer still won't boot, the problem is with the hardware.

4. If you suspect the hard disk problem is a hardware failure:

   For IDE drives:
   - Check for bad cables and connectors.
   - Verify the driver for the disk controller is not corrupt or missing.
   - Verify the jumpers are connected correctly.
   - Verify the hard disk's BIOS settings.

Boot into the system BIOS, verify the # of heads, cylinders, and sectors per track are set correctly.

For SCSI drives:

- Check for bad cables.
- Check for incorrect termination.
- Verify the SCSI identifier for the hard disk is correct.
- Disable sync negotiation in the SCSI BIOS.

5. If the computer boots from an MS-DOS boot disk, run Fdisk and complete the following steps:

   a. Verify that a primary partition exists on the C drive.

   b. Verify that the primary partition is marked active (bootable).

   c. Test to see if the computer can boot now.

⚠ If you create a new partition, any data that was previously stored on the hard disk will be erased.

6. If Fdisk doesn't find any partitions on the hard disk, complete the following steps:

   a. Create a primary partition.

   b. Mark the primary partition active.

   c. Exit Fdisk and restart the computer.

   d. At the A: prompt, enter `format c: /s` to format the C drive and make it bootable.

   e. Test to see if the computer can boot now.

7. If Fdisk finds a primary partition that is marked active, complete the following steps:

   a. At the A: prompt, enter `fdisk /mbr` to repair the master boot record on the C drive.

   b. At the A: prompt, enter `sys c:` to re-copy the system files to the C drive.

   c. Test to see if the computer can boot now.

8. If the computer attempts to boot but hangs, use the boot options:

   a. Restart the computer (turn the power off and on if necessary).

   b. After the POST phase of the boot sequence, when you see a flashing cursor at the top of the screen, press and hold F8 (if you have configured the computer to dual-boot, you can press F8 when you see the boot menu).

   c. Select the desired boot option from the menu. Use Table 12-9 as a guide.

   d. Log on as a local administrator.

   e. Click Yes in the Safe Mode message box.

   f. Use the appropriate troubleshooting steps to correct the problem. For example, re-install or update a corrupt device driver, copy or delete files, modify a system setting, or uninstall a service or application.

   g. Reboot to normal mode.

Table 12-9: *Windows 98 Boot Options*

Option	Description	Use When
Command Prompt Only	Does not load the Windows 98 graphical interface.	You want to access the computer's hard disk in order to copy new files to the disk or delete files.
Logged (\Bootlog.txt)	Starts Windows 98 normally, but stores a record of whether Windows 9x components loaded successfully in the Bootlog.txt file.	You want to determine if a device driver isn't loading successfully.
Safe Mode	Starts the computer with a minimal set of drivers and services, including the mouse, keyboard, VGA display, and hard disk.	The problem might be with the networking components.
Safe Mode with Networking Support	Starts the computer with the Safe Mode drivers and services, along with the networking drivers and services.	You need to access the network to repair the problem.
Safe Mode Command Prompt Only	Starts the computer with the Safe Mode drivers and services, and a command prompt interface.	A problem is preventing Windows from displaying the graphical desktop.
Step-by-Step Confirmation	Loads drivers in Config.sys, Autoexec.bat, and Windows 98 one line at a time, enabling you to select which drivers should load.	You suspect that a faulty driver is preventing Windows 98 from booting.

9. If the above steps don't resolve the problem, suspect a problem with the computer's hardware. Things to check include:

   - Replacing the hard disk with a hard disk that you know to be good. If the computer boots successfully from this new hard disk, replace the failed hard disk with a new hard disk.

   - If the computer does not boot successfully from a hard disk that you know to be good, try replacing the drive cable and plugging in a different power cable.

   - If the computer still does not boot successfully, try installing the hard disk you suspect has failed into a computer that you know boots successfully. If the new computer boots from the hard disk, the problem is with the old computer's hardware. If the new computer does not boot successfully from the hard disk, replace it.

10. If the computer hangs during the startup of Windows 98, complete the following steps:

    a. Check the computer's CMOS settings for a virus protection feature. Some computers have a BIOS setting that prevents applications from modifying the boot sector of the startup disk. Windows 9x must modify the boot sector during Setup or the first time it runs. Disable the virus protection feature by using the computer's CMOS setup.

b. Use an MS-DOS boot disk to boot the computer. Disable any real-mode drivers in the autoexec.bat and config.sys files. If this resolves the problem, make sure that the devices with real-mode drivers aren't using the same system resources as other devices. Try to obtain new Windows 9x drivers for these devices.

c. If the problem occurs after you installed device drivers intended for an older version of Windows (such as Windows 3.1), use Sysedit to remove the entries in the System.ini that were added by the device driver's installation software. If the device is displayed in Device Manager, delete it. Restart Windows 98 and use the Add New Hardware Wizard to re-install the device using Windows 98-compatible drivers.

11. If you see the message *Bad or missing <filename>* during startup, complete the following tasks:

a. Use Sysedit to check the syntax of the entry in the startup file (for example, config.sys).

b. Verify that the file Windows 98 is attempting to load is stored in the right folder.

c. Verify that the file is the correct version.

d. If you suspect that the file might be corrupted, try replacing the file with a known good version from another computer or from a backup set.

12. If you receive a message stating that the Registry is missing or corrupt and you are unable to access Windows 98, complete these steps:

a. Restart Windows 98.

b. During the boot process, press and hold the Ctrl key until the Microsoft Windows 98 Startup menu is displayed.

c. Select Command Prompt only.

d. At the MS-DOS command prompt, enter `scanreg /restore`.

e. Select the backup set you want to restore and click Restore.

13. If you receive a message stating that the Registry is missing or corrupt and you are able to access Windows 98, complete these steps:

a. Restart Windows 98 using the Restart In MS-DOS Mode option.

b. At the MS-DOS command prompt, enter `scanreg /restore`.

c. Select the backup set you want to restore and click Restore.

14. If you have a particular device that isn't functioning correctly, perform the following steps:

a. Run Device Manager and display the device's Properties dialog box (from the Start menu, choose Settings→Control Panel. Double-click System. Select the Device Manager tab).

b. In the Properties dialog box for the device, select the Resources tab.

c. Look at the Conflicting Device List. Verify that there aren't any resource conflicts.

    d.   If you see a resource conflict, try changing the settings as needed. You can also run the Hardware Troubleshooter in Windows Help to obtain assistance in troubleshooting resource conflicts.

    e.   If you are unable to resolve the conflicts, remove the device in Device Manager and re-install it by using the Add New Hardware Wizard.

15. If the computer boots to a command prompt instead of Windows 9x, complete the following steps:

    a.   Verify the operating system is installed on the computer by entering `ver`.

    b.   Make sure that the Msdos.sys file is present in the C:\ folder. If necessary, use `dir C:\ /ah` to display hidden files.

    c.   Verify that the Msdos.sys file has not been corrupted:

        1.   From the Start menu, choose Programs→Accessories→System Tools→ System Information.

        2.   Choose Tools→System File Checker.

        3.   Select Scan For Altered Files and click Start. If the System File Checker detects an altered system file, it will prompt you to restore the original file from the Windows 98 installation CD-ROM.

    d.   Verify that a virtual device driver (VxD) is not the cause of the problem. (If a VxD is preventing Windows 98 from booting, you'll see an error message stating which VxD is causing the problem.) If a VxD is the problem, re-install Windows 98 and choose the Verify or Safe Recovery option to restore the faulty VxD.

16. If the computer boots into Windows 98 but reports disk errors, try the following:

    •   Run ScanDisk to examine your disk for invalid file names, file dates, and times, bad sectors, and invalid compression structures, as well as lost, invalid, and cross-linked clusters.

    •   If you are running Windows 98, run the Maintenance Wizard to check your hard disk for problems.

Run ScanDisk in Windows 9x

To run ScanDisk from an MS-DOS prompt:

1. Boot to MS-DOS.

2. Enter `scandisk` *drive:*, where *drive* is the drive letter of the partition you're troubleshooting.

 A version of scandisk is in the \Windows folder.

3. Press Enter.

4. If prompted to perform a surface scan, use the arrow keys to select either Yes to perform the scan or No to skip the scan.

5. Use the arrow keys to select Exit.

To run ScanDisk from Windows 9x:

1. Choose Start→Programs→Accessories→System Tools→ScanDisk.

2. In the drives list box, select the drive(s) you want to check for errors.

You can use the Shift or Ctrl keys to select multiple disks in the drives list box.

3. In the Type Of Test box, select Standard or Thorough.

4. If you select Thorough, click the Options button to select the following:

- Change the area of the disk to scan from System And Data Areas to either System Area Only or Data Area Only.

- Disable write-testing by checking the Do Not Perform Write Testing check box.

- Disable repairing bad sectors in hidden and system files by checking the Do Not Repair Bad Sectors In Hidden And System Files check box.

Click OK to close the Surface Scan Options dialog box.

5. Click the Advanced button to change the following default options:

- Change Display Summary from Always to either Never or Only if Errors Found.

- Change Log File from Replace Log to either Append To Log or No Log.

- Change Cross-linked Files from Make Copies to either Delete or Ignore.

- Change Lost File Fragments from Convert To Files to Free.

- Change Check Files For Invalid File Names to also include Invalid Dates and Times and/or Duplicate Names, or to disable Invalid File Names.

- Disable Check Host Drive First.

- Enable Report MS-DOS Mode Name Length Errors.

Click OK to close the ScanDisk options dialog box.

6. If you want Window 9x to automatically fix errors that it finds, check the Automatically Fix Errors check box.

7. Click Start.

8. Click Close to close the ScanDisk Results dialog box.

9. Click Close to close the ScanDisk dialog box.

Run the Maintenance Wizard in Windows 9x

To run the Maintenance Wizard on a Windows 98 computer:

1. Choose Start→Programs→Accessories→System Tools→Maintenance Wizard.

2. Select either Express or Custom. Express completes the following tasks:

- Defragments your hard disk to speed up your most frequently used programs.

- Checks your hard disk for errors.

- Deletes unnecessary files from the hard disk.

Custom allows you to select your own maintenance tasks.

3. Select one of the following times to run maintenance tasks:

- Nights—Midnight to 3:00 A.M.

- Days—Noon to 3:00 P.M.

- Evenings—8:00 P.M. to 11:00 P.M.

- Custom—Use current settings (this option is available only if you select Custom in Step 2).

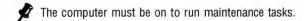 The computer must be on to run maintenance tasks.

Click Next.

4. If you selected Custom, select either Yes, Defragment My Disk Regularly or No, Do Not Defragment My Disk.

   If you selected Yes, Defragment My Disk Regularly, use the Reschedule button to alter the default schedule for the defragmentation task. Use the Settings button to change the default drive to defragment.

   Click Next.

5. If you selected Custom, select either Yes, Scan My Hard Disk For Errors Regularly or No, Do Not Scan My Hard Disk For Errors.

   If you selected Yes, Scan My Hard Disk For Errors Regularly, use the Reschedule button to alter the default schedule for the disk scan task. Use the Settings button to change the default drive to scan and scan options.

   Click Next.

6. If you selected Custom, select either Yes, Delete Unnecessary Files Regularly or No, Do Not Delete Unnecessary Files.

   If you selected Yes, Delete Unnecessary Files Regularly, use the Reschedule button to alter the default schedule for the file removal task. Use the Settings button to change the default types of files to remove. Check the check boxes of the file types you want Windows 98 to delete.

   Click Next.

7. If you want to run the maintenance tasks immediately, check the When I Click Finish, Perform Each Scheduled Task For The First Time check box.

8. Click Finish.

ACTIVITY 12-2

Troubleshooting Hard Disk Problems

Scenario:

As the in-house technician for a company, you're responsible for troubleshooting any problems users encounter with their Windows 2000 and Windows 98 computers. You've received four troubleshooting requests.

Troubleshooting Request #1

1. A user reports that he was exploring his Windows 2000 computer and opened Computer Management. He found some free space on his hard disk so he created and formatted a new partition. Now, his computer won't boot.

   What do you think is the problem? How should you fix it?

Troubleshooting Request #2

2. Another user reports that she is unable to boot her Windows 2000 computer. You attempt to boot her computer using a boot disk with no success. After referring to your documentation of the configuration of the user's computer, you know that the computer's hard disk is an IDE disk that contains only a single partition.

   What should you try next? Why?

Troubleshooting Request #3

3. You've received a computer from a new employee, Dave. He complains that his computer was terribly slow and now he can't boot into Windows 98. You try to boot with an MS-DOS boot disk and can get MS-DOS to load from the floppy disk.

   What can you eliminate as the problem?

4. **What should you try next to fix Dave's computer?**

Troubleshooting Request #4

5. Jane calls to say that her computer is slow to start up in Windows 98 and periodically the screen will go blue on her and she has to reboot. You receive Jane's computer and can boot into Windows 98, but it is very slow.

   What should you do to try to fix Jane's computer?

TOPIC C

Restore Data

In Lesson 11, you learned how to back up data so that it's available to you to restore on a user's computer. You'll need this backup in the event the computer crashes or the computer's user accidentally deletes files that he needs. In this topic, you'll learn how to go about restoring your backup of the data.

Nothing will panic a user more than the thought that he's lost some (or even all) of his data. In fact, most users consider the loss of their data the worst possible thing that can happen to them on a computer. As an A+ technician, your job requires that you know how to restore data in just such an emergency.

How to Restore Data

Procedure Reference: Restore Data in Windows 2000

To restore data in Windows 2000:

1. Log on as a user who's either a member of the Backup Operators or Administrators groups, owner of a file, or a user who has at least the Write NTFS permissions to restore file data.

2. Load your backup media.

3. Run Backup.

4. Click Restore Wizard.

5. Click Next.

6. Below What To Restore, expand the backup media (File or Tape).

7. Check the backup set stored on the backup media that you want to restore.

8. Click Next.

9. If you want to configure advanced options such as the destination for the restored files, what you want Backup to do if the files already exist on the computer's hard disk, and whether you want to restore security permissions, click Advanced.

10. Click Finish to restore the backup.

11. Click OK to confirm that you have inserted the backup media.

12. Click Close to close the Restore Progress dialog box.

13. Close Backup.

14. Verify that the files, folders, or both were restored successfully.

Procedure Reference: Restore Data in Windows XP

To restore data in Windows XP:

1. Log on as a user who's either a member of the Backup Operators or Administrators groups, owner of a file, or a user who has at least the Write NTFS permissions to restore file data.

2. Load your backup media.

3. Run Backup.

4. Click Next.

5. Select Restore Files And Settings and click Next.

6. Below Items To Restore, expand the backup media (File or Tape).

7. Expand the backup set you want to restore.

8. Check the files and folders you want to restore from the backup set.

9. Click Next.

10. If you want to configure advanced options such as the destination for the restored files, what you want Backup to do if the files already exist on the computer's hard disk, and whether you want to restore security permissions, click Advanced.

11. Click Finish to restore the backup.

12. Click Close to close the Restore Progress dialog box.

13. Close Backup.

14. Verify that the files, folders, or both were restored successfully.

Procedure Reference: Restore Data in Windows NT

To restore data in Windows NT:

1. Log on as a user who's either a member of the Backup Operators or Administrators groups, owner of a file, or a user who has at least the Write NTFS permissions to restore file data.

2. Load your backup media.

3. Run Backup.

4. Click Restore Wizard.

5. Click Next.

6. Below What To Restore, expand the backup media (File or Tape).

7. Check the backup set stored on the backup media that you want to restore.

8. Click Next.

9. If you want to configure advanced options such as the destination for the restored files, what you want Backup to do if the files already exist on the computer's hard disk, and whether you want to restore security permissions, click Advanced.

10. Click Finish to restore the backup.

11. Click OK to confirm that you have inserted the backup media.

12. Click Close to close the Restore Progress dialog box.

13. Close Backup.

14. Verify that the files, folders, or both were restored successfully.

Procedure Reference: Restore Data in Windows 98

To restore data in Windows 98:

1. Load your backup media.

2. Run Backup (Msbackup.exe) from the System Tools menu.

3. Select Restore Backed Up Files and click OK.

4. From the Restore From drop-down list, select your backup media.

5. If necessary, in the text box, type the path and name of the backup file.

6. Click Next.

7. In the Select Backup Sets dialog box, check the backup set(s) you want to restore and click OK.

8. Below What To Restore, check the files and folders you want to restore.

9. Click Next.

10. From the Where To Restore drop-down list, select where you want to restore the files and click Next.

11. On the How To Restore page, select one of the following:

   • Do Not Replace The File On My Computer (Recommended), if you don't want to restore the backup over the files currently on your computer's hard disk.

   • Replace The File On My Computer Only If The File Is Older, to have Backup restore the files over the copies on your computer only if the files on your computer are older than the ones within the backup set.

   • Always Replace The File On My Computer, if you want to have the files in the backup set replace the files on your computer (regardless of the date stamp on the files).

12. Click Start to begin the restore.

13. Click OK to confirm that you have inserted the backup media.

14. Click OK to close the Operation Completed message box.

15. Click OK to close the Restore Progress dialog box.

16. Close Backup.

17. Verify that the files, folders, or both were restored successfully.

ACTIVITY 12-3

Restoring Data

Setup:
You have a backup set containing a backup of the D:\Data\Personnel folder on a floppy disk. The name of the backup file is personnel.bkf.

Setup:
Before you start this activity, complete the following steps:

1. Log on to Windows 2000 as Admin#.

2. Make sure you have a backup of D:\Data\Personnel on floppy disk.

3. In Windows Explorer, delete the D:\Data\Personnel folder.

4. Close Windows Explorer.

Scenario:
You have been hired as an A+ technician to perform system maintenance and management tasks for a client. You have configured each user's Windows 2000 computer to back up on a weekly basis. You want to test a backup you made to verify that you're getting valid backups.

What You Do	How You Do It
1. Restore the backup of the D:\Data\ Personnel folder.	a. Insert the floppy disk containing the backup into the floppy disk drive.

b. **Run Backup.**

c. **Click Restore Wizard.**

d. **Click Next.**

e. Below What To Restore, **expand File and then the backup media.**

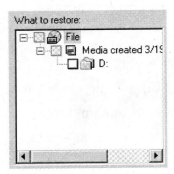

f. **Expand D.**

g. When prompted, in the Backup File Name text box, **verify that the correct path and backup file name is displayed.**

h. **Click OK.**

i. **Check the D:\Data\Personnel folder.**

j. **Click Next.**

k. **Click Finish.**

l. **Click OK** to confirm that you have inserted the backup media.

m. **Click Close** to close the Restore Progress dialog box.

n. **Close Backup.**

2. **Verify that the D:\Data\Personnel folder restored successfully.**

a. In Windows Explorer, **verify that you see the D:\Data\Personnel folder.**

b. **Select the D:\Data\Personnel folder.**

c. **Verify that you see the Salary.doc file within it, along with a Reports folder.**

d. **Close Windows Explorer.**

Topic D

Restore the Registry

In Topic 12C, you learned how to restore a user's data in the event of a computer crash or accidental deletion of files. But restoring user data files doesn't restore the operating system's configuration information. If you need to restore the operating system's configuration, one technique you can use is to restore a backup of the Registry—and that's what you'll learn how to do in this topic.

Without the Registry, or if the Registry becomes corrupt, a user's computer won't have the information it needs to properly load the operating system. Losing the Registry is like losing the detailed driving directions you got from the American Automobile Association for a month-long cross country trip. Without these directions, you won't know which roads to take. Without the Registry, a computer won't know what device drivers and services to load, nor will it know how the user's applications are configured. Because the Registry is so critical to the Windows operating systems, it's essential that you as an A+ technician know the steps to restore it so that you can get the computer back up and running.

How to Restore the Registry

Procedure Reference: Restore the Registry from a Registry Editor Backup

To restore the Registry from a Registry Editor backup:

1. If you can't start Windows in normal mode, boot to Safe Mode.

2. If you're using Windows 2000, Windows XP, or Windows NT, log on as a local administrator.

3. Verify that you have a backup of the Registry that was created with Registry Editor (regedit.exe).

4. Run Regedit.exe (from the Start menu, choose Run. In the Open text box, type regedit.exe and click OK).

5. In the left pane, select My Computer.

6. Choose Registry→Import Registry File.

7. From the Look In drop-down list, select the drive on which you stored the Registry backup.

> 🖉 You might see an error message stating that not all Registry keys were imported. Registry Editor can't overwrite the portions of the Registry that are currently in use.

8. Select the backup file and click Open. Registry Editor will import the Registry backup.

9. Click OK to close the Successful Import message.

10. Close Registry Editor.

11. Restart the computer.

12. When the computer has restarted, log back on and verify that the problem has been corrected.

Procedure Reference: Restore the Registry from a Windows NT Backup

To restore the Registry from a Windows NT Backup:

1. Insert the media with your Registry backup.

2. Open Backup.

3. Click Close to close the Microsoft Backup dialog box.

4. Select the Restore tab.

5. Click Yes to have Backup refresh the information it displays in the Restore window.

6. In the Select Backup Sets dialog box, check the backup set containing the Registry backup and click OK.

7. Below What To Restore, select at least one file to restore.

8. Click Options.

9. Select the Advanced tab.

10. Check Restore Windows Registry and click OK.

11. Click Start to begin the restore.

12. Click OK to confirm that you have inserted the backup media.

13. Click Yes to confirm that you want to restore the Windows Registry.

14. In the Microsoft Backup message box, select one of the following:
    - Click Yes if you want to restore the hardware and system settings configuration in the Registry. You don't have to restore these settings if they haven't changed since the last Registry backup.

- Click No if you do not want to restore the hardware and system settings configuration in the Registry.

15. Click OK to close the Operation Completed message box.

16. If any errors are reported, click Report to view the log file. Close the log file when you're done reviewing it.

17. Click OK to close the Restore Progress dialog box.

18. Click Yes to restart the computer.

Procedure Reference: Restore the Registry from a Windows 98 Backup

To restore the Registry from a Windows 98 backup:

1. Insert the media with your Registry backup.

2. Open Backup.

3. Click Close to close the Microsoft Backup dialog box.

4. Select the Restore tab.

5. Click Yes to have Backup refresh the information it displays in the Restore window.

6. In the Select Backup Sets dialog box, check the backup set containing the Registry backup and click OK.

7. Below What To Restore, select at least one file to restore.

8. Click Options.

9. Select the Advanced tab.

10. Check Restore Windows Registry and click OK.

11. Click Start to begin the restore.

12. Click OK to confirm that you have inserted the backup media.

13. Click Yes to confirm that you want to restore the Windows Registry.

14. In the Microsoft Backup message box, select one of the following:
    - Click Yes if you want to restore the hardware and system settings configuration in the Registry. You don't have to restore these settings if they haven't changed since the last Registry backup.
    - Click No if you do not want to restore the hardware and system settings configuration in the Registry.

15. Click OK to close the Operation Completed message box.

16. If any errors are reported, click Report to view the log file. Close the log file when you're done reviewing it.

17. Click OK to close the Restore Progress dialog box.

18. Click Yes to restart the computer.

ACTIVITY 12-4

Restoring the Registry

Setup:

You have backed up the HKEY_LOCAL_MACHINE\Software\Microsoft key within Registry Editor.

Scenario:

You have installed a new Microsoft application on a Windows 2000 computer that's causing other applications to hang. You've already tried restoring the Last Known Good configuration from the boot menu, but it didn't fix the problem. Fortunately, before you installed the new application, you backed up the HKEY_LOCAL_MACHINE\Software\Microsoft key by using Registry Editor. You now want to restore the backup.

What You Do	How You Do It
1. Restore the Registry backup.	a. **Restart the computer.**
	b. When the boot menu is displayed, **press F8** to open the Advanced Options menu.
	c. From the Windows Advanced Options Menu, **select Safe Mode and press Enter.**
	d. From the operating system menu, **select Microsoft Windows 2000 Professional and press Enter.**
	e. **Log on as Admin#.**
	f. **Run Registry Editor** (from the Start menu, choose Run. In the Open text box, type regedit.exe and click OK).
	g. **Click OK.**

h. In the left pane, **select HKEY_LOCAL_ MACHINE\Software\Microsoft.**

```
HKEY_LOCAL_MACHINE
    HARDWARE
    SAM
    SECURITY
    SOFTWARE
        Classes
        Clients
        InstallShield
        INTEL
        KasperskyLab
        Iameme
        McAfee
        Microsoft
```

i. **Choose Registry→Import Registry File.**

j. **Open the C:\Backup folder.**

k. **Select the RegBack.reg file and click Open.**

l. **When the import is complete, click OK** to close the Registry Editor message box.

m. **Close Registry Editor.**

2. **Verify that the computer boots successfully.**

a. **Shut down and restart the computer.**

b. **Choose Windows 2000 Professional from the boot menu.**

c. **Log on as Admin#.**

TOPIC E

Restore System State Data

In Topic 12D, you learned how to restore a computer's Registry in case disaster strikes. In Windows 2000 and Windows XP, however, you have another choice for restoring the Registry (along with other critical operating system information): restoring a system state data backup. In this topic, you'll master the steps for doing just that.

A computer's system state data provides the "how to" instructions for configuring the operating system when the computer boots. Without this information, the computer potentially won't have what it needs to load the necessary drivers and services for the computer to function. In fact, it's possible that the computer won't even boot if the system state data is lost. Enter you, the A+ technician, to the rescue: By mastering the skills in this topic, you'll know just what to do to restore the system state data quickly so that the computer functions normally.

How to Restore System State Data

Procedure Reference: Restore System State Data in Windows 2000

To restore System State data in Windows 2000:

1. If you can't start Windows 2000 in normal mode, boot to Safe Mode.

2. Log on as a local administrator.

3. Load your backup media.

4. Run Backup.

5. Click Restore Wizard.

6. Click Next.

7. If you don't see the backup set containing the System State Data backup, click Import File. In the Catalog Backup File text box, type the path and file name for the backup file and click OK.

8. Below What To Restore, complete the following steps:

    a. Expand the backup media (File or Tape).

    b. Expand the backup set you want to restore.

    c. Check System State.

9. Click Next.

10. Click Finish to restore the backup.

11. Click OK to confirm that you have inserted the backup media.

12. Click Close to close the Restore Progress dialog box.

13. Click Yes to restart the computer (you might need to close some processes manually).

14. When the computer reboots, log on and verify that the problem has been corrected.

Procedure Reference: Restore System State Data in Windows XP

To restore System State Data in Windows XP:

1. Log on as a local administrator.

2. If you can't start Windows XP in normal mode, boot to Safe Mode.

3. Load your backup media.

4. Run Backup.

5. Click Next.

6. Select Restore Files And Settings and click Next.

7. If you don't see the backup set containing the System State Data backup, click Import File. In the Catalog Backup File text box, type the path and file name for the backup file and click OK.

8. Below What To Restore, complete the following steps:

    a. Expand the backup media (File or Tape).

    b. Expand the backup set you want to restore.

    c. Check System State.

9. Click Next.

10. Click Finish to restore the backup.

11. Click Close to close the Restore Progress dialog box.

12. Click Yes to restart the computer. (You might need to close some processes manually.)

13. When the computer reboots, log on and verify that the problem has been corrected.

ACTIVITY 12-5

Restoring System State Data

Setup:

You have backed up the System State Data for Windows 2000 to C:\Backup\SystemState.bkf.

Scenario:

A programmer just installed a custom application he developed on one of your client's computers. The client has contacted you because he's now experiencing problems with his computer. You aren't sure what the custom application changed on the computer. Fortunately, you scheduled a System State Data backup to take place on a regular basis; the last backup occurred last night.

What You Do	How You Do It
1. Restore the System State Data.	a. Open Backup.

b. Click Restore Wizard.

c. Click Next.

d. Expand the media set and check System State.

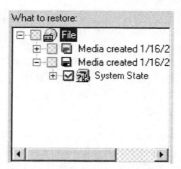

e. Click Next.

f. Click Advanced.

g. On the Where To Restore page, **click Next** to accept the default of Original location.

h. On the How To Restore page, **select Always Replace The File On Disk and click Next.**

i. On the Advanced Restore Options page, **click Next.**

j. **Click Finish.**

k. **Browse to C:\Backup and double-click System State.bkf.**

l. **Click OK.**

m. When the restore is complete, **click Close.**

n. When prompted, **click Yes** to restart the computer. The restart might take longer than usual.

Topic F

Recover Boot Sector Files

In Topic 12E, you learned how to recover a computer's System State Data, part of which includes the computer's boot sector files. If you have a computer that won't boot and you know it's due to one or more missing boot files, or the computer has one of the older operating systems such as Windows NT or Windows 9x, you can use other techniques to repair the computer. In this topic, you'll learn how to recover corrupt or missing boot files in all of the Windows operating systems.

It's not uncommon for a user to accidentally delete some of the files his computer needs to boot the operating system. Or, in another scenario, a virus can corrupt a computer's boot files. In a third example, installing and partitioning a new hard disk might make Windows 2000, Windows NT, or Windows XP unable to find the operating system files to complete loading the operating system. In all of these cases, your best and quickest method for repairing these computers is to recover their boot sector files.

How to Recover Boot Sector Files

Procedure Reference: Use Recovery Console to Repair Windows XP

To use Recovery Console to Repair Windows XP:

1. Boot to the Recovery Console.
    *   If you have installed the Recovery Console as a boot option, restart the computer and select Recovery Console from the boot menu.
    *   If you haven't installed the Recovery Console as a boot option, boot the computer from the Windows XP Professional CD-ROM. On the Welcome To Setup screen, press R to boot to the Recovery Console.

2. When prompted, enter the number of the Windows XP Professional installation to which you want to log on.

3. Enter the Administrator user's password to log on.

4. Use the appropriate Recovery Console commands to correct the system problem. Refer to Table 12-10 for examples.

5. Enter `exit` to end your Recovery Console session and restart the computer.

6. Verify that Windows XP works correctly by logging on.

Table 12-10: *Recovery Console Examples*

Situation	How to Fix
You need to re-create the boot sector or the master boot record.	Use the `fixboot` or `fixmbr` commands.
A boot file is missing or corrupt and you don't have a boot disk.	Replace the missing file by using the `expand` command to extract a compressed copy of the file from the installation CD-ROM, or the `copy` command to copy the file from another location.
A system file or a device driver file is missing or corrupt.	Replace the file from the installation media for Windows XP Professional or for the device.
There is a problem with a Safe Mode driver or service.	Use the `disable` command to disable the service or driver, and then replace the files.
The pagefile is corrupt.	Use the `delete` command to delete the pagefile.sys file.

Procedure Reference: Perform an Emergency Repair in Windows 2000

To perform an emergency repair in Windows 2000:

 Do not attempt an emergency repair on a computer configured to dual boot between Windows 2000 or Windows NT and Windows XP. Doing so will replace the system files installed by Windows XP with the older Windows 2000 or Windows NT system files—which will prevent Windows XP from loading.

1. Boot the computer from the Windows 2000 Professional installation CD-ROM.

    If you don't have a bootable CD-ROM drive, use the `makeboot.exe` (if you're using a 16-bit operating system) or `makeboot32.exe` (if you're using a 32-bit operating system) command to create the three setup boot floppies. Boot the computer from the first floppy disk.

2. When prompted, press R to repair a Windows 2000 installation.

3. Press M to select a manual repair.

4. Select the repair tasks you want to perform:
   - Inspect Startup Environment
   - Verify Windows 2000 System Files
   - Inspect Boot Sector

   By default, all three repair tasks are selected. Press Enter to deselect a task.

5. Select Continue.

    You can press L to perform a repair using files on the hard disk if you do not have an ERD.

6. Press Enter to indicate that you have an Emergency Repair Disk (ERD).

7. Insert the ERD and press Enter. Setup begins the emergency repair process.

8. Remove the ERD when you see the countdown bar for the system to restart.

9. Boot to Windows 2000 and verify that you can log on.

10. Re-apply any Service Packs or hotfixes for Windows 2000 (when you run an emergency repair, it will replace any updated Windows 2000 files with the original versions from the installation CD-ROM. This means that if you've updated Windows 2000 with a Service Pack, the emergency repair process will replace those files with the original files. You should always re-apply any Service Packs or hotfixes after performing an emergency repair).

Procedure Reference: Performing an Emergency Repair in Windows NT

To perform an emergency repair in Windows NT:

1. Insert the Windows NT installation CD-ROM into the computer's CD-ROM drive.

2. Insert the Windows NT Setup boot disk.

3. If the computer is currently running, restart the computer. Otherwise, turn on the computer.

4. When prompted, press R for Repair.

5. Select the desired repair options by using the check boxes. The four options are described in Table 12-11.

Table 12-11: *Windows NT Repair Options*

Option	Description
Inspect Registry Files	You are able to select the Registry trees you want to repair. The Setup program will replace the selected trees with the backup copies contained on your emergency repair disk (this means that all changes made to the Registry since you last updated the emergency repair disk will be lost).
Inspect Startup Environment	If you have Windows NT 4.0 installed on your computer and it does not appear in the list of bootable systems, select this option.
Verify Windows NT System Files	This option verifies the existence and integrity of all Windows NT system files. The repair process has the ability to replace the missing or corrupt files after verification from the user, or to automatically replace all missing or corrupt files.
Inspect Boot Sector	When you cannot boot to any operating system installed on your computer, use this option to replace the boot sector on your disk.

6. When prompted, insert the emergency repair disk.

7. Verify, replace, or reinstall files as necessary.

8. Remove the ERD when the repair is complete.

9. Boot to Windows NT and verify that you can log on.

10. Re-apply any Service Packs or hotfixes for Windows NT.

ACTIVITY 12-6

Recovering Boot Sector Files

Setup:

You have installed the Windows XP Recovery Console as an option on the boot menu. The Windows XP installation is in E:\Windows.

Scenario:

One of your clients reports that he is unable to boot his Windows XP computer. You suspect that he used a utility that modified either his computer's boot sector or the master boot record. On a previous visit to the client's office, you installed the Recovery Console on all Windows XP computers.

What You Do	How You Do It
1. Repair the boot sector and master boot record on the computer.	a. Restart the computer and choose the Microsoft Windows Recovery Console from the boot menu.
	b. When prompted for the Windows installation you want to repair, **enter 2**
	c. For the Administrator's password, **enter password**
	d. At the E:\Windows prompt, **enter fixboot** to repair the boot sector.
	e. When prompted, **enter Y** to confirm that you want to update the boot sector on the C drive. You should see a message stating that the boot sector was successfully written.
	f. **Enter fixmbr** to repair the computer's master boot record.
	g. When prompted, **enter Y** to confirm that you want to write a new master boot record on the C drive. You should see a message stating that the master boot record was successfully written.
	h. **Enter exit** to restart the computer.

2. Verify that you can log on to Windows XP.

a. From the boot menu, **choose Windows XP Professional.**

b. **Log on as Admin#.**

Topic G

Perform an Automated System Recovery

In Lesson 11, you learned the steps for creating an Automated System Recovery (ASR) backup set for a Windows XP-based computer. In this lesson, you've learned the steps you can take to attempt to recover the computer without performing an ASR. But if all else fails and you're unable to recover the computer, it's time for you to perform an ASR. In this topic, you'll learn the procedures for recovering a computer with ASR.

If you're unable to recover a Windows XP computer by restoring user and system state data, you have two choices to get the computer up and running: You can completely re-install the computer's operating system and then attempt to restore whatever user and system state data backups you have, or you can perform an Automated System Recovery (ASR). Although an ASR is essentially a process for re-installing the operating system, it does offer you one distinct advantage: ASR will attempt to salvage whatever it can of the operating system's configuration.

How to Perform an Automated System Recovery

Procedure Reference: Perform an ASR

To perform an ASR:

1. Run the Windows Setup program by booting from the Windows XP Professional installation CD-ROM, or by running the `winnt32.exe` command manually.

2. When the Press [F2] To Run Automated System Recovery (ASR) message is displayed in the status bar, press F2. This message disappears quickly.

3. When prompted, insert the ASR boot floppy disk and press any key (you can also start the ASR with this disk already in the floppy disk drive).

4. If prompted, press C to confirm that your disk partitions will be deleted and re-created. This is necessary on dynamic disks to prepare them for operating system installation (you can't install Windows XP Professional on a dynamic disk). ASR will convert the disks back to dynamic later on.

5. When prompted, after the disk is scanned and configured, Windows Setup runs, and the Automated System Recovery Wizard runs, insert the ASR backup media.

6. Complete the Automated System Recovery Wizard; ASR will automatically restore the ASR backup set.

To support unattended system recovery, the screens in the Automated System Recovery Wizard will automatically advance after a time-out.

7. If you are prompted for an installation directory (for example, if ASR is restoring to a clean hard disk), provide the path (typically, C:\Windows). When the installation and restoration are complete, the computer will restart.

8. Log on and verify the computer works properly.

OPTIONAL DISCOVERY ACTIVITY 12-7

Performing an Automated System Recovery

Setup:

You have created an ASR backup set and floppy.

Scenario:

You have been called in by a client to repair his Windows XP computer. You have tried just about everything to fix it, including re-writing the master boot record and boot sector information in the Recovery Console, restoring a backup of the Registry, and even restoring a System State Data backup. The computer still won't boot. When you initially installed the computer and configured the user's applications, you created an ASR backup set and floppy disk for just such an emergency.

---

1. **Initiate an ASR.**

     The ASR message appears only briefly in the status bar at the bottom of the screen (after the screen turns blue). You'll first see a message prompting you to press F6 to install third-party drivers; the next message is the ASR prompt. If you miss the ASR prompt, restart the computer and start over.

---

2. **Complete the ASR.**

     After the disks are scanned and configured, you might see a prompt that you need to restart because Setup has performed system maintenance. Restart the computer and initiate the ASR process again by pressing F2.

---

3. **Verify that Windows XP was successfully restored.**

Lesson 12 Follow-up

In this lesson, you learned how to perform the tasks necessary to recover after a disaster. Specifically, you learned how to troubleshoot problems with applications and computers' hard disks. You also learned how to restore backups of data, the Registry, and System State data, and how to perform an emergency repair. Finally, you learned how to recover a failed Windows XP computer by performing an Automated System Recovery. As an A+ technician, you'll need these skills so that you can respond to troubleshooting support calls and get your clients' computers back up and running after a failure.

1. **What types of disasters have you encountered with regards to computers? How did you respond?**

2. **What is your experience with restoring data from backup?**

LESSON 13

Installing Client Operating Systems

Lesson Time
3 hour(s), 30 minutes

Lesson Objectives:

In this lesson, you will install client operating systems.

You will:

- Install a Windows client operating system.
- Upgrade from an older Windows operating system to a newer Windows operating system.
- Troubleshoot operating system installations.
- Add or remove operating system components.

Introduction

Throughout this course, you've been learning how to configure and troubleshoot all of the Windows operating systems. You've learned how to connect these operating systems to a network, how to secure their resources, manage and share file and print resources, and manage their hard disks. Now, it's time to use this knowledge you've gained in how to configure these operating systems by learning how to install them from scratch or upgrade them. So, in this lesson, you'll learn how to install the Windows 98, Windows 2000, and Windows XP operating systems. You'll also learn how to upgrade Windows 98 to Windows 2000 or Windows XP, and how to upgrade Windows 2000 to Windows XP.

Without a properly installed operating system, your users' computers will not function. Although most new computers come straight from the manufacturer with an operating system loaded, you will encounter situations in which the operating system will need to be re-installed or upgraded on existing systems.

The following CompTIA A+ Operating System Technologies (2003) Examination objectives are covered in this lesson:

- Topic A:
    - 1.1 Contrasts between Windows 9x/Me, Windows NT 4.0 Workstation, Windows 2000 Professional, and Windows XP.
    - 2.1 Verify hardware compatibility and minimum requirements.
    - 2.1 Determine OS intallation options: Installation type (typical, custom, other), Dual Boot Support.
    - 2.1 Disk preparation order (conceptual disk preparation): Start the installation, Partition, Format drive.
    - 2.1 Run appropriate set up utility: Setup, Winnt.
    - 2.1 Installation methods: Bootable CD, Boot floppy, Network installation.
    - 2.2 Upgrade paths available, Determine correct upgrade startup utility (e.g. WINNT32 vs WINNT), Verify hardware compatibility and minimum requirements, Apply OS service packs, patches, and updates.
    - 2.3 Alternative Boot Methods: Dual Boot.
- Topic C:
    - 2.1 Identify common symptoms and problems.
- Topic D:
    - 2.2 Install additional Windows components.

TOPIC A

Install a Windows Client Operating System

So far in this course, you've learned the steps you must take to configure the various components of each Windows operating system. For example, you learned how to manage Windows 98, Windows 2000, and Windows XP computers' file and print resources. Now it's time for you to learn the steps for installing each operating system from scratch, and that's what you'll learn in this topic.

Knowing how to perform a Windows 98, Windows 2000, or Windows XP installation from scratch is an important part of an A+ technician's toolkit. You need to know how to install a computer from scratch in case you're redeploying a computer from one user to another. You also need to know how to re-install a Windows client operating system when all of your other troubleshooting techniques fail. Although re-installing a Windows client operating system should be your last option for recovering a failed computer, it's an invaluable option nonetheless.

Windows Operating Systems Features

Each new release of the Windows operating systems brings you new and enhanced features. In Table 13-1, you see a list of the features available in Windows 98. Windows 2000 supports all of the features in Windows 98 and adds new features. In Table 13-2, you'll find a list of the features of Windows 2000. Likewise, Windows XP supports all of the features in Windows 2000—but adds new features. You'll find the features of Windows XP in Table 13-3.

Table 13-1: *Features of Windows 98*

Feature	Enables You To
Active Desktop	Display Web pages on your desktop.
Easier Internet Access	Connect to the Internet by typing a URL in any window in Windows 98 or even the taskbar and save Web pages for offline use.
Multiple Monitor Support	Increase the size of your desktop by configuring the computer to display on two monitors.
Outlook Express	Send and receive POP3, IMAP, and HTTP email.
Quick Launch Toolbar	Run applications by clicking their icons in the taskbar.
Task Scheduler	Automate tasks on your computer.
Tighter Integration with Internet Features	Open items on the computer by clicking a link instead of double-clicking it; navigate through folders using the Forward and Back buttons; and use a Web page as the background for a window.
Troubleshooters	Quickly diagnose problems.
USB Support	Easily install (or remove) devices from USB ports.

Table 13-2: *Features of Windows 2000*

Feature	Description
Active Directory	A directory service that provides access to all objects and resources in a Windows 2000 domain environment.
Backup	Backup supports a wide variety of storage media, such as tape drives, external hard disks, Zip drives, recordable CD-ROMs, and logical drives.
Disk Quotas	Provides a method for managing storage space by enabling you to limit users' disk space.
Encrypting File System (EFS)	Enables you to encrypt files on an NTFS partition.
Microsoft Management Console	Microsoft's new standard interface for all system administration tools. It's the framework that supports specialized tools, called snap-ins, each of which is designed to provide specific management capabilities.
Plug and Play support	Provides support for automatic and dynamic reconfiguration of installed hardware, removable devices, a New Hardware Wizard, and an enhanced Device Manager.
Power management functionality	These features include system power management, device power management, processor power management, battery management, thermal management, and application-level power management.
Task Scheduler	A graphical utility that makes it easy for you to automate tasks such as backing up the computer.

 Windows NT does not support disk quotas, file encryption, backing up to media other than tapes, and Plug and Play. In addition, Windows NT does not include the Microsoft Management Console or Task Scheduler utilities.

Table 13-3: *Features of Windows XP*

Feature	Description
Adaptive Start menu	The Start menu automatically adapts to the way you work. The programs you use most frequently are listed first on the Start menu.
Consolidated taskbar	If you open multiple files within the same application (such as Microsoft Word), Windows XP consolidates all open windows for that application on the taskbar.
Dramatically reduced reboot requirements	In Windows 2000, many changes you make to the computer's configuration require you to reboot the computer. In Windows XP, many of these same scenarios no longer require you to reboot the computer.

Feature	Description
New visual design	The user interface is redesigned in Windows XP to make it easier to perform tasks. For example, common management tasks are grouped together in Control Panel. In addition, Microsoft added new visual cues to help you navigate more easily.
User State Migration Tool	A utility that enables you to easily migrate a user's data, application settings, and operating system settings from an old computer to a new Windows XP computer.
Windows Installer service	A service that helps you track, upgrade, and remove software programs correctly from the computer.

Installation Requirements

Each Windows operating system has different hardware requirements. In Table 13-4, we list the hardware requirements for installing Windows 98. In Table 13-5, you'll find the minimum hardware requirements for Windows 2000 Professional; in Table 13-6, you see the hardware requirements for Windows XP Professional. Keep in mind that these tables list the minimum requirements for installing the respective operating system. For optimal performance, your computer should exceed these hardware requirements. You should also check the Windows Hardware Compatibility List on Microsoft's Web site at **http://www.microsoft.com/hwdq/hcl/**.

Table 13-4: *Windows 98 Hardware Requirements*

Hardware	Minimum Requirement
Processor	486DX 66 MHz
RAM	16 MB
Hard disk	At least 225 MB of free space
Video adapter	VGA
Installation source	CD-ROM or DVD-ROM (without one of these drives, you must install Windows 98 using floppy disks)
Pointing device	Mouse

Table 13-5: *Windows 2000 Professional Hardware Requirements*

Hardware	Minimum Requirement
Processor	Pentium 133 MHz
RAM	32 MB (64 MB recommended)
Hard disk	2 GB with 1 GB free space
Video adapter	VGA
Installation source	12X CD-ROM
Pointing device	Mouse

Table 13-6: *Windows XP Professional Hardware Requirements*

Hardware	Minimum Requirement
Processor	Pentium 233 MHz
RAM	64 MB
Available disk space	1.5 GB
Video adapter	Super VGA
Installation source	CD-ROM or DVD-ROM
Pointing device	Mouse

In addition to the hardware requirements listed in Table 13-4, Table 13-5, and Table 13-6, you might find that you need the following hardware regardless of which Windows operating system you're installing:

- A sound card and speakers (or headphones).

- A modem for accessing the Internet or faxing purposes.

   In many cases, you'll find that choosing an operating system for a computer is dictated by the computer's hardware. If you support users that have older hardware, using the Windows 98 operating system will typically be the best choice because of its low hardware requirements. On the other hand, if you have users with newer (and faster hardware), using either Windows 2000 or Windows XP will offer them better performance on those systems, with the added benefit of increased security.

Multiple Boot Computer

In certain environments, you might find it necessary to configure a computer with more than one operating system. This type of computer is called multiple boot because it enables you to boot the computer to more than one operating system. If you plan to configure a multiple boot computer with the Windows 98 and Windows 2000, Windows NT, or Windows XP operating systems, you must:

- Configure the C drive to use the FAT file system.

- Install Windows 98 first, and then install Windows 2000, Windows NT, or Windows XP.

If you plan to configure a multiple boot computer with the Windows 2000 and Windows NT or Windows XP operating systems, you must install the older operating system(s) first. Install the most recent operating system last. For example, if you plan to install the Windows 2000 and Windows XP operating systems on a computer, you must install Windows 2000 first, and then install Windows XP.

Windows Setup Programs

If you install a version of Windows by inserting the installation CD-ROM or by booting from a bootable CD-ROM, you'll find that the installation starts automatically for you. But what if you're connecting to installation files on a network share to perform a network installation or if you're performing an upgrade? In this scenario, you'll need to know which file to double-click to start the installation. In Table 13-7, you see the appropriate setup file to use based on the operating system you're currently using and the operating system you want to install.

Table 13-7: *Windows Setup Programs*

Operating System You're Currently Using	Operating System You're Installing	Installation File
MS-DOS	Windows 98	Setup.exe
MS-DOS	Windows 2000 or Windows XP	Winnt.exe
Windows 95	Windows 98	Setup.exe
Windows 98, Windows 2000, Windows NT, or Windows XP	Windows 2000 or Windows XP	Winnt32.exe

Windows Upgrade Paths

As technology changes and newer operating systems are released, at some point you'll probably find yourself as part of the process of deploying a new operating system. Whether you perform an upgrade or a fresh installation depends in part on whether your current operating system supports an upgrade. Table 13-8 described the upgrade paths for the Windows operating systems. If an upgrade path isn't supported, then an upgrade is not possible; the newer operating system will have to be installed over the older operating system, with the older operating system and its settings being deleted in the process.

Table 13-8: *Windows Upgrade Paths*

Current Operating System	Can be Upgraded To
Windows 95	Windows 98, Windows 2000 Professional
Windows 98	Windows 2000 Professional, Windows XP Professional
Windows NT Workstation 4.0	Windows 2000 Professional, Windows XP Professional
Windows 2000 Professional	Windows XP Professional
Windows XP Professional	None at this time

Windows Update

After you have installed an operating system on a computer, you can obtain the latest updates for that operating system by connecting to Microsoft's Windows Update Web site. This Web site is located at **windowsupdate.microsoft.com**. You can also connect to the Windows Update Web site by choosing Windows Update from the Start menu in Windows 98, Windows 2000, and Windows XP.

How to Install a Windows Client Operating System

Procedure Reference: Install Windows 98

To install Windows 98 as the only operating system on the computer:

📌 This procedure assumes that you do not currently have an operating system on the computer.

1. Verify that the computer's hardware meets the requirements for Windows 98.

2. If necessary, create a Windows 98 Startup disk.

- If you have access to a Windows 98 computer, use these steps to create a Startup Disk:

  a. In Control Panel, double-click Add/Remove Programs.

  b. Select the Startup Disk tab.

  c. Click Create Disk.

  d. When prompted, insert the Windows 98 installation CD-ROM and click OK.

  e. Insert a floppy disk into the floppy disk drive.

  f. Click OK.

  g. Close Add/Remove Programs and Control Panel.

- If you do not have access to a Windows 98 computer, but you do have access to a computer, use these steps to create a Startup Disk:

  a. On a working computer, insert the Windows 98 CD-ROM.

  b. If you see a Welcome To Windows 98 dialog box, click Exit to close it.

  c. Open Windows Explorer.

  d. Access the \Tools\Mtsutil\Fat32ebd folder.

  e. Double-click Fat32ebd.exe to create the Startup disk.

  f. When prompted, press Y and Enter to continue.

  g. When you see the message "Done," close the MS-DOS Prompt window.

  h. Write protect and label the floppy disk.

3. Insert the Windows 98 Startup disk into the computer on which you want to install Windows 98.

4. Turn on the computer. If necessary, configure the computer to attempt to boot from floppy disk first.

> You won't need to access the CD-ROM at this point in the installation.

5. When prompted, choose Start Computer Without CD-ROM Support and press Enter.

6. Use Fdisk to partition the computer's hard disk.

   a. If the computer has any existing partitions you no longer need, delete the partitions.

   b. If you want to use the FAT32 file system, enable large disk support.

   c. Create at least one primary partition and mark it active.

   d. When prompted, restart the computer (press Ctrl+Alt+Delete).

7. When prompted, choose Start Computer With CD-ROM Support and press Enter.

8. Format the computer's partitions.

   a. At the A: prompt, enter `format c: /s`.

   b. Format any additional logical drives you created by entering `format drive letter:`. For example, `format d:`.

9. Insert the Windows 98 installation CD-ROM into the computer's CD-ROM drive.

10. At the A: prompt, enter `x:\setup`, where x is the letter assigned to the computer's CD-ROM drive.

11. Press Enter to continue. ScanDisk runs to verify that the disk has no errors.

12. In ScanDisk, press X to exit.

13. The Windows 98 Setup Wizard starts. Complete the following tasks:

    a. On the License Agreement page, select I Accept The Agreement and click Next.

    b. Enter the Windows 98 product key and click Next.

    c. On the Select Directory page, choose one of the following:

       • Select C:\WINDOWS to install Windows 98 in the default folder.

       • Select Other Directory if you want to choose a different folder in which to install Windows 98.

    d. Click Next.

    e. If you chose Other Directory, enter the path to the folder in which you want to install Windows 98, and then click Next.

    f. On the Setup Options page, select one of the following options:

       • Typical

       • Portable

       • Compact

       • Custom

    g. Click Next.

    h. On the User Information page, enter the user's name and the company name. Click Next.

    i. On the Windows Components page, select one of the following:

       • Install The Most Common Components (Recommended).

       • Show Me The List Of Components So I Can Choose.

    j. Click Next.

    k. If you selected Show Me The List Of Components So I Can Choose, check the Windows components you want to install on the computer and then click Next.

    l. Select your country or region and click Next.

    m. Click Next to create a Windows 98 Startup disk.

    n. When prompted, insert a blank floppy disk and click OK.

    o. When the Startup disk creation is complete, remove the floppy disk and label it. Click OK.

    p. Click Next. Setup will now copy the Windows 98 files to your hard disk.

       The file copy process will take several minutes.

    q. When the file copy is complete, click Restart Now.

       Setup will automatically restart the computer after 15 seconds.

14. After the computer restarts, Setup will attempt to detect the hardware. When hardware detection is complete, click Restart Now to restart the computer again.

15. Click OK to close the Network message box reminding you to define a workgroup name.

16. If Setup detected a network card in the computer, on the Identification page, complete the following tasks:

    a. In the Computer Name text box, type a name for the computer.

    b. In the Workgroup Name text box, type the name of the workgroup to which you want the computer to belong.

    c. Optionally, in the Computer Description text box, type a description for the computer.

    d. Click Close.

17. In the Date/Time Properties dialog box, configure the appropriate date, time, and time zone for your location. Click Close.

18. When the installation is complete, click Restart Now.

> By default, Windows 98 assumes you want to use the name you typed on the User Information page as your user name.

19. In the User Name text box, type the user name you want to use for the computer.

20. In the Password text box, type the password you want to assign to this user.

21. Click OK.

22. In the Confirm New Password text box, re-type the password and click OK.

23. Configure the computer to connect to the Internet.

24. If necessary, install any hardware drivers that were not automatically installed during setup. For example, make sure that the drivers for devices such as sound cards, modems, and display adapters were installed correctly.

    a. Use Device Manager to view the status of these devices and to look for any devices for which Setup did not install the drivers.

    b. If you need new drivers, connect to the manufacturer's Web site to download the drivers for Windows 98.

    c. Use Add New Hardware in Control Panel to install the drivers that weren't installed or to install drivers for non-Plug and Play devices. To open Add New Hardware, double-click it. After Windows searches for the hardware and reports that it can't find it, select No, I Want To Select The Hardware From A List. Then select the type of hardware device and click Next. Then click Have Disk if you have the drivers on floppy disk, in a folder on the hard disk, or in a location on the network. Browse to the correct drivers and complete the wizard.

25. Update Windows 98.

    a. From the Start menu, choose Windows Update.

    b. Click Yes to install and run the Windows Update Control Package.

    c. If necessary, click Yes again.

    d. Click Scan For Updates.

e.   Click Review And Install Updates.

f.   Click Yes to continue.

g.   Follow the prompts to install the updates you want. You'll find that some of the updates are "exclusive," which means they can't be installed with other updates. If you choose to install an exclusive update, be sure to go back to the Windows Update Web site to check for other updates.

26.   If necessary, restart the computer after the updates are installed.

27.   If you have enough available disk space, copy the Windows 98 installation files to a folder on the hard disk.

Procedure Reference: Install Windows 2000 Professional

To install Windows 2000 Professional as the only operating system on the computer:

 This procedure assumes that you do not currently have an operating system on the computer.

1.   Verify that the computer's hardware meets the requirements for Windows.

2.   Start the installation.

- If the computer does not have a bootable CD-ROM drive, boot the computer from the first Setup disk. Use the following steps to create and use the Setup disks if you don't have them:

    a.   Verify that you have three blank floppy disks.

    b.   At a working computer, insert the Windows 2000 CD-ROM.

    c.   If you're using Windows 9x or MS-DOS, run \bootdisk\makeboot.exe from the Windows 2000 CD-ROM to create the Setup disks.

    d.   If you're using Windows 2000, Windows XP, or Windows NT, run \bootdisk\makebt32.exe from the Windows 2000 CD-ROM to create the Setup disks.

    e.   Insert each disk when prompted.

    f.   Label the disks.

    g.   Insert the first Windows Setup disk and start the computer. When prompted, insert each additional disk as required.

- If the computer has a bootable CD-ROM drive, insert the Windows 2000 CD-ROM and start the computer. If prompted, press a key to boot from CD.

- If the installation files are on a network share, complete the following steps:

    a.   Connect the computer to the network.

    b.   Access the network share containing the installation files.

    c.   Double-click the appropriate Setup program file (use winnt.exe if you're using MS-DOS to access the network share; use winnt32.exe if you're using Windows 98 to connect to the network share).

3.   On the Welcome To Setup page, press Enter to install Windows 2000.

4.   Press F8 to agree to the Microsoft Windows 2000 Professional license.

5.   Partition and format the computer's hard disk.

a. If the computer has any existing partitions you no longer need, highlight the partition and press D to delete each partition. Press L to confirm that you want to delete the partition.

b. To create a partition, highlight Unpartitioned Space and press C. In the text box, type the size for the partition and press Enter.

c. Highlight the partition in which you want to install Windows 2000 and press Enter.

d. Select from the following choices to format the new partition:
   - Format The Partition Using The NTFS File System.
   - Format The Partition Using The FAT File System.

e. Press Enter.

When the format is complete, Setup checks the partitions and then copies some of the Windows 2000 files to the hard disk.

For detailed steps on how to use Fdisk, see Lesson 8.

6. Press Enter to restart the computer. Do not boot from the CD-ROM.

7. On the Welcome page, click Next.

Setup now detects and installs the devices in the computer.

8. When the hardware detection is complete, on the Regional Settings page, configure the locale and keyboard layout if necessary (the default settings are English (United States) for the locale and US for the keyboard layout).

9. Click Next.

10. On the Personalize Your Software page, complete the following:
   - In the Name text box, type the user of the computer's name.
   - In the Organization text box, type the company name.
   - Click Next.

11. On the Your Product Key page, enter your product key and click Next.

12. On the Computer Name And Administrator Password page, complete the following:
   - In the Computer Name text box, type a name for the computer.
   - In the Administrator password text box, type the password you want to assign to the Administrator's user account.
   - In the Confirm Password text box, re-type the password.
   - Click Next.

13. If Setup detected a modem in the computer, on the Modem Dialing Information page, complete the following:
   - From the What Country/Region Are You In Now drop-down list, select the appropriate country or region.
   - In the What Area Code (Or City Code) Are You In Now text box, type the area code.

- In the If You Dial A Number To Get An Outside Line text box, type a value if applicable.

- Select either Tone Dialing or Pulse Dialing.

- Click Next.

14. On the Date And Time Settings page, configure the date, time, time zone, and whether your location adjusts for Daylight Savings Time. Click Next.

15. On the Networking Settings page, select one of the following:

- If you want to install the network components with TCP/IP as the only protocol and you want the IP address to be assigned dynamically, select Typical Settings.

- If you want to configure TCP/IP manually, or you want to install additional protocols, select Custom Settings.

16. Click Next.

17. If you select Custom Settings, use the Networking Components page to customize the network connection.

- Click Install to add additional network components such as protocols.

- Highlight Internet Protocol (TCP/IP) and click Properties to manually configure the IP addressing information.

- Click Next when you're finished.

18. On the Workgroup Or Computer Domain, complete the following steps:

    a. If you want the computer to be a member of a workgroup, select No, This Computer Is Not On A Network. In the Workgroup Or Computer Domain text box, type the name of the workgroup.

    b. If you want the computer to be a member of a domain, select Yes, Make This Computer A Member Of The Following Domain. In the Workgroup Or Computer Domain text box, type the NetBIOS name of the domain (for example, if the Active Directory domain name is company.com, type company for the NetBIOS domain name).

    c. Click Next.

    d. If you're joining the computer to a domain, in the Join Computer To *Domain* dialog box, type the user name and password of a user with administrative rights for the domain. Click OK.

Setup now completes copying the Windows 2000 files to the hard disk. This process may take 15 to 20 minutes.

19. Click Finish. The computer automatically restarts.

20. If you configured the computer as a member of a workgroup and not a domain, Windows automatically starts the Network Identification Wizard. Use the following steps to complete the wizard:

    a. On the Welcome page, click Next.

    b. On the Users Of This Computer page, select one of the following options:

    - Users Must Enter A User Name And Password To Use This Computer, if you want each user to have to log on to the computer whenever it boots.

- Windows Always Assumes The Following User Has Logged On To This Computer, if you want Windows 2000 to automatically log on as a specific user whenever the computer boots. In the appropriate text boxes, enter a user name and password, and confirm the password.

    c.   Click Next.

    d.   Click Finish.

21. If you configured Windows 2000 to require each user to log on, log on as Administrator with the password you defined for the account during installation.

22. Configure the computer to connect to the Internet.

23. If necessary, install any hardware drivers that were not automatically installed during setup. For example, make sure that the drivers for devices such as sound cards, modems, and display adapters were installed correctly.

    a.   Use Device Manager to view the status of these devices and to look for any devices for which Setup did not install the drivers.

    b.   If you need new drivers, connect to the manufacturer's Web site to download the drivers for Windows 2000.

    c.   Use Add/Remove Hardware in Control Panel to install the drivers that weren't installed or to install drivers for non-Plug and Play devices. To open Add New Hardware, double-click it. Select Add/Troubleshoot Device. After Windows searches for Plug and Play hardware, in the list of devices, select the type of hardware device you want to add and click Next. Select No, I Want To Select The Hardware From A List. Select the type of hardware you want to install. Then click Have Disk if you have the drivers on floppy disk, in a folder on the hard disk, or in a location on the network. Browse to the correct drivers and complete the wizard.

24. Update Windows 2000.

    a.   From the Start menu, choose Windows Update.

    b.   Click Yes to install and run the Windows Update Control Package.

    c.   If necessary, click Yes again.

    d.   Click Scan For Updates.

    e.   Click Review And Install Updates.

    f.   Click Yes to continue.

    g.   Follow the prompts to install the updates you want. You'll find that some of the updates are "exclusive," which means they can't be installed with other updates. If you choose to install an exclusive update, be sure to go back to the Windows Update Web site to check for other updates.

25. If necessary, restart the computer after the updates are installed.

26. If you have enough available disk space, copy the Windows 2000 installation files to a folder on the hard disk.

27. If necessary, use Computer Management to create any additional user accounts needed on the computer.

Procedure Reference: Install Windows XP Professional

To install Windows XP Professional as the only operating system on the computer:

This procedure assumes that you do not currently have an operating system on the computer.

1. Verify that the computer's hardware meets the requirements for Windows XP.

2. Start the installation.

   - If the computer does not have a bootable CD-ROM drive, boot the computer from the first Setup disk. Use the following steps to create and use the Setup disks if you don't have them:

     a. Verify that you have three blank floppy disks.

     b. At a working computer, insert the Windows XP CD-ROM.

     c. If you're using Windows 9x or MS-DOS, run \bootdisk\makeboot.exe from the Windows XP CD-ROM to create the Setup disks.

     d. If you're using Windows 2000, Windows XP, or Windows NT, run \bootdisk\makebt32.exe from the Windows XP CD-ROM to create the Setup disks.

     e. Insert each disk when prompted.

     f. Label the disks.

     g. Insert the first Windows Setup disk and start the computer. When prompted, insert each additional disk as required.

   - If the computer has a bootable CD-ROM drive, insert the Windows XP CD-ROM and start the computer. If prompted, press a key to boot from CD.

   - If the installation files are on a network share, complete the following steps:

     a. Connect the computer to the network.

     b. Access the network share containing the installation files.

     c. Double-click the appropriate Setup program file (use winnt.exe if you're using MS-DOS to access the network share; use winnt32.exe if you're using Windows 98 to connect to the network share).

3. On the Welcome To Setup page, press Enter to install Windows XP.

4. Press F8 to agree to the Microsoft Windows 2000 Professional license.

5. Partition and format the computer's hard disk.

   a. If the computer has any existing partitions you no longer need, highlight the partition and press D to delete each partition. Press L to confirm that you want to delete the partition.

   b. To create a partition, highlight Unpartitioned Space and press C. In the text box, type the size for the partition and press Enter.

   c. Highlight the partition in which you want to install Windows XP and press Enter.

   d. Select from the following choices to format the new partition:

      - Format The Partition Using The NTFS File System (Quick)
      - Format The Partition Using The FAT File System (Quick)
      - Format The Partition Using The NTFS File System
      - Format The Partition Using The FAT File System

LESSON 13

e. Press Enter.

When the format is complete, Setup checks the partitions and then copies some of the Windows XP files to the hard disk.

6. Press Enter to restart the computer. Do not boot from the CD-ROM.

Setup now detects and installs the devices in the computer.

7. When the hardware detection is complete, on the Regional Settings page, configure the locale and keyboard layout if necessary (the default settings are English (United States) for the locale and US for the keyboard layout).

8. Click Next.

9. On the Personalize Your Software page, complete the following:
   - In the Name text box, type the user of the computer's name.
   - In the Organization text box, type the company name.
   - Click Next.

10. Enter the Product Key and click Next.

11. On the Computer Name And Administrator Password page, complete the following:
    - In the Computer Name text box, type a name for the computer.
    - In the Administrator password text box, type the password you want to assign to the Administrator's user account.
    - In the Confirm Password text box, re-type the password.
    - Click Next.

12. If Setup detected a modem in the computer, on the Modem Dialing Information page, complete the following:
    - From the What Country/Region Are You In Now drop-down list, select the appropriate country or region.
    - In the What Area Code (Or City Code) Are You In Now text box, type the area code.
    - In the If You Dial A Number To Get An Outside Line text box, type a value if applicable.
    - Select either Tone Dialing or Pulse Dialing.
    - Click Next.

13. On the Date And Time Settings page, configure the date, time, time zone, and whether your location adjusts for Daylight Savings Time. Click Next.

14. On the Networking Settings page, select one of the following:
    - If you want to install the network components with TCP/IP as the only protocol and you want the IP address to be assigned dynamically, select Typical Settings.
    - If you want to configure TCP/IP manually, or you want to install additional protocols, select Custom Settings.

15. Click Next.

16. If you select Custom Settings, use the Networking Components page to customize the network connection.

    - Click Install to add additional network components such as protocols.

    - Highlight Internet Protocol (TCP/IP) and click Properties to manually configure the IP addressing information.

    - Click Next when you're finished.

17. On the Workgroup Or Computer Domain, complete the following steps:

    a. If you want the computer to be a member of a workgroup, select No, This Computer Is Not On A Network, Or Is On A Network Without A Domain. In the Make This Computer A Member Of The Following Workgroup text box, type the name of the workgroup.

    b. If you want the computer to be a member of a domain, select Yes, Make This Computer A Member Of The Following Domain. In the text box, type the NetBIOS name of the domain (for example, if the Active Directory domain name is company.com, type company for the NetBIOS domain name).

    c. Click Next.

    d. If you're joining the computer to a domain, in the Join Computer To *Domain* dialog box, type the user name and password of a user with administrative rights for the domain. Click OK.

    Setup now completes copying the Windows XP files to the hard disk. This process may take 25 to 30 minutes. The computer automatically restarts when the copy process completes.

18. In the Welcome To Microsoft Windows page, click Next.

19. Select one of the following options to configure how the computer connects to the Internet:

    - Yes, This Computer Will Connect Through A Local Area Network Or Home Network.

    - No, This Computer Will Connect Directly To The Internet.

20. Click Next.

21. On the Ready To Register With Microsoft page, select whether you want to register the computer with Microsoft at this time. If you select Yes, click Next and complete the steps to register the computer.

22. Click Next.

23. If you configured the computer as a member of a workgroup and not a domain, on the Who Will Use This Computer page, type the names of the users who will use the computer and click Next. Windows XP will automatically create user accounts for these users.

24. Click Finish.

> For more information on how to configure an Internet connection in Windows XP, see Lesson 8.

25. Configure the computer to connect to the Internet.

26. If necessary, install any hardware drivers that were not automatically installed during setup. For example, make sure that the drivers for devices such as sound cards, modems, and display adapters were installed correctly.

   a. Use Device Manager to view the status of these devices and to look for any devices for which Setup did not install the drivers.

   b. If you need new drivers, connect to the manufacturer's Web site to download the drivers for Windows XP.

   c. Use the Add Hardware Wizard to install the drivers that weren't installed or to install drivers for non-Plug and Play devices. Select Yes, I Have Already Connected The Hardware. Select Add A New Hardware Device. Select Install The Hardware That I Manually Select From A List. Select the type of hardware you want to install. Then click Have Disk if you have the drivers on floppy disk, in a folder on the hard disk, or in a location on the network. Browse to the correct drivers and complete the wizard.

27. Update Windows XP.

   a. From the Start menu, choose All Programs→Windows Update.

   b. Click Yes to install and run the Windows Update Control Package.

   c. If necessary, click Yes again.

   d. Click Scan For Updates.

   e. Click Review And Install Updates.

   f. Click Yes to continue.

   g. Follow the prompts to install the updates you want. You'll find that some of the updates are "exclusive," which means they can't be installed with other updates. If you choose to install an exclusive update, be sure to go back to the Windows Update Web site to check for other updates.

28. If necessary, restart the computer after the updates are installed.

29. If you have enough available disk space, copy the Windows XP installation files to a folder on the hard disk.

30. If necessary, use Computer Management to create any additional user accounts needed on the computer.

Procedure Reference: Install Windows 98 and Windows 2000/XP on a Single Computer

To install both Windows 98 and Windows 2000 or Windows XP on a single computer:

⚠ You must install Windows 98 first.

1. Install Windows 98 first. Make sure the installation meets the following requirements:

   • The C drive must be formatted to be no larger than 2 GB and must use the FAT file system.

   • If you want to create an NTFS partition, you must leave free space on the hard disk when you install Windows 98.

2. Install Windows 2000 or Windows XP. Make sure that you complete the following during installation:

    a.   In Windows 98, insert the Windows 2000 Professional or Windows XP Professional CD-ROM.

    b.   If you're installing Windows 2000, when you're prompted to upgrade Windows 98, click No.

📌 Microsoft strongly recommends that you install each operating system in its own partition.

    c.   Click Advanced Options. Check I Want To Choose The Installation Partition During Setup so that you can create a new partition on which to store Windows 2000 during installation.

    d.   Follow the prompts to complete the Windows 2000 or Windows XP installation (refer to the procedures for installing these operating systems for more information).

3.   In Windows 2000 or Windows XP, select the default operating system.

    a.   Open Control Panel.

    b.   Double-click System.

    c.   Select the Advanced tab.

    d.   Click Startup And Recovery.

    e.   From the Default Operating System drop-down list, select the operating system you want to load by default on the computer.

    f.   Click OK twice.

    g.   Close Control Panel.

4.   Verify that you can start each operating system from the boot menu.

Procedure Reference: Install Windows 2000 and Windows XP on a Single Computer

To install Windows 2000 and Windows XP on a single computer:

⚠ You must install Windows 2000 first.

1.   Install Windows 2000. If you want to install Windows XP into a separate partition, make sure that you leave free space on the hard disk.

2.   Install Windows XP Professional. Make sure that you complete the following during installation:

    a.   In Windows 2000, insert the Windows XP Professional CD-ROM.

    b.   When you're prompted to upgrade Windows 2000, click No.

📌 Microsoft strongly recommends that you install each operating system in its own partition.

    c.   Click Advanced Options. Check I Want To Choose The Installation Partition During Setup so that you can create a new partition on which to store Windows 2000 during installation.

    d.   Follow the prompts to complete the Windows XP installation (refer to the procedures in Topic A for more information).

3.   In Windows 2000 or Windows XP, select the default operating system.

    a.   Open Control Panel.

b. Double-click System.

c. Select the Advanced tab.

d. Click Startup And Recovery.

e. From the Default Operating System drop-down list, select the operating system you want to load by default on the computer.

f. Click OK twice.

g. Close Control Panel.

4. Verify that you can start each operating system from the boot menu.

Installation Types

During the installation of the Windows 98 and Windows Me operating systems, you'll get to choose which type of installation you want to perform. Generally, there are four types to choose from, all of which are described in Table 13-9.

Table 13-9: *Installation Types*

Installation Type	Description
Typical	This is the default option and is recommended for most users. A Typical installation provides the least customization. It was designed for the least user intervention; thus, it performs most installation steps automatically. The most common Windows 9x components are installed.
Portable	This installation option is recommended for portable or mobile computers. In addition to many of the default options installed with a Typical installation, it installs the Windows 9x features that are designed specifically for mobile computing, such as the Briefcase.
Compact	This installation option installs the minimum files required to run Windows 9x. It is recommended for users who have minimal disk space available on their hard drives, but who cannot run a network-shared copy of Windows 9x.
Custom	This installation option provides the greatest customization, enabling the user to select from every available option provided by the Setup program.

ACTIVITY 13-1

Installing Windows 98 and Windows 2000 on a Single Computer

Setup:

You have created a Windows 98 Startup disk. You have the Windows 98 CD-ROM. The Windows 2000 Professional installation files are shared on \\2000srv\win2000.

Setup:

You will need two blank floppy disks to complete this activity.

Scenario:

Your client, Applications Developers, Inc., has asked you to install both Windows 98 and Windows 2000 on several computers. Applications Developers, Inc., is located in San Francisco. This company does custom programming, so Mike Jones (the president) wants to have Windows 98 and Windows 2000 available for programmers to test applications they develop. Because the computers will be used for testing purposes, Mike would like you to make sure that all the default configuration options are set in both Windows 98 and Windows 2000. These computers have existing operating systems, applications, and data files, so he has asked you to make sure to remove them before installing Windows 98 and Windows 2000.

Your client would like you to name each computer Win98–# and Win2000–# (in the appropriate operating systems), where # is a unique number. His existing workgroup is named AppDev. Each computer should have a user named Admin# for each operating system, where # is the same number assigned to the computer. The password for each user should be password. Mike's network has a DHCP server for configuring TCP/IP.

Mike has mentioned to you that the users will primarily work in Windows 2000. For this reason, he would like you to make as much disk space as possible available to the Windows 2000 operating system. He also would like you to make sure that the files the users create in Windows 2000 are secure.

What You Do	How You Do It
1. Remove all old operating systems and data from the computer.	a. Insert the Windows 98 Startup disk and turn on the computer.
	b. When prompted, **choose Start Computer Without CD-ROM Support and press Enter.**
	c. Enter **fdisk**
	d. Enter **N** twice to disable large disk support.
	e. Delete all partitions.

2. **Create and format a primary partition.**

    a. In Fdisk, **enter 1** to create a DOS partition.

    b. **Enter 1** to create a primary DOS partition.

    c. **Enter N** to specify that you want to manually enter a size for your primary partition and manually mark it active.

    d. **Enter 2048** or the maximum allowed size to create the partition for the partition size.

    e. **Press Esc.**

    f. **Enter 2** to mark a partition active.

    g. **Enter 1** to make the partition active.

    h. **Press Esc** until you exit Fdisk.

    i. **Press Ctrl+Alt+Delete** to restart the computer.

    j. When prompted, **choose Start Computer With CD-ROM Support and press Enter.**

    k. At the A: prompt, **enter format c: /s**

    l. **Enter Y** to confirm that you want to format the C drive.

    m. **Press Enter** to accept a blank volume label.

3. Install Windows 98.

a. Insert the Windows 98 installation CD-ROM into the computer's CD-ROM drive.

b. At the A prompt, **enter x:\setup** (where x is the letter of the computer's CD-ROM drive).

c. **Press Enter to continue.**

d. When ScanDisk completes, **press X** to exit.

e. **Click Continue.**

f. On the License Agreement page, **select I Accept The Agreement and click Next.**

g. **Enter the Windows 98 product key and click Next.**

h. On the Select Directory page, **verify that C:\WINDOWS is selected and click Next.**

i. On the Setup Options page, **verify that Typical is selected and click Next.**

j. In the User Name text box, .type *Mike Jones*

k. In the Company Name text box, **type** *Application Developers, Inc.*

l. **Click Next.**

m. **Verify that Install The Most Common Components (Recommended) is selected and click Next.**

n. In the Computer Name text box, **type** *Win98-#*, where # is your assigned number.

o. In the Workgroup Name text box, **type** *AppDev* **and click Next.**

p. **Verify that United States is selected and click Next.**

q. **Click Next** to create a Windows 98 Startup disk.

r. When prompted, **insert a blank floppy disk and click OK.**

s. When the Startup disk creation is complete, **remove the floppy disk and label it. Click OK.**

t. **Click Next.** Setup now copies the necessary Windows 98 files to the hard disk.

📌 The file copy process will take several minutes.

u. If neccessary, when the file copy is complete, **click Restart Now.**

📌 The hardware detection process will take several minutes.

v. Setup now performs hardware detection. If neccessary, when the process is complete, **click Restart Now.**

w. If neccessary, **click OK** to close the Network message box.

x. **Click Close.**

y. In the Date/Time Properties dialog box, **configure the appropriate date, time, and time zone for San Francisco.**

z. **Click Close.**

aa. If neccessary, when the installation is complete, **click Restart Now.**

ab. In the User Name text box, **type** *Admin#*

ac. In the password text box, **type** *password* **and click OK.**

ad. In the Confirm New Password text box, **type** *password* **and click OK** to log on.

ae. **Uncheck Show This Screen Each Time Windows 98 Starts and close the window.**

4. Configure an Internet connection.

    a. Choose Start→Programs→Accessories→ Internet Tools→Internet Connection Wizard.

    b. Select I Want To Set Up My Internet Connection Manually, Or I Want To Connect Through A Local Area Network (LAN).

    c. Click Next.

    d. Select the appropriate connection option.

    e. Click Next.

    f. If you selected to connect to the Internet through a local area network (LAN), configure the proxy server information as needed.

    g. Click Next.

    h. Select No to skip configuring an Internet email account.

    i. Click Finish.

LESSON 13

5. Verify that all hardware drivers installed correctly.

a. In Device Manager, **view the status of all devices.** An exclamation point within a yellow circle indicates that the driver for a device is not working properly.

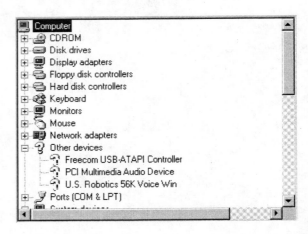

b. If necessary, **use Add/Remove Hardware** in Control Panel to install drivers for hardware devices or **connect to the hardware manufacturer's Web site** to download the appropriate drivers.

6. **Update Windows 98.**

a. From the Start menu, **choose Windows Update.**

b. **Click Yes** to install and run the Windows Update Control Package.

c. If necessary, **click Yes** again.

d. **Click Scan For Updates** to look for all updates to Windows 98.

Welcome to Windows Update

Get the latest updates available for your computer's operating system, software, and hardware.

Windows Update scans your computer and provides you with a selection of updates tailored just for you.

 Scan for updates

e. **Click Review And Install Updates.**

f. **Click Yes** to continue.

g. **Follow the prompts to install the updates you want.**

h. If necessary, **restart the computer when prompted.**

i. **Log back on as Admin#.**

7. **Install Windows 2000 Professional.**

a. In Windows 98, **access \\2000srv\ win2000.**

b. **Double-click winnt32.exe.**

⚠ Do not upgrade Windows 98.

c. On the Welcome page, **verify that Install A New Copy Of Windows 2000 (Clean Install) is selected and click Next.**

d. **Select I Accept This Agreement and click Next.**

e. On the Select Special Options page, **click Advanced Options.**

⚠ Make sure that you specify that you want to choose the installation partition during setup.

f. **Check I Want To Choose The Installation Partition During Setup and click OK.**

☑ I want to choose the installation partition during Setup

g. **Click Next.**

h. **Click Finish** to restart the computer.

i. On the Welcome page, **press Enter.**

j. **Highlight the unpartitioned space on the hard disk and press C** to create a new partition.

k. **Press Enter** to accept the default partition size of all remaining free space on the hard disk.

l. **Highlight the new partition and press Enter** to install Windows 2000 on this partition.

m. **Verify that Format The Partition Using The NTFS File System is selected and press Enter.**

n. **Press Enter** to restart the computer.

o. On the Welcome page, **click Next.**

p. On the Regional Settings page, **click Next** to accept the default locale and keyboard layout.

q. On the Personalize Your Software page, in the Name text box, **type** *Mike Jones*

    In the Organization text box, **type** *Application Developers, Inc.*

r. **Click Next.**

s. On the Computer Name And Administrator password page, in the Computer Name text box, **type** *WIN2000—#*, where # is your assigned number.

t. In the Administrator password text box, **type** *password*

    In the Confirm Password text box, **type** *password*

u. **Click Next.**

v. If Setup detected a modem, in the What Area Code (Or City Code) Are You In Now text box, **type** *415*

w. **Click Next.**

x. On the Date And Time Settings page, **configure the date, time, and time zone. Click Next.**

y. On the Networking Settings page, **verify that Typical Settings is selected and click Next.**

z. On the Workgroup Or Computer Domain page, **verify that No, This Computer Is Not On A Network is selected.**

aa. In the Workgroup Or Computer Domain text box, **type** *APPDEV*

ab. **Click Next.** Setup now installs the Windows components.

 Setup now copies the necessary files to the

hard disk. This process will take 15 or 20 minutes to complete.

ac. **Click Finish.** The computer restarts.

8. **Require users to log on to the computer.**

a. **Select Windows 2000 Professional and press Enter.**

b. **In the Network Identification Wizard, click Next.**

c. **Select Users Must Enter A User Name And Password To Use This Computer.**

d. **Click Next.**

e. **Click Finish.**

f. **Log on as Administrator with a password of password.**

g. **Uncheck Show This Screen At Startup.**

h. **Click Exit.**

9. Configure an Internet connection.

a. Run the Internet Connection Wizard.

b. **Specify that you want to configure the Internet connection manually and click Next.**

c. **Select the appropriate connection option.**

d. **Click Next.**

e. If you selected to connect to the Internet through a local area network (LAN), **configure the proxy server information as needed.**

f. **Click Next.**

g. **Select No** to skip configuring an Internet email account. **Click Next.**

h. If neccessary, **uncheck the To Connect To The Internet Immediately check box.**

i. **Click Finish.**

---

10. Verify that all hardware drivers installed correctly.

a. In Device Manager, **view the status of all devices.**

```
WIN2000-1
├── Computer
├── Disk drives
├── Display adapters
├── DVD/CD-ROM drives
├── Floppy disk controllers
├── Floppy disk drives
├── IDE ATA/ATAPI controllers
├── Keyboards
├── Mice and other pointing devices
├── Modems
├── Monitors
├── Network adapters
├── Other devices
│   └── Freecom USB-ATAPI Controller
├── Ports (COM & LPT)
├── Sound, video and game controllers
├── System devices
└── Universal Serial Bus controllers
```

b. If necessary, **use Add/Remove Hardware** in Control Panel to install drivers for hardware devices, **or connect to the Manufacturer's Web site(s)** to download and install the appropriate drivers.

11. **Update Windows 2000.**

    a. From the Start menu, **choose Windows Update.**

    b. **Click Yes** to install and run the Windows Update Control Package.

    c. If necessary, **click Yes** again.

    d. **Click Scan For Updates** to look for all updates to Windows 2000.

    Scan for updates

    e. **Click Review And Install Updates.**

    f. **Click Yes** to continue.

    g. **Follow the prompts to install the updates you want.**

    h. If necessary, **restart the computer when prompted.**

    i. **Log back on as Administrator.**

12. Create Admin#.	a. In Computer Management, **expand Local Users And Groups.**
	b. **Right-click Users and choose New User.**
	c. In the User Name text box, **type** *Admin#*
	d. In the Password text box, **type** *password*
	e. In the Confirm Password text box, **type** *password*
	f. **Uncheck User Must Change Password At Next Logon.**
	g. **Click Create.**
	h. **Click Close.**
	i. **Close Computer Management.**

TOPIC B

Upgrade a Windows Client Operating System

In Topic 13A, you learned how to install a Windows client operating system from scratch on a computer. A user has used this computer to install her applications and has stored quite a bit of data on it. Now, you've been asked to upgrade this computer to a later version of Windows. In this topic, you'll learn the steps for upgrading from an earlier version of Windows to a newer version.

Upgrading a computer's operating system to a newer one enables the computer's user to take advantage of the new features and capabilities added to the newer version. And as you've seen, performing such an upgrade offers you, the A+ technician, the benefit of saving a lot of time. You won't have to completely install the new operating system from scratch along with all of the user's applications. You also won't have to spend time restoring the user's data into the new operating system.

How to Upgrade a Windows Client Operating System

Procedure Reference: Upgrade from Windows 98 to Windows 2000

To upgrade from Windows 98 to Windows 2000:

1. Verify that the computer meets the hardware requirements for Windows 2000 (use Table 13-5 or go to **www.microsoft.com/windows2000/professional/evaluation/ sysreqs/default.asp**).

2. Back up the user data files.

3. In Windows 98, insert the Windows 2000 Professional CD-ROM.

4. When prompted, click Yes to upgrade Windows 98.

5. On the Welcome page, select Upgrade To Windows 2000 (Recommended) and click Next.

6. Select I Accept This Agreement and click Next.

7. If necessary, enter the Windows 2000 product key and click Next.

8. On the Preparing To Upgrade To Windows 2000 page, click Click Here to connect to the Windows Compatibility Web site to check your computer's hardware. When you're done, close Internet Explorer.

9. Click Next.

10. On the Provide Upgrade Packs page, select one of the following:
    *   Yes, I Have Upgrade Packs. Click Add to add to the Upgrade Pack List.
    *   No, I Don't Have Any Upgrade Packs.

11. Click Next.

12. On the Upgrading To The Windows 2000 NTFS File System page, select Yes, Upgrade My Drive if you want to upgrade the hard disk to NTFS. Otherwise, select No, Do Not Upgrade My Drive. Click Next.

13. Review the Upgrade Report. Click Save As if you want to save it. You can also click Print if you want to print the report.

14. Click Next.

15. Click Next to begin the upgrade.

16. When prompted, restart the computer. Do not boot from the Windows 2000 CD. Setup copies some of the Windows 2000 files to the hard disk.

17. Press Enter to restart the computer. Do not boot from the CD-ROM.

18. If you chose to upgrade the disk to NTFS, Setup converts the disk at this point. When the conversion is complete, your computer restarts.

    Setup now detects and installs the devices in the computer. It also automatically installs networking components and adds the computer as either a member of a workgroup or a domain (based on the configuration of Windows 98). Setup now completes copying the Windows 2000 files to the hard disk. This whole automated process may take 20 to 30 minutes.

19. Click Restart Now.

20. In the Password Creation dialog box, type a temporary password to assign to each user account created during the upgrade (at a minimum, you should see one user account plus the Administrator account).

21. Click OK.

22. Log on as Administrator with the password you just defined.

    🖈 For more information on how to configure an Internet connection in Windows 2000, see Lesson 8.

23. If necessary, configure the computer to connect to the Internet.

24. If necessary, install any hardware drivers that were not automatically installed during setup. For example, make sure that the drivers for devices such as sound cards, modems, and display adapters were installed correctly.

    a. Use Device Manager to view the status of these devices and to look for any devices for which Setup did not install the drivers.

    b. If you need new drivers, connect to the manufacturer's Web site to download the drivers for Windows 2000.

    c. Use Add New Hardware in Control Panel to install the drivers. When prompted, do not have Windows 2000 search for the device. Instead, select the driver from the files you downloaded.

25. Update Windows 2000.

    a. From the Start menu, choose Windows Update.

    b. Click Yes to install and run the Windows Update Control Package.

    c. If necessary, click Yes again.

    d. Click Scan For Updates.

    e. Click Review And Install Updates.

    f. Click Yes to continue.

    g. Follow the prompts to install the updates you want. You'll find that some of the updates are "exclusive," which means they can't be installed with other updates. If you choose to install an exclusive update, be sure to go back to the Windows Update Web site to check for other updates.

26. If necessary, restart the computer after the updates are installed.

27. If you have enough available disk space, copy the Windows 2000 installation files to a folder on the hard disk.

28. If necessary, use Computer Management to create any additional user accounts needed on the computer.

Procedure Reference: Upgrade from Windows 2000 to Windows XP

To upgrade from Windows 2000 to Windows XP:

1. Verify that the computer meets the hardware requirements for Windows XP (use Table 13-6 or go to **www.microsoft.com/windowsxp/pro/evaluation/sysreqs.asp**).

2. Back up the user data files.

3. In Windows 2000, insert the Windows XP Professional CD-ROM.

4. Click Install Windows XP.

5. From the Installation Type drop-down list, select Upgrade (Recommended) and click Next.

6. Select I Accept This Agreement and click Next.

7. Enter the Product Key and click Next.

8. On the Get Updated Setup Files page, select one of the following:
   - Yes, Download The Updated Setup Files (Recommended).
   - No, Skip This Step And Continue Installing Windows.

9. Click Next.

   If you selected to download updated setup files, Setup will connect to Microsoft's Web site and download updates for installing Windows XP. Your computer will automatically restart after downloading the updates. Do not boot from the CD.

10. After copying files, Setup will restart the computer again. Do not boot from the CD.

11. When the installation is complete, the computer will restart again.

12. On the Welcome To Microsoft Windows page, click Next.

13. On the Ready To Register With Microsoft page, select whether you want to register the computer with Microsoft at this time. If you select Yes, Click Next and complete the steps to register the computer.

14. Click Next.

15. On the Let's Get On The Internet page, select one of the following:
    - Get Online With MSN.
    - Do Not Set Up An Internet Connection At This Time.

    Click Next.

16. If you selected Get Online With MSN, complete the steps to create an account.

17. Click Finish.

18. Log on to Windows XP.

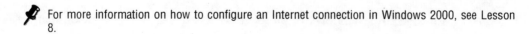 For more information on how to configure an Internet connection in Windows 2000, see Lesson 8.

19. If necessary, configure the computer to connect to the Internet.

20. If necessary, install any hardware drivers that were not automatically installed during setup. For example, make sure that the drivers for devices such as sound cards, modems, and display adapters were installed correctly.

    a. Use Device Manager to view the status of these devices and to look for any devices for which Setup did not install the drivers.

    b. If you need new drivers, connect to the manufacturer's Web site to download the drivers for Windows XP.

    c. Use Add New Hardware in Control Panel to install the drivers. When prompted, do not have Windows XP search for the device. Instead, select the driver from the files you downloaded.

21. Update Windows XP.

a. From the Start menu, choose All Programs→Windows Update.

b. Click Yes to install and run the Windows Update Control Package.

c. If necessary, click Yes again.

d. Click Scan For Updates.

e. Click Review And Install Updates.

f. Click Yes to continue.

g. Follow the prompts to install the updates you want. You'll find that some of the updates are "exclusive," which means they can't be installed with other updates. If you choose to install an exclusive update, be sure to go back to the Windows Update Web site to check for other updates.

22. If necessary, restart the computer after the updates are installed.

23. If you have enough available disk space, copy the Windows XP installation files to a folder on the hard disk.

Replacing an Operating System

If you want to completely replace the operating system on a computer, you'll need to complete the following steps:

1. Back up all data on the computer that you want to retain after changing the operating system.

2. Install the new operating system. During the installation, delete all partitions on the hard disk, and then create a new partition for the operating system.

3. Restore the backed up files to the computer.

ACTIVITY 13-2

Upgrading Windows 98 to Windows 2000

Setup:

Before you can complete this activity, you will need to remove the dual-boot environment. Use the following steps to do so:

1. In Windows 98, use Windows Explorer to access the C:\Windows\Command folder.

2. Copy the sys.com file to your Windows 98 Startup disk.

3. Boot the computer with the Windows 98 Startup disk.

4. Overwrite the hard disk's Master Boot Record by entering sys C:.

5. Restart the computer to Windows 98.

⚠ Do not delete the Windows 2000 partition.

Setup:

You will need a Windows 98 Startup disk to complete this activity. The Windows 2000 Professional installation files are in \\2000srv\win2000.

Scenario:

A client has asked you to upgrade her computer from Windows 98 to Windows 2000 Professional. She's interested in implementing the security features that are available in Windows 2000 and not Windows 98. She also wants to make sure that she won't have to re-install her applications or lose any of her data. The client also tells you that she has copied the Windows 98 installation files to C:\Win98 and backed up portions of Windows 98 to C:\Backup; she will no longer need these files.

What You Do	How You Do It
1. Verify that the computer's hardware meets the minimum Windows 2000 Professional requirements.	a. In Internet Explorer, **connect to *www.microsoft.com/windows2000/ professional/evaluation/sysreqs/ default.asp*.**
	b. **Review the minimum hardware requirements.**
	c. On the desktop, **right-click My Computer and choose Properties** to display information about the computer's processor and RAM. **Verify that the processor and RAM meet the minimum requirements.**
	d. **Click Cancel** to close the System Properties dialog box.
	e. **Use Windows Explorer** to verify that you have enough free disk space.
	f. **Close all open windows.**

2. **Upgrade Windows 98 to Windows 2000.**

a. **Connect to \\2000srv\win2000.**

b. **Double-click winnt32.exe.**

c. If neccessary, **click Yes** to upgrade Windows 98.

d. **Select Upgrade To Windows 2000 (Recommended) and click Next.**

e. **Select I Accept This Agreement and click Next.**

f. **Click Next** to skip connecting to the Windows Compatibility Web site to check the computer's hardware.

g. **Select No, I Don't Have Any Upgrade Packs and click Next.**

h. **Select Yes, Upgrade My Drive** to upgrade the hard disk to NTFS.

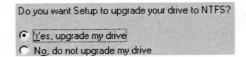

Do you want Setup to upgrade your drive to NTFS?

◉ Yes, upgrade my drive
○ No, do not upgrade my drive

i. **Click Next.**

j. **Review the Upgrade Report for any problems.**

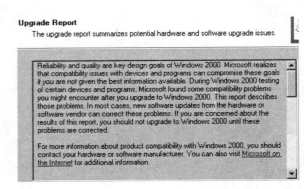

Upgrade Report

The upgrade report summarizes potential hardware and software upgrade issues.

Reliability and quality are key design goals of Windows 2000. Microsoft realizes that compatibility issues with devices and programs can compromise these goals if you are not given the best information available. During Windows 2000 testing of certain devices and programs, Microsoft found some compatibility problems you might encounter after you upgrade to Windows 2000. This report describes those problems. In most cases, new software updates from the hardware or software vendor can correct these problems. If you are concerned about the results of this report, you should not upgrade to Windows 2000 until these problems are corrected.

For more information about product compatibility with Windows 2000, you should contact your hardware or software manufacturer. You can also visit Microsoft on the Internet for additional information.

k. **Click Next.**

l. **Click Next** to begin the upgrade.

⚠ Do not boot from the Windows 2000 CD-ROM.

m. When prompted, **restart the computer.**
Setup will now copy some of the Windows
2000 files to the hard disk.

n. When prompted, **press Enter** to restart
the computer.

Setup will now convert the hard disk to
NTFS. After the conversion, your computer will automatically restart. Setup
will then continue with detecting hardware, installing the network components,
and copying the rest of the Windows 2000
files. This process can take up to 30
minutes.

o. When the installation is complete, **click
Restart Now.**

p. In the New Password Creation dialog box,
in the Password text box, **type** *password*

q. In the Confirm New Password text box,
type *password*

r. **Click OK.**

3. Verify that all hardware drivers installed correctly.

   a. **Log on as Administrator with a password of password.**

   b. **Uncheck Show This Screen At Startup and click Exit.**

   c. In Device Manager, **view the status of all devices.**

   d. If necessary, **use Add/Remove Hardware** in Control Panel to install drivers for hardware devices **or connect to the Manufacturer's Web site** to download and install the appropriate drivers.

4. **Update Windows 2000.**

   a. From the Start menu, **choose Windows Update.**

   b. **Click Yes** to install and run the Windows Update Control Package.

   c. If necessary, **click Yes** again.

    d. **Click Scan For Updates** to look for all updates to Windows 2000.

       Scan for updates

    e. **Click Review And Install Updates.**

    f. **Click Yes** to continue.

    g. **Follow the prompts to install the updates you want.**

    h. If necessary, **restart the computer when prompted.**

    i. From the boot menu, **choose the first Windows 2000 Professional option** (the second Windows 2000 Professional option is the installation of Windows 2000 you completed in the previous activity).

    j. **Log back on as Administrator.**

---

5. **Delete any files the client no longer needs.**

    a. **Open Windows Explorer.**

    b. **Access C:\.**

    c. **Right-click C:\Win98 and choose Delete** to delete the Windows 98 installation files.

    d. **Click Yes** to confirm deleting the folder.

    e. **Delete the C:\Backup folder.**

    f. **Close Windows Explorer.**

ACTIVITY 13-3

Upgrading Windows 2000 to Windows XP

Setup:

The Windows XP installation files are in \\2000srv\winxp.

Setup:

To complete this activity successfully, perform the following tasks:

1. Restart the computer.

2. From the boot menu, choose the second Windows 2000 Professional installation.

3. Log on as Administrator#.

Scenario:

One of your clients calls to tell you that he's just purchased Windows XP Professional. He's currently running Windows 2000 Professional on his computer.

What You Do	How You Do It
1. Verify that the computer's hardware meets the minimum Windows XP Professional requirements.	a. In Internet Explorer, **connect to** *www.microsoft.com/windowsxp/pro/ evaluation/sysreqs.asp.*
	b. **Review the minimum hardware requirements.**
	c. On the desktop, **right-click My Computer and choose Properties** to display information about the computer's processor and RAM. **Verify that the processor and RAM meet the minimum requirements.**
	d. **Click Cancel** to close the System Properties dialog box.
	e. **Use Windows Explorer** to verify that you have enough free disk space.
	f. **Close all open windows.**

2. **Upgrade Windows 2000 to Windows XP.**

    a. In Windows 2000, **access \\2000srv\ winxp\i386.**

    b. **Double-click winnt32.exe.**

    c. **Click Install Windows XP.**

    d. From the Installation Type drop-down list, **select Upgrade (Recommended) and click Next.**

    e. **Select I Accept This Agreement and click Next.**

    f. **Enter the Product Key and click Next.**

    g. **Verify that Yes, Download The Updated Setup Files (Recommended) is selected and click Next** to connect to Microsoft's Web site and download updates for installing Windows XP. Your computer will automatically restart after downloading the updates.

        After copying files, Setup will automatically restart the computer again. Setup completes the upgrade, which can take from 30 to 45 minutes. Your computer will automatically restart again.

    h. If necessary, in the Display Settings message box, **click OK. Click OK** again to confirm the adjusted display settings.

    i. **Click Next.**

    j. On the Ready To Register With Microsoft page, **select No and click Next.**

    k. **Click Finish.**

3. **Verify that all hardware drivers installed correctly.**

    a. **Log on to Windows XP as Administrator.**

b. In Device Manager, **view the status of all devices.**

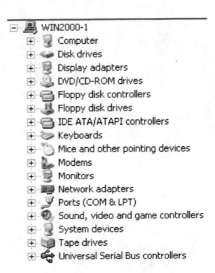

c. If necessary, **use Add Or Remove Hardware** in Control Panel to install drivers for hardware devices **or connect to the Manufacturer's Web site** to download and install the appropriate drivers.

4. **Update Windows XP.**

a. From the Start menu, **choose Windows Update.**

b. **Click Yes** to install and run the Windows Update Control Package.

c. If necessary, **click Yes** again.

d. **Click Scan For Updates** to look for all updates to Windows XP.

> ⟶ Scan for updates

e. **Click Review And Install Updates.**

f. **Click Yes** to continue.

g. **Follow the prompts to install the updates you want.**

h. If necessary, **restart the computer when prompted.**

i. **Log back on as Administrator.**

TOPIC C

Troubleshoot Operating System Installations

So far in this lesson you've learned how to install operating systems from scratch. Unfortunately, sometimes an installation will fail. As an A+ technician, you'll be expected to troubleshoot problems with installing an operating system so that you're able to successfully install the operating system. So, in this lesson, you'll learn the common problems that can occur during installation and how to go about troubleshooting them.

In some cases, you'll wish that you could just walk away when you encounter a problem during an installation. Unfortunately, that's not how it works in the real world. As an A+ technician, it's your job not only to attempt to install a computer's operating system, but also to install it successfully. Mastering the skills for troubleshooting installations will enable you to quickly and successfully handle any problem that might crop up during an operating system installation.

Common Problems

Regardless of which Windows operating system you're installing, you'll find that the problems you can encounter are very similar. In Table 13-10, you see a list of common installation problems you can encounter, along with potential solutions for those problems.

Table 13-10: *Common Installation Problems*

Problem	Potential Solution
Media errors	Try using a different CD-ROM or a different set of shared installation files on the network.
Unsupported CD-ROM drive	Try replacing your CD-ROM drive with one that's supported, or install using another method such as connecting to a network share.
Insufficient disk space	Try using Setup to create a partition out of free space on your disk that's large enough. You can also try deleting files or folders, moving files or folders to another partition, compressing an NTFS partition, or creating a larger NTFS partition.
Failure of Windows to install or start	Check that all of the hardware on your computer is detected and is compatible with Windows 2000.
Failure of a dependency service to start (in Windows 2000 or Windows XP only)	Use the Back button in the Setup wizard to return to the Network Settings page. Verify that you have installed the correct network card driver and protocol. You'll also need to check the configuration settings for your adapter. Make sure that the computer name is unique on the network.

How to Troubleshoot an Operating System Installation

Procedure Reference: How to Troubleshoot an Operating System Installation

To troubleshoot an operating system installation:

1. If you're installing a Windows operating system on a computer with no existing operating system, and the installation is failing, verify that the computer's hardware is compatible with the version of Windows you're attempting to install. If necessary, upgrade the hardware.

2. If you're upgrading to a new version of Windows and you're receiving errors when Setup tries to write to the hard disk, disable any anti-virus software on the computer. Also, make sure that the computer's CMOS setup is not configured to perform any boot sector virus detection.

   For more information on how to troubleshoot hard disks in Windows 2000, Windows XP, and Windows NT, see Lesson 6. To learn how to troubleshoot hard disks in Windows 9x, see Lesson 5.

3. If you're experiencing hard disk errors, troubleshoot the hard disks. If necessary, replace the hard disks.

4. If the Setup program for the version of Windows you're installing does not recognize the computer's CD-ROM drive and the computer has an existing operating system (or is configured to boot with network support from a floppy disk), install Windows by connecting to a network share with the installation files.

5. If the Setup program for the version of Windows you're installing does not recognize the computer's CD-ROM drive and the computer does not have an existing operating system, install Windows by using the Setup boot disks.

ACTIVITY 13-4

Troubleshoot Operating System Installations

Scenario:

As an A+ technician, you've been hired by a computer retailer to work in their Service department. As part of your job, you're expected to install and troubleshoot operating systems on a daily basis.

What You Do	How You Do It
1. A customer bought the Windows XP Professional upgrade. He brought in his Windows 98 computer to the Service department to have the upgrade installed. One of the technicians reports that the installation is failing after Setup copies files to the hard disk and reboots the computer. **What might be the problem? How should you fix it?**	
2. A customer brought in a computer on which she would like you to remove all existing data and install Windows 2000 Professional. You have deleted the partitions on the computer's hard disk. You insert the Windows 2000 CD-ROM but the computer won't boot from it. **What should you do?**	

TOPIC D

Add or Remove Operating System Components

Up to this point in the lesson, you've learned how to install operating systems using the typical installation option. In some cases, though, the Windows components Setup installs when you perform a typical installation won't meet the needs of a particular user. For this reason, in this topic, you'll learn how to add or remove operating system components on a computer.

Tailoring an operating system to meet a particular user's needs is just like custom building a house. One homeowner might like blue walls and grey carpeting, while another homeowner might prefer off-white walls and beige carpeting. Just as you can tailor a house to the homeowner's tastes, so can you tailor the Windows environment to a user's tastes or needs. For example, you might encounter a situation where the owner of a company requires that you remove all games from users' computers. To do so, you'll need to know how to remove an operating system component.

Operating System Components

Each Windows operating system comes with a variety of components. These include Accessories (such as the Calculator and Notepad), Communications, Games, and so on. Depending on how you install Windows, you might find that your installation does not include a component that you need. You can install that component by using Control Panel.

How to Add or Remove Operating System Components

Procedure Reference: Add or Remove Operating System Components

To add or remove operating system components:

1. Log on as a local administrator.

2. If you're using Windows XP, in Control Panel, click Add Or Remove Programs.

    If you're using Windows 2000, Windows NT, or Windows 98, in Control Panel, double-click Add/Remove Programs.

3. If you're using Windows 2000 or Windows XP, click Add/Remove Windows Components.

    In Windows NT, click Windows Setup.

    In Windows 98, select the Windows Setup tab.

4. To install a component, check its check box in the Components list.

    To uninstall a component, uncheck its check box.

5. To install or remove a component within a category, select the component category (such as Accessories) and click Details.

   Check or uncheck the component's check box, and then click OK.

6. Click Next.

7. If prompted, insert the Windows installation CD-ROM and click OK.

8. If necessary, click Finish.

9. Close all open windows.

10. Verify that the component was installed or removed.

ACTIVITY 13-5

Removing Operating System Components

Scenario:

You recently installed Windows XP Professional on a client's computers. The owner of the company feels that users are spending too much time playing the games included with Windows XP.

What You Do	How You Do It
1. **Remove the games from Windows XP.**	a. In Control Panel, **click Add Or Remove Programs.**
	b. **Click Add/Remove Windows Components.**
	c. In the Components list, **select Accessories And Utilities and click Details.**
	d. **Uncheck Games and click OK.**

	e. **Click Next.**
	f. **Click Finish.**
	g. **Click Close** to close Add Or Remove Programs.
	h. **Close Control Panel.**

2. **Verify that the computer no longer has games.**

a. From the Start menu, **choose All Programs→Games.** There are no games available on the menu.

b. **Close the Start menu.**

Lesson 13 Follow-up

In this lesson, you learned how to install the Windows 98, Windows 2000, and Windows XP Professional computers. You also learned how to upgrade to the Windows 2000 or Windows XP operating system, how to add or remove any of the operating system components, and how to troubleshoot the problems you can encounter during installation. These skills will prepare you to quickly respond to clients' requests for installing or upgrading their computers' operating systems.

1. **Have you ever installed an operating system? If so, which one? What was your experience with the installation?**

2. **What is your experience with upgrading computer operating systems? Did you encounter any problems? If so, how did you resolve them?**

LESSON 14

Automating Client Operating System Installations

Lesson Time
3 hour(s)

Lesson Objectives:

In this lesson, you will automate client operating system installations.

You will:

- Perform an unattended installation.
- Create a computer image.
- Install a computer image.

Introduction

In Lesson 13, you learned the exact steps you must perform to install an operating system from scratch, and how to upgrade an operating system. But installations and upgrades are time-consuming tasks. In this lesson, you'll learn how to automate installations and upgrades.

You've been asked to install Windows XP on 100 client computers. The installations need to be completed over a single weekend. You timed the installation on one of the computers, and it took almost two hours. Automating the installations will enable you to reduce the amount of time you need to complete the installations and meet your client's needs.

The following CompTIA A+ Operating System Technologies (2003) Examination objectives are covered in this lesson:

- Topic B:
  - 2.1 Installation methods: Drive Imaging.

TOPIC A

Perform an Unattended Installation

Another technique you can use to automate the installation of computer operating systems is to perform unattended installations. In this topic, you'll learn how to create the files you need for an unattended installation along with how to perform the actual unattended installation.

Just as you saw with creating and deploying computer images, performing unattended installations can also save you hours of setup time. One reason is because you won't have to sit at each computer and respond to the prompts you see during a manual installation. Instead, the unattended installation process will use files you've configured with the answers to each of these prompts to automate the installation. This means that you can perform an unattended installation on several computers at once.

Given that performing an unattended installation requires more configuration on your part as compared to deploying a computer image, you might be wondering when you would choose to perform an unattended installation instead of imaging. Here are some reasons: First, you might choose to perform an unattended installation instead of deploying a computer image if the computers on which you want to install the operating system have significantly different hardware. Another reason why you might perform an unattended installation is if your company doesn't have money in its budget to purchase the necessary imaging software. In both scenarios, performing an unattended installation offers you a faster method for installing the operating system on multiple computers as compared to performing a manual installation.

Answer File

Definition:

An *answer file* is a setup file that provides the answers needed by the Windows Setup program during an unattended installation. An answer file is divided into sections that group together the settings that are required to complete the various phases of Windows Setup. An answer file must conform to the following general syntax:

```
[section name]
keyname = value
keyname = value
```

You can create an answer file by using the Setup Manager utility or any text editor (such as Notepad). You can save the answer file with the extension .sif or .txt. Table 14-1 lists the required sections in an answer file and the types of settings to specify in each section.

Table 14-1: *Required Sections in an Answer File*

Section Name	Contains Information For
[Unattended]	The text-mode portion of Setup, such as the installation folder, and the file system type. The Unattended mode key determines the level of user interaction permitted during the unattended installation.
[UserData]	System-specific information, including the name and organization, computer name, and product key. You must provide a computer name or configure Setup to automatically generate a name.
[GuiUnattended]	The GUI portion of Setup, including the time zone and administrator password.
[Display]	Display settings for the computer, such as the screen resolution and refresh rate.
[Networking]	Typical or custom networking settings. Required if you want to configure custom settings during the unattended installation.
[Identification]	The domain or workgroup this computer will join.

Example:

Figure 14-1 shows you an example of an answer file.

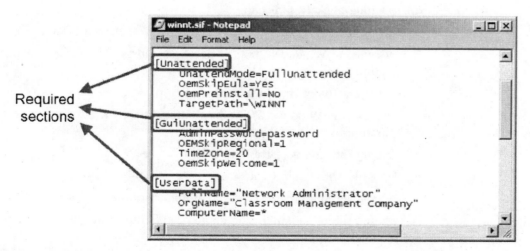

Figure 14-1: *An unattended answer file.*

Setup Command Syntax for Unattended Installations

When you're ready to perform an unattended installation, you begin the installation by using the appropriate Windows Setup program, followed by the option specifying the answer file you want to use. Here's the syntax:

```
winnt32 /s:\\server\share /unattend:answer_file
```

In this syntax, replace `\\server\share` with the name of the server and the shared folder name that contains the Windows installation files (you'll want to run an unattended installation using files on a network server so that you can install multiple computers at the same time). Replace `answer_file` with the name of the answer file you created.

Setup Batch Files

Instead of manually typing the commands to begin an unattended installation, you might choose to create a setup batch file to specify the appropriate commands for you. Inserting the correct command syntax in a file reduces the chance you might make a mistake in the command. You can then run the batch file yourself, or distribute it to users as a file so that they can launch the unattended setup.

How to Perform an Unattended Installation

Procedure Reference: Perform an Unattended Installation of Windows 2000

To perform an unattended installation of Windows 2000:

1. Use Setup Manager to create an unattended answer file.

   a. If you're using Windows XP, if necessary, install the Setup Manager Wizard (Setupmgr.exe).

      1. Create a folder in which to store Setup Manager.
      2. Access the Windows XP installation files (if necessary, insert the appropriate CD-ROM).
      3. Select the \Support\Tools folder.
      4. Double-click Deploy.cab.
      5. Copy the Setupmgr.exe and Setupmgx.dll files to a folder.

   b. If you're using Windows 2000, if necessary, install the Setup Manager Wizard (Setupmgr.exe).

      1. Create a folder in which to store Setup Manager.
      2. Access the Windows 2000 installation files (if necessary, insert the appropriate CD-ROM).
      3. Select the \Support\Tools folder.
      4. Double-click Deploy.cab.
      5. Copy the Setupmgr.exe and Setupmgr.chm files to a folder.

   c. Access the folder to which you copied the Setup Manager Wizard files and double-click Setupmgr.exe to run the wizard.

   d. In the Windows Setup Manager Wizard, click Next.

   e. Verify that Create A New Answer File is selected and click Next.

f.   If you're using Windows 2000's Setup Manager, select Windows 2000 Unattended Installation and click Next.

g.   If you're using Windows XP's Setup Manager, select Windows Unattended Installation and click Next.

h.   On the Platform page, if you're using Windows 2000's Setup Manager, select one of the following:

   •   Windows 2000 Professional

   •   Windows 2000 Server

i.   On the Platform page, if you're using Windows XP's Setup Manager, select one of the following:

   •   Windows XP Home Edition

   •   Windows XP Professional

   •   Windows 2000 Server, Advanced Server, or Data Center

j.   Click Next.

k.   Select the level of user interaction you want during the unattended installation and click Next.

   •   Provide Defaults—Answers you provide in the answer file are the default answers and Windows Setup prompts the user to review them. The user can change any answer.

   •   Fully Automated—Windows Setup doesn't prompt the user for any answers during installation. You must provide all answers in the answer file.

   •   Hide Pages—Hides the pages for which you have provided all answers in the answer file.

   •   Read Only—If a page isn't hidden from the user, the user can't make any changes to the answers you supplied in the answer file.

   •   GUI Attended—Automates only the text-mode portion of the installation. The user will be prompted to provide the necessary answers in the graphical portion of installation.

l.   Follow the prompts to complete the information you want to include in the answer file. These prompts will vary depending on which user interaction level you select.

m.   On the Computer names page, enter multiple computer names or check Automatically Generate Computer Names Based On Organization Name to have the unattended installation automatically name the computer for you.

n.   Select the installation source. Use one of the following:

   •   To copy the installation files from their current location to a shared distribution folder:

      a.   Select Yes, Create Or Modify A Distribution Folder. Click Next.

      b.   Specify the current location of the installation files. The source folder, usually the \i386 folder, should contain the Dosnet.inf information file. Click Next.

      c.   Specify the target folder name and share name for the distribution folder. Click Next.

- To use an existing distribution folder, whether on a network share or on a CD-ROM:

    a. Select No, This Answer File Will Be Used To Install From A CD.

    b. Click Next.

o. When you have finished entering settings, select the Additional Commands page and click Finish.

p. Enter a path and file name for your answer file and click OK. The wizard will create the answer file and the associated UDF and setup batch files in this folder.

- If you will be installing directly from the Windows XP or Windows 2000 CD-ROM, you must save the answer file to a floppy disk as A:\Winnt.sif. Be sure that the [Data] section of the answer file contains the required parameters.

- For all other types of installations, you can name the answer file anything you like.

q. Close Setup Manager by clicking the Close box.

r. Open the answer file and setup batch file in a text editor to verify your custom settings.

2. If necessary, edit the setup batch file to provide the path to the network installation shared folder.

3. Perform an unattended installation. Use the following steps:

a. Verify that the target computer's hardware meets the minimum Windows 2000 hardware requirements.

b. If your answer file is on a floppy disk, insert the floppy disk.

c. Launch the setup by using one of the following methods:

- Boot the computer from the Windows 2000 installation CD-ROM. The Setup program will automatically locate and run the A:\Winnt.sif file (make sure you configure the computer to boot from the CD-ROM first).

- Run the appropriate version of the Windows Setup program (Winnt.exe or Winnt32.exe) with the appropriate unattended setup switches.

- Run a setup batch file. The batch file command syntax is `batch_file_name [ID]`, where `[ID]` is the appropriate ID code for this computer installation as defined in the [Unique IDs] section of the UDF.

d. Respond to any prompts in Windows Setup to complete the installation.

Procedure Reference: Perform an Unattended Installation of Windows XP

To perform an unattended installation of Windows XP:

1. Use Setup Manager to create an unattended answer file.

a. If you're using Windows XP, if necessary, install the Setup Manager Wizard (Setupmgr.exe).

    1. Create a folder in which to store Setup Manager.

    2. Access the Windows XP installation files (if necessary, insert the appropriate CD-ROM).

    3. Select the \Support\Tools folder.

    4.   Double-click Deploy.cab.

    5.   Copy the Setupmgr.exe and Setupmgr.chm files to the folder.

b.   Access the folder to which you copied the Setup Manager Wizard files and double-click Setupmgr.exe to run the wizard.

c.   In the Windows Setup Manager Wizard, click Next.

d.   Verify that Create A New Answer File is selected and click Next.

e.   Select Windows Unattended Installation and click Next.

f.   On the Platform page, select one of the following:

- Windows XP Home Edition
- Windows XP Professional
- Windows 2000 Server, Advanced Server, or Data Center

g.   Click Next.

h.   Select the level of user interaction you want during the unattended installation and click Next.

- Provide Defaults—Answers you provide in the answer file are the default answers and Windows Setup prompts the user to review them. The user can change any answer.

- Fully Automated—Windows Setup doesn't prompt the user for any answers during installation. You must provide all answers in the answer file.

- Hide Pages—Hides the pages for which you have provided all answers in the answer file.

- Read Only—If a page isn't hidden from the user, the user can't make any changes to the answers you supplied in the answer file.

- GUI Attended—Automates only the text-mode portion of the installation. The user will be prompted to provide the necessary answers in the graphical portion of installation.

i.   Select the installation source. Use one of the following:

- To copy the installation files from their current location to a shared distribution folder:

    a.   Select Yes, Create Or Modify A Distribution Folder. Click Next.

    b.   Specify the current location of the installation files. The source folder, usually the \i386 folder, should contain the Dosnet.inf information file. Click Next.

    c.   Specify the target folder name and share name for the distribution folder. Click Next.

- To use an existing distribution folder, whether on a network share or on a CD-ROM:

    a.   Select No, This Answer File Will Be Used To Install From A CD.

    b.   Click Next.

j.   Check I Accept The Terms Of The License Agreement and click Next.

k.   Complete the data required for each of the items listed in the left pane. For example, below General Settings, select Customize The Software. In the right pane, enter the Name and Organization for the user who will use the computer. Move to the next item in the left pane and complete the required information, and so on. When you have completed all required information, click Finish.

l. Enter a path and file name for your answer file and click OK. The wizard will create the answer file and the associated UDF and setup batch files in this folder.

- If you will be installing directly from the Windows XP or Windows 2000 CD-ROM, you must save the answer file to a floppy disk as A:\Winnt.sif. Be sure that the [Data] section of the answer file contains the required parameters.

- For all other types of installations, you can name the answer file anything you like.

m. Open the answer file and setup batch file in a text editor to verify your custom settings.

2. If necessary, edit the setup batch file to provide the path to the network installation shared folder.

3. Perform an unattended installation. Use the following steps:

a. Verify that the target computer's hardware meets the minimum Windows XP hardware requirements.

b. If your answer file is on a floppy disk, insert the floppy disk.

c. Launch the setup by using one of the following methods:

- Boot the computer from the Windows XP installation CD-ROM. The Setup program will automatically locate and run the A:\Winnt.sif file (make sure you configure the computer to boot from the CD-ROM first).

- Run the appropriate version of the Windows Setup program (Winnt.exe or Winnt32.exe) with the appropriate unattended setup switches.

- Run a setup batch file. The batch file command syntax is `batch_file_name [ID]`, where `[ID]` is the appropriate ID code for this computer installation as defined in the [Unique IDs] section of the UDF.

d. Respond to any prompts in Windows Setup to complete the installation.

ACTIVITY 14-1

Performing an Unattended Installation

Setup:

The Classroom Management Company is located in Rochester, New York. The client uses the 585 area code.

Setup:

Restart the computer to Windows 2000 Professional.

Scenario:

The network administrator at one of your clients, Classroom Management Company, has asked you to automate the installation of Windows 2000 Professional for her. She would like you to prepare an answer file that will enable anyone in the IT department to install Windows 2000 Professional on a computer without having to sit at the computer during the installation process. After reviewing the client's network environment, you have determined the following information:

- The client has an Active Directory domain named class.com. All Windows 2000 computers are members of this domain.

- The Admin1 domain user account with a password of password has sufficient permissions to add computers to a domain.

- Classroom Management Company uses DHCP servers to assign IP addresses to its clients.

- The network administrator is not concerned about the names of the computers. She says you can use whatever naming convention is the easiest when automating the installations.

- The network administrator wants all administrator accounts to have the same password.

- The Windows 2000 installation files have been shared on the company's Windows 2000 server at \\2000srv\win2000. The Windows 2000 Support Tools have been shared in \\2000srv\support.

- All of the computers the network administrator purchases have monitors and video cards that support true color (32 bit) and at least 800 x 600 screen resolution.

- All computers on the network print to the \\2000srv\netprint shared network printer.

- The network administrator would like you to save the files you create to automate installations on a floppy disk.

Your client would like you to test the unattended installation files you create to verify that they work.

What You Do	How You Do It
1. **Install Setup Manager.**	a. **Log on as Administrator.**
	b. In Windows Explorer, **create a folder named C:\Setup.**
	c. **Access \\2000srv\support.**
	d. **Double-click Deploy.cab.**
	e. **Copy the Setupmgr.exe and Setupmgx. dll files to C:\Setup.**

2. **Create the unattended installation files.**	a. In Windows Explorer, **access the C:\Setup folder.**
	b. **Double-click setupmgr.exe.**
	c. **Click Next.**
	d. **Verify that Create A New Answer File is selected and click Next.**

Do you want to create a new answer file or modify an existing one?

- Create a new answer file
- Create an answer file that duplicates this computer's configuration
- Modify an existing answer file

e. **Verify that Windows 2000 Unattended Installation is selected and click Next.**

This answer file is for:

- Windows 2000 Unattended Installation
- Sysprep Install
- Remote Installation Services

f. **Verify that Windows 2000 Professional is selected and click Next.**

g. On the User Interaction Level page, **select Fully Automated.**

> Select the level of user interaction during Windows Setup:
>
> ○ Provide defaults
>
> ● Fully automated

h. **Click Next.**

i. **Check I Accept The Terms Of The License Agreement and click Next.**

j. In the Name text box, **type** *Network Administrator*

k. In the Organization text box, **type** *Classroom Management Company* and **click Next.**

l. On the Computer Names page, **check Automatically Generate Computer Names Based On Organization Name.**

> ☑ Automatically generate computer names based on organization name

m. **Click Next.**

n. In the Password and Confirm Password text boxes, **type** *password* and **click Next.**

o. On the Display Settings page, from the Colors drop-down list, **select True Color (24 bit).**

p. From the Screen Area drop-down list, **select 800 x 600.**

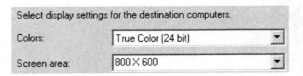
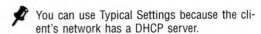

q. **Click Next.**

📌 You can use Typical Settings because the client's network has a DHCP server.

r. On the Network Settings page, **verify that Typical Settings is selected and click Next.**

s. On the Workgroup Or Domain Page, **select Windows Server Domain.**

t. In the Domain text box, **type** *class*

u. **Check Create A Computer Account In The Domain.**

v. In the User Name text box, **type** *Admin1*

w. In the Password and Confirm Password text boxes, **type** *password*

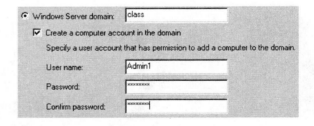

x. **Click Next.**

y. From the Time Zone drop-down list, **select (GMT-05:00) Eastern Time (US & Canada) and click Next.**

z. **Verify that Yes, Edit The Additional Settings is selected and click Next.**

aa. On the Telephony page, in the What Area

(Or City) Code Are You In text box, **type 585 and click Next.**

ab. On the Regional Settings page, **click Next** to accept the default settings.

ac. On the Languages page, **click Next** to skip adding any additional language groups.

ad. On the Browser And Shell Settings page, **click Next** to accept the default settings.

ae. On the Installation Folder page, **click Next** to accept the default folder name of \Winnt.

af. On the Install Printers page, in the Network Printer Name text box, **type *2000srv\\netprint* and click Add.**

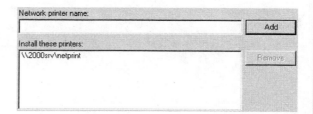

ag. **Click Next.**

ah. On the Run Once page, **click Next.**

ai. **Select No, This Answer File Will Be Used To Install From A CD.** You can choose this option even though you will be using a network share to install Windows 2000.

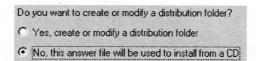

aj. **Click Next.**

ak. **Insert a blank, formatted floppy disk into the floppy disk drive.**

al. On the Answer File Name page, in the Location And File Name text box, **enter A:\Unattend.txt and click Next.** Setup Manager also names the setup batch file unattend.bat by default.

am. **Click Finish.**

an. In Windows Explorer, **access the A drive.**

ao. **Right-click unattend.bat and choose Edit.**

ap. In the set SetupFiles = line, **change the path to set SetupFiles = \\2000srv\ win2000.**

aq. **Change the line to run the winnt32 command to read \\2000srv\win2000\ winnt32 /s:%SetupFiles% /unattend:%AnswerFile%**

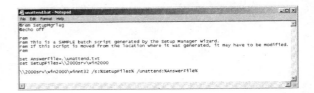

ar. **Save your changes and close Notepad.**

3. **Test the unattended installation.**

    a. In Windows Explorer, **verify that you're accessing the A drive.**

    b. **Double-click unattend.bat** to start the installation. **Remove the floppy disk when prompted.**

    c. When the installation is complete, **log on as Administrator** to verify that the installation completed successfully.

    d. **Check to see that the computer has the NetPrint network printer installed and that the display settings are set to 800 x 600 and true color (24 bit).**

TOPIC B

Create a Computer Image

In the last lesson, you learned how to perform a manual installation of an operating system. But what if you're responsible for installing an operating system along with all application software on 20 computers? One technique you can use to cut down on the amount of time you'll have to spend installing the operating system on these computers is to create an image of one computer and then install it on the remaining 19 computers. In this topic, you'll learn the first part of the imaging process by mastering the steps for creating a computer image.

Simply downloading a computer image is the fastest possible method for installing an operating system on a computer. Using a computer image to install an operating system on several computers also enables you to easily standardize their configuration. Because you'll be using a computer image over and over to install the operating system on so many computers, it's critical that you create a good image that contains everything you need. Configuring the image properly will help you avoid having to spend time recreating an image and then downloading it again to the computers for which you're responsible for installing.

Computer Image

For ease of installing multiple computers, you can "clone" a computer's hard disk onto a network server, and then download that clone onto other computers' hard disks. When you clone a computer's hard disk, you create an exact duplicate image of it. Installing this *computer image* onto other computers enables you to avoid having to install the operating system and all applications on each computer. Most companies use one of two tools for creating and downloading computer images: Symantec Ghost or Windows 2000/Windows XP Remote Installation Services (RIS). Because Symantec Ghost is so commonly used, you'll sometimes hear the process of imaging a computer referred to as *ghosting* a computer.

The Computer Image Deployment Process

The image-deployment process contains two main phases: the preparation phase and the deployment phase. First, you must prepare the image:

1. Prepare the computer of which you want to create an image:

   a.   Install the operating system.

   b.   Configure the operating system and applications while logged on as the user account you want to preserve in the image.

   c.   Copy this user account's profile to the Default User profile.

   d.   Test to verify the installation and configuration.

   e.   If you're creating an image of a Windows 2000 or Windows XP computer, prepare the computer with a system-preparation utility such as Sysprep. This utility enables each computer that receives the cloned image to have its own unique security identifier number (SID).

   f.   Shut down the computer.

2. Restart the computer by using a custom boot disk for your own network or by using a startup disk from the computer image utility (Ghost or RIS).

3. Run the computer image utility to duplicate the computer installation to a file.

4. Store the image on easily accessible media, such as a CD-ROM or a network share.

After you have prepared the image, you can deploy it to multiple computers:

1. Verify that the computer on which you want to install the image has identical hardware to the computer you cloned.

2. Start this computer by using a custom boot disk for your own network or by using a startup disk for the computer image utility.

3. Use the computer image utility to download the image onto the computer.

4. If you downloaded the image to a Windows 2000 or Windows XP computer, use the Sysprep mini-Setup routine to customize settings for the newly installed computer.

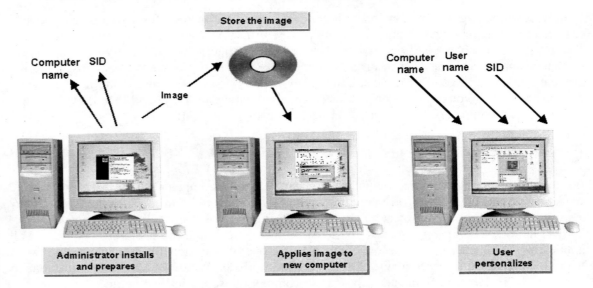

Figure 14-2: *Preparing and deploying a computer image.*

How to Create a Computer Image

Procedure Reference: Create a Computer Image and Store it on a Network Share

To create an image of a computer running Windows 2000, Windows XP, Windows NT, or Windows 98 and store it on a network share:

1. Install the Windows operating system.

2. Connect to the Windows Update Web site to update the operating system.

3. If you're using Windows 2000, Windows XP, or Windows NT, log on as a user account with administrative permissions and configure operating system settings. Install and configure all applications.

4. If necessary, install Ghost. (See the following procedure for how to install Ghost.)

5. Create a Ghost boot disk. (See the Create a Ghost Boot Disk procedure.)

6. Uninstall any applications you don't want to include in the computer image. For example, if you don't want to include the Ghost application on the image of the computer, uninstall Ghost.

7. If you're using Windows 2000, Windows XP, or Windows NT, copy this user's profile to the Default User profile.

   a. Log on as a local administrator.

   b. Open Windows Explorer.

   c. If you're using Windows 2000 or Windows XP, select the x:\Documents And Settings folder (replace x: with the drive letter on which Windows 2000 or Windows XP is installed). Configure this folder to display System and hidden files.

   If you're using Windows NT, select the x:\Winnt\Profiles folder (replace x: with the drive letter on which Windows 2000 or Windows XP is installed). Configure this folder to display System and hidden files.

   d. Close Windows Explorer.

   e. In Control Panel, double-click System.

   f. Select the User Profiles tab.

   g. In the Profiles Stored On This Computer list, select the profile you want to copy.

   h. Click Copy To.

   i. Below Copy Profile To, type or click Browse to enter the path x:\Documents And Settings\Default User. (replace x: with the drive letter on which Windows 2000 or Windows XP is installed).

   j. If you receive a warning stating that the Default User folder already exists, click Yes to overwrite the files.

   k. Below Permitted To Use, click Change.

   l. In the Name list, double-click Everyone.

   m. Click OK to copy the reference user's profile to the default user.

   n. Click OK to close the System Properties dialog box.

   o. Close Control Panel.

> 📌 If you use Setup Manager to create a Sysprep answer file, the mini-setup will automatically generate a unique name for the computer.

8. If you're using Windows 2000 or Windows XP and you want to automate the setup routine that will run after you deliver the computer to the user, use Setup Manager to create a Sysprep answer file. Save the file as \Sysprep\Sysprep.inf. The Sysprep answer file uses the same syntax as an unattended installation answer file, but supports only the necessary subset of sections and keys required by the mini-setup routine.

9. If you're using Windows 2000 or Windows XP, extract the Sysprep.exe and Setupcl.exe files from the \Support\Tools\Deploy.cab folder on the Windows XP or Windows 2000 installation CD-ROM to \Sysprep on the computer you want to image (the Sysprep and Setup Manager Wizard files must be in the same folder if you want to use an answer file to automate the mini-setup routine).

10. If you're cloning Windows XP, prepare the computer by running Sysprep with the appropriate parameters. See Table 14-2 for a list and description of the parameters you can use when preparing a computer for imaging. You can do either of the following:

   - Run Sysprep at the command line with the appropriate switches. Use this syntax: `sysprep [-switch]...[-switch]`

   - Run Sysprep.exe and make the appropriate selections in the System Preparation Tool graphical utility.

Table 14-2: *Windows XP Sysprep Parameters*

Switch	Graphical Equivalent	Purpose
—msoobe (default setting)	Leave MiniSetup unchecked	Uses Windows Welcome as the mini-setup routine.
—mini	Check MiniSetup	Runs an abbreviated version of the Windows XP Professional Setup Wizard as the mini-setup routine; detects and uses a Sysprep.inf file if present.
—quiet	None	Prevents the confirmation dialog boxes from being displayed.
—forceshutdown	From the Shutdown drop-down list, select Shutdown	Forces shutdown of the computer.
—reboot	From the Shutdown drop-down list, select Reboot	Forces a reboot of the computer after Sysprep is run.
—pnp	Check PnP	Runs Plug and Play detection when the computer is restarted after the computer image is downloaded.

11. If you're cloning Windows 2000, prepare the computer by running Sysprep with the appropriate parameters. See Table 14-3 for a list and description of the parameters you can use when preparing a computer for imaging. You can Run Sysprep at the command line with the appropriate switches. Use this syntax: `sysprep [-switch]...[-switch]`.

Table 14-3: *Windows 2000 Sysprep Parameters*

Switch	Purpose
–quiet	Prevents the confirmation dialog boxes from being displayed.
–reboot	Forces a reboot of the computer after Sysprep is run.
–pnp	Runs Plug and Play detection when the computer is restarted after the computer image is downloaded.

12. Insert the Ghost boot disk and turn the computer on.

13. When prompted to log on, press Enter to log on as the user you specified when you created the boot disk.

14. When prompted, enter the user account's password.

15. Access the mapped network drive letter.

16. Enter `ghost` to run the Ghost utility.

17. On the License Agreement Warning page, press Enter to mark the computer's hard disk.

18. Press Enter again.

19. Verify that Local is selected and press Enter.

20. Verify that Disk is selected and press Enter.

21. Select To Image and press Enter.

22. Press Enter to select the computer's hard disk.

23. In the File Name text box, type a name for the computer image.

24. Press Alt+S to save the name.

25. Select a compression setting and press Enter.
    - Fast
    - High

26. Press Alt+Y to create the image.

27. Press Enter to continue.

28. Press Q to quit.

29. Press Y to quit.

Procedure Reference: Install Ghost

To install Ghost:

1. Insert the Norton Ghost installation CD-ROM or connect to a network share containing the installation files.

2. If necessary, double-click Ghost to start the installation.

3. In the InstallShield Wizard, click Next.

4. Select I Accept The Terms In The License Agreement and click Next.

5. If necessary, enter a name and company name in the User Name and Organization text boxes.

6. Click Next.

7. On the Destination Folder page, select the folder in which you want to install Ghost or click Next to accept the default path.

8. Click Install to begin the installation.

9. When the installation is complete, follow the pages in the wizard to register the software or click Skip to skip registration.

10. On the Installation Completed Successfully page, click Next.

11. Click Finish.

Procedure Reference: Create a Ghost Boot Disk

To create a Ghost boot disk:

1. If necessary, install Ghost (see the Install Ghost procedure).

2. Verify the driver used by the computer's network card. Use these steps:
   a. On the desktop, right-click My Computer and choose Properties.
   b. Select the Hardware tab.
   c. Click Device Manager.
   d. Expand Network Adapters.
   e. Record the name of the driver.
   f. Close Device Manager.
   g. Click OK to close the System Properties dialog box.

3. Run Norton Ghost (from the Start menu, choose Programs or All Programs→ Norton Ghost 2003→Norton Ghost).

4. In the left pane, click Ghost Utilities.

5. Click Norton Ghost Boot Wizard.

6. Select Drive Mapping Boot Disk and click Next.

7. In the list of network card drivers, select the computer's network card driver if available (if the driver isn't available, click Add and follow the prompts to load the driver from the network card manufacturer's floppy disk or CD-ROM).

8. Click Next.

9. Verify that Use PC-DOS is selected and click Next.

10. In the Client Computer Name text box, type a name to use when you boot the computer from the boot disk. If you plan to run Ghost simultaneously on multiple computers, make sure that you configure each boot disk with a different computer name.

11. In the User Name text box, type a user name for the server on which you plan to store the computer image.

12. In the Domain text box, type the NetBIOS domain name for this server.

> Using G for this drive letter will make it easier for you to remember what letter to use when accessing the images.

13. Below Mapped Drive, from the Drive Letter drop-down list, select a drive letter.

14. In the Maps To text box, type the UNC share name for the folder in which you want to store the Ghost image.

15. Click Next.

16. Configure the TCP/IP addressing settings. Use one of the following:
    - Select DHCP Will Assign The IP Settings if you want to use a DHCP server to assign the IP address to the client when it boots from the boot disk.
    - Select The IP Address Settings Will Be Statically Defined if you want to manually assign the IP address, subnet mask, gateway, and DNS address to the client.

17. Click Next.

18. On the Destination Drive page, verify that the correct drive letter for the computer's floppy drive is specified.

19. Click Next.

20. On the Review page, click Next.

21. Click Start to format the floppy disk.

22. Click OK to confirm.

23. Click OK to close the Format Complete message box.

24. Click Close.

25. Click Finish.

26. Close Norton Ghost.

27. Remove the floppy disk and label it.

28. Copy Ghost.exe from the \Program Files\Symantec\Norton Ghost 2003 folder to the shared folder in which you plan to store the computer image.

Procedure Reference: Uninstall Ghost

To uninstall Ghost:

1. In Control Panel, double-click Add/Remove Programs.

2. In the list of currently installed programs, select Norton Ghost.

3. Click Remove.

4. Click Yes to remove Norton Ghost.

5. Close Add/Remove Programs and Control Panel.

ACTIVITY 14-2

Creating an Image of Windows 2000

Scenario:

The network administrator at one of your clients, Classroom Management Company, has asked you to automate the installation of Windows 2000 for her. This company teaches training courses in Windows 2000 and would like an easy way to wipe out and re-install Windows 2000 on classroom computers when a course completes. To facilitate this goal, the network administrator would like you to create an image of one of the classroom computers. After reviewing the client's network environment, you have determined the following information:

- The client has an Active Directory domain named class.com. All Windows 2000 computers are members of this domain.

- The Admin1 domain user account with a password of password has sufficient permissions to add computers to a domain.

- Classroom Management Company uses DHCP servers to assign IP addresses to its clients.

- The network administrator wants all administrator accounts to have the same password.

- The Windows 2000 installation files have been shared on the company's Windows 2000 server at \\2000srv\win2000. This share contains both the \i386 folder and the \Support\Tools folders.

- All computers use the Windows 2000 background as their wallpaper.

- All computers on the network print to the \\2000srv\netprint shared network printer.

- Each computer should be named Win2000–1. The network administrator will rename the computers whenever she installs the image.

- The network administrator does not want Norton Ghost or any system preparation tools included in the image. Because you won't be leaving Ghost on the computer, you don't need to register it.

Your client's network administrator has purchased Norton Ghost 2003 and copied its installation files to \\2000srv\ghost. In addition, she has created a share named \\2000srv\images on the server for storing cloned computer images for the network. She copied the Ghost executable files to \\2000srv\images.

The network administrator has already installed Windows 2000 Professional on the computer she wants you to clone. She would like you to install the latest Service Pack on this computer before you clone it.

What You Do	How You Do It
1. If neccessary, **install the latest Windows 2000 Service Pack.**	a. **Open Internet Explorer.** If necessary, **configure the Internet connection.**
	b. In the Address text box in Internet Explorer, **enter** *www.microsoft.com/ windows2000/downloads/servicepacks*
	c. In the Service Packs list, **click the link for the most recent Service Pack.**
	d. **Click Download Windows 2000 SP#,** where # is the number of the most recent Service Pack.
	e. **Click Go.**
	f. **Click Yes.**
	g. Below Download, **click SP# Express Installation.**
	h. **Select Run This Program From Its Current Location and click OK.**
	i. **Click Yes.**
	j. **Follow the prompts to install the Service Pack.**
	k. When the Service Pack installation is complete, **click Finish.**

2. **Install Ghost.**

    a. **Log on as Administrator.**

    b. **Access the \\2000srv\ghost share.**

    c. **Double-click Ghost** to install Norton Ghost 2003.

    d. **Click Next.**

    e. **Select I Accept The Terms In The License Agreement and click Next.**

    f. If necessary, in the User Name and Organization text boxes, **enter the appropriate names.**

    g. **Click Next.**

    h. **Click Next** to accept the default installation folder.

    i. **Click Install.**

    j. If you're prompted to register the software, **click Skip and then click Yes.**

    k. **Click Next.**

    l. **Click Finish.**

3. **Create a Ghost boot disk.**

    a. **Use Device Manager** to determine the driver for the computer's network card.

    b. **Record the name of the network adapter driver: _____**

    c. **Close Device Manager.**

    d. From the Start menu, **choose Programs→ Norton Ghost 2003→Norton Ghost.**

    e. In the left pane, **click Ghost Utilities.**

    f. **Click Norton Ghost Boot Wizard.**

    g. **Select Drive Mapping Boot Disk and click Next.**

h.   In the Name list, **select the driver for the computer's network card.**

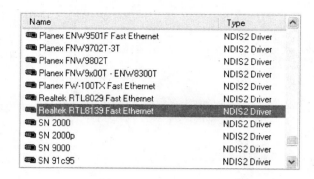

i.   **Click Next.**

j.   On the DOS version page, **click Next.**

k.   In the Client Computer Name text box, **type *computer#*** where # is your assigned number.

l.   In the User Name text box, **type *Admin#***

m.   In the Domain text box, **type *class***

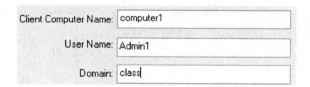

n.   From the Drive Letter drop-down list, **select G:**

o.   In the Maps To text box, **type *\\2000srv\ images***

p.   **Click Next.**

q. Verify that DHCP Will Assign The IP Settings is selected and click Next.

⦿ DHCP will assign the IP settings
◯ The IP settings will be statically defined:

r. On the Destination Drive page, **click Next.**

s. **Click Next.**

t. **Click Start** to format the disk.

u. **Click OK** to begin the format.

v. **Click OK** when the format is complete.

w. **Click Close.**

x. When the boot disk is created, **click Finish.**

y. **Close Norton Ghost.**

z. **Remove the floppy disk and label it.**

4. **Uninstall Norton Ghost.**

a. In Control Panel, **double-click Add/Remove Programs.**

b. **Select Norton Ghost.**

c. **Click Remove.**

d. **Click Yes.**

e. **Close Add/Remove Programs and Control Panel.**

5. **Configure the necessary operating system settings.**

a. If neccessary, **create an administrative user named Admin# with a password of password.** You're going to use this account to configure the default user profile.

b. **Log on as Admin#.**

 If you don't disable this wizard, it will show up each time you download the computer image to a computer.

c. In the Getting Started With Windows 2000 window, **uncheck Show This Screen At Startup and click Exit.**

d. On the desktop, **right-click the background and choose Properties.**

e. In the Select A Background Picture list, **select Windows 2000.**

f. **Click OK** to save your changes.

g. If necessary, **click Yes** to enable Active Desktop.

h. In the Printers folder, **use the Add Printer wizard to install the \\2000srv\ Netprint network printer.**

i. If necessary, **configure the computer as a member of the class.com domain** (right-click My Computer and select the Network Identification tab). **Restart the computer** when prompted.

6. **Update the default user profile.**

⚠️ You must log on as an administrative user other than Admin# to copy the user profile.

a. **Log on to the local computer as administrator with a password of password.**

b. In Windows Explorer, **configure the Documents And Settings folder to display hidden files and folders** (access the C:\Documents And Settings folder. Choose Tools→Folder Options. Select the View tab, choose Show Hidden Files And Folders and click OK).

c. **Close Windows Explorer.**

d. **Right-click My Computer and choose Properties.**

e. **Select the User Profiles tab.**

f. In the Profiles Stored On This Computer list, **select Admin#.**

g. **Click Copy To.**

h. When you're prompted to log on to the domain, **click Cancel.**

i. **Click Browse.**

j. Below My Computer, **select the C:\Documents And Settings\Default User.**

k. **Click OK** to specify that you want to copy the Admin# user's profile to the Default User profile.

l. Below Permitted To Use, **click Change.**

m. When you're prompted to log on to the domain, **click Cancel.**

n. From the Look In drop-down list, **select your local computer.**

o. In the Name list, **double-click Everyone.**

p. **Click OK** to close the Copy To dialog box.

q. **Click Yes** to confirm that you want to copy the profile.

r. **Click OK** to close the System Properties dialog boxes.

7. Create the sysprep answer file.

a. In Windows Explorer, **create a folder named C:\Sysprep.**

b. **Access \\2000srv\Support.**

c. **Double-click Deploy.cab.**

d. **Copy the all files to C:\Sysprep.**

e. In Windows Explorer, **access the C:\Sysprep folder.**

f. **Double-click setupmgr.exe.**

g. **Click Next.**

h. **Verify that Create A New Answer File is selected and click Next.**

i. **Select Sysprep Install and click Next.**

j. **Verify that Windows 2000 Professional is selected and click Next.**

k. **Select Yes, Fully Automate The Installation and click Next.**

l. In the Name text box, **type** *Network Administrator*

m. In the Organization text box, **type** *Classroom Management Company* and **click Next.**

n. In the Computer Name text box, **type** *Win2000—#*

o. **Click Next.**

p. In the Password and Confirm Password text boxes, **type** *password* and **click Next.**

q. On the Display Settings page, **click Next to accept the default settings.**

r. On the Network Settings page, **verify that Typical Settings is selected and click Next.**

s.   On the Workgroup Or Domain Page, **select Windows Server Domain.**

t.   In the Domain text box, **type *class***

u.   **Check Create A Computer Account In The Domain.**

v.   In the User Name text box, **type *Admin1***

w.   In the Password and Confirm Password text boxes, **type *password***

x.   **Click Next.**

y.   From the Time Zone drop-down list, **select (GMT-05:00) Eastern Time (US & Canada) and click Next.**

z.   **Select No, Do Not Edit The Additional Settings and click Next.**

aa. **Verify that Yes, Create Or Modify The Sysprep Folder is selected and click Next.**

ab. On the Additional Commands page, **click Next.**

ac. On the OEM Branding page, **click Next.**

ad. On the Additional Files Or Folders page, **click Next.**

ae. On the OEM Duplicator String page, **click Next.**

af. On the Answer File Name page, **click Next** to accept the default answer file name of sysprep.inf.

ag. **Click Finish.**

8. **Prepare the computer for cloning.**

    a. In Windows Explorer, **access the C:\Sysprep folder.**

    b. In the C:\Sysprep folder, **double-click sysprep.exe.**

    c. **Close the C:\Sysprep folder.**

    d. In the Windows 2000 System Preparation Tool message box, **click OK.** Your computer will shut down when the system preparation is complete.

9. Clone the computer.

a. Insert the Ghost boot disk and turn the computer on.

b. When prompted, **press Enter** to log on as the user account you specified when you created the boot disk.

c. **Enter** *password*

d. **Enter G:**

e. **Enter ghost**

f. If necessary, **press Enter** to mark the computer's hard disks.

g. **Press Enter again.**

h. **Verify that Local is selected and press Enter.**

i. **Verify that Disk is selected and press Enter.**

j. **Select To Image and press Enter.**

k. On the Select Local Source Drive page, **press Enter.**

l. In the File Name text box, **type** *Admin#*

m. **Press Enter.**

n. **Verify that No is selected and press Enter.**

o. **Press Alt+Y to create the image.**

p. If neccessary, **press Enter** in the New Media dialog box.

q. When the image creation is complete, **press Enter** to continue.

r. **Press Q to close Ghost.**

s. **Press Y** to confirm you want to close Ghost.

TOPIC C

Install a Computer Image

In Topic 14B, you learned the skills necessary to create an image of a standard computer. Now you're ready to install that image on other computers. In this topic, you'll learn how to deploy an image onto a target computer.

Imagine the following scenario: You've been asked to install the Windows 2000 operating system, Microsoft Office, and the Lotus Notes client on 250 computers—all over the course of a single weekend. If it takes you three hours to install one computer's operating system and the applications, it will take you a total of 750 man hours to complete this task if you install all of the computers manually. Instead, you can dramatically reduce the amount of time you'll need to perform these installations by creating and then installing a computer image instead. Knowing how to create an image, as you saw in Topic 14B, and how to deploy an image will save you untold hours when you're responsible for installing and configuring a number of computers.

How to Install a Computer Image

Procedure Reference: Install a Computer Image

To install a computer image:

1. If necessary, create a Ghost boot disk (see the Create a Ghost Boot Disk procedure).

2. Insert the Ghost boot disk and turn the computer on.

3. When prompted to log on, press Enter to log on as the user you specified when you created the boot disk.

4. When prompted, enter the user account's password.

5. Access the mapped network drive letter.

6. Enter ghost to run the Ghost utility.

7. Press Enter.

8. Verify that Local is selected and press Enter.

9. Verify that Disk is selected and press Enter.

10. Select From Image and press Enter.

11. Use the arrow keys to highlight the image file you want to install and press Alt+O.

12. Press Enter to select the computer's hard disk.

13. If necessary, make any changes to the size of the computer's partitions.

14. Press Alt+O.

15. Press Alt+Y to install the image.

16. Press Enter to restart the computer.

17. Remove the boot disk.

18. If you used Sysprep to prepare the computer, complete the necessary pages in the mini-Setup wizard.

19. When prompted, log on to the computer. Verify that the computer is functioning correctly.

ACTIVITY 14-3

Installing a Computer Image

Scenario:

Your client, Classroom Management Company, has asked you to prepare their Windows 2000 classroom for class next week. You don't know how the computers are currently configured, but the client has an image of exactly how the computers must be configured for the class in the \\2000srv\images folder. The network administrator has installed Ghost in this share and provided you with a Ghost boot disk.

This image has the following settings:

- The computer is a member of the class.com Active Directory domain.
- It uses DHCP servers to obtain its IP address.
- The computer uses the Windows 2000 background as its wallpaper.
- It's configured to print to the \\2000srv\netprint shared network printer.

What You Do	How You Do It
1. Install the computer image.	a. Shut down the computer.
	b. Insert the Ghost boot disk and turn on the computer.
	c. When prompted, **press Enter** to log on as the user account you specified when you created the boot disk.
	d. Enter *password*
	e. Enter G:
	f. Enter ghost
	g. Press Enter.
	h. Verify that Local is selected and press Enter.
	i. Verify that Disk is selected and press Enter.
	j. Select From Image and press Enter.
	k. Use the arrow keys to highlight the Admin#.GHO image file and press Alt+O.
	l. On the Select Local Destination Drive page, **press Enter.**
	m. Press Alt+O.
	n. **Press Alt+Y** to install the image.
	o. **Press Enter** to restart the computer.
	p. Remove the boot disk.

2. Verify the computer installation.

   a. The mini-setup process now runs. When the process is complete, **log on locally as Admin#.**

   b. **Verify that the desktop wallpaper is Windows 2000.**

   c. **Make sure that the computer is configured to print to the \\2000srv\netprint network printer.**

   d. **Verify that the computer is a member of the class.com domain.**

   e. **Verify that the computer is configured to obtain its IP address from a DHCP server.**

Lesson 14 Follow-up

In this lesson, you learned how to automate installations by performing tasks such as an unattended installation, cloning a computer, and downloading the clone image to another computer. Because the process of installing an operating system is so time-consuming, using these techniques will help you to install computers much faster and save you quite a bit of work.

1. **Have you ever performed an unattended installation? If yes, what was your experience with it?**

2. **Have you ever cloned a computer? If yes, how did it go? Were you able to successfully download the computer image to another computer? Why or why not?**

Follow-up

In this course, you learned how to perform the tasks an A+ technician must perform to manage the Windows operating systems on computers. Specifically, you learned how to:

- Manage both Windows and non-Windows application.
- Install and configure a network connection.
- Implement security.
- Manage file and print resources.
- Manage disk resources.
- Connect computers to the Internet and an intranet.
- Implement virus protection.
- Prepare for disaster recovery.
- Recover from disaster.
- Install client operating systems.
- Automate client operating system installations.

Throughout the course, you learned how to perform these tasks in the Windows 98, Windows 2000, Windows NT, and Windows XP operating systems. Mastering the skills necessary to complete these tasks will enable you to respond to any operating system technical support calls you encounter. By combining the class experience with review, study, and hands-on experience, you'll also be prepared to demonstrate your knowledge on the A+ exam.

1. **What operating system(s) do you think you will be supporting?**

2. **Give some examples of technical support calls you think you'll encounter.**

What's Next?

A+ Certification: Operating Systems prepares you for the A+ OS Technologies certification exam. If you haven't done so already, you should take the *A+ Certification: Hardware* course.

APPENDIX A

Upgrade From Windows 95 to Windows 98

At some point you might be asked to upgrade a Windows 95 computer to Windows 98 to take advantage of Windows 98's larger set of features. Before you attempt to upgrade a Windows 95 computer to Windows 98, make sure that your computer's hardware meets the minimum requirements for Windows 98. In Table A-1, we list the hardware requirements your computer must meet.

Table A-1: *Windows 98 Hardware Requirements*

Hardware	Minimum Requirement
Processor	486DX 66 MHz
RAM	16 MB
Hard disk	At least 225 MB of free space
Video adapter	VGA
Installation source	CD-ROM or DVD-ROM (without one of these drives, you must install Windows 98 using floppy disks)
Pointing device	Mouse

To upgrade Windows 95 to Windows 98:

1. Verify that your hardware meets the hardware requirements for Windows 98 (use Table A-1).
2. Verify that any applications you're running on Windows 95 will work on Windows 98.
3. Back up the data files.
4. In Windows 95, close all programs, including any anti-virus programs.
5. Start the Windows 98 installation.
   - If you're installing from a CD-ROM, insert the CD-ROM. If you're prompted to upgrade, click Yes.
   - If you're installing from a network share and inserting the CD-ROM does not prompt you to upgrade, from the Start menu, choose Run. In the Open text box, type the command to start the installation.

— Type $x:\backslash$Setup (where x is the drive letter assigned to your computer's CD-ROM drive). Click OK.

— Type $\backslash\backslash$computer$\backslash$share_name$\backslash$setup to install from a shared network folder. Click OK.

6. The Windows 98 Setup Wizard starts. Complete the following tasks:

a. On the License Agreement page, select I Accept The Agreement and click Next.

b. Enter the Windows 98 product key and click Next.

c. On the Select Directory page, choose one of the following:

- Select C:\WINDOWS to install Windows 98 in the default folder.

- Select Other Directory if you want to choose a different folder in which to install Windows 98.

d. Click Next.

e. If you chose Other Directory, enter the path to the folder in which you want to install Windows 98, and then click Next.

f. On the Save System Files page, select the appropriate option.

- Choose Yes if you want Setup to save your original Windows 95 installation so that you can later uninstall Windows 98 if necessary. Be aware that if you save your Windows 95 installation files, you will need an additional 110 MB of disk space to install Windows 98.

- Choose No if you want to overwrite your Windows 95 installation.

g. Click Next.

h. If you have multiple hard disks or partitions in your computer, select the drive letter on which you want to store the uninstall files and click OK.

i. On the Setup Options page, select one of the following options:

- Typical

- Portable

- Compact

- Custom

j. Click Next.

k. On the User Information page, verify the user's name and the company name. Click Next.

l. On the Windows Components page, select one of the following:

- Install The Most Common Components (Recommended).

- Show Me The List Of Components So I Can Choose.

m. Click Next.

n. If you selected Show Me The List Of Components So I Can Choose, check the Windows components you want to install on the computer and then click Next.

o. Verify your country or region and click Next.

p. Click Next to create a Windows 98 Startup disk.

q. When prompted, insert a blank floppy disk and click OK.

r. When the Startup disk creation is complete, remove the floppy disk and label it. Click OK.

s. Click Next. Setup will now copy the Windows 98 files to your hard disk.

The file copy process will take several minutes.

t.   When the file copy is complete, click Restart Now.

Setup will automatically restart the computer after 15 seconds.

7.   After the computer restarts, Setup will attempt to detect the hardware. When hardware detection is complete, click Restart Now to restart the computer again.

8.   Setup will automatically use your previously defined Windows 95 settings such as the computer name, workgroup name, and date/time properties.

9.   When the installation is complete, click Restart Now.

10. If necessary, log on to Windows 98.

11. If necessary, install any hardware drivers that were not automatically installed during setup. For example, make sure that the drivers for devices such as sound cards, modems, and display adapters were installed correctly.

   a.   If the Add New Hardware Wizard prompts you to install a new driver, click Next and follow the prompts to install the driver.

   b.   Use Device Manager to view the status of these devices and to look for any devices for which Setup did not install the drivers.

   c.   If you need new drivers, connect to the manufacturer's Web site to download the drivers for Windows 98.

   d.   Use Add New Hardware in Control Panel to install the drivers. When prompted, do not have Windows 98 search for the device. Instead, select the driver from the files you downloaded.

12. Install any additional Windows 98 components. In Control Panel, open Add/Remove Programs and select the Windows Setup tab.

13. Install any operating system updates that are available on Microsoft's Web sites. These updates include patches and add-ons that increase functionality and make the operating system more secure.

APPENDIX B

Upgrade From Windows NT to Windows 2000 or Windows XP

Because Microsoft is phasing out Windows NT support, you might be asked to upgrade a Windows NT computer to Windows 2000 or Windows XP, Microsoft's newest operating systems in the Windows NT line. Before you upgrade Windows NT to Windows 2000 or Windows XP, you should make sure that your computer's hardware meets the requirements for the appropriate operating system. You'll find the hardware requirements for each operating system in Table B-1 and Table B-2.

Table B-1: *Windows 2000 Professional Hardware Requirements*

Hardware	Minimum Requirement
Processor	Pentium 133 MHz
RAM	32 MB (64 MB recommended)
Hard disk	2 GB with 1 GB free space
Video adapter	VGA
Installation source	12X CD-ROM
Pointing device	Mouse

Table B-2: *Windows XP Professional Hardware Requirements*

Hardware	Minimum Requirement
Processor	Pentium 233 MHz
RAM	64 MB
Available disk space	1.5 GB
Video adapter	Super VGA
Installation source	CD-ROM or DVD-ROM
Pointing device	Mouse

To upgrade from Windows NT to Windows 2000, complete the following steps:

1. Verify that the computer's hardware meets the requirements for Windows 2000 (see Table B-1).

2. Verify that any applications you're running on Windows NT will work on Windows 2000.

3. Back up the computer's data.

4. Start the installation.

   - If the computer does not have a bootable CD-ROM drive, boot the computer from the first Setup disk. Use the following steps to create and use the Setup disks if you don't have them:

     a. Verify that you have three blank floppy disks.

     b. At a working computer, insert the Windows 2000 CD-ROM.

     c. Run \bootdisk\makebt32.exe from the Windows 2000 CD-ROM to create the Setup disks.

     d. Insert each disk when prompted.

     e. Label the disks.

     f. Insert the first Windows Setup disk and start the computer. When prompted, insert each additional disk as required.

   - If the computer has a bootable CD-ROM drive, insert the Windows 2000 CD-ROM and start the computer. If prompted, press a key to boot from CD.

   - If the installation files are on a network share, complete the following steps:

     a. Connect the computer to the network.

     b. Access the network share containing the installation files.

     c. Double-click winnt32.exe.

5. When prompted, click Yes to upgrade to Windows 2000.

6. On the Welcome page, select Upgrade To Windows 2000 (Recommended) and click Next.

7. When prompted, click Finish to restart the computer. At this point, Setup copies the files it needs to your computer. The file copy process will take several minutes.

8. Press Enter to restart your computer when the file copy process is complete.

9. Setup now detects and installs the device drivers it needs for your computer. This process will take several minutes.

10. When setup is complete, restart the computer.

11. Log on as a local administrator.

12. Uncheck Show This Screen At Startup and click Exit to close the Getting Started With Windows 2000 message box.

13. If necessary, configure the computer to connect to the Internet.

14. If necessary, install any hardware drivers that were not automatically installed during setup. For example, make sure that the drivers for devices such as sound cards, modems, and display adapters were installed correctly.

    a. Use Device Manager to view the status of these devices and to look for any devices for which Setup did not install the drivers.

    b. If you need new drivers, connect to the manufacturer's Web site to download the drivers for Windows 2000.

    c. Use Add New Hardware in Control Panel to install the drivers. When prompted, do not have Windows 2000 search for the device. Instead, select the driver from the files you downloaded.

15. Install any additional Windows 2000 components. In Control Panel, open Add/Remove Programs and click Add/Remove Windows Components.

16. Update Windows 2000.

    a. From the Start menu, choose Windows Update.

    b. Click Yes to install and run the Windows Update Control Package.

    c. If necessary, click Yes again.

    d. Click Scan For Updates.

    e. Click Review And Install Updates.

    f. Click Yes to continue.

    g. Follow the prompts to install the updates you want. You'll find that some of the updates are "exclusive," which means they can't be installed with other updates. If you choose to install an exclusive update, be sure to go back to the Windows Update Web site to check for other updates.

17. If necessary, restart the computer after the updates are installed.

18. Log back on to the computer.

You can upgrade Windows NT Workstation only to Windows XP Professional (not Windows XP Home Edition). To upgrade a computer from Windows NT Workstation to Windows XP Professional, complete the following steps:

1. Verify that the computer meets the hardware requirements for Windows XP (use Table B-2 or go to **www.microsoft.com/windowsxp/pro/evaluation/sysreqs.asp**).

2. Verify that any applications you're running on Windows NT will work on Windows XP.

3. Back up the computer's data.

4. Start the upgrade.

    • If the computer does not have a bootable CD-ROM drive, boot the computer from the first Setup disk. Use the following steps to create and use the Setup disks if you don't have them:

        a. Verify that you have three blank floppy disks.

        b. At a working computer, insert the Windows XP CD-ROM.

        c. If you're using Windows 9x or MS-DOS, run \bootdisk\makeboot.exe from the Windows XP CD-ROM to create the Setup disks.

        d. If you're using Windows 2000, Windows XP, or Windows NT, run \bootdisk\ makebt32.exe from the Windows XP CD-ROM to create the Setup disks.

        e. Insert each disk when prompted.

        f. Label the disks.

        g. Insert the first Windows Setup disk and start the computer. When prompted, insert each additional disk as required.

    • If the computer has a bootable CD-ROM drive, insert the Windows XP CD-ROM and start the computer. If prompted, press a key to boot from CD.

    • If the installation files are on a network share, complete the following steps:

        a. Connect the computer to the network.

        b. Access the network share containing the installation files.

        c. Double-click winnt32.exe.

5. Click Install Windows XP.

6. On the Welcome To Windows Setup page, verify that Upgrade (Recommended) is selected and click Next.

7. Choose I Accept This Agreement and click Next.

8. Enter your product key and click Next.

9. When prompted, restart the computer.

10. Setup now copies some of the necessary files for the upgrade to your computer. This file copy process will take several minutes. When Setup completes the copying, your computer will automatically restart.

11. Setup now installs Windows XP using the configuration settings you selected for Windows NT. When the installation is complete, your computer will automatically restart.

12. On the Welcome To Microsoft Windows page, click Next.

13. If you want to register your copy of Windows XP with Microsoft, choose Yes, I'd Like To Register With Microsoft Now and click Next. Follow the prompts to register Windows XP. If not, choose No, Not At This Time and click Next.

14. If you want to use MSN to connect to the Internet, choose Get Online With MSN, click Next, and follow the prompts to establish an account. If you don't want to use MSN, choose Do Not Set Up An Internet Connection At This Time and click Next.

15. On the Who Will Use This Computer dialog box, use the text boxes to create any new user accounts you need and then click Next (if you don't want to create any new user accounts, click Skip).

16. Click Finish.

17. Log on as a local administrator.

18. If necessary, configure the computer to connect to the Internet.

19. If necessary, install any hardware drivers that were not automatically installed during setup. For example, make sure that the drivers for devices such as sound cards, modems, and display adapters were installed correctly.

    a. Use Device Manager to view the status of these devices and to look for any devices for which Setup did not install the drivers.

    b. If you need new drivers, connect to the manufacturer's Web site to download the drivers for Windows 2000.

    c. Click Printers And Other Hardware in Control Panel. In the left pane, click Add Hardware to install the drivers. When prompted, do not have Windows XP search for the device. Instead, select the driver from the files you downloaded.

20. Install any additional Windows XP components. In Control Panel, open Add/Remove Programs and click Add/Remove Windows Components.

21. Update Windows XP.

    a. From the Start menu, choose Windows Update.

    b. Click Yes to install and run the Windows Update Control Package.

    c. If necessary, click Yes again.

    d. Click Scan For Updates.

    e. Click Review And Install Updates.

    f. Click Yes to continue.

g. Follow the prompts to install the updates you want. You'll find that some of the updates are "exclusive," which means they can't be installed with other updates. If you choose to install an exclusive update, be sure to go back to the Windows Update Web site to check for other updates.

22. If necessary, restart the computer after the updates are installed.

23. Log back on to the computer.

A+™ Certification: Operating Systems Third Edition – A CompTIA Certification

APPENDIX C
Dynamic Disks

Windows 2000 and Windows XP support dynamic disks. In this appendix, you'll learn the procedures for:

- Converting a basic disk to a dynamic disk.
- Reverting to a basic disk.
- Creating a simple volume.
- Extending a simple volume.

Converting a basic disk to a dynamic disk enables you to take advantage of the advanced features of dynamic disks such as modifying the partitions on the disk without having to delete the disk's partitions and create new ones. For example, one feature of dynamic disks is that you can increase the available space in a partition—something you might do if a user is running out of space in a partition and there's free disk space available on the hard disk. The advantage to using a dynamic disk in this scenario is that the computer will use the same drive letter for the expanded partition and the user will simply see a larger partition. In contrast, if you have only a basic disk in the computer, your only choice is to create an additional partition with a different drive letter. This means that the user will have to get used to accessing two different drive letters in order to retrieve or save her files. To convert a basic disk to a dynamic disk, complete the following steps:

1. Log on as a local administrator.
2. Open Computer Management.
3. In the console tree, select the Disk Management folder.
4. Verify that you have at least 1 MB of free space on the disk.
5. If you're using Windows 2000, right-click the disk you want to convert and choose Upgrade To Dynamic Disk.

   If you're using Windows XP, right-click the disk you want to convert and choose Convert To Dynamic Disk.
6. Verify that the check box for the disk you want to convert is checked. Click OK.
7. The message box shows you a list of all the partitions on the disk that will be converted. Click Convert.
8. Click Yes twice to confirm the conversion.
9. Click OK to restart the computer and perform the conversion.
10. After the computer restarts, log on.

11. When prompted, click Yes to restart a second time (the system detects the converted disk as a new device; you need to reboot to install it).

12. After the computer restarts, log on.

13. In Disk Management, verify that the disk type is listed as Dynamic, and that all partitions on the original disk have been converted to simple volumes on the dynamic disk.

If you want to revert a dynamic disk to a basic disk, complete the following steps:

1. Log on as a local administrator.

2. Back up data in all volumes on the disk.

3. In Disk Management, delete all volumes on the disk.

4. Right-click the disk and choose Convert To Basic Disk.

5. After the conversion, create any partitions you need on the disk and restore your data.

Just as you saw earlier in the course with partitions, creating a volume makes a dynamic disk accessible to the user of the computer. As an A+ technician, there are several reasons why you might need to create volumes. For example, the user might have a dynamic disk with free space that you want to make accessible to the user. Another example might be if you need to redeploy an old computer for another user and you've determined that a dynamic disk is the best choice for the new user. In this scenario, you'll need to be able to create at least one volume within the dynamic disk to make it accessible to the new user. The bottom line? Without volumes in a dynamic disk, the hard disk might as well be considered an expensive paperweight because the user won't be able to store any data on the disk. To create a simple volume on a dynamic disk, complete the following steps:

1. Log on as a local administrator.

2. Open Computer Management (right-click My Computer and choose Manage).

3. In the console pane, select the Disk Management folder.

4. If you're using Windows 2000, right-click the available free space in the dynamic disk on which you want to create a new volume and choose Create Volume. The Create Volume Wizard starts.

   If you're using Windows XP, right-click the available free space in the disk on which you want to create a new partition and choose New Volume. The New Volume Wizard starts.

5. Click Next.

6. On the Select Partition Type page, select Primary Partition.

7. Click Next.

8. If you're using Windows 2000, in the Amount Of Disk Space To Use text box, type the size of the partition you want to create.

   If you're using Windows XP, in the Partition Size In MB text box, type the size of the partition you want to create.

9. Click Next.

10. On the Assign Drive Letter Or Path page, select one of the following:

    • If you want to assign a permanent drive letter to the new partition, choose a drive letter from the drop-down list.

    • If you want to mount the partition into an empty NTFS folder, enter the path to the folder or click Browse to select a folder.

    • If you do not want to assign a drive letter or mount path, select Do Not Assign A Drive Letter Or Drive Path.

11. Click Next.

12. Select whether or not to format this partition. If you choose to format the partition, you can select from the following options:

   - The file system to use (FAT, FAT32, or NTFS).

   - The allocation unit size. This is the size of the smallest available file-storage unit on the disk, and determines the size of the file clusters.

   - The volume label, a name that's assigned to the partition.

   - Check Perform A Quick Format if you want to perform a quick format instead of a full format.

   - Check Enable File And Folder Compression to enable compression on the entire partition.

13. Click Next.

14. Click Finish.

15. Close Computer Management.

16. Verify that the new partition is accessible by using a utility such as Windows Explorer or My Computer.

Imagine the following scenario: You've been called in as an A+ technician to support a Windows 2000 computer you didn't initially install; the user of this computer reports that he's running out of disk space. After some investigation, you determine that the original installer of the computer created a system volume that's 2 GB in size, a 4 GB data volume, and left over 12 GB of free disk space. You want to make all of this free space available to the user, but you don't want the user to have to learn to access a new drive letter (which is what would happen if you created a new volume). What's the best solution? Extend the existing data volume to include the 12 GB of free disk space. Extending the data volume enables the user to access the data volume using the same drive letter. In addition, you can extend the volume without having to worry about losing any of the existing files on the data volume. As you can see, extending a volume offers you a quick and painless solution to increasing the user's available disk space. To extend a simple volume, complete the following steps:

1. Log on as a local administrator.

2. Open Computer Management.

3. In the console tree, select the Disk Management folder.

4. In the details pane, right-click the volume you want to extend and choose Extend Volume.

5. In the Extend Volume Wizard, click Next.

6. Verify that the disk that contains the free space you want to use appears in the Selected list. If not, add it from the Available list.

7. In the Select The Amount Of Space In MB text box, enter the amount of free space you want to add. Click Next.

8. Click Finish. The two areas of space will appear with the same volume label. The total capacity of the volume appears in the list of volumes in the upper-right pane of Disk Management.

There are a few restrictions you should be aware of before attempting to extend a volume. You can extend a volume if:

- You have administrative privileges.

- You have unallocated free space available.

- The volume is not formatted to FAT or FAT32 (you can extend NTFS volumes, or volumes that are not formatted).

- The volume does not contain the Windows 2000 or Windows XP Professional system files or the system boot information.

APPENDIX D

A+ OS Technologies Exam Objectives

Table D-1 lists the test domains and objectives for the A+ OS Technologies examination, and where they are covered in this course.

Table D-1: *Mapping Exam Objectives to Course Content*

A+ OS Test Domains and Objectives	Element K Course Lessons and Topics
Domain 1.0: Operating System Fundamentals	
1.1 Identify the major desktop components and interfaces, and their functions. Differentiate the characteristics of Windows 9x/ME, Windows NT 4.0 Workstation, Windows 2000 Professional, and Windows XP.	• Lesson 1 • Operating system features: Lesson 13, Topic A • Operating system components: — Lesson 2, Topics A and B — Lesson 5, Topic A • Major Operating System Interfaces — Lesson 2, Topics A, B, C, and D — Lesson 3, Topics B and D — Lesson 7, Topic A
1.2 Identify the names, locations, purposes, and contents of major system files.	• Windows 9x-specific files: — Lesson 2, Topics A and D — Lesson 11, Topic A • Windows NT-based specific files: — Lesson 2, Topic A — Lesson 11, Topic A
1.3 Demonstrate the ability to use command-line functions and utilities to manage the operating system, including the proper syntax and switches.	• Lesson 3, Topic B • Lesson 11, Topics A and E • Lesson 12, Topics A and B

APPENDIX D

A+ OS Test Domains and Objectives	Element K Course Lessons and Topics
1.4 Identify basic concepts and procedures for creating, viewing, and managing disks, directories, and files. This includes procedures for changing file attributes and the ramifications of those changes (for example, security issues).	• Disks: — Lesson 4, Topic D — Lesson 5, Topics A through D — Lesson 6, Topics A through D • Directory Structures: — Lesson 2, Topic C • Files: — Lesson 11, Topic D — Lesson 4, Topics D and E — Lesson 7, Topic C — Lesson 8, Topic B
1.5 Identify the major operating system utilities, their purpose, location, and available switches.	• Lesson 1 • Disk Management Tools: — Lesson 7, Topic D — Lesson 8, Topic D — Lesson 11, Topics D, E, and F — Lesson 12, Topics B, C, D, and E • System Management Tools: — Lesson 3, Topic A — Lesson 4, Topic A — Lesson 12, Topics A and B — Lesson 2, Topic A • File Management Tools — Lesson 12, Topic B — Lesson 2, Topic A
Domain 2: Installation, Configuration, and Upgrading	
2.1 Identify the procedures for installing Windows 9x, Windows ME, Windows NT 4.0 Workstation, Windows 2000 Professional, and Windows XP, and bringing the operating system to a basic operational level.	• Lesson 13, Topics A and C • Lesson 12, Topics C, D, and E
2.2 Identify steps to perform an operating system upgrade from Windows 9x/ME, Windows NT 4.0 Workstation, Windows 2000 Professional, and Windows XP. Given an upgrade scenario, choose the appropriate steps.	Lesson 13, Topic B

A+ OS Test Domains and Objectives	Element K Course Lessons and Topics
2.3 Identify the basic system boot sequences and boot methods, including the steps to create an emergency boot disk with utilities installed for Windows 9x/ME, Windows NT 4.0 Workstation, Windows 2000 Professional, and Windows XP.	• Lesson 11, Topics A, B, and C • Lesson 12, Topics B, F, and G
2.4 Identify procedures for installing/adding a device, including loading/adding/configuring device drivers and required software.	• Lesson 3, Topic A • Lesson 13, Topic D • Lesson 5, Topic A
2.5 Identify procedures necessary to optimize the operating system and major operating system subsystems.	• Lesson 2, Topics B and D • Lesson 7, Topic D • Lesson 8, Topic D
Domain 3: Diagnosing and Troubleshooting	
3.1 Recognize and interpret the meaning of common error codes and startup messages from the boot sequence, and identify steps to correct the problems.	• Lesson 11, Topics A and B • Lesson 12, Topics A and B
3.2 Recognize when to use common diagnostic utilities and tools. Given a diagnostic scenario involving one of these utilities or tools, select the appropriate steps needed to resolve the problem.	• Lesson 3, Topic C • Lesson 11, Topics A, B, and C • Lesson 12, Topics A, B, E, and F
3.3 Recognize common operational and usability problems and determine how to resolve them.	• Lesson 5, Topic E • Lesson 6, Topic # • Lesson 12, Topic A • Lesson 10, Topics A, B, C, D, and E
Domain 4: Networks	
4.1 Identify the networking capabilities of Windows. Given configuration parameters, configure the operating system to connect to a network.	• Lesson 3, Topics A, B, C, D, E, F, and G • Lesson 4, Topics C and D • Lesson 5, Topics A and D • Lesson 6, Topics B, C, and D
4.2 Identify the basic Internet protocols and terminologies. Identify procedures for establishing Internet connectivity. In a given scenario, configure the operating system to connect to and use Internet resources.	• Lesson 9, Topics A, B, C, D, and E

LESSON LABS

Due to classroom setup constraints, some labs cannot be keyed in sequence immediately following their associated lesson. Your instructor will tell you whether your labs can be practiced immediately following the lesson or whether they require separate setup from the main lesson content.

LESSON 1 LAB 1

Identifying Graphical and Command-line Tools

Scenario:

You've been asked to help a new Windows user identify some common tools you'd use to manage a Windows computer. The user has a list of tools he's been told he should know about, and he's asked you to describe the tools to him.

1. **Match the tool to its description.**

___	Taskbar	a.	Tool used to connect to other computers in Windows 98.
___	Start button	b.	Command used to display a text file.
___	Deltree	c.	Command used to display the operating system version.
___	Disk Manager	d.	Tool located at the bottom of the Windows screen; contains the Start button and system tray.
___	Type	e.	Command used to configure environment variables.
___	User Manager	f.	Tool used to access almost any tool on a Windows computer.
___	Set	g.	Tool used to manage hard disks in Windows NT 4.0.
___	Ver	h.	Tool used to create user account in Windows NT 4.0.
___	Disk Management	i.	Tool used to manage hard disks in Windows XP.
___	Network Neighborhood	j.	Command used to delete a directory and all the files and subdirectories it contains.

LESSON 2 LAB 1

Installing and Configuring Applications in Windows 98

Scenario:

You have been called in as an A+ technician to install and configure applications on a client's Windows 98 computer. The client has two applications that she wants to use: the tools in the Windows 98 Resource Kit, and the AutoShop MS-DOS application. After meeting with the client, you've discovered that the tool she uses most often from the Resource Kit is Clip Tray. For this reason, she would like you to make it as easy as possible for her to access and run Clip Tray. You have also reviewed the documentation for the AutoShop application and have determined that it needs 480 KB of conventional memory and 2048 KB of extended memory in order to perform adequately.

1. **Install the Windows 98 Resource Kit.**

2. **Create a shortcut to the Clip Tray Resource Kit utility on the desktop.**

3. **Install the AutoShop application.**

4. Configure the necessary memory requirements for AutoShop.

LESSON 3 LAB 1

Configuring a Network Connection in Windows XP

Scenario:

One of your clients has just purchased a new laptop. This laptop came with the Windows XP Professional operating system already installed. Your client would like you to configure this computer so that he can connect to all of the resources on his network. He reports that he is experiencing some problems with his computer and is getting error messages referring to the network card. After interviewing the client, you've determined that:

- His network is using a DHCP server for providing IP addresses.
- Your client plans to periodically access a Novell NetWare 3.12 server. This server is using the default Ethernet frame type of 802.2.

1. **Update the network card driver.**

2. **Configure TCP/IP.**

3. **Test the TCP/IP configuration.**

4. **Install NWLink IPX/SPX.**

5. **Install the Client Service for NetWare.**

LESSON 4 LAB 1

Implementing Local Security in Windows XP

Scenario:

As an A+ technician, you have been called in by one of your clients, Consulting Architects, Inc., to configure a new user's computer. The network administrator for your client's network tells you that this new user is named William Murphy, and that he would like you to assign a password of *password* to the user account. He would like Windows XP to prompt the new user to change his password when he first logs on to the computer. Mr. Murphy works for the Design department at Consulting Architects, Inc. All the computers within this department are members of a workgroup named Design.

The network administrator also tells you that this new user should be able to install applications on the computer, but that he should not have the full privileges of an administrator. In addition, the new user will be working on sensitive proposals so the network administrator wants you to make sure that no users other than Mr. Murphy will be able to access his data files.

1. Configure the computer as a member of the Design workgroup.

2. Create and configure William Murphy's user account.

3. Add the new user account to the appropriate group.

4. Implement encryption on the new user's My Documents folder.

LESSON 5 LAB 1

Managing File and Print Resources in Windows XP

Scenario:

As a member of the IS department for your company, Classroom Management, you have been asked to configure a new user's Windows XP computer. This user, Sarah Vance, will be logging on to your company's Windows 2000 domain, class.com. In addition, Sarah will be creating templates for documents such as reports and proposals on her computer; these templates must be accessible by all authorized users in your company. However, the network administrator has told you that no-one should be able to modify the templates other than Sarah. The network administrator would like you to name this folder \Templates and store it on the drive containing Windows XP.

Sarah will need the ability to print from her computer. Your company has a network printer named \\2000srv\netprint. She will also be printing to this printer from an MS-DOS application.

1. **Configure the computer as a member of the class.com domain.**

2. **Create and share a folder for storing the templates.**

3. **Connect to the network printer.**

4. **Capture the lpt1 port to the network printer.**

LESSON 6 LAB 1

Managing File and Print Resources

Scenario:

You've been hired by AlphaBeta Company to move one of their older Windows 98 computers to the production floor. On the production floor, many engineers will be logging in, running diagnostic programs and then storing the report files in the local My Documents folder. The engineers have expressed a desire to have a personalized work environment when they work on the production floor computer. They complain that things get moved around all the time on them and when they are in a hurry, it takes too much time to re-adjust to the modified environment.

The engineers also need access to the files in this folder from their office computers so that they can pull data from the report files into other database and statistical programs. All the office computers are members of a workgroup called Production. Security is not a large concern at AlphaBeta, but they would like to restrict access to the share on this computer. They would like to give managers the ability to read the reports, and only allow those who run the reports full control of the folder. They would like you to change the name displayed in Network Neighborhood from My Documents to Prod Reports, so they don't confuse the folder with their local My Documents folder.

In addition, there is an HP Laser Jet 4si they'd like to print the reports on. Many times it is inconvenient to run down to the production floor computer to print, so they'd like you to make it so they can print the reports on this printer from their office computers. Because the reports are a high priority, they don't want other employees to use the printer.

1. **Set the computer's workgroup to Production.**

2. **Enable user profiles on the computer.**

3. **Verify security is set to share-level.**

4. **Share the My Documents folder with two passwords: one for ReadOnly access and the other for Full.**

5. On the computer, **install the HP LaserJet 4si printer.**

6. **Share the printer and protect it with a password.**

7. **Test the share permissions on the file and the printer.**

LESSON 7 LAB 1

Managing Disk Resources in Windows XP

Scenario:

You have been asked by a client to manage the hard disks on some Windows XP computers. After reviewing the configuration of the computers, you have determined that whoever installed Windows XP did not use all available disk space. The company representative tells you that the company is very concerned about two things: the security of the users' files and making sure that users have enough available disk space. When asked, the company representative also tells you that according to his knowledge, the computers' hard disks have never been defragmented.

1. **Create a new partition from the remaining free space on the hard disk.**

2. **Format the new drive to NTFS.**

3. **Compress the new drive.**

4. **Defragment the hard disk.**

LESSON 8 LAB 1

Managing Disk Resources in Windows 98

Scenario:

You've been called to AlphaBeta Company to help get more life out of some older Windows 98 computers. The users have been complaining that they just don't have enough space to store their files. However, the company can't afford to upgrade the components in the computers at this time. When you examine the computers in question, you see that the hard disks are larger than 2 GB in size, but Windows 98 was installed using FAT and the extra disk space was never partitioned and formatted for use. When asked, the company representative also tells you that according to his knowledge, the computers' hard disks have never been defragmented.

1. **Create a new extended partition from the remaining free space on the hard disk.**

2. **Create a logical drive within the extended partition that uses all the available disk space.**

3. **Format the new partition to FAT32.**

4.   Convert the existing partition to FAT32.

5.   Defragment the hard disk.

LESSON 9 LAB 1

Connecting to Internet/Intranet Resources

Activity Time:

1 hour(s)

Data Files:

• ABhome.htm

Setup:

You will need to obtain the mail server name and email account name from your instructor or the person setting up the lab for you.

AlphaBeta Company's new remote access server is running the TCP/IP protocol exclusively with server assigned addressing information. The phone number for access is (985)555–5555.

AlphaBeta purchased a Creative Labs Modem Blaster 28.8 modem for each of the computers. They have been physically installed in the computers, but Windows 98 does not recognize then and the drivers aren't installed yet.

Scenario:

AlphaBeta Company is a small, not-for-profit company. They've been operating with older Windows 98 computers that were donated to them. They recently received a grant so that they can get all their client computers Internet access and email. The staff, who all work from their homes, is very excited to start using Outlook Express to communicate with each other and Internet Explorer to do their some of their initial research tasks.

When you talk with the staff, each of them tells you that their phone service is tone and none of them needs to dial anything special to dial out. You've created a simple local home page called ABHome.htm, so that when the staff opens up Internet Explorer, it doesn't need to make the dial-in connection to load the home page.

 When you've finished the lab, to check your work, refer to the Connecting to Internet Intranet Resources Lab Results.txt file.

1.   **Manually install the modem drivers.**

2.   **Create the dial-up connection.**

3. **Set up an Internet connection.**

4. **Configure Outlook Express for your users' email access.**

5. **Configure Internet Explorer to use Outlook Express as its default mail client and to use the ABHome.htm file as the home page.**

LESSON 10 LAB 1

Implementing Virus Protection

Activity Time:

1 hour(s)

Data Files:

- FixKlez.com

- W32_Klez Removal Tool.doc

- W32_Klez_E@mm.doc

Scenario:

AlphaBeta Company was hit hard by the W32.Klez.E@mm worm. They've called you for assistance in recovering their Windows 98 computers. They have purchased licenses for Norton AntiVirus 2003. The company has asked you to check each computer for the worm, remove the worm if you find it, and install Norton AntiVirus 2003 on all the computers. They want to make sure that their clients are automatically getting protection updates at least every week to help prevent an attack of this scope in the future.

You've gone to Norton's Security Response Web site and found two documents regarding W32.Klez.E@mm and a W32.Klez search and removal tool. W32_Klez_E@mm.doc and W32_Klez Removal Tool.doc are the pertinent security documents and FixKlez.com is the search and removal tool.

 When you've finished the lab, to check your work, refer to the Implementing Virus Protection Lab Results.txt file.

1. **Read the W32_Klez_E@mm.doc file for general information on the Klez worm.**

2. **Read the W32_Klez Removal Tool.doc file for instructions on using the FixKlez. com tool.**

3. Per the directions in the W32_Klez Removal Tool.doc file, **run FixKlez.com.**

4. **Install Norton AntiVirus 2003.**

5. **Obtain the latest virus definiton files.**

6. **Scan the computer for viruses.**

7. **Configure LiveUpdate to run automatically every 7 days.**

LESSON 11 LAB 1

Preparing for Disaster Recovery

Scenario:

You have been asked to take whatever steps you can to prepare a client's computer for any disaster she might encounter. This client does custom programming, so she uses a computer configured to dual-boot between Windows 2000 and Windows XP; this configuration enables her to test the programs she writes in both operating systems. She stores all of the programs she creates in the C:\Data folder. Because time is money to your client, she is very concerned about preparing her computer so that she can quickly recover if disaster strikes. She would like you to store any backups you create in the partition on the computer that does not contain the Windows 2000 or Windows XP operating systems. She is planning to buy a tape backup drive this week, and will back up the contents of this partition when she has the tape drive.

1. **Create a boot disk.**

2. **Create an emergency repair disk for Windows 2000.**

3. **Install the Recovery Console.**

4. **Back up the C:\Data folder.**

5. **Back up the Windows XP System State Data.**

6. **Back up the Windows XP Registry.**

7. **Create an ASR Backup Set.**

LESSON 12 LAB 1

Recovering from Disaster

Data Files:

- Templates.bkf

Scenario:

You work for the Help Desk at AlphaBeta Company. After returning from lunch, you discover that you have three trouble tickets waiting for you.

Trouble Ticket #1

1. One of the users reports that she is getting a "Windows Protection Error" message when she attempts to shut down her computer in Windows 98. **Research the error at Microsoft's Support Web site (*support.microsoft.com*) and create a plan for solving the problem.**

Trouble Ticket #2

2. A user reports that when he turned on his Windows 2000 computer, he received the error message "NTLDR is missing." **Research the error at Microsoft's Support Web site (*support.microsoft.com*) and create a plan for solving the problem.**

3. After researching the user's problem with the missing NTLDR file, you have determined that your best course of action is to repair the computer's boot files. **Perform an emergency repair.**

Trouble Ticket #3

4. A user tells you that she accidentally deleted the C:\Templates folder on her Windows 2000 computer. This folder contains files that are critical to her job. Because the files are so important to her, she backs them up regularly to a file named Template.bkf in the C:\Data folder. **Restore the backup file.**

LESSON 13 LAB 1

Installing Client Operating Systems

Scenario:

One of your clients has asked you to configure a new computer on her network. She does custom programming, so she would like to have both the Windows 2000 and Windows XP operating systems on the computer for testing purposes. After interviewing the client, you've determined that her network contains the following:

- A Windows 2000 Server domain named class.com.
- A Novell NetWare 3.12 server.
- A DHCP server to provide IP address leases.

1. **Install Windows 2000 and Windows XP.**

2. **Update both operating systems.**

LESSON 14 LAB 1

Automating Client Operating System Installations

Scenario:

Your client would like you to install Windows XP on 50 new computers he has purchased. Because some of the computers have different hardware, you can't use Ghost to install the computers. These computers will all be members of the Research workgroup. The network is TCP/IP-based and clients obtain IP addresses from a DHCP server. Your client would like you to install Windows XP in as little time as possible.

1. **Perform an unattended installation of Windows XP.**

2. **Update Windows XP.**

SOLUTIONS

Lesson 1

Activity 1-1

1. **Match the tool with its description.**

  h Windows Explorer

  a. Found in Windows 2000 and Windows XP, this tool contains just about every system administration or information tool you'd need to manage both operating systems.

  f My Computer

  b. Found in Windows 98 and Windows NT 4.0, this tools is used to connect to other computers on the network.

  e Control Panel

  c. This tool, found in the lower-left corner of a Windows desktop, contains all the tools you'd need to manage the computer.

  a Computer Management

  d. Found in Windows 98, Windows 2000, and Windows XP, this tool is used to gather information about the hardware attached to a computer.

  g My Network Places

  e. Opened directly from the Start menu in Windows XP, this tool contains programs used to configure the Windows operating system or the computer's hardware.

  b Network Neighborhood

  f. Opened from the desktop in Windows 98, Windows NT 4.0, and Windows 2000, this tool is used to manage files and folders on your computer.

  d Device Manager

  g. Found in Windows 2000 and Windows XP, this tool is used to connect to other computers on the network.

  c Start menu

  h. Opened from the Programs menu in Windows 98 and Windows NT 4.0, this tool is used to manage files and folders on your computer.

Activity 1-2

1. **Match the command-line tool with its description.**

_c_	Md	a.	Copies files, folders, and directory trees.
_g_	Deltree	b.	Displays the operating system version.
_b_	Ver	c.	Creates a new directory.
_a_	Xcopy	d.	Displays the memory usage on a computer.
_h_	Dir	e.	Configures environment variables.
_d_	Mem	f.	Changes file attributes.
_f_	Attrib	g.	Deletes a specified directory structure (a directory and all its subdirectories).
_e_	Set	h.	Displays the contents of a directory.

Lesson 1 Follow-up

Lesson 1 Lab 1

1. **Match the tool to its description.**

_d_	Taskbar	a.	Tool used to connect to other computers in Windows 98.
_f_	Start button	b.	Command used to display a text file.
_j_	Deltree	c.	Command used to display the operating system version.
_g_	Disk Manager	d.	Tool located at the bottom of the Windows screen; contains the Start button and system tray.
_b_	Type	e.	Command used to configure environment variables.
_h_	User Manager	f.	Tool used to access almost any tool on a Windows computer.
_e_	Set	g.	Tool used to manage hard disks in Windows NT 4.0.
_c_	Ver	h.	Tool used to create user account in Windows NT 4.0.
_i_	Disk Management	i.	Tool used to manage hard disks in Windows XP.
_a_	Network Neighborhood	j.	Command used to delete a directory and all the files and subdirectories it contains.

Lesson 3

Activity 3-5

1. **What should you try next to attempt to solve the problem?**

    a) Have the client open a Command Prompt window and enter `ping 127.0.0.1`.

    b) Have the client open a Command Prompt window and enter `ping 192.168.200.1`.

    ✓ c) Have the client open a Command Prompt window and enter `ipconfig /release` and `ipconfig /renew`.

    d) Have the client manually configure his IP address to one on the 192.168.200.# network, a subnet mask of 255.255.255.0, and a default gateway address of 192.168.200.1.

2. **What might be the problem?**

    a) Her network's WINS server is down.

    ✓ b) Her network's DNS server is down.

    c) Her computer is configured with the wrong default gateway address.

    d) Her computer is configured with the wrong subnet mask.

3. **Which step should you take first?**

    a) Ask the client to ping another computer on his network.

    ✓ b) Ask the client if any of the other users on the network are experiencing problems.

    c) Ask the client to verify that the DHCP server is running.

    d) Ask the client to run `ipconfig /release` and `ipconfig /renew`.

4. **What should you check next?**

    ✓ a) That his computer's network cable is plugged in to both the network card and the wall jack.

    b) That the router is on and functioning properly.

    c) That the hub is on and functioning properly.

    d) That the DHCP server is on and functioning properly.

5. **Which configuration parameter might be the cause of this problem?**

    ✓ a) The server's IP address

    b) The users' IP addresses

    c) The users' subnet masks

    d) The server's default gateway address

Activity 3-6

2. **How do you verify connectivity after installing the NetBEUI protocol?**

    You can verify that the NetBEUI protocol is installed and working by browsing the Network Neighborhood. If you see other NetBEUI-based computers, the NetBEUI protocol is working on the computer.

Activity 3-8

2. How can you verify that the NWLink IPX/SPX protocol is installed successfully?

You can verify that the NWLink IPX/SPX protocol is installed successfully by attempting to communicate with other NWLink IPX/SPX-based computers (such as by browsing the Network Neighborhood). If you're able to connect to another NWLink IPX/SPX-based computer, you have installed the protocol successfully.

Lesson 4

Activity 4-1

3. What would happen if you attempted to log on as JeffB to the class.com domain?

You wouldn't be able to log on. The user account JeffB exists only on the local computer, not on the domain.

Lesson 5

Activity 5-5

1. When you get to her desk, what step should you take next to troubleshoot the problem?

You should print a test document from Notepad. If the page prints successfully, Mary's problem might be with Excel, not the printer or print driver.

2. What should you try next?

If printing directly to the printer succeeds, try stopping and starting the Print Spooler service. If resetting the Print Spooler service doesn't resolve the problem, try adjusting the spool settings on the printer until you can print from all Windows programs. You should try changing the printer's settings so that Windows prints directly to the printer instead of spooling the print job.

3. What might be the problem and how can you fix it?

Suzanne's local printer is installed on lpt1. When she executed the `net use lpt1 \\2000srv\netprint`, *she redirected the print jobs that would normally print on the local printer to the network printer.*

To fix the problem, you should:

a. *Execute the* `net use lpt1 /delete`.

b. *Capture the printer port lpt2 to the network printer by executing* `net use lpt2 \\2000srv\netprint`.

c. *Configure the non-Windows application to print to lpt2.*

Lesson 6

Activity 6-5

1. **What do you suspect the problem is and how would you correct it?**

   The problem might be caused by incorrect spool or bi-directional printer settings.

   Test the spool settings:

   a. *From the Start menu, choose Settings→Printers.*

   b. *Right-click the printer and choose Properties.*

   c. *Click the Details tab.*

   d. *Click Spool Settings.*

   e. *Select Print Directly To The Printer.*

   f. *Click OK twice.*

   g. *Print a test page from Notepad.*

   If the page prints successfully, try different combinations of spool settings until you can print from all Windows programs.

   Disable bi-directional support.

   a. *From the Start menu, choose Settings→Printers.*

   b. *Right-click the printer and choose Properties.*

   c. *Click the Details tab.*

   d. *Click Spool Settings.*

   e. *Select Disable Bi-Directional Support For This Printer.*

   f. *Click OK twice.*

   g. *Print a test page from Notepad.*

   If the page prints successfully, replace the printer cable with one that conforms with the 1284 IEEE specification.

2. **What do you suspect the problem might be and how do you fix it?**

   The Windows 9x update may have altered the printer driver installed on Sarah's computer. You remove and re-install the printer driver from the Windows 9x CD-ROM.

3. **What do you suspect the problem might be and how do you fix it?**

   You suspect the printer port might not be working correctly.

   You need to verify the printer port is working properly:

   a. *Right-click My Computer and choose Properties.*

   b. *Click the Device Manager tab.*

   c. *Expand Ports (COM & LPT) by clicking the plus sign (+).*

   d. *Select the printer port.*

   e. *Click Properties.*

   f. *Verify the Device Status reads This Device Is Working Properly.*

   g. *Select the Resources tab.*

h. *Verify the Conflicting Devices List reads No Conflicts.*

If the port is not working correctly, try removing and re-installing the port. If another device is conflicting with the printer port, you need to correct the device conflict.

If the port is not working correctly, you need to remove and re-install the printer port:

a. *Right-click My Computer and choose Properties.*

b. *Click the Device Manager tab.*

c. *Expand Ports (COM & LPT) by clicking the plus sign (+).*

d. *Select the printer port.*

e. *Click Remove.*

f. *Click OK.*

g. *Restart your computer.*

h. *When the port is detected by Windows, follow the prompts to re-install the port.*

Lesson 7

Activity 7-1

1. Given that your client wants the partition to be accessible to both Windows 98 and Windows 2000, what type of partition must you create (given the current configuration of the hard disk)? Why?

    You must create an extended partition. Windows 98 recognizes only one primary and one extended partition on each hard disk.

2. What file system(s) can you use on this partition? Why?

    Because the partition must be accessible to both Windows 98 and Windows 2000, you must use either the FAT or the FAT32 file systems on this partition.

Activity 7-5

3. What will happen if your client downloads a new file to the D:\Data\NASA folder?

    The new file will be compressed because you have configured compression on the folder itself.

4. What will happen if your client moves one of the files from the D:\Data\NASA folder to another folder on the same partition?

    The file will still be compressed if she moves a file to another folder on the same partition.

5. What will happen if your client copies one of the files from the D:\Data\NASA folder to another uncompressed folder on the same partition?

    The copy of the file will no longer be compressed if she copies the file to an uncompressed folder. The original file will remain compressed in its original location.

Activity 7-6

2. Based on the analysis you see in the report, should you defragment this disk?

   Answers will vary depending on the student computers.

Lesson 9

Activity 9-4

1. Obtain the email account information.

Full name:	*Answers will vary according to the classroom setup.*
Email address:	*Answers will vary according to the classroom setup.*
Incoming mail server type:	*Answers will vary according to the classroom setup.*
Incoming mail server name (if necessary):	*Answers will vary according to the classroom setup.*
Outgoing mail server name (if necessary):	*Answers will vary according to the classroom setup.*
Account password:	*Answers will vary according to the classroom setup.*

Activity 9-5

1. What questions would you ask to define the problem?

   Some questions that would be helpful in defining the problem would be:
   - *Can you access other sites through Internet Explorer?*
   - *Were you ever able to access sites through Internet Explorer?*
   - *If so, when did IE stop being able to access other sites?*
   - *At that time, were there any configuration changes made to the computer?*
   - *Can you send email through Outlook Express?*
   - *Can you ping the site name?*
   - *Can you ping the site's IP address?*
   - *Is the physical connection working?*

2. What do you suspect is the problem?

   A physical problem.

3. What are your next steps for troubleshooting John's computer?

   Check the physical components of the Internet connection:

- *Verify modems are properly installed and connected to the computer and turned on.*

- *If John is using a VPN connection utilizing a network card and cable, verify the network card is functioning and the cable is connected.*

- *Try pinging another internal computer to test the physical link.*

- *If John has multilinked devices in his connection object, test the physical connectivity of each device.*

- *Once you narrow the problem to a specific physical component, check all physical components for hardware failure, look for patches on the manufacturer's Web site, and re-install the device's driver.*

4. **What do you suspect is the problem?**

   Ken's outgoing mail protocol is not set correctly. He needs to set it to SMTP.

5. **What do you suspect is the problem?**

   The Web master of the HR department's intranet has placed permissions on the Performance Reviews page that do not allow Carolyn access.

Lesson 10

Activity 10-9

1. **What is your response?**

   Select the Restore Your Master Boot Record option in the alert—you are sure there has not been a legitimate change to the system files.

2. **What is your response?**

   Use the Rescue Disk set to repair or replace infected files.

3. **What is your response?**

   Examine the log file to view the details of the incident and its resolution to make sure the file was cleaned and to identify the virus to communicate and protect against it on other computers in the company.

4.

   You choose to submit quarantined files to AVERT via WebImmune because you suspect the file is infected with a new, unknown virus.

Lesson 12

Activity 12-1

1. **What utility should you use to edit the user's Registry?**

   ✓ a) Registry Editor (regedt32.exe)

   b) Registry Editor (regedit.exe)

   c) System Configuration Editor (sysedit.exe)

   d) Microsoft Configuration Utility (msconfig.exe)

2. **What's the most efficient way to solve this user's problem?**

   a) Identify which files she deleted and copy them from another computer to the user's computer.

   ✓ b) Re-install Microsoft Office.

   c) Determine which files the user deleted. Copy the files from the Microsoft Office installation CD-ROMs and expand them by using Expand.exe.

   d) Remove Microsoft Office. Reboot the computer, and then re-install Microsoft Office.

3. **What utility can you use to capture detailed information about the problem?**

   You should use Dr. Watson to capture information about the application.

Activity 12-2

1. **What do you think is the problem? How should you fix it?**

   The user's problem is that the partition he created re-numbered his existing partitions. As a result, the ARC path in the Boot.ini file no longer points to the correct partition. You should fix the problem by:

   - *Attempting to boot the computer using a Windows 2000 boot disk. If the boot is successful, copy the Boot.ini file from the boot disk to C:*

   - *If you can't boot the computer from the boot disk, edit the Boot.ini on the floppy disk. Try increasing the number of the partition by one in the ARC path. Try booting from the boot disk. If successful, copy the Boot.ini file from the boot disk to C:*

2. **What should you try next? Why?**

   You should attempt to re-create the files necessary to boot Windows 2000 by performing an emergency repair. If the emergency repair fails, the problem is probably a hardware failure. Troubleshoot the hardware failure by:

   - *Checking for bad cables and connectors.*

   - *Verifying the jumper configuration.*

   - *Checking the hard disk's BIOS settings.*

   - *Trying the hard disk in a known good computer.*

3. **What can you eliminate as the problem?**

   You can eliminate hardware failure problems.

4. **What should you try next to fix Dave's computer?**

You could try either or both of the following solutions when you suspect a software problem and can boot to MS-DOS:

- *Use **Fdisk** to verify the active partition is set to the partition of the operating system you want to boot to.*

- *At a command prompt, enter* `chkdsk drive:` *(if not current volume) plus any desired switches to run the **Chkdsk** utility to examine your file and directory structure for errors and inconsistencies, mark bad disk sectors and recover readable information.*

5. **What should you do to try to fix Jane's computer?**

You could try either of the following solutions when you suspect a software problem and can boot into Windows 9x:

- *Run **ScanDisk** to examine your disk for invalid file names, file dates, and times, bad sectors, and invalid compression structures, as well as lost, invalid, and cross-linked clusters.*

- *If you are running Windows 98, run the **Maintenance Wizard** to check your hard disk for problems.*

Lesson 13

Activity 13-4

1. **What might be the problem? How should you fix it?**

The computer is probably configured to detect any attempts to update the boot sector and master boot record as a virus. Disable the virus protection in CMOS setup, restart the computer, and begin the installation again.

2. **What should you do?**

Use the Windows 2000 CD-ROM to create the Setup boot disks. Start the installation by using the Setup boot disks.

GLOSSARY

answer file
A setup file that provides the answers needed by the Windows Setup program during an unattended installation.

APIPA
(Automatic Private IP Addressing) The private IP address range from 169.254.0.1 to 169.254.255.254 used by Microsoft to provide temporary IP connectivity between Windows computers that are part of a single network segment and are not connected to the Internet.

ASR
Automated System Recovery is a process that uses backup data and the Windows XP Professional installation source files to rebuild a failed computer.

Autoexec.bat
A file used by the MS-DOS operating system to automatically load software whenever the computer boots.

basic disk
A physical hard disk that is divided logically into partitions. A basic hard disk can contain a maximum of four partitions, of which, a maximum of one can be extended.

boot partition
The hard disk partition that contains the \Windows or \Winnt folder.

boot sector
The reserved area on a hard disk or floppy disk where the information for booting the computer is stored.

boot sequence
The portion of the Windows 2000/NT/XP startup process where the computer physically starts up and the system hardware is initialized.

Bootsect.dos
A Windows 2000/NT/XP boot file that loads a non-Windows 2000, Windows XP, or Windows NT operating system on a dual-boot computer.

buffers
A configuration setting that enables you to specify how much memory is reserved for transferring temporary information between a non-Windows application in RAM and I/O devices.

built-in groups
The security groups created automatically when you install Windows 2000, Windows XP, or Window NT.

built-in user accounts
The user accounts created automatically when you install Windows 2000, Windows XP, or Windows NT.

cluster
The smallest unit of disk space used when the operating system writes to the hard disk.

Command.com
An MS-DOS operating system file that provides the command line interface. Also called the command interpreter and the DOS shell.

computer image
An exact duplicate copy of a computer hard disk's information.

Config.sys

A file used by the MS-DOS operating system to perform tasks such as load device drivers, configuring the operating system environment, and optimizing memory management.

conventional memory

The first 640 KB of RAM in the computer. MS-DOS uses this portion of memory whenever you run an application such as the MS-DOS Edit program. If you run a DOS application within Windows, Windows uses some of the computer's memory to simulate conventional memory.

data

The configuration information stored within a Registry value.

default gateway

An IP address used to identify a TCP/IP-based router that provides access to a remote network. When you configure a computer's default gateway, the computer forwards any communications for remote networks to the IP address of the default gateway.

DHCP

(Dynamic Host Configuration Protocol) A protocol which enables a Windows NT or Windows 2000 serve to dynamically assign IP addresses to clients.

dial-up connection

An outbound connection that uses WAN transmission media such as modems and phone lines to connect a client on one physical network to a Remote Access Server (RAS) on a remote network.

DNS

(Domain Name System) A static, distributed, hierarchical database system used to map computer (host) names to IP addresses.

domain

A Microsoft network model that an administrator implements by grouping computers together for the purpose of sharing a centralized user account database. Sharing this user account database enables users to use these accounts to log on at any computer in the domain.

domain controller

A server that stores the user account database for the domain and is responsible for authenticating users when they log on to the domain.

driver

A software component that you install in Windows to enable the operating system to communicate with specific hardware. For example, you install a printer driver to enable a Windows computer to print to that printer.

dynamic disk

A physical hard disk that is divided logically into volumes. A dynamic disk can contain an unlimited number of volumes.

emm386.exe

A driver that must be loaded before DOS can access expanded memory. You load this driver by modifying the computer's config.sys file and adding the line `device = c:\dos\emm386.exe`. You can also use the emm386.exe driver to make the upper memory area accessible for storing TSRs by adding (or modifying) the line in config.sys to read `device = c:\dos\emm386.exe noems`.

EMS

(expanded RAM) The first technology that enabled computers and MS-DOS to access more than 1 MB of memory; this goal was accomplished by installing an expansion card in the computer with additional memory chips. MS-DOS accessed expanded RAM by swapping it in and out of the upper memory area, 64 KB at a time. This type of memory is also referred to as EMS, which is short for"expanded memory specification."

encryption

The process of using an encryption key to translate data into a coded version that cannot be read without access to the required decryption key.

ERD

(emergency repair disk) A disk that contains information about the current configuration of the operating system and that can be used to repair problems with the operating system.

extended partition

A partition used simply for storing data. You cannot use an extended partition to boot a computer.

FAT32

A file system that provides support for disks larger than 2 GB on Windows 95 OSR2, Windows 98, and Windows ME systems.

files

A configuration setting that enables you to specify how much memory is reserved for the number of files opened by a DOS application.

fragmentation

The degree to which the pieces that make up files are spread across the hard disk.

frame type

Specifies the format in which the computer sends data and expects to receive data. Two computers must be using not only the NWLink IPX/SPX protocol but also the same frame type in order to communicate across a network.

group policy object

A collection of settings, applied within the Active Directory, that are used primarily to restrict users' actions on computers within an Active Directory domain.

Hal.dll

A Windows 2000/NT/XP driver that isolates the computer's hardware and device drivers from the operating system so that the same operating system can be used on a variety of hardware.

high memory area

The first 64 KB of RAM immediately after the first megabyte of RAM in the computer (this is the memory between 1024 KB and 1088 KB). In DOS, you can use the high memory area to store a single terminate-and-stay-resident (TSR) program, a device driver, or DOS itself. Windows does not simulate the high memory area when you run a non-Windows application.

himem.sys

A driver that must be loaded before DOS can access extended memory. You load this driver by modifying the computer's config.sys file and adding the line `device = c:\dos\himem.sys`.

hoax

Tricks users into believing there is a malicious code threat to their systems

HTML

HyperText Markup Language (HTML) is the authoring language used to create documents on the Web. HTML defines the structure and layout of a Web document as it should present itself in a Web browser.

Io.sys

An MS-DOS operating system file that enables the operating system to access the computer's hardware.

IP address

Four numbers that uniquely identify a computer on the network. This address is typically shown in the format 192.168.200.200. A portion of the IP address is used to identify the network on which the computer resides (similar to the street name in a mailing address); the remaining portion of the IP address is used to identify the computer itself (similar to the house number portion of a mailing address.)

key

A folder that appears in the left pane of the Registry Editor window. A key can contain other keys (also called subkeys) and values.

L2TP

(Layer Two Tunneling Protocol) An Internet standard VPN protocol for connecting a variety of VPN servers, including RRAS servers running L2TP.

load phases

The portion of the Windows 2000/NT/XP startup process where the operating system is loaded.

malicious code attack

A type of software-based attack where an attacker inserts malicious code into a user's system to disrupt or disable the operating system or an application.

MBR

(Master Boot Record) Contains the instructions for finding and loading the computer's operating system.

Msdos.sys

An MS-DOS operating system file that enables the computer to access disks.

NetBEUI

A small network protocol, developed by Microsoft, that enables computers to communicate over a network. You can use NetBEUI in place of a network protocol such as TCP/IP as long as the computers on the network do not need to access the Internet.

network client

A software component you install that enables a computer to access shared files and printers on another computer across the network. For example, if you want a Windows 2000 computer to access shared files on a Novell NetWare 4.12 server, you must install the Client Service For NetWare on the Windows 2000 computer first.

network-attached printer

A printer with an installed network card that is connected directly to the network cabling that you connect to by specifying its IP address.

non-routable

Refers to network protocols that cannot send data across routers.

Ntbootdd.sys

A Windows 2000/NT/XP boot file that initializes support for SCSI hard disks on which the BIOS is disabled.

Ntdetect.com

A Windows 2000/NT/XP boot file that performs hardware detection on the computer.

Ntldr

A Windows 2000/NT/XP boot file that loads the operating system.

Ntoskrnl.exe

A Windows 2000/NT/XP boot file that loads the basic Windows 2000, Windows NT, or Windows XP operating system.

NWLink IPX/SPX

Microsoft's version of Novell NetWare's proprietary network protocol, IPX/SPX. This protocol enables computers to communicate over a network (including across routers). The NWLink IPX/SPX protocol does not, however, enables computers to communicate on the Internet.

outbound connection

A network connection that connects clients on one physical network to resources on a remote network.

paging file

The file used by Windows to implement virtual memory. This file is also known as a swap file.

partition

An area of hard disk that is treated logically as a single unit of storage.

path

An environment variable that enables you to specify the folders in which you want the operating system to search for executable files.

Plug and Play

The ability of a computer to automatically configure hardware devices such as network cards and printers to work. The computer's BIOS, operating system, and the hardware device must support Plug and Play in order for it to be successful. Windows 9x, Windows 2000, and Windows XP all support Plug and Play.

PPP

(Point-to-Point Protocol) A remote access protocol used to transmit data across phone lines.

PPTP

(Point-to-Point Tunneling Protocol) A Microsoft proprietary VPN protocol for connecting to Microsoft Routing and Remote Access Service (RRAS) servers running PPP.

primary network logon types

A configuration setting that determines how Windows 98 will attempt to log users on to the computer.

primary partition

A partition that can be used to boot the computer.

print driver

A software component you install in Windows to configure the operating system to communicate with a specific printer.

print spooler

The print process component that receives the job from the print driver and stores it until it can be produced on the printer.

Recovery Console

A command-line utility for repairing a computer.

Registry

A database of system and application configuration information.

remote connection

A network connection that connects clients on one physical network to resources on a remote network.

remote-access connection

A network connection that connects clients on one physical network to resources on a remote network.

share-level security

Enables you to set a password on each individual shared resource.

SLIP

(Serial Line Internet Protocol) A remote access protocol used to transmit data across serial lines.

spools

The process of storing a print job on a hard disk; this print job is then later sent to the printer.

static IP address

An IP address that is configured manually, not using DHCP. Static IP addresses are not meant to change frequently.

Subnet mask

Four numbers used to distinguish the network portion of the IP address from that of the computer portion. For example, if a computer's IP address is 192.168.200.200 and the subnet mask is 255.255.255.0, this means that the network portion of the address is 192.168.200, and the computer portion is the remaining byte (200).

System

The Windows 2000/NT/XP Registry file that contains the system configuration information and a list of the device drivers to be loaded during the boot process.

system partition

The hard disk partition that contains the files necessary for booting the Windows 2000, Windows NT, or Windows XP operating system.

system policy

A collection of settings used to restrict users' actions on computers within a Windows NT domain. These settings are applied through the use of a system policy file on the domain controllers.

system state data

The Windows 2000 or Windows XP boot files, Registry, COM+ object registrations, and all files installed during the installation of Windows 2000 or Windows XP that have the .sys, .dll, .ttf, .fon, .ocx, and .exe extension.

System.ini

A Windows initialization (.ini) file that's used to configure specific parameters used by DOS and Windows 9x.

TCP/IP

(Transmission Control Protocol/Internet Protocol) A suite of protocols that enables computers to communicate across a network and over the Internet. This protocol suite consists of many different protocols, most notably, TCP and IP. In addition, it includes SNMP for sending email and HTTP for connecting to and downloading Web pages.

Trojan Horse

A piece of malicious code that masquerades as a harmless file.

GLOSSARY

TSR program
(terminate-and-stay-resident program) An MS-DOS program that remains in memory after you initially run it. A TSR stays in memory until you reboot the computer. You typically run TSR programs only on computers that are using MS-DOS as the operating system.

UMB
(upper memory blocks) Blocks of memory that are not in use within the upper memory area.

upper memory area
The 384 KB of RAM between 640 KB and 1 MB in a computer. This segment of RAM is reserved in MS-DOS for use by the computer's hardware devices. If you run a DOS application within Windows, Windows simulates the upper memory area for the application.

user-level security
Enables you to specify which users and groups have access to each individual shared resource.

value
An entry in the Registry database that contains configuration information. A value consists of three parts: a name, data type, and the data stored in the value.

Virtual Device Driver
A type of device driver used in Windows 9x. You sometimes see virtual device drivers referred to as VxDs because their associated files have the extension .vxd.

virus
A piece of malicious code that spreads from one computer to another by attaching itself to other files.

VPN connection
(Virtual Private Network connection) An outbound connection that uses existing local or outbound connection objects to connect a client on one physical network, through a private connection over a public network, to a VPN server on a remote network.

Win.com
A file used by Windows 9x to start the operating system.

Win.ini
A Windows 9x initialization (.ini) file used to set environment parameters for older applications that were written for Windows 3.1.

Windows 9x share permission
A collection of defined rights that allow access to a shared resource.

WINS
(Windows Internet Naming System) A Windows NT or Windows 2000 service used to enable clients to obtain the IP address for a given computer name.

workgroup
A Microsoft network model that simply groups computers together for ease of finding shared resources such as folders and printers. A workgroup does not share a centralized user account database.

worm
A piece of malicious code that spreads from one computer to another on its own, not by attaching itself to another file.

XMS
(extended RAM) All of the memory in the computer after the first 1,088 KB. This segment of memory is also referred to as XMS, which is short for "extended memory specification."

INDEX

INDEX